ROGER BILES AND MARK H. ROSE

D1231200

# A Good Place to Do Business

*The Politics of Downtown Renewal since 1945*

TEMPLE UNIVERSITY PRESS

*Philadelphia* • *Rome* • *Tokyo*

TEMPLE UNIVERSITY PRESS
Philadelphia, Pennsylvania 19122
tupress.temple.edu

Chapter 2 credit: Mark H. Rose and Roger Biles, "Arthur Rubloff and the
Grinding Politics of Renewal in Chicago, 1947 to 1986," *Journal of Urban
History* 46, no. 6 (November 2020): 1341–67.

Chapter 10 credit: Roger Biles and Mark H. Rose, "'Gilbertville,' 'Ilitchville,' and the Redevelopment of Detroit," *Journal of Planning History* 20,
no. 1 (February 2021): 3–27.

Library of Congress Cataloging-in-Publication Data

Names: Biles, Roger, 1950– author. | Rose, Mark H., 1942– author.
Title: A good place to do business : the politics of downtown renewal since
   1945 / Roger Biles and Mark H. Rose.
Other titles: Urban life, landscape, and policy.
Description: Philadelphia : Temple University Press, 2022. | Series: Urban
   life, landscape, and policy | Includes bibliographical references and
   index. | Summary: "This book looks at the politics of downtown business
   promotion as an urban renewal strategy from the end of World War II to
   the present, with a focus on five case cities: Philadelphia, Chicago,
   Detroit, St. Louis, and Cleveland"— Provided by publisher.
Identifiers: LCCN 2022011190 | ISBN 9781439920817 (cloth) | ISBN
   9781439920824 (paperback)
Subjects: LCSH: Urban renewal—United States—History—Case studies. |
   Urban policy—United States—Case studies. | Central business
   districts—United States—History—Case studies. | Industrial
   promotion—United States—Case studies. | Shrinking cities—Political
   aspects—United States.
Classification: LCC HT175 .B47 2022 | DDC 307.3/4160973—dc23/
   eng/20220610
LC record available at https://lccn.loc.gov/2022011190

Printed in the United States of America

9  8  7  6  5  4  3  2  1

# A Good Place to Do Business

In the series *Urban Life, Landscape, and Policy,* edited by David Stradling, Larry Bennett, and Davarian Baldwin. Founding editor, Zane L. Miller.

A list of additional titles in this series appears at the back of this book.

*In honor of Mary Claire and Marsha Lynn and*

*in memory of Ray Mohl, our friend and collaborator*

# Contents

## PART III DOWNTOWN'S CONTINUING ALLURE, 2000–2020

# Preface

In January 2003, we attended the 117th annual meeting of the American Historical Association. Chicago was and remains a diverse and interesting place to grow up, and it was a treat to return for a few days. We stayed at a hotel on South Michigan Avenue. During that meeting, we attended a dinner at the Chicago Historical Society (now the Chicago History Museum). Rather than make the trip by subway, bus, or taxi, we decided to walk the 2.5 miles. Urban historians regularly encourage their students to take walking tours of cities. We made the correct decision. As a light snow fell around us, we crossed the Chicago River, skirted the affluent crowds window-shopping along the Magnificent Mile, and strolled through a swank residential area aptly named the Gold Coast. In the soft glow of the streetlights, we gazed at multimillion-dollar mansions and elegantly appointed brownstones on State Street north of the city's dazzling skyline. By the time we reached the stately Chicago Historical Society at the southern edge of beautifully landscaped Lincoln Park, we were amply reminded of how decades of undivided attention to the financial health and attractive appearance of the urban core had succeeded in creating a wonderful setting for the Windy City's most fortunate residents to reside and work.

As children and young adults in Chicago during the 1950s and 1960s, however, we resided in neighborhoods far removed from the central business district and the fabulous Gold Coast. Our families and our neighbors were mostly first- and second-generation descendants of immigrant people. Some grandparents spoke English with East European accents. We also re-

membered the less enthralling aspects of Chicago life in middling and working-class communities on the North Side. Apart from the occasional trip
downtown for special occasions or shopping excursions in search of items
unavailable at nearby shops, our families stayed close to home and made do
in smallish houses and modest apartments. Our neighbors, as we recall,
relied on the beneficence of Mayor Richard J. Daley and his foot soldiers in
the potent Democratic machine to patch the streets and sidewalks, remove
the snow, construct nearby parks with swings and sandboxes, and restore
quiet when Saturday night revelers celebrated too loudly well into Sunday
morning. Our parents, reliable Democratic party voters, admired Daley for
making Chicago "the city that works." All in all, local government played an
important role in maintaining our neighborhoods and in creating attachments
among neighbors and with far-off City Hall. During those years, however,
we were not alert to the disparities between the city's spending in our neighborhoods—Lakeview and Rogers Park—and the vast sums of money invested on
downtown's upkeep. Recalling our experiences in Chicago of many decades
earlier, we understood that downtown's exalted status had not only persisted
but intensified across the postwar decades, right up to our visit in 2003.

As urban historians, we determined to study the politics that had brought
downtown into such prominence, always to the detriment of the city's lower-
income residents in less glitzy neighborhoods. Dramatic changes in the city's
population and economy were part of the story. Between 1950 and 1980,
Chicago's population declined by a whopping 600,000 persons. Remaining
residents were often poorer than those who had departed for leafy suburbs
or the booming cities of the nation's southwest such as Los Angeles, Houston, and Phoenix. Dramatic population losses during those decades accompanied profound economic and political changes. During the late 1940s and
extending for decades, the rapid diminution of manufacturing resulted in
unemployment for thousands of industrial workers. Vacated factories, abandoned warehouses, and empty retail shops pockmarked the cityscape.

Policies conceived in Washington, DC contributed to the changed fortunes
of the largest U.S. cities. Beginning in the 1930s, funding for such federal
programs as slum clearance and public housing paled in comparison with
government aid for suburbanization. Low-interest mortgage insurance, Veterans Administration loans, tax breaks for homeowners instead of renters,
and high-speed expressways that whisked commuters and shoppers in and
out of downtowns made possible the sprawl of ranch houses and apartment
complexes throughout the crabgrass frontier. Suburban construction of shopping centers and other commercial properties likewise benefited from federal policies because tax write-offs for new construction far exceeded the
amount allowed for the renovation of aging structures. As big-city mayors

complained, federal policies underwrote metropolitan decentralization to the detriment of inner cities.

Urban renewal, the most important federal effort to aid metropolises in the post–World War II years, fell short of undoing the damage in two landmark pieces of legislation. The Taft-Ellender-Wagner Housing Act of 1949 provided for a modicum of public housing only as an adjunct to slum clearance and downtown revitalization. Coupled with the Housing Act of 1954, which decreased requirements for residential projects and increased the amount of funds that could be spent on office towers, hospitals, universities, and stadiums, the 1949 law became largely a vehicle for constructing office buildings, parking garages, swank apartment complexes, and retail outlets. Disillusionment with urban renewal grew in the 1950s and 1960s amid ongoing population loss and racial conflict. Most Americans judged President Lyndon B. Johnson's urban reform efforts, especially the Great Society and Model Cities programs, as little more than costly failures.

As conditions in cities deteriorated in the 1970s, Washington, DC, retreated from its urban engagement rooted in the 1930s and capped by Johnson's War on Poverty in the 1960s. Trumpeting a series of "new federalisms" that put the onus for urban reform squarely on local government, a series of presidential administrations sharply reduced aid to cities. The Ronald W. Reagan White House inflicted draconian budget cuts in the 1980s, but the support from other administrations was nearly as meager. Eliminating entire urban programs and drastically trimming budgets for others, the Department of Housing and Urban Development and other federal agencies sent a clear message to local officials that they needed to procure their own funding sources. The need for public-private partnerships and creative fiscal management took on a new importance. And at the same time, federal policies still permitted mayors and local business leaders to make important decisions both about whether to develop public housing, expressways, and urban renewal projects and where those vast undertakings would be located. Here were all the makings for a vast assault on African American and low-income neighborhoods, even before the financial squeeze hit full force.

In the hardening political economy of the postwar decades, Mayor Richard J. Daley and his business allies scrambled for economic solutions. But their search never included a quest for citywide projects, or even projects that would have applied equally among an increasingly diverse population that included recent arrivals from Mexico, Puerto Rico, southern-born African Americans, and Pacific Rim nations. Instead, the city's business and political leaders had started to believe that upscale shopping, fancy offices, convention centers, new sports arenas, and the like would soon return visitors and suburbanites back downtown, one still populated by white persons.

Indeed, if redevelopment proved successful, well-heeled members of the middle class would return to live in upscale apartments and condominiums. Surely, the fabulous shops and offices along North Michigan Avenue, the developer Arthur Rubloff's Miracle Mile, offered a daily and incontrovertible statement about how catering to well-off shoppers and businesspeople seeking prestigious office space led to rising property values, improved tax revenues, more jobs, and impressive sales increases. White women were supposed to shop on North Michigan Avenue—with heavy shopping bags delivered to their homes by uniformed drivers. Like New York's Fifth Avenue, Rubloff's Miracle Mile was a brand, a gendered lifestyle, and a demographic that many sought to emulate.

North Michigan Avenue was only one among Rubloff's successful investments. Yet comparatively few took notice of the fact that Rubloff located another development, Evergreen Plaza Shopping Center, just beyond the city's border on the Far South Side. As early as the 1950s, Rubloff and countless developers like him were already creating a zero-sum game for the affluent shoppers' attention, dollars, and prestige. Whether on North Michigan Avenue or at Evergreen Plaza, moreover, Rubloff-style prosperity for white families extended only a short distance in any direction. Chicagoans, we recognized, were increasingly poor and nonwhite. Even as high school students staring out of windows from the city's buses and subway trains, we and our peers could not fail to identify the stark divides of wealth and race that characterized Chicago's neighborhoods. In later years, we came to understand that residence in any number of South Side communities guaranteed that no bank would make a home or business loan. Job losses and racial hatreds abided in the realms in which the city's growing African American population reached young adulthood. Regardless of neighborhood, Chicago's racial politics were unyielding, no more so than when Chicagoans elected Harold L. Washington the city's first African American mayor (1983–1987). Washington attempted to shift resources to impoverished neighborhoods but achieved few successes during his brief time in office.

To put the matter in bluntest form, Chicago's business and political leaders had determined to invest in downtown and disinvest in African American neighborhoods. During the course of more than seventy years since World War II, city officials delivered basic services irregularly to Austin, West Garfield Park, Englewood, Pullman, and other declining communities; young black males suffered constant harassment and severe beatings (some lethal) from white police officers given carte blanche authority to administer a harsh and unyielding street justice to people of color. Racial inequality and segregation took a heavy toll in another zero-sum game. City hall kept the lion's share of the city's resources close to home, to spend in pursuit of downtown improvements. Using urban-renewal projects such as new hospitals, wide highways like the Congress Street Expressway, and other measures, Daley and city officials sought to isolate the downtown from black incursions. Such policies and practices aimed at exclusion meant not only keeping unwanted minorities from residing too close to the central business district but also limiting the number of black shoppers on downtown streets. As the city's demographics changed in the last decades of the twentieth century, the same strictures applied to the rapidly growing Latinx population. In the minds of the mayor and the city's commercial elite, the Loop, North Michigan Avenue, and the adjacent area north of the Chicago River needed to remain the privileged domain of white bankers, lawyers, commodities traders, merchants, and shoppers. As we began this study, our understanding of Chicago's downtown and neighborhood politics served as a point of departure for understanding an identical focus in five other American cities. Years spent in musty archives, library stacks, and online sources also guided our research in new and exciting directions. Pittsburgh, we learned, served as an important idea center for downtown-oriented politics.

After World War II, the nation's business and political leaders regularly sought to emulate the Pittsburgh Renaissance. By the early 1950s, a sparkling lineup of skyscrapers in the Steel City stood as the undisputed showpiece of a modern and prosperous downtown. During the next twenty years, photographs of those new buildings, bathed in sunlight, circulated widely in the United States and overseas, attracting appreciative visitors. Delegations of business executives and politicians traveled by train and airplane to Pittsburgh to learn how Richard King Mellon, a wealthy executive, and Mayor David L. Lawrence, with his strong political and union connections, had collaborated to bring the Renaissance into existence. Visitors heard a consistent report. From 1943 on, Mellon and Lawrence were laser-focused on eliminating the city's choking smoke, preventing periodic floods, and making the downtown a center of business and cultural life once again. Mellon occupied the senior position in contact with Mayor Lawrence and in relationships with Pittsburgh's business leaders. A note or telephone call from Mellon was certain to rivet the attention of a holdout executive, especially in the first years of renewal, when reducing the use of coal in factories and locomotives loomed as the day's largest political battle. By any calculus, the Mellon-Lawrence combination presented a difficult-to-beat combination in fostering Pittsburgh's downtown redevelopment. But controlling smoke and floods were not the only topics on the lists of concerns for visitors to big-city downtowns, or even the most important ones. Sophisticated politicians like Daley and St. Louis mayor Raymond R. Tucker had not trekked to Pittsburgh only to relearn dull ideas about city departments and the formal workings of city councils, taught routinely in high school civics classes.

Pittsburgh's visitors included mayors Daley and Tucker, along with top business leaders such as beer baron August A. "Gussie" Busch Jr. During dinners over thick steaks, mixed drinks, cigars, and cigarettes, the visitors inquired at length about how the unusual Mellon-Lawrence combination actually held such wide sway in Pittsburgh politics. Lawrence and Mellon cooperated with one another and top business leaders to clear small shops and aging stores from prime downtown property. Equally, executives and politicians from every city asked how Pittsburgh officials and planners had acquired the legal and political muscle that were prerequisite to moving and keeping African Americans away from downtown. In short, Mayors Daley and Tucker and every member of their large delegations wanted a list of ingredients in Mellon and Lawrence's political sauce.

Yet those big plans conceived on Pittsburgh tours seldom turned into equally grand projects in the visitor's home cities. The fruits of the visits to Pittsburgh's aluminum-sheathed buildings and dinnertime conversations with prosperous Pittsburgh business executives possessed a limited shelf life once visitors returned to the hubbub of daily politics and dealmaking. And still more important, advice about creating vast, racially charged clearance projects did not translate easily and directly into hoped-for renewal in downtown St. Louis, Chicago, Detroit, Cleveland, or Philadelphia, the five cities in this case study.

Downtown renewal programs in each of our cities nonetheless lurched forward, often without cohesive and coherent leadership. Bulldozers in African American neighborhoods launched massive highway projects. Detroit mayor Albert E. Cobo and Cleveland planner Ernest J. Bohn countenanced the removal of thousands of poor and working-class residents for the construction of expressways they deemed essential to downtown redevelopment. From the late 1950s, St. Louis mayor Tucker and his business allies presided over the clearance of a vast African American area adjoining downtown; and, in the mid-1960s, Tucker approved clearance of another area—right in downtown—to construct a new stadium for the Cardinals baseball club. In Philadelphia, William L. Rafsky, a political activist and long-time city employee, guided expressway construction, built public housing, and coordinated construction of downtown skyscrapers and upscale housing near Independence Hall. Up to the 1970s, Rafsky also presided over programs that relocated thousands of African American households and lured a small number of upper-income white households downtown.

All in all, mayors and council members in each of our cities, including Philadelphia and Pittsburgh, still searched for resources to support police and fire departments and aging schools. Nor during those postwar years had sophisticated city leaders like Philadelphia's Rafsky figured out ways to reverse financial losses, halt their city's population exodus, or stop the disappearance of jobs to suburbs or into nonexistence. None of these harsh changes was racially neutral, moreover. The cost of building downtowns during those years as well as the steep job losses fell most heavily on each city's residents of color. After World War II, race was a visible and ineradicable part of the policy regimes that governed the nation's aging industrial cities.

From the 1970s and extending for the next five decades, members of succeeding generations of business and political leaders in our five cities sought once again to remedy population losses, unrelieved poverty, and racial hatreds. In each city, we learned, mayors like Detroit's Coleman A. Young and Cleveland's Michael R. White still awarded precedence to downtown renewal rather than to the repair of aging neighborhoods and dilapidated schools. But in their singular focus on downtown, we discovered, city officials no longer routinely sanctioned the bulldozing of African American neighborhoods. The emphasis in every city, however, remained on development of flashy stadiums, additional expressways, and upscale hotels. In Cleveland, each mayor starting with George V. Voinovich (1980–1989) worked with business leaders to make downtown a fun place to gamble, watch a baseball game or a regatta, and visit the Rock and Roll Hall of Fame.

Money, prestige, jobs, taxes, race, and a desire to remain a factor in an unending scramble toward urban greatness resided at the center of this downtown-centered politics. In any city, few white executives or top political officials (white as well as black) doubted that the path to downtown's restored image had to include a refurbished convention center and airport improvements. Lacking funds to maintain even basic services like police and schools, however, leaders such as Detroit Mayor Kwame Kilpatrick (2002–2008) approached bankers and credit-rating agencies such as Standard and Poor's almost hat in hand. And, as yet an additional approach to securing a steady income, or at least a cash infusion, Chicago mayor Richard M. Daley (1989–2011) sold municipal assets such as parking meters and the Chicago Skyway (a toll bridge). From the 1970s on, every Detroit mayor promised that casinos would shore up the city's diminished finances, but gambling riches proved illusory. And from the 1990s on, a succession of Detroit mayors simply turned over downtown redevelopment to wealthy businesspeople such as Daniel Gilbert of Quicken Loans and Michael Ilitch Sr. of Little Caesars. Gilbert, at the mayor's request, led an audacious—but ultimately unsuccessful—effort to win one of Amazon's planned headquarters sites for his city. Detroit, by Gilbert's reckoning, still deserved a place on a list of important U.S. cities.

In this environment, officials in every city also adopted a softer tone in their dealings with financial agencies and wealthy executives. During the mid-1990s, business-friendly Philadelphia mayor Edward G. Rendell "developed a kind of cult status among analysts and investors, who associate[d] virtually all of the city's turnaround to his dynamic personality and optimism." Still, critics—and there were many—described these newer approaches to downtown development with words such as *privatization* and *neoliberal*, a concept that historian Harold James contended in 2020 was "a go-to term for denunciation."[1] But there is no doubt that mayors like Rendell awarded high marks to any program that would raise their city's credit rating from the B to the A range.

From the 1970s on, hospital growth appeared to offer a long-sought-after device to ease urban finances and to short-circuit job and population losses. Hospitals such as Barnes-Jewish in St. Louis managed urban renewal projects, including efforts to coax wealthier families back to the city—and, better still, those costly renewal programs resided off the city's books. Hospitals created jobs. Rush Medical Center in Chicago and the world-renowned Cleveland Clinic employed thousands, including well-paid administrators and medical specialists. They purchased supplies locally, creating more jobs and taxpaying businesses. Small wonder that top hospital administrators took their place on city leadership committees.

No one or two themes explain the tumult and complexity of urban change across more than seven decades. We are certain, however, that politics—informed each day by ideas about race—resided at the center of that change. The elected officials and powerful businessmen who worked in tandem gained the upper hand in local government and made the decisions that shaped urban redevelopment. We are equally certain that those leaders, amid the nonstop upheavals, continued to make downtown the focal point of that politics. Accordingly, we have highlighted the inestimable role played by key individuals—entrepreneurs and politicians—whose decisions largely determined the fortunes of the five cities. Neither remote global forces nor the unknowable operation of "the market" accounted for the decisions made in city after city to prioritize downtown redevelopment.

# Acknowledgments

Scholarly books mature across decades. That maturation process starts in undergraduate and graduate classes and extends right up to the moment we press "submit" and, at last, send the manuscript to our editors. Historians and other scholars regularly acknowledge the singular process of writing a book. Yet we also recognize that writing a book involves our colleagues, families, teachers, editors, and friends during the course of many years. They engage in sharing time-worn stories about archival visits and kindly listen to our partially formed ideas. This large community's presence, wisdom, support, and love helped bring us to this moment.

Early on, we had the privilege of studying with graduate and undergraduate faculty who oriented us toward cities, social structures, urban ecology, and political economy. We remember Meyer Weinberg, Don Kirschner, Helena Znaniecki Lopata, Ellis Hawley, August Meier, John Burnham, Herbert Slutsky, Mel Holli, and Perry Duis. Their deep engagement with ideas and generosity of spirit live on with us, we hope. Glenda Riley and Austin Kerr, now retired, were wonderful seminar instructors.

University officials generously supported our work. At Illinois State University, history department chairs Tony Crubaugh and Ross Kennedy provided an office for Roger, so that he could continue his research and writing after retirement. At FAU, faculty committees kindly made awards in support of Mark's research travels. History department chairs Steve Engle, Patty Kollander, and Ben Lowe were enthusiastic advocates.

Librarians and archivists make book publishing possible. At Illinois State University's Milner Library, Vanette Schwartz and Angela Bonnell provided able assistance, as always; and at Florida Atlantic University, Holly Hargett, April Porterfield, Steven Matthew, Renata Johnson, Garrett Goode, Kim Preston, Melanie Poloff, and Larry Mello went out of their way multiple times to connect Mark with the library's resources.

We were equally well served during our research travels by Romie Minor at the Detroit Public Library's Burton Historical Collection and by Ann K. Sindelar and Vicki Catozzi at the Western Reserve Historical Society. Roger Horowitz and Carol Lockman arranged a comfortable room for Mark at the Hagley Museum and Library, enabling several days in their superb archives. Kristen Chinery at Wayne State University's Walter Reuther Library guided us toward useful collections. Kellee Warren at the University of Illinois at Chicago's Archives and Special Collections and Elizabeth Clemens at the Reuther Library made it easy to acquire photographs. We also had excellent research visits at University of Illinois at Chicago's Archives and Special Collections, the University of Pennsylvania's Architectural Archives, the University of Chicago Library's Special Collections, the University of Missouri at St. Louis Archives, Washington University Archives, and the Harold Washington Public Library in Chicago. Temple University's Urban Archives is a singularly wonderful place to conduct research. During his lengthy tenure at the Chicago History Museum, Archie Motley was every researcher's favorite archivist.

Conversations with colleagues about cities, politics, and social processes benefited our thinking in ways too numerous and subtle to place on a list. Early on, John Nolan provided a tour of St. Louis's down-and-out North Side and a glimpse into the lives of the city's dispossessed. After that, generous colleagues probably did not realize the degree to which we were engaged with their ideas. Steve Engle, Barbara Ganson, Boyd Breslow, Kelly Shannon, Chris Silver, Mary Sies, David Schuyler (deceased), Liz Cohen, Virginia Price, Paul Barrett (deceased), Dominic Vitiello, Bob Fairbanks, Todd Swanstrom, Louise Dyble, Joseph Heathcott, Todd Michney, Pam Laird, Terry Jones, Mark Wilson, Dick Hopkins, Tim Gilfoyle, Zach Schrag, Chris Klemek, Clifton Hood, Maire Murphy, Francesca Ammon, Alex von Hoffman, Eric Sandweiss, Margaret Marsh, Howard Gillette, Al Churella, Eric Avila, Josh Salzmann, Vicki Howard, Wendell Pritchett, Jack Bauman, Brian Balogh, Gary Miller, Lana Stein, Arnold Hirsch (deceased), and our dear friend and collaborator Raymond A. Mohl (deceased).

David Goldfield published an early version of our Arthur Rubloff chapter in the *Journal of Urban History*. Around the same time, *Journal of Planning History* editors Nicholas Bloom and Sonia Hirt published our preliminary conclusions on Dan Gilbert and Mike Ilitch's powerful positions in

Detroit politics. Nick, Sonia, and David's focused comments proved valuable in our thinking; and we appreciated their confidence in our fledgling enterprise. Megan Maher prepared the excellent maps that appeared in those journals; and Dennis McClendon added equally well done maps to the book.

Several colleagues took time from busy schedules to comment on parts of our manuscript. We are pleased to thank Ted Muller, Joel Tarr, Amanda Seligmann, Drew Simpson, Tracy Neumann, Joel Rast, Dom Pacyga, Christy Chapin, Andrew Hurley, Guian McKee, Dan Amsterdam, Kristin Szylvian, Mark Souther, Colin Gordon, Huping Ling, and Marsha Rose for careful and wise comments. At nearly every meeting, Ted and Joel added to our decades-long conversation about Pittsburgh politics. Finally, Arnie Kanov, Mark's cousin, kindly rectified our software problems.

Temple University Press editors and readers provided able support at every juncture. Aaron Javsicas supported this project enthusiastically from the start and showed great patience with two historians who were constantly angling for additional words and illustrations. Aaron selected deeply informed readers. Their reports remain models for how to engage authors' examples and concepts. Larry Bennett, an expert on Chicago politics, dazzled us with his intuitive understanding of other cities as well. He was the perfect series editor—knowledgeable, prompt in providing comments, and always willing to help without being intrusive. Geof Garvey, our copyeditor, played every note right; and, like twice before, Melissa Stearns Hyde prepared a valuable index.

We reached adulthood during another moment of dramatic change in Chicago's demographics. Our parents, Lloyd W. Biles and Irene F. Biles and Albert S. Rose and Bertha B. Rose, never studied the contours of urban history. They stood against the trend of lamenting those changes. Roger's children (Brian, Jeannie, and Grant) and Mark's children (Amy and Liana) came of age with the idea that their fathers were always writing and traveling for research and meetings. Our children are adults now—Amy and Liana are parents—and we still think about each of them every day. Mary Claire Biles and Marsha Lynn Shapiro Rose managed their careers alongside the domestic responsibilities we should have undertaken. Between us, we have been married to Mary Claire and Marsha Lynn for more than ninety years. They remain the loves of our lives.

# A Good Place to Do Business

# I

# Downtown Politics after World War II

After World War II, Pittsburgh was another smoky, racially conflicted, and declining city. During the next several decades, however, Pittsburgh's political and business leaders determined to remodel their city's downtown. These leaders—all white and male—labeled their program the Pittsburgh Renaissance, an ambitious term that analogized a program of vast destruction and equally vast rebuilding to the Italian Renaissance centuries earlier. We are not able to judge whether Pittsburghers' comparison of their city to the literature, art, and architecture of Milan, Rome, and Florence during the course of earlier centuries is apt or overblown. And yet, starting in the 1940s and extending for decades, business and political leaders in the great industrial cities we examine in this book—St. Louis, Chicago, Detroit, Cleveland, and Philadelphia—followed the Pittsburgh Renaissance in detail.

They had good reasons to do so. Pittsburgh, they recognized, had taken drastic steps to reduce smoke and remake downtown into an attractive place in which to invest, shop, and have fun. Visiting politicians in that era were equally certain that removal of African Americans from areas in and near downtown comprised another important feature in their cities' future restoration program. During the 1950s, mayors and high-level executives from as far away as St. Louis traveled to Pittsburgh to hear at first-hand about the policies, cash, and removal programs that were prerequisite to restoring downtown to an equal level of clear skies and a burgeoning, mostly white prosperity. Between 1945 and 1970, Pittsburgh's political and business leadership committed to making the Renaissance a success, sometimes at a high cost to their firms. One person, however, was singularly important in bringing the Renaissance into being and keeping his city's leaders focused on making it a success.

Richard King Mellon was seemingly born to remodel downtown Pittsburgh. Starting in the 1930s and extending into the 1960s, Mellon's remarkable combination of wealth, influence, and a deep desire to change parts of the city placed him at the center of Pittsburgh politics. As a start, Mellon, a white male, was also extraordinarily rich. When Mellon died, age 70, on June 4, 1970, he left behind a family estate valued at $3 billion. ($21.7 billion in 2022) Mellon was by one account the second wealthiest person in the United States, richer in fact than the better-known Rockefeller family. The Mellon family's wealth had increased with American industrialization and financial growth. Richard King, the family patriarch, had held a controlling interest in several of the nation's largest corporations, including the Gulf Oil Company, the Aluminum Company of America (Alcoa), and General Reinsurance. In 1970 Mellon's First Boston Corporation remained the nation's leading investment banking syndicate, handling a larger dollar value of new stock market issues than the better-known Merrill Lynch and Lehman Brothers. Up to 1967, Mellon also served as chairman of the board at the Mellon National Bank and Trust Company, Pittsburgh's largest bank and the thirteenth largest in the United States. A writer for *Time* Magazine described Mellon's passing as the "Death of a King."[1]

Mellon enjoyed little by way of formal training for business. He had a weekly tutorial at home about business successes and failures. His father and his uncle, Andrew W. Mellon, the U.S. Secretary of the Treasury between 1921 and 1932, met at the young Mellon's house prior to church services on Sundays, where they insisted that he listen to their business-focused discussions. Uncle Andrew also brought Alcoa and Gulf Oil Company executives with him to weekly Sunday dinners. Mellon's father ran his own set of businesses. He directed the construction of impressive buildings located in downtown Pittsburgh, including the Mellon National Bank Building (1924) and the 44-story Gulf Building, which opened in 1932. Not all of his father's investments shined. During the 1920s, he held a large interest in the declining Pittsburgh Coal Company. Coal executives engaged in numerous conflicts with unionized miners.[2]

As the young Richard King Mellon came of adulthood, his father's and uncle's experiences taught a larger set of lessons. Mellon had adopted the idea that his family's wealth and reputation rested in some measure on working successfully with other leaders. Whether his family's male leaders directed skyscraper construction, made decisions about a declining coal company, presided over a large bank, or considered the many problems afflicting the Pennsylvania Railroad, the senior Mellons recognized that lawmakers and union leaders often played a decisive role in shaping the nation's business environment, each of their firms' operating rules, and the family's prosperity. As one example, federal officials regulated the interest rate that the Mellon bank (and every bank holding a federal charter) paid on savings accounts; and in fact, those same federal officials made regular visits to bank headquarters to check on compliance with the government's many financial rules. As a second example, Pennsylvania Railroad executives had long negotiated with union leaders about wages and working conditions for locomotive engineers and other top-level operating employees. Starting in 1920, moreover, members of the powerful Interstate Commerce Commission determined whether the Pennsylvania Railroad could serve customers located in a new territory or purchase trucking and steamship companies to extend service and acquire additional shipments.[3] To maintain and enhance the value of businesses that each day participated in a tumultuous political economy, the younger Mellon had surely learned, required solid partnerships with union leaders and lawmakers as well the presence of an engaged, determined, and precise executive hand exercised on a near-daily basis. Knowledge about government regulators and union leaders represented only Richard King Mellon's first step toward successful management of Pittsburgh's renewal.

## Mellon and Public Affairs

Both at school and at home, future business leaders like Richard King Mellon also acquired the idea that they were to achieve prominence in directing public affairs. He had a lot of practice. During World War I, Mellon enlisted in the U.S. Army. In 1936 he married Constance Prosser, the widow of a wealthy New York banker. Marriage to a socially prominent family widened Mellon's network of persons on whom he could rely for advice and to whom he could turn to add to his storehouse of political capital—a storehouse that was fundamental to the process of assembling and closing large deals.[4]

Mellon also developed experience in command positions. In 1934, following his father's death, Mellon Bank's board of directors elected him president. By 1937, Mellon served as a director of thirty-four corporations. During World War II, he rose to the rank of assistant chief of the War Department's international division. Following the war, Mellon remained in the army reserves, where he achieved the rank of lieutenant general. Friends and colleagues often called him General, his preferred nickname. Again, men like Richard Mellon expected to preside over important financial and civic organizations. And yet, a wealthy and prominent person like Mellon might have chosen among a large number of areas in which to invest his energy and considerable talent. Pittsburgh, by one account, was an inherited passion.[5]

Starting in the 1940s, Mellon focused on two projects that were intimately related. He reorganized the family's enterprises, many of which were located in Pittsburgh, and he sought with equal energy to clean Pittsburgh's smoke-laden air, unclog snarled traffic, and construct new office towers downtown. Mellon, like any real estate manager sizing up his properties' future values and earnings potential, wanted to replace aging and dirty structures that had long suffered neglect, vacancies, falling property values, low prestige tenants, and declining rental rates. But the younger Mellon was no small-scale landlord seeking only to boost rental and occupancy rates in a few dilapidated buildings. By training and habit, Mellon expected to direct the nation's most important and most visible social and economic changes.

Mellon was one among many business leaders in the nation's largest cities who wanted to alter the American political economy. During and after the war, businessmen, lawmakers, and ordinary residents throughout the United States talked and planned for an economy that would not fall into another depression, and they planned with equal fervor to build cities that were sunny, prosperous, and growing again. Most of those plans yielded only modest results, or none at all. During the two decades after World War II, Mellon possessed the know-how, networks, authority, and the political as well as financial resources to undertake major changes in his family's corporations as well as in a large industrial city. At the same time, Mellon served as a senior partner with the mayor in every downtown construction project. Mellon was Pittsburgh's city planner in all but title. By the late 1960s, Mellon and his business and political associates had made Pittsburgh's postwar renewal program one of the most successful and certainly one of the most visible in the United States. That renewal started with creation of a key organization.

## The Allegheny Conference on Community Development

In 1943 Mellon played a central role in creating the Allegheny Conference on Community Development (ACCD) and making it the prime vehicle for directing Pittsburgh's postwar renewal. Robert E. Doherty, the president of the Carnegie Institute of Technology, served as the committee's first chair. Pittsburgh residents knew the institute as Carnegie Tech (the future Carnegie Mellon University). At a luncheon held at a downtown hotel, attendees listened as Doherty spoke about the "resuscitation of a devitalized and deteriorating metropolitan area" as the new organization's core goal. ACCD members would coordinate the studies and planning that were prerequisite to such a massive undertaking. But in its first year, with the World War taking precedence, the ACCD remained a modest affair set in humble circumstances.

On December 1, the *Pittsburgh Press* ran a notice that Dr. Willard E. Hotchkiss, director of Carnegie Tech's Social Studies Division, would present a lecture titled "Educational Aspects of Post-War Community Planning" at the Downtown YMCA. Hotchkiss, in addition to his duties at Carnegie Tech, was chairman of the ACCD's Study Planning Commission. Hotchkiss and Doherty were exceptions among Carnegie Tech's faculty and senior officials. In the 1940s, Carnegie Tech remained a school where most faculty and administrators harbored few aspirations to serve among the city's intellectual and political leaders. Carnegie Tech faculty worked with a limited budget to educate local students. The YMCA, for that matter, was not a place at which the city's business and political leaders gathered to hear professors' lectures.[6]

Nor were Mellon and the ACCD's ideas about postwar planning unique. Business executives and lawmakers in many cities were making plans to deal with choking smoke, miserable traffic congestion, falling property values, the outmigration of businesses and households to the suburbs, and diminished retail sales, especially downtown. Faculty such as Hotchkiss also sought to create devices to maintain full employment after the war rather than a return to gloomy depression days and government sponsored projects that, according to critics, produced nothing useful. Negative assessments of government programs were standard rhetorical fare among American business leaders. At the same time, those businessmen, including Mellon and his ACCD colleagues, depended on government to bestow contracts, offer favorable regulatory rulings, trim union authority, invest in roads and airports, and foster development of a growing national economy once the war ended.

Race was also a central factor in Mellon's postwar planning. Like business leaders in St. Louis, Chicago, Detroit, and countless other cities, Mellon and his ACCD members wanted to remove African American households and entire neighborhoods from areas around downtown. ACCD officials also targeted aging, white-occupied buildings located in downtown's heart. Such vast renewal projects required the authority of state, federal, and city governments. Despite their dependence on government in areas as different as building highways, clearing smoke, leveling aged buildings, and demolishing African American neighborhoods, businessmen like Mellon relied on anti-government rhetoric to foster the idea that they were the city's productive citizens, in contrast with seemingly inept and venal politicians and self-serving union leaders. Mellon's rhetorical strategy, which came naturally, was to cast businessmen like himself as the only persons who could be trusted to manage urban revival. All in all, Mellon and his ACCD colleagues sounded and behaved no differently than their racially focused counterparts in large and small cities located throughout the United States.[7]

In Pittsburgh, Mellon and his top Allegheny Conference officials developed connections to political and business leaders throughout the city and region. At the start, Mellon created an ACCD parent committee and a series of neighborhood committees. Members of the earliest parent committee, his most important set of connections by far, included Edgar J. Kaufmann, owner of one of Pittsburgh's largest department stores, and Frank Buchanan, a member of the U.S. Congress from Pittsburgh and a Democratic Party stalwart. Mellon and his family members were avid Republicans. Buchanan's addition to the ACCD's leadership gave Mellon another advocate for Pittsburgh's share of federal highway, water, and renewal programs. Among Allegheny Conference members, political and financial resources to support Pittsburgh's regeneration took precedence over party allegiance. Above all, Mellon wanted ACCD members and ordinary residents to promote Pittsburgh as a place in need of restoration and as a city in which to invest and raise a family. And again, Mellon's Pittsburgh, once reinvented and rebuilt, would feature skyscrapers, well-paid corporate employees, fewer blocks housing saloons, cigar stores, and boarding houses, a reduced number of African Americans, and a far larger number of middle-income, white residents.[8]

## Mayor David L. Lawrence and the Pittsburgh Renaissance's First Days

Mellon's connection to the young ACCD was important. But the Pittsburgh financial titan made a second and perhaps more important connection with Pittsburgh's mayor, David L. Lawrence, who was also the leader of the local Democratic Party. Mellon needed Lawrence's support to build roads, change zoning ordinances, and complete other tasks that only the municipality could accomplish. Lawrence, for his part, exercised tight control over members of Pittsburgh's city council. At the same time, Lawrence needed Mellon and the business community's support to finance the immense expense of cleaning up the city. Pittsburgh's business executives also held the option of taking their firms to the suburbs, or to another city. Mayor Lawrence wanted those executives, including Mellon, to remain downtown, where they paid taxes and employed thousands of his constituents. Even before his election, Lawrence already favored a renewal program tailored to Mellon and the ACCD's approach. As much as Mellon and Lawrence shared an outlook about how to repair Pittsburgh, they rarely met in person, but instead communicated through subordinates. Mellon, with his vast wealth and with equally large sums of cultural and political capital at his disposal, served as the senior partner in negotiations with Lawrence. Mellon would have dominated any relationship, other than perhaps those with top corporate executives in New York and Chicago or with the president of the United States. Mellon's involvement changed the ACCD from a "'luncheon club' into the city's most effective organization," a local journalist reported years later. On a day-to-day basis, however, the fundamentally shy Mellon left hard, wrenching tasks such as negotiating with lawmakers to seasoned hands like Mayor Lawrence and to his top officials and staff members at the Allegheny Conference.[9]

Mellon's Pittsburgh Renaissance commenced with a comprehensive campaign against air pollution. Smoke permeated the Steel City, often necessitating the use of streetlights throughout the day. The shirt collars of downtown office workers turned gray by noon, and homemakers washed curtains every week to remove the accumulated soot. Airline pilots dreaded landing at the local airport because of limited visibility. The smog issue had become so serious that executives of large firms headquartered in Pittsburgh listed the desire to live in a cleaner city as a major reason that they were considering relocation elsewhere. By 1945, senior executives at giant corporations such as U.S. Steel, the Westinghouse Electric Corporation, and Mellon's Alcoa had begun to draft plans to build skyscrapers for their new administrative offices in other cities. Pittsburgh, known widely for its unrelieved gloom and grime, also had a reputation as an unhealthy place to reside and raise a family, as a poor place in which to invest, and as a difficult location to recruit and retain senior executives. Mellon and members of the ACCD had clearly tabulated the financial cost of a degraded environment.[10]

In its inaugural project, ACCD officials modeled their solution to the air-pollution problem after the St. Louis smoke control ordinance of 1940. Drafted by Washington University engineering professor Raymond R. Tucker, who had been appointed city smoke commissioner in 1937, the St. Louis ordinance prohibited the use of coal with high ash and sulfur content, established exacting inspection procedures, and adopted stiff penalties for emission offenders. In 1941 Pittsburgh Mayor Cornelius D. Scully sent the city's health director to St. Louis to observe the smoke control measures taken there. The Pittsburgh city council passed a smoke abatement ordinance in short order but declined to implement it during World War II. In 1946 Mayor Lawrence announced his intention to enforce the overlooked ordinance, and the ACCD rallied behind him. Even Mellon, the director of the Consolidated Coal Company, the largest supplier of fuel to the region, supported the mayor.

Converting a large city and thousands of customers to less smoky devices for cooking, heating, and manufacturing was never easy or automatic. Smoke reduction required homeowners and businesses to change from cheap coal to cleaner (and more expensive) coals, or to natural gas, either way putting miners' jobs at stake. (In 1947, natural gas pipelines reached Pittsburgh, supplying vast quantities of the inexpensive and cleaner burning fuel to the local gas company). Miners (and the countless employees who transported coal and worked with it in each of the city's factories) comprised an important base of Lawrence's support, but still, he went forward with smoke reduction plans. Lawrence prioritized smoke control's benefits for the city's future prosperity over coal workers' immediate fears about the elimination of their jobs. Business executives seeking to change Pittsburgh's smoky image demanded that local, coal-using businesses switch to gas. When coal companies and railroads in the county and surrounding region threatened to ignore the restrictions, top ACCD officials successfully lobbied for a smoke control bill in the state legislature. And when the Pennsylvania Railroad's president objected to the smoke legislation, Mellon threatened to use his influence with corporate executives to shift their freight shipments to competing railroads. Before long, the president of the massive U.S. Steel Corporation joined Mellon in pushing the railroad to go along with the pending legislation. In retrospect, Allegheny Conference leaders including Lawrence judged their successful showdown with the president of the Pennsylvania Railroad an important test of their ability to surmount political divisions and win a face-off with a major corporation. In future years, corporate executives, large property owners, and political leaders in other struggling industrial cities, including Detroit, Chicago, and Philadelphia, looked to the Steel City for fruitful examples of business-government cooperation. Above all, as political scientist Barbara Ferman observes, the Pittsburgh model's apparent success in coming years also fostered "a political culture centered around civic mindedness [and] corporate participation in public affairs."[11] During the next decade, sunny days appeared more regularly in the Pittsburgh region. A less smoky city represented only the first step in Mellon and Lawrence's efforts to rehabilitate downtown Pittsburgh.

Mellon perceived that a united and vibrant ACCD (known to locals simply as "the Conference") held the key to a successful renewal program. With wartime strictures and responsibilities disappearing behind them, Mellon and a few others remodeled the Conference into the shape it took for the next decade and more. They created an executive committee composed of attorneys, bankers, university administrators, and top corporate officials, including Henry J. Heinz II, the president and chair of the H.J. Heinz Corporation; Robert C. Downie, the president of Peoples First National Bank and Trust; and Edgar Kaufmann, the department-store executive. In subsequent years, additional corporate leaders such as Gwilym Price, the Westinghouse Electric Corporation's Chair and CEO, joined the ACCD's executive committee. Those executive committee members pledged in advance to attend Conference meetings in person rather than send a representative or surrender their right to vote. Personal involvement was part of the ACCD ethos and added to their collective ability to accomplish renewal goals. As well, executive committee members and the organization's more than 100 active members enjoyed solid connections to local and state officials who directed and legislated about most aspects of Pittsburgh's urban redevelopment program.[12] Like Mellon and Lawrence, Conference members were native Pittsburghers largely. Those interwoven ACCD relationships grew still more extensive with Lawrence's tenure as Pennsylvania's governor from 1959 to 1963.

Park H. Martin, the ACCD's long-time executive director, had also developed extensive relationships among Pittsburgh's corporate and political leaders. Martin was a Carnegie Tech engineering graduate who was director of planning for the Allegheny County government and then ran his own consulting firm. While still employed by the county, he set aside the land that became the Greater Pittsburgh Airport and assembled a $72 million development program that included a parkway, bridges, and roads. Richard King Mellon, still an army colonel, hired Martin at a meeting in Harrisburg, Pennsylvania, the state capital.[13] From the start, Martin shared Mellon's commitment to the transformation of downtown Pittsburgh.

## The Focus on Downtown Pittsburgh

During the first years after World War II, downtown Pittsburgh, like downtowns in most American cities, continued to suffer deterioration and a failure to invest in new buildings and updated stores. In March 1946, a fire of mysterious origin destroyed the Wabash Railroad's three, block-long train sheds and warehouses that had blocked full development of Pittsburgh's downtown. Firefighters needed more than 42 hours to extinguish the blaze, a record. A massive fire, ever-present smoke, and occasional floods only reinforced the conviction among many that the central business district was an unattractive place to conduct business or spend the day shopping.[14]

The Wabash Railroad fire created an opportunity for Conference leaders to coalesce around a large-scale restoration plan, their first. During the summer of 1946, the president of the Pittsburgh and West Virginia Railroad (which owned the Wabash Railroad) traveled to New York City with several ACCD officials to visit the Metropolitan Life Insurance Company. They sought funds to redevelop an area much larger than the railroad's properties. Buildings—many still housing residents and small businesses—would be demolished to make way for downtown office towers fronting on the junction of the Allegheny, Monongahela, and Ohio Rivers, an area known to Pittsburgh residents as The Point. The Metropolitan's president turned them down, but he recommended that the group visit with the president of Equitable Life Assurance Society of the United States, who approved. By one participant's account, "Equitable wanted to know definitely if the smoke ordinance was going to be effective. [And], when we answered, 'yes,' [downtown restoration] was made." Members of the City Planning Commission, an ACCD ally, certified a 59-acre site as eligible for renewal.[15]

Public authority was crucial in other ways. The city's Urban Renewal Authority, chaired by Mayor Lawrence, also approved the redevelopment plan, making it possible to use Equitable Life's funds in this public-private partnership. As part of the negotiations leading up to this moment, Edgar Kaufmann, the department store executive and a Conference activist, acquiesced to redevelopment plans despite the fact that a competitor's store would remain located closer to the Point. Construction started in 1950, after Mayor Lawrence and city council members approved the plan.[16]

During the next decade and beyond, corporate leaders, always working in close alliance with ACCD officials, constructed high-rise office towers and a high-rent apartment building. In June 1960, Equitable Life executives and David Lawrence, now Pennsylvania's governor, were on hand to dedicate the opening of yet another building. Designers clad the new, 22-story tower, named Four Gateway Center, in glass and stainless steel. A local reporter, keeping with the booster rhetoric that accompanied Pittsburgh's renewal program, described Four Gateway Center as "one of the most distinguished business addresses in America."[17] All in all, it appeared, Mellon, Lawrence, and Allegheny Conference leaders like Park Martin had converted the smoky and ramshackle Point into a handsome collection of corporate offices called the Gateway Center. That name evocatively suggested the presence of an equally remodeled city located just beyond those gateway buildings.

In truth, Mellon and other conference leaders had focused all or most of their attention on downtown Pittsburgh's physical restoration. As a start, they judged construction of underground parking a crucial factor in the Point's successful development. Attracting downtown visitors was another priority. Pittsburgh's Convention Bureau encouraged free-spending business and professional groups to meet in the city and stay at a downtown hotel, especially the new, 22-story Hilton Hotel that opened in December 1959. Governor Lawrence was on hand to remind opening day guests, including hotel chain president Conrad N. Hilton, about the many skeptics in Pittsburgh who had doubted the Mellon-Lawrence partnership and the ACCD's vision for converting the shabby Point into the spectacular Gateway Center.[18] History was a useful device to further legitimate past developments and recruit succeeding generations of listeners to the importance of maintaining that partnership and vision.[19]

## The Pittsburgh Idea and the Racialized Politics of Urban Renewal in American Cities

By the 1960s, Mellon's Allegheny Conference and the Pittsburgh Renaissance (as it was labeled) had achieved recognition among business and political leaders in cities throughout the United States. Newspaper and magazine writers regularly published before-and-after photos of the Point. Accompanying stories described the methods that citizens, politicians, and business leaders acting in concert had employed. Just as Lawrence and other ACCD leaders liked to repeat, who, upon viewing those photos, could fail to distinguish between the earlier smoke and grime and the contemporary assembly of gleaming office towers? [20]

Visitors also marveled at Pittsburgh's ability to eliminate "blighted" areas in and around the Gateway Center. *Blighted* was a word that developers and lawmakers used to characterize dilapidated buildings, as for instance the unrepaired and abandoned buildings that surrounded downtown Pittsburgh and every other central business district. Many of those buildings, however, also housed modest businesses such as saloons and rooming houses. The owners of residential buildings sometimes supplemented modest incomes by taking in boarders. With renewal programs looming on the political horizon, many property owners and residents sought the assistance of political leaders to protect their investments, their small businesses, or simply the places where they lived. But those Pittsburghers, never well organized, were no match for a united business and political leadership bent on creating a different downtown. Language helped their cause. Pittsburgh's leadership as well as ordinary citizens judged large parts of downtown "blighted." And "blighted" was in turn a profoundly racialized term, one that white Pittsburgh residents and white residents located in any other city did not require a dictionary or formal instruction to understand. Blight was another word for slum, which by the 1950s almost always designated an area occupied by African Americans, Puerto Ricans, or poor (white) southerners who had recently moved north. Blight could also be applied to areas of the city that many Pittsburghers no longer visited, or perhaps even feared. [21]

In Pittsburgh, as in every American city, race was always at or near the center of politics. As early as 1945, Mellon, Lawrence, and other top ACCD officials had agreed that they would no more tolerate a blighted area in their city than they would tolerate a cancer on their bodies. Only a radical resection, as every adult recognized, could return a cancer patient to a full and prosperous health. Blight's elimination and the first stages of urban restoration, however, started not with anesthetics and surgical knives but with noisy bulldozers that leveled older buildings and evicted unwanted residents, blacks and a smaller number of whites. [22]

Journalists visiting downtown Pittsburgh took an identical stance. Pittsburgh's Lower Hill was located east of downtown, and it was also "blighted" and scheduled for demolition. The "slums" in Pittsburgh's Lower Hill, a news writer reported in November 1956, "compare with the worst in Cincinnati," his newspaper's hometown. Was the Pittsburgh slum clearance program "a blueprint for Cincinnati?" the reporter asked rhetorically. By the mid-1950s, with sparkling skyscrapers reaching toward the clear sky and nearby slums soon to be demolished, Mellon and Lawrence's Pittsburgh Renaissance emerged as a must-see inspection site for business executives and as a brand name that urban political leaders sought to replicate in their hometowns.[23]

Large delegations of business and professional leaders made pilgrimages to view Pittsburgh's Renaissance. In October 1953, Raymond R. Tucker, now mayor of St. Louis, led a delegation of his city's top executives to Pittsburgh, where they met with ACCD director Martin and a number of Pittsburgh's business and political leaders. In June 1956, as another example, Chicago Mayor Richard J. Daley led fifty-nine business executives to Pittsburgh. Mayor Lawrence and other officials provided a guided tour of the Gateway Center, the new parking garages, and Lower Hill, the area scheduled for demolition. "We can't have a strong democracy," Daley announced, "unless we rid our cities of slums." During the 1950s and 1960s, members of more than seventy groups, international and domestic, toured downtown Pittsburgh.[24]

Daley and civic leaders in other cities had no need to undertake time-consuming and exhausting trips to Pittsburgh's buildings and parking lots only to pronounce on academic themes like slums and democracy. Nor did they have reason to make an arduous journey solely to inspect the Hilton Hotel, sample from its tasty menu, and walk around the Gateway Center's office towers. Photos, plans, and architectural renderings, including cost estimates, were always available to businessmen and lawmakers who, each day, bought and sold buildings, sought higher rent tenants, scrutinized reports about construction prices, and looked for ways to boost their city's tax base.

Daley, Tucker, and the other visitors traveled to Pittsburgh to talk about the politics of urban renewal. As members of visiting delegations smoked cigars and cigarettes, imbibed mixed drinks, and dined at Pittsburgh's fancier restaurants, they maintained one question front and center. Daley and members of those seventy delegations wanted to know how had David Lawrence, Richard King Mellon, and Park Martin managed to overcome the political and economic obstacles that delayed or stopped identical redevelopment plans in their hometowns? Not even Daley, an autocratic boss whose supposedly unchecked power allowed him to dominate Chicago's government and politics, had yet managed to launch a redevelopment program in the city's central business district. That retail sales in downtown Pittsburgh continued to fall during the 1950s and the fact that Lawrence, Mellon, and Martin had directed the demolition of lively manufacturing areas did not matter to Daley or to members of his entourage. Pittsburgh was building skyscrapers, eliminating blight, reducing smoke, constructing new highways, and pushing African Americans farther from downtown.[25] A trip to Pittsburgh, Daley and his associates clearly hoped, would allow them to uncover a political formula to launch their cities into equally rapid and successful recovery programs.

Civic notables seeking to uncover Pittsburgh's magic recipe for urban resuscitation returned home with a list of preconditions essential to halting rapid decline, and journalists ratified their conclusions. First and foremost, business and political leaders in St. Louis, Chicago, and other cities unconditionally accepted the necessity of reviving the central business district as the first step toward reinvigorating the entire municipality. Although property owners, corporate moguls, and executives at banks and insurance companies may have had diverging interests in some cases, they could all agree on the indispensability of the central business district to reviving their city's property values, retail sales, and tax bases. Those early Pittsburgh tourists also glimpsed the exhilarating prospect of using new roads such as Pittsburgh's Crosstown Boulevard to reduce congestion, speed wealthy shoppers downtown, and at the same time protect new skyscrapers from residents still housed in blighted areas within eyesight. In Pittsburgh, high-rent units frequently replaced the crumbling structures leveled by the wrecker's ball. Housing for the poor would have to wait for another day. As Mellon, Lawrence, Martin, and Pittsburgh's enthusiastic visitors agreed, full attention to the neighborhoods could be realized only once the largest property owners, corporate renters (banks and law firms), and cultural pace setters such as art museums and concert halls had arrested decline and set the city again on a healthy financial course.

The success of Mellon's Allegheny Conference contained implications that no executive in any city could ignore. Corporate officials, bankers, merchants, and other stakeholders in every city's downtown revival planning learned that they must act in concert with local officials who controlled the municipal purse strings and possessed the authority and political connections to secure aid from state and federal agencies. The Pittsburgh Renaissance, in which the Republican ACCD and Democratic Mayor Lawrence made common cause, underscored the importance of bipartisan cooperation in which businessmen and politicians put aside their mutual distrust and worked together for a common goal. Mellon proved willing to challenge the interests of the mighty Pennsylvania Railroad, for example, just as Lawrence took positions criticized by the trade unions that served as crucial components of his electoral base. "This is a new kind of blending of public and private enterprise," Lawrence gushed in 1951. "It is the most promising and rewarding program in our public life today."[26]

In Pittsburgh, observes historian Gabriel Winant, "the drama of industrial decline [had] appeared in particularly stark and visible form." But in turn, the remarkable reconstruction of downtown Pittsburgh, effusively praised in the national press and confirmed by visiting dignitaries from around the country, pointed the way for business leaders in declining industrial cities determined to forge their own urban renaissance. Great metropolises laid low after World War II by the loss of industry, population, and retail sales saw a common set of problems in Pittsburgh and took heart in that city's ability to refashion a tired landscape. The grand public-private partnership in Pittsburgh provided a blueprint for halting the spread of blight and breathing life into ailing central business districts. Fighting against popular perceptions that rotting Rust Belt cities were doomed to continue losing ground to verdant suburbs and thriving Sunbelt communities, local elites and government officials took their cues from Richard King Mellon and David Lawrence to offset the declension narrative.[27]

## Government and Growth in Five American Cities

This first part of this study follows the unrelenting efforts of urban and political leaders in five cities to replicate the heralded Pittsburgh story. We follow those developments in St. Louis, Chicago, Detroit, Cleveland, and Philadelphia—five major metropolises that held vital positions in the growth of American trade and manufacturing during the previous century. Starting even before World War II, however, those cities were already caught in the undertow of industrial change—fewer manufacturing jobs, loss of retail sales, falling property values, and intense racial conflict. Whether in the 1920s and 1930s or in the 1960s and 1970s, leaders in these cities identified their downtown's skyscrapers, giant department stores, and upscale shops (and their mostly white employees and shoppers) as the unchangeable building blocks for regional prosperity. The Pittsburgh model came naturally to leaders in these five cities. And that Pittsburgh model evolved from a lengthy history of national and urban politics.

Detroit, Chicago, and the other cities we chose to study developed originally as trade hubs and became industrial powerhouses. All five cities benefited from the sustained support of government, which played a critical role in creating conditions favorable to the rise of manufacturing. Entrepreneurs offered unstinting praise to the virtues of unbridled capitalism and the unerring wisdom of the market, but all the while fiercely pursued aid from city halls, state legislatures, and especially Washington, DC. Whether distributing land that could be sold to generate capital or building infrastructure to boost commerce, government leaders in every decade pursued an approach made famous by Alexander Hamilton, the first Secretary of the Treasury.

Hamilton, seeking to build a large and prosperous nation, sought to promote business interests. City and state leaders, especially in the northern states, were quick to follow Hamilton's ideas.

Public spending for private development occurred repeatedly as a national trade and transportation network developed during the nineteenth century. Government largess funded the building of canals, docks, wharves, piers, roads, bridges, and railroads; state and federal dollars paid for the dredging of harbors and the removal of sandbars to enable local waterways to handle increasingly larger vessels. In the process, these five cities became integral components of the emerging national political economy. The Pennsylvania Railroad, for example, tied Philadelphia to developing markets in the urban west, including Cleveland, Detroit, Chicago, and even distant St. Louis. Decades earlier, the opening of the Erie Canal proved crucial in placing Cleveland, Detroit, and Chicago at the heart of the Great Lakes network. Thanks to government-funded improvement of its docks, St. Louis assumed primacy of the steamboat trade on the Mississippi River. No one could deny the links between government beneficence and the growth of the five cities during the crucial decades of phenomenal economic expansion. Long before the advent of automobiles, trucks, and airlines, railroads linked these five cities to a burgeoning economy. As Americans moved west, they carried with them innovative ideas about how to set up businesses, speculate in real estate, and engage in diverse and profitable activities such as forging steel and manufacturing shop tools. No fact mattered more to urban development than the arrival of millions of immigrants from Europe and migrants from the Deep South.

The populations of the five cities exploded during the industrial age as Europeans left behind the economic stagnation and political and religious persecution in their homelands for work in a rapidly industrializing America. In the twentieth century, poor whites departed rural southern states for the opportunity offered in northern factories; beginning during the First World War, African Americans fled the danger and economic uncertainty of the Jim Crow South for jobs and the promise of freedom in northern and western cities. Latin Americans and Asians also migrated to these five cities. They took up a similar process of clustering in neighborhoods composed largely of people who spoke their language, ate similar foods, and practiced their religion in like fashion.

These new arrivals from every part of the globe often lived near downtown for easy access to jobs and municipal services. Central business districts served as the financial and cultural epicenters of urban life. Mass transit networks in turn radiated outward from downtown into expanding neighborhoods, permitting factories, shops, and households to spread across the landscape. During the years between 1900 and 1940, these vast, sprawling cities of shops and mills produced the railroads, steel, lamps, radios, shoes, and other products that boosted living standards for many. Starting in 1939–1940, factories located in these five cities provided essential industrial goods as part of the nation's "Arsenal of Democracy." After World War II, returning soldiers pushed populations still higher, with each city reaching a peak in 1950. But in the decades that followed, residents and their employers moved to suburbs or to other cities in the west and south. St. Louis's population sank from 856,000 in 1950 to 453,000 in 1980; and Philadelphia's population declined from 2.07 million to 1.68 million during that same period. Each city lost not only residents and jobs, but also a whopping part of their tax base as higher income residents moved away. Starting as early as 1945, leaders in these five cities desperately sought solutions to their declining fortunes. They focused their recovery programs almost exclusively on downtown revival, exactly the path that businessman Richard King Mellon and Mayor David Lawrence pursued in Pittsburgh.

Philadelphia, Detroit, Cleveland, St. Louis, and Chicago shared a number of common experiences during the era of rapid industrial expansion—smoke, for one example, and diverse populations for another. But unique local circumstances also produced a varied set of inheritances in the communities by the time that the Second World War concluded. Machine tools comprised a large part of Cleveland's economy. Philadelphia's postwar economy still included a large number of knitting mills. But without doubt, one item transcended these differences. In every city, black and white residents lived in different parts of town; they occupied different jobs; they shopped in different stores; they dined separately; they rarely socialized after work; they experienced diseases at different rates; and they judged that an advantage awarded to another part of the city came at their expense. In each of our cities, these seemingly intractable differences informed politics across many decades. And yet, white Americans were sometimes reluctant to explain their city's social and economic geography in harsh racial terms. Instead, they preferred to describe their hometown's housing arrangements or talk about who secured which high-wage jobs in terms of abstractions such as hard work, natural affinities, and the market's sovereign workings. As historians Stefan Link and Noam Maggor remind us, however, "'the market' never shed its deeply political nature."[28] And for most of the time, that politics was limited to a grinding, zero-sum affair.

## Philadelphia

The busiest port and most affluent community in England's North American Empire by the mid-eighteenth century, Philadelphia served as an entrepôt linking its rich agricultural hinterland with markets in Europe and the Caribbean. By the 1770s, only London surpassed Philadelphia in the volume and value of maritime trade. Philadelphia merchants saw shipping tonnage of incoming and outgoing vessels decline sharply after the opening in 1825 of the Erie Canal, which provided east coast shippers and merchants with easy access through the Great Lakes to the fertile lands west of the Appalachian Mountains and elevated New York City to primacy among seaport cities. Avoiding permanent decline, however, Philadelphia's political and business leaders successfully engineered the transition from a commercial to an industrial city. Exploiting its many assets—convenient location near waterpower; ready access to coal and iron deposits; abundant capital in the nation's premier financial institutions, including the Bank of the United States; technical expertise; and a ready supply of skilled labor—the city became the manufacturing capital of the nation by the end of the nineteenth century. Philadelphia's burgeoning industries yielded a variety of goods ranging from iron and steel to cigars, from pharmaceuticals to shoes, but garment and textile factories became the most important segment of the local economy.[29]

By the late 1870s, although Philadelphia remained a leading manufacturing center, the development of new modes of transportation, the appearance of new commodities, and the demise of some industries altered the industrial landscape. The rising popularity of synthetic fabrics and the loss of business to the American South and other locations where factories paid extraordinarily low wages undermined the competitiveness of the city's textile mills. The decline of the textile industry, which began in earnest in the 1920s, occurred gradually enough that forty thousand workers still labored in the mills during World War II. As late as the mid-twentieth century, people around the world still thought of Philadelphia as an industrial juggernaut, the home of Baldwin Locomotive, the Pennsylvania Railroad, Midvale Steel, Stetson Hat, Keystone Knitting Mills, and countless smaller enterprises that produced large quantities of high-quality products.[30]

Philadelphia's political leadership came almost exclusively from the Republican Party, which predominated for more than a half-century. Unlike in many northern industrial cities where local elites and good government reformers supported the Republican Party and Democratic machines represented the interests of the immigrant masses, Philadelphians of all stripes consistently supported the Grand Old Party. Periodic reform outbursts registered public indignation but failed to unseat local Republican bosses "King" James McManes, Israel Durham, Boies Penrose, and William Vare, all of whom answered to Matthew Quay and other Republican politicians in Harrisburg who firmly controlled state politics in the last decades of the nineteenth century. Characterizing Philadelphia as both "the worst-governed city in the country" and remarkably prosperous, Lincoln Steffens, muckraking author of the best-selling exposé, *The Shame of the Cities*, called the city "corrupt and contented."[31] We might debate the precise accuracy of Steffens's account of Philadelphia's corruption. But we should never doubt that the city's manufacturers and bankers helped build a downtown composed of magnificent shops and adjoining neighborhoods composed of hardworking and impoverished newcomers of every nationality and race.

## Detroit

Another city that began as a remote outpost of empire for a European nation, Detroit grew rapidly along with the automobile industry and surpassed Philadelphia in industrial production by the early 1920s (ranking third then behind New York City and Chicago). Situated on the Detroit River between Lake St. Clair and Lake Erie, Detroit provided New France with a strategic location for controlling the lucrative fur trade in the Upper Great Lakes region. After burning to the ground in 1805, the city recovered slowly until the opening of the Erie Canal in 1825 sparked a sharp increase in immigration to the Old Northwest in the decades before the Civil War. As the fur trade disappeared, Detroit became the primary mercantile center for the Michigan Territory, importing manufactured goods from the east coast and exporting fish, farm products, lumber, copper, iron, and lead from Michigan's Upper Peninsula. Long before the onset of the automobile industry, Detroit established a solid if unspectacular industrial base through copper smelting and the manufacture of iron and steel, cast-iron stoves, ships, and railroad cars.[32]

Detroit's rapid industrial development and explosive population growth in the early decades of the twentieth century owed to the mass production of motor vehicles. Applying the lessons of shipbuilding and meatpacking technology, Henry Ford, Ransom Olds, Henry Leland, David Buick, John and Horace Dodge, and others devised the critical breakthroughs necessary for the usage of internal combustion engines. By 1914, when Ford activated moving assembly lines in his Highland Park factory, Detroit and surrounding communities had become the leading automakers in the world. Detroit's preeminence in the industry, assured by the time of the Great Depression, began to dissolve thereafter as automobile corporations decentralized their assembly and parts production enterprises. In the years before World War II, however, Detroit stood alone as the Motor City.[33]

When Henry Ford adopted the eight-hour workday and doubled the wages he paid his employees to five dollars a day in 1914—and competitors found it necessary to follow his lead—the motor vehicle industry became a magnet for laborers worldwide. Immigration from southern and eastern Europe, especially Poland, Russia, Italy, and Hungary, accounted for the lion's share of the increase, with the foreign-born constituting fully half of the city's population by 1925. African Americans migrated to Detroit seeking jobs in the auto factories that paid wages much higher than they could earn in the Jim Crow South. From the thirteenth largest U.S. city in 1900 to the ninth largest in 1910 and the fourth largest in 1920, Detroit's population grew rapidly. By 1930, Detroit had nearly supplanted Philadelphia as the nation's third largest city.[34]

The extreme privations of the Great Depression, most evident in cities overly dependent upon one industry, proved to be especially devastating in Detroit. (With its singular reliance on iron and steel, Pittsburgh had also proved particularly vulnerable). In desperation, autoworkers evidenced a new militancy and enjoyed such remarkable breakthroughs that the city became known as a union stronghold. Effectively utilizing a new tactic, the sit-down strike, the United Auto Workers (UAW) and other unions netted huge membership gains among the rank-and-file in Detroit factories. No such success followed in their attempts to influence municipal politics, however, as the city's Protestant elite had imposed a nonpartisan electoral system with at-large city council elections that favored conservative candidates opposed to the redistributive policies favored by the unions. The local Republican Party, dominated by the owners and chief executive officers of the major auto companies, controlled city government while its leadership resided in leafy bedroom communities surrounding Detroit. Without doubt, however, many of those same executives willingly promoted campaigns to boost the city's borrowing to construct libraries, schools, and wide roads. In this period, Detroit's leaders supported beautification projects that presumably improved property values and the city's image. No one among the city's top executives, however, had any reason to countenance the idea of building a partnership with detested workers or their poorly organized unions.[35]

## Cleveland

Like Detroit, Cleveland grew as part of the transportation and trade network that developed along the Great Lakes and later became one of the nation's foremost industrial cities. The tiny settlement on the banks of Lake Erie languished until the opening of the Erie Canal and its selection as the northern terminus of the Ohio and Erie Canal, which opened Great Lakes commerce to Akron, Columbus, Cincinnati, and a number of other Ohio communities along the 308-mile route. The shift from commercial to industrial city came in the mid-nineteenth century as vast quantities of iron ore from the Lake Superior region arrived in Cleveland along with coal mined in Pennsylvania, Ohio, and West Virginia. By the 1870s and 1880s, manufacturers used the steel produced in the city's foundries to make railroad equipment, stoves, furnaces, tools, machinery, electrical apparatus, and ore boats.

Detroit's rise to prominence in motor vehicle production also benefited Cleveland, which developed such ancillary industries as steel, paint, electrical wiring, and automobile parts. Following the discovery of oil in Pennsylvania in 1859, railroad connections made the city a leading center for oil refining; in 1870, John D. Rockefeller established the Standard Oil Corporation in Cleveland. Coming to maturity during the golden age of Fordism, its mills and factories mass-producing durable goods for distribution in world markets, Cleveland became an industrial behemoth by the turn of the twentieth century.[36]

The city's striking economic growth paralleled an equally remarkable population surge. Surpassing Cincinnati in 1900 as Ohio's largest city, Cleveland's population grew by 47 percent on average each decade between 1870 and 1930. With a total of 900,429 residents in 1930, Cleveland had become the nation's sixth largest city. The influx of Poles, Hungarians, Czechs, Italians, Greeks, Russian Jews, and other groups from southern and eastern Europe, nestled into a patchwork quilt of ethnic neighborhoods, made Cleveland such a cosmopolitan city that the total of foreign-born and first-generation immigrants equaled three-fourths of the population in 1920. The industries located along the Cuyahoga River, which sliced through the city to Lake Erie, befouled the air and left a layer of soot and ash in nearby working-class enclaves. Oil refineries, steel mills, and paint and chemical factories dumped waste materials into the meandering river, already contaminated by untreated runoff from sewers. The river caught fire "from time to time" in the late nineteenth century, long before the celebrated episode in 1969 that became one of the iconic examples of industrial despoliation invoked by late twentieth century environmentalists.[37]

Troubled by the environmental and social costs of industrialism, Cleveland residents clamored for improvements to urban life. Tom L. Johnson, a wealthy businessman who became an ardent reformer and served four terms as mayor (1901–1909), constructed public bathhouses and playgrounds in poor neighborhoods, professionalized city agencies, and built a municipally owned electric plant to generate light for homes and streets. During Johnson's mayoralty, according to Lincoln Steffens, Cleveland became "the best governed city in the United States," but the estimable mayor lost the battle for municipal control of street railways and then his bid for a fifth term. Coalitions of businessmen and reformers sought to deliver city services more efficiently though a series of structural reforms, including the adoption of a city manager system from 1924 to 1931, but voluntary civic organizations consistently exercised the most influence in local governance. As the institutional voice of the business community, representing prominent industrialists, merchants, bankers, and real estate developers, the Cleveland Chamber of Commerce set the policy agenda for local government. The Cleveland

Foundation, created in 1914 to underwrite social surveys, fund charitable enterprises, and improve local public institutions, emerged as a powerful force for economic growth and downtown development in the next decade and again later in the century.[38]

## Chicago

Like Detroit and Cleveland an early beneficiary of Great Lakes commerce, Chicago became the axis of the transcontinental railroad network and the great marketplace for an immense western hinterland—in historian William Cronon's apt phrase, "nature's metropolis." Chicago's imperialistic reach across the interior of the continent owed in large measure to the fearless entrepreneurship exhibited by a relentless business elite that seemed superior to its Midwestern urban rivals in its vision, innovation, willingness to take risk, and hard-headed deal making. The advantages in human capital and business acumen, which observers have cited repeatedly in explaining Chicago's meteoric rise and sustained prosperity, surfaced from the beginning of the city's growth and development.[39]

Between the 1850s and 1920s, Chicago became the industrial leviathan of the Midwest. As historian Cronon has shown, three commodities in particular—grain, meat, and lumber—launched its dramatic growth. Chicago owed its spectacular economic rise to other industries as well. Iron ore from Minnesota's Mesabi Range fueled the growth of the city's iron and steel industry, which by 1900 ranked third among U.S. cities. Chicago entrepreneurs pioneered in the mail order catalog business, as Sears, Roebuck, and Company and Montgomery Ward's revolutionized retailing in the modern era. Mail order marketers and local clothing stores sold garments manufactured in factories and sweatshops wedged into the periphery of the city's downtown. And of course, the growth of all these industries relied firmly upon the links forged by the railroads between the city fortuitously situated at the southern end of Lake Michigan and an expanding hinterland. By 1930, having surpassed Philadelphia forty years earlier as the nation's second largest city, Chicago and surrounding communities in northeastern Illinois and northwestern Indiana trailed only the New York City metropolitan area (which contained more than twice as many people) among the country's manufacturing regions.[40]

Radiating out from the central business district (known locally as "the Loop"), a mosaic of ethnic neighborhoods made Chicago one of the nation's most heterogeneous cities. In 1870 more than half of the city's residents identified themselves as foreign-born; twenty years later, first- and second-generation immigrants constituted more than three-fourths of the population. The Germans and Irish remained the largest immigrant groups in Chicago as late as 1880, but thereafter the "new immigrants" from southern and Eastern Europe arrived by the hundreds of thousands. Poles, Italians, Czechs, Lithuanians, Greeks, Bohemians, Russians, and other Slavs provided the muscle for the ravenous industrial machine's assembly lines and blast furnaces, opened small businesses that served local clienteles, and persevered to get ahead in a society fraught with hardship but full of opportunity. Having initially dominated the city's economic, social, and political life, the Protestant Yankee elites vacated their exclusive enclaves when large numbers of immigrants and southern blacks arrived and resettled in tony railroad suburbs such as Oak Park, Evanston, and several North Shore communities strung along Lake Michigan.[41]

While the elites fled the inner city and abdicated responsibility for local governance, at a time when urban political machines predominated in many other large industrial cities, Chicago sustained a strong two-party tradition in which neither Democrats nor Republicans could consolidate power across the metropolitan region. Several mayors enjoyed loyal followings but failed to translate personal popularity into lasting organizational strength. The political terrain changed dramatically with the coming of the Great Depression, however, when the potent Democratic machine that dominated local politics for nearly a half-century formed under the leadership of Anton Cermak. A Bohemian immigrant of working-class origins, Cermak built a "house for all peoples" that merged Irish, German, Polish, Czech, and Jewish factions into an unbeatable coalition and won election as mayor in 1931. After Cermak's death two years later, the Kelly-Nash machine maintained Democratic suzerainty through the Second World War, doling our patronage jobs, political appointments, and favors to a broad spectrum of ethnic groups. Providing order and pursuing pro-growth policies that delighted the business community, the Chicago Democratic organization became the nation's most powerful urban political machine by the middle of the twentieth century.[42]

## St. Louis

Chicago's triumphant rise came largely at the expense of St. Louis—its leading competitor to become the gateway to the American west—which nevertheless emerged as one of the nation's largest cities and the commercial center for the south-central region. Located between the sites where the Missouri and Ohio Rivers flowed into the Mississippi River, the city grew in conjunction with increasing steamboat trade. By 1840, more than two thousand steamboats stopped each year at the city's Mississippi River levees, and the volume of trade continued to surge well into the 1880s. St. Louis lost its battle with Chicago for economic supremacy due to the increasing importance of railroads. While Chicago businessmen skillfully utilized the flow of capital from New York City investors to underwrite railroad construction, St. Louis's location in a slave state and close commercial ties with the southern plantation economy made Wall Street lenders skittish about financing new enterprises there. Eastern financiers began steering capital away from St. Louis in the 1850s, a decision vindicated during the Civil War when the Confederacy's blockade of the Mississippi River severed connections with northern financial institutions and disrupted the economies of St. Louis and other border towns. St. Louis remained the larger city until the 1870s, but Chicago's business leaders had already established commercial hegemony in the West by then.[43]

With excellent transportation providing access to nearby agricultural and mineral resources, St. Louis developed into a formidable regional manufacturing center. Food processing (flour milling, sugar refining, and meatpacking, especially) led the way, followed by brewing and distilling, chemicals, pharmaceuticals, and iron and steel products. In the late nineteenth century, taking advantage of inexpensive land and superb railroad connections across the river, many industries relocated in the broad Illinois flood plain. The 656-acre National Stockyards in East St. Louis, along with a thriving area of iron and steel production in the Illinois communities of Alton, Granite City, and Madison created an impressive manufacturing sector in the shadow of the area's principal city. On the eve of the Great Depression, despite the difficulties experienced by the brewing and distilling industries caused by prohibition, the St. Louis metropolitan region ranked seventh nationally in manufacturing.[44]

Throughout the nineteenth century, population increase in St. Louis owed largely to the influx of rural migrants from the surrounding countryside and to immigrants from Germany and Ireland. Unlike the situation in many industrial cities, which attracted large contingents of newcomers from eastern and southern Europe, the numbers of Italian, Greek, Jewish, and Slavic immigrants arriving in St. Louis remained small. Because of its location and accessibility, the city proved to be a popular destination for African Americans fleeing the Deep South, and its black population stood third nationally in 1880. Rigid racial segregation persisted, with many whites residing in or moving to the western edge of the city and the suburbs. A local ordinance passed in 1916 legalized residential segregation through racial zoning. When the U.S. Supreme Court invalidated such laws the following year, St. Louis realtors and property owners turned to restrictive deed covenants to maintain racial separation.[45]

Following an annexation of adjacent land in 1876, the final expansion of the city's boundaries permitted by state law, St. Louis became a compact city of sixty-six square miles bordered by the Mississippi River on the east and by autonomous suburbs on all other sides. That same year, the Missouri legislature disjoined St. Louis from the surrounding county and granted the city the nation's first home rule charter. The political separation of city and county left a legacy of political fragmentation and egregiously uneven economic development. County leaders and suburban officials openly conspired to starve the central city of resources—often in racist language that reflected the increasing African American presence in the inner city—in a manner unseen in other metropolitan areas until much later in the twentieth century. For more than a century, the areas of the city distant from the river absorbed the growing population as neighborhoods farther east filled to capacity, then deteriorated, and finally lost residents. The nation's fourth largest city in 1910, St. Louis experienced slight population growth in the first decades of the twentieth century and saw its population rank drop to sixth in 1920, seventh in 1930, and eighth in 1940; the city's population declined from 1930 to 1940, its first loss in 120 years.[46]

The population loss that plagued St. Louis in the fourth decade of the twentieth century mirrored the economic collapse that undermined conditions during the Great Depression in all five industrial cities. The nationwide economic crisis damaged urban America everywhere, but took a particularly heavy toll in large industrial cities where the ubiquity of shuttered factories, bread lines, soup kitchens, and Hoovervilles affixed a human face to the catastrophe. Astronomical unemployment rates, which remained disturbingly high throughout the 1930s, reached extreme levels in cities where the largest number of workers had been employed in manufacturing and mechanical industries. By all accounts, Detroit became the hardest hit big city in the United States with more than half of the labor force in November 1932 lacking regular employment and many others finding only part-time work. If the unemployment crisis reached its peak in the Motor City, the situation in Chicago, Philadelphia, Cleveland, and St. Louis became nearly as acute. In Philadelphia, for example, the panicked governor of Pennsylvania reported that approximately a quarter of a million people "faced actual starvation."[47]

The sorrowful condition of the central business districts in the five cities, the most visible portions of the suffering communities, vividly illustrated the extent of decline. Construction ground to a halt in the urban core and, as property values nosedived, vacancy rates increased in office buildings and other commercial properties. Land values in Chicago's Loop declined by half from 1928 to 1933. Department store sales fell nearly 50 percent in Chicago and Detroit between 1929 and 1933. With fewer businessmen on the road, occupancy rates in downtown hotels also fell. Looking to reduce costs and minimize losses, property owners sold devalued real estate and replaced demolished buildings with parking garages and parking lots—a process that historian Alison Isenberg termed "the paradox of unbuilding Main Street." By the end of the Depression decade, a fatalistic Cleveland real estate investor exhorted downtown businessmen and property owners to save "what we have left of the central business district."[48]

## Five Cities and Postwar Renewal Politics

World War II brought temporary relief. A decade of economic torpor and fear of permanent industrial decline gave way within a year to an urgent demand for military goods, and to rising production, renewed investment, and full employment. Downtowns recovered, initiating a brief period of metropolitan recentralization. The diversion of resources into military production slowed suburban building, while shortages and rationing augmented the convenience of downtown locations for consumers. Reduced automobility, owing to the dearth of new cars being manufactured, gasoline shortages, and the wartime proscription against using rubber for tires, likewise elevated real estate values in the urban core. Workers suddenly blessed with disposable income once again shopped in downtown department stores. In sum, the wartime emergency rekindled life in abandoned industrial districts, brought customers back to somnolent central business districts, and returned a measure of prosperity to communities that had recently been mired in debt and disillusionment.[49]

The renewal of economic activity proved to be a godsend to the inert industrial cities. Yet, increased investment, full employment, and rebounding retail sales in the World War II boomtowns failed to dispel concerns about the future. Local officials and business elites in Chicago, Philadelphia, Detroit, Cleveland, and St. Louis, just as in Pittsburgh, began preparing plans for bolstering their downtowns in the postwar years. In each city, pro-growth coalitions made downtown revitalization the centerpiece of their efforts to forestall decentralization and decline. In 1940, for example, the Chicago city council approved the construction of a network of expressways radiating outward from downtown—a system completed under Mayor Richard J. Daley in the 1950s and 1960s. New expressways, went the reasoning, would bring the well-off shopper back downtown; and those same expressways, circling the Loop, would knock down "slum" buildings increasingly occupied by black and brown residents. Engineers and planners spoke knowingly about "two birds with one stone." The promise of this quick and cheap path to prosperity caught on quickly as part of much larger renewal plans. A 1944 study commissioned by Detroit to plan postwar improvements called for construction of limited access highways, a civic center on the riverfront, a large medical center, and a new municipal airport, as well as extensive landscaping to improve the appearance of downtown. In 1945 St. Louis sponsored a design competition for a memorial to commemorate the city's key role in westward expansion; a distinguished panel of architects chose Eero Saarinen's rendering of a massive arch as a symbol of the city's storied past and imminent rebirth. City notables felt the need for dramatic innovations and large-scale investments after World War II to safeguard against the resumption of economic contraction.[50]

Armed with the plans sketched out during the war, local officials and business elites prepared to do battle against the forces of blight and disinvestment. Urban business leaders, much as political scientist Clarence N. Stone observes, excel[led] in getting strategically positioned people to act together, thereby expanding . . . [their] realm of allies." Buoyed by the stunning success achieved in Pittsburgh, businessmen in each of our remaining five cities set out to save their central business districts by launching a series of projects: The construction of expressways and parking garages to improve automobile access, the replacement of aging structures with new buildings for work and leisure, better housing nearby to keep middle-class taxpayers from fleeing to the suburbs, refurbished municipal infrastructures (streets, sidewalks, bridges, waterworks, and the like) that had been left unattended for so long because of the Depression and the war, and new and expanded airports to enhance national and international commerce. In the process, they sought both to restore many of the downtown's traditional functions and to adapt to the changing perquisites of an emerging service economy. Determined to make the downtown the engine of civic rebirth, they formulated new designs that helped to transform the nature of urban life. During the years between 1945 and the early 1970s, bold plans and massive spending produced remodeled downtowns populated by towering skyscrapers and surrounded by complex freeway networks, enormous convention centers, and gleaming sports stadiums. Those massive changes were never meant for the enjoyment of the many in each city who were displaced. "The poor, near poor, and other nonaffluent residents of the central city were thoroughly marginalized," observe several political scientists writing in 2015.[51]

Yet even the sacrifice of neighborhoods and livelihoods failed to bring about the hoped-for improvements in downtown's trajectory. Large-scale renewal projects and massive spending failed to restore central business districts in Detroit, Cleveland, and our other cities to the economic surge of the World War II years or to the prosperity of previous decades. A profoundly racialized politics had built these downtowns, and now, no amount of equally racialized politics could restore their downtown populations, property values, or sales. That same politics added each day to the racial antagonisms that visibly guided almost every decision made in these five cities. St. Louis's political and business leaders were ardent in their advocacy for Pittsburgh-style renewal.[52]

# 1

# St. Louis, Stan "The Man" Musial, and the Politics of Destruction

For a decade and more after World War II, city leaders made national news whenever they spoke about economic progress. Assertions about more jobs, rising wages, reopened stores, and a widening American affluence comprised important elements in that progress talk. And in turn, business executives and politicians in St. Louis, Pittsburgh, Chicago, and elsewhere who promised to lead their diminished cities and their low-income residents to restored prosperity always enjoyed flattering attention. During the 1950s and 1960s, St. Louis remained sufficiently visible on the nation's political and economic maps to merit visits by journalists in search of energetic businessmen and forceful mayors promising to convert smoke, grime, and store closures into new skyscrapers and restored economic growth in city centers.

Reporters who arrived with a modicum of knowledge about the city's history never had to look far for a lead on a good story. In 1910 St. Louis was the nation's fourth largest city; and as late as 1929, the city's industrial district ranked seventh in manufacturing after cities like Chicago, Philadelphia, Detroit, and of course, New York. St. Louis firms, with their Midwest location and superb rail connections to Chicago, Detroit, Cleveland, and Philadelphia, played a major role in supplying manufactured goods such as shoes, chemicals, and drugs to urban and rural dwellers throughout the United States. Ralston-Purina, for instance, was among the nation's standard producers of chow for farm animals and cereals for the American breakfast table far into the postwar years. Anheuser-Busch, a brewery that labeled itself the world's largest, was also headquartered in St. Louis.

Despite the presence of large and respected firms like Ralston-Purina and Anheuser-Busch, the glamour and hype that once surrounded downtown St. Louis's booming growth had faded into textbook stories for school children. By the 1950s, St. Louis was by any standard a city and a region with a lengthy history of economic deterioration, racialized poverty, and an unswerving history of racial segregation. "Protestant churches . . . continue to retreat from the heart of the city as Negro residential areas expand," a writer for *The Christian Century* announced in June 1953. Not only churches and their congregants left St. Louis. In 1952 Brown Shoe, a Fortune 500 company, relocated from downtown to Clayton, a high-income and fast-growing suburb west of the city. Only five years later, Edgar Monsanto Queeny, long active in St. Louis politics, moved the headquarters of his worldwide Monsanto Chemical to Creve Coeur, a small and upscale town six miles west of downtown Clayton.[1]

Parts of downtown were also well advanced in an undeniable economic downturn that took the form of declining retail sales, falling property values, and abandoned buildings. Members of no group had a greater stake in maintaining downtown property values than members of the St. Louis Real Estate Board, which included the owners and managers of large office and manufacturing buildings. "The soundness of the city's core is threatened," board president J. Ben Miller told members in January 1953 and "requires a rebuilding of much of its older area." Those same real estate operators complained about high taxes collected on their buildings and then spent on services provided to residents of lower-income neighborhoods. Race stood at the center of those laments, especially as low income, African American shoppers replaced wealthier, white patrons at major department stores and smaller shops in the city's downtown.[2]

Starting in the late 1940s, higher-income shoppers in St. Louis, like their counterparts in every American city, initiated a decades-long process of shifting their buying from large and prestigious downtown department stores like Famous-Barr and Stix, Baer and Fuller to suburban shops located closer to home. In 1948, managers at Famous-Barr added to the suburban rush, opening a branch store in Clayton, where Brown Shoe moved four years later. Downtown jewelers and furriers, dependent on the department stores' drawing power, went out of business. And once again, racial animosities resided at or near the center of these changes. Managers at Stix, Baer and Fuller had only recently desegregated their restaurants; and, Famous-Barr's managers postponed integrating their tearoom until 1958. These changes in the racial divides accompanying lunch and tea no doubt added another reason for many white shoppers to reduce their patronage or stop going to the central business district altogether. Remaining stores were often old, stodgy, and lacking in contemporary appeal. With so much change at hand, sober retailers even questioned the seemingly fundamental idea of downtown as the city's natural retail center. The era for building downtown department stores had passed, announced T. V. Hauser, head of Sears, Roebuck and Co. late in 1954. In 1956, however, the F. W. Woolworth Co. opened a three-story building, the first new development in downtown St. Louis during the past twenty years.[3] All in all, large retailers and major property developers expressed little confidence in the future of the nation's downtowns. It is difficult to estimate precisely which large American city had the sorriest reputation among property owners, store managers, and shoppers. But for many of St. Louis's retailers and property managers, the sentiment about the central business district's prospects was mostly downbeat.

Flat and declining sales among retailers comprised only the most visible and easily measured part of the changes taking place in downtown St. Louis. By the 1950s, the city's residents, especially in higher income white households, no longer judged downtown the best place to go on a movie date or simply for an evening comprised of eating and drinking with friends and family. During the 1940s and 1950s, St. Louis's business and political leaders attributed all or part of these dismal changes to traffic congestion, inadequate highways, and the growing presence of low-income African Americans who resided in deteriorated properties adjoining the central business district.[4]

Residents and visitors to Chicago, Cleveland, Detroit, and many other cities regularly made identical observations about the apparent relationships among racial change, diminished patronage, choked highways, and the absence of fresh investments in their cities. Reports of falling sales and diminished property values in distant cities proved no comfort to St. Louis businessmen. Almost each quarter, store managers wrote off the cost of unsold suits and dresses; and reports prepared for investors and property managers showed stores and office buildings that continued to decline in value. Our bank "has $20,000,000 worth of real estate under its fiduciary care," David R. Calhoun Jr., the president of the St. Louis Union Trust Co., told Missouri's governor in January 1953, and "the value of that property is seriously threatened by the city's deterioration."[5]

## Civic Progress Visits Pittsburgh

St. Louis leaders believed that political action could arrest this threatening set of developments. In January 1953, Joseph M. Darst, the outgoing mayor, appointed a small number of his city's top business executives to membership in a new, private group titled Civic Progress, Inc. Raymond R. Tucker, the city's newly elected mayor, made additional appointments to Civic Progress. The group's catchy name linked the welcome idea that the St. Louis economy could be made to grow faster with the equally hopeful idea that downtown St. Louis could retain or even restore its customary and deserved place as the region's corporate and cultural center. Tucker and his business associates in Civic Progress had only to follow the clear example of the path to economic and urban revival that Pittsburgh's leaders had already established for all to see. In St. Louis and in other cities, committees made up of business executives tasked to devise ways to improve roads, schools, and air quality were a standard feature of urban political life in every decade. St. Louis's business leaders started their renewal program with a visit to Pittsburgh.[6]

In October 1953, eleven Civic Progress members toured Pittsburgh, the nation's unofficial temple of urban renewal politics. Civic Progress delegates included Mayor Tucker and August Busch Jr., president of his family's Anheuser-Busch Co. and the new owner of the St. Louis Cardinals baseball club. Morton B. May, president of Famous-Barr department store, joined the group, as did Powell B. McHaney, president of the General American Life Insurance Company. Banker David Calhoun was naturally one of the visiting dignitaries. "Progress is contagious," announced a news reporter who accompanied the delegation to Pittsburgh.[7] Urban progress, in that rendition, was akin to the corporate goals that executives like Busch and Calhoun outlined each year for their firms, with the expectation that employees would faithfully carry out directives and share their bosses' enthusiasm for achieving stated outcomes.

Allegheny Conference executive director Park H. Martin guided Mayor Tucker and the visiting St. Louis executives through his standard tour. They toured the ongoing demolition of "blighted" areas as well as the new, skyscraping towers in the Gateway Center and other sites that had attracted national attention as part of the emerging Golden Triangle. Thirteen years earlier, Tucker, then the St. Louis smoke commissioner, met with Pittsburgh visitors to talk about his city's success in reducing smoke. But on this trip to Pittsburgh, the talk among Martin, Tucker, Busch, Calhoun, and other top-level St. Louis executives revolved around how Pittsburgh leaders had accumulated the political, legal, and financial resources to launch expensive and politically fraught projects such as expressways, office towers, high-rent apartments, and "blight" reduction. Lunches and dinners with Pittsburgh's renewal leaders and even Mayor David Lawrence provided time for face-to-face conversations about how they had overcome such a large number of political obstacles. "Don't think it's easy to carry out a program like this," Martin admonished his guests at their tour's start. Cooperation between public and private groups and among government officials at every level was indispensable, Martin added. "We hope to lick our paralleling problems as successfully as you have," Busch announced to Martin and his other hosts.

As Busch observed, Pittsburgh and St. Louis confronted identical problems, including declining populations, racialized poverty, and a deteriorating downtown. But, as Busch, Tucker, and their cohort discovered, the political organization in those two cities differed in marked ways.[8]

Civic Progress was an undertaking handicapped from the start by politics. The practice of politics in St. Louis, as long-time leaders like Busch and Tucker recognized, was not amenable to Pittsburgh-style cooperation between government, business, and organized labor. Mayor Lawrence in Pittsburgh had built strong relationships with the city's union leaders; they trusted him to watch out for their interests, most of the time at least. In St. Louis, by contrast, Mayor Tucker had never developed long-term connections with local unions or with the city's large African American population. Nor had the mayor cultivated relationships with most aldermen. Tucker, in fact, detested aldermen's local concerns such as constituent jobs. Tucker, who had studied and then taught engineering at Washington University in St. Louis, conceived the city as a large economic organism rather than as a cluster of ethnic neighborhoods built around intense local connections.[9]

Politics also limited Tucker's ability to revivify the St. Louis economy and remake downtown into a vital business center. St. Louis operated on a weak mayor system, which meant that substantial authority rested with the city's fractious Board of Aldermen. Journalists and local residents reduced the city's politics to a simple aphorism, "banks vs. unions." Banks in this adage served as a stand-in term for businessmen like beer company president Busch and others who failed to appreciate the lives that ordinary citizens—presumably union members—lived in neighborhoods close to work but politically and culturally far from the mayor's office and his talk about progress. The city's racial geography added another dimension to these sharp divisions. St. Louis was a rigidly segregated city. African Americans resided on the North Side and whites on the South Side. Racially conscious St. Louisans judged every city action such as a road improvement or a new school in terms of whether black or white residents benefited.[10]

Civic Progress leaders, characterized as the bankers, were in many ways interchangeable socially and politically with their Pittsburgh counterparts. Like the Allegheny Conference's membership, Civic Progress included top executives at the city's largest firms, as for instance Ralston-Purina, Anheuser-Busch, and Union Electric Company, which supplied electricity to homes and factories in St. Louis and across a large portion of Missouri. In July 1956, a writer for *Fortune* described Civic Progress members as "six manufacturers, five bankers, two department store executives" and other visible and seemingly influential leaders. Civic Progress members were the city's "leading citizens," that writer added, signaling not only their prestige but also their acknowledged role as economic and political leaders and as cultural arbiters. Many Civic Progress members held a stake in downtown property; and still others, owners or not, had devoted a large portion of their adult lives to bringing about important changes in the city's environment, including the successful smoke reduction program and further development of the zoo and substantial park system. In addition, business executives like banker Calhoun and insurance company president McHaney had donated countless hours to persuading skeptical voters to approve multiple bond issues to fund schools and other projects in the years prior to Civic Progress's formation. With their city already in the throes of economic and racial changes that threatened investments and prestige, Civic Progress members planned to apply the same energetic leadership and executive decision making to the city's problems that they had long brought to their corporate offices and to their past actions in behalf of St. Louis's growth and prestige. Like Richard King Mellon and his business colleagues in Pittsburgh's Allegheny Conference, Civic Progress members built their careers, their professional networks, and their public images around the idea that downtown St. Louis could be upgraded and that it was worth their personal and collective effort to do so. And with all the wealth, visibility, energy, political know-how, and apparent authority assembled in and around Civic Progress, who could have doubted members' ability to create and manage a downtown renewal program modeled on Pittsburgh's?[11]

And yet, Civic Progress members determined at the outset that they lacked the capacity to create a strong, top-down organization identical to Mellon's. August Busch acknowledged Mellon's commanding presence in the Allegheny Conference as a key element in Pittsburgh's successful renewal program. In St. Louis, Busch told Mayor Tucker and Civic Progress members during their Pittsburgh visit, "we don't have a big Mellon." Busch was not referencing Mellon's obvious wealth or suggesting that St. Louis's business leaders and the banks, insurance companies, and manufacturing firms they headed such as Monsanto and Ralston-Purina enjoyed limited financial and political resources. The St. Louis business community was a crucial actor in the city's politics. And, in future years, St. Louis leaders like Mayor Tucker regularly acknowledged Civic Progress as a key factor behind "every major civic improvement since its organization." The plainspoken and savvy Busch merely articulated a political fact that Civic Progress leaders recognized at the start of their renewal program. Insiders like Busch understood that his Civic Progress colleagues had multiple and often conflicting business, urban, and professional interests that were not easily remolded to line up behind any one program or person. In Pittsburgh, a note or telephone call from Richard King Mellon commanded the prompt attention of mayors and any business leader who sought to advance in the region's politics, board memberships, and high-prestige clubs. In contrast, St. Louis business leaders, including

Civic Progress members, had in past years failed to create a united front on how to deal with the city's many racial and economic problems. Busch's observation that St. Louis lacked a person capable of exercising Mellon's insistent presence was exactly on target. But still, according to Busch, their fractiousness did not have to become an insurmountable obstacle to St. Louis's version of progress. "We'll succeed," Busch contended, "if we go at it right and split up a lot of little melons."[12]

## A Bond Issue with Black and White Support

Put in practical terms, Busch's idea about splitting melons actually meant getting one Civic Progress member to volunteer to direct each renewal activity. St. Louis leaders had relied on a single person, usually a visible business executive, to preside over earlier projects. Results of that approach produced mixed results. The city's varied history of winning voter approval for bond issues was a case in point. As a start, two-thirds of participating voters had to endorse any bond issue, setting a high bar for winning approval and gaining additional funds for improvement projects. In 1944, St. Louis voters approved a bond campaign led by future Civic Progress members Powell McHaney, an insurance company president, and J. Wesley McAfee, head of the region's electric light company. Expressway construction and the promise of public-works jobs for returning veterans helped win voter approval. In 1948, however, leaders of a bond campaign to raise funds for sewers and urban renewal failed. African American voters in particular feared destruction of their targeted neighborhoods, and white voters worried that displaced black residents would relocate to their neighborhoods. Race and realistic fears of neighborhood destruction informed all or most of St. Louis politics.[13]

By 1953, the unpredictable results of those bond proposals had been a key factor in Mayor Darst's decision to create Civic Progress. Now, with a bond proposal again before voters, McHaney and other Civic Progress leaders determined on a more ecumenical approach to winning approval. By September, they had recruited the city's Roman Catholic archdiocese and the rabbinical association to support approval of a bond issue totaling $1.5 million to pay for downtown improvements. On September 15, one of the Catholic prelates even spoke on a radio broadcast about the ways that progress in civic affairs could influence spiritual progress, thus bringing yet another dimension to the progress talk that enveloped downtown enthusiasts. Only a few days later, having secured passage, the inexhaustible McHaney described the appearance of a "favorable climate" for yet another bond issue, valued at $100 million.[14]

Banker Calhoun took charge of promoting that vastly larger bond issue, which actually totaled $110.6 million. If voters approved, Calhoun and his small Civic Progress organization promised money for twenty-three projects, including street improvements, bridges, parks, hospitals, flood control, schools, and of course three expressways. Calhoun even asked African Americans to vote in favor of one of the bond issues that promised vast demolition in their neighborhoods. According to a newspaper report, 950 organizations, including the League of Women Voters and the Teamsters' Union, endorsed the bond proposals and spread positive word among their membership. Calhoun also rallied supporters to speak in favor of the bond issue. As in past campaigns, McHaney made speeches to local groups. Leading up to the vote, the archbishop of St. Louis asked priests in eighty-three area churches to urge support among parishioners attending mass. A parade that included five bands and eighty-five vehicles and floats marched along a fifteen-mile route to generate additional awareness and enthusiasm.[15]

On May 26, despite afternoon wind and rain, voters approved each of the twenty-three bond issues by margins of up to 80 percent. Long-stymied construction plans for downtown expressways and a massive clearance program in the nearby African American area west of downtown could go forward. Busch described the outpouring of support as "a proud day for a proud city." In plain terms, Civic Progress members, led in this instance by Calhoun, had assembled a vast coalition aimed largely at restoring downtown property values, sales, and prestige to the center of St. Louis.[16] During the next decade, the bond issue's success and the resulting demolition and highway programs also created an opportunity to initiate additional projects, as, for instance, a new stadium for the St. Louis Cardinals baseball club. And as with any large undertaking in St. Louis, the political struggle started with another election, this one to select members of a board of freeholders.

## Racial Distrust and the Freeholder's Election

After World War II, leaders in St. Louis, including Mayor Tucker and Civic Progress executives such as August Busch, began to identify big-league sports as another tool in their downtown redevelopment plans. The idea, not fully formed at the time, was that sports would return high-spending fans to downtown. The city's famous Gateway Arch, which opened to the public in June 1967, was one part of a decades-long interest among business and political leaders in making high-spending visitors a main element propelling downtown's renewal.[17] But first, voters had to have their say in yet two more elections. Between those votes in 1956 and 1957 and the stadium's opening in 1966, downtown's deterioration and sharply drawn white animosities helped guide stadium politics in detail.

On May 8, 1956, St. Louisans voted in a special election to choose members of a board of freeholders to revise the city's charter. At first glance, the city's charter—old or revised—was a topic likely to induce somnolence among all but the most civic-minded residents. In St. Louis, however, any change pressed by the city's white leadership was certain to raise African American suspicions about a power grab. A St. Louis committeeman identified the charter revision effort as "a stealthy move to 'cut the Negro's throats.'" Only a few days before the election, St. Louis's Republican and Democratic leaders also joined forces to oppose the Civic Progress slate, fearing a loss of influence in local affairs. Nevertheless, voters elected thirteen freeholders, including two African Americans. Mayor Tucker and Civic Progress leaders had endorsed each of the winners, highlighting their heft in city politics when they coalesced around a project and their opponents remained poorly organized. The newly elected freeholders promptly got about the business of writing a new charter.[18]

No sooner was the election concluded than African American leaders expressed concern about protecting and expanding civil rights in the charter to be written. In February 1957, nine of the recently elected freeholders proposed a change to the charter that threatened to reverse even the limited influence the city's African American community exercised in the city's politics. Under the existing charter, city government revolved around twenty-eight, ward-based aldermen. With that system, African Americans held four aldermanic seats; and, with their growing population, African Americans actually dominated politics in two additional wards. In all, the presence of the four officeholders guaranteed a modicum of representation in efforts to pry open city jobs and to advance civil-rights legislation. Now, however, a majority of freeholders proposed to change the board of aldermen to what they described as the 7-7-1 plan. Put simply, seven members of the revised aldermanic board would be elected to represent the city as a whole, and another seven were to be elected from wards that would be greatly expanded in size and number of voters. Such an arrangement would almost certainly submerge even a united African American vote under the weight of a much larger white vote. As well, the mayor in this new plan would have a vote. Altogether, seven aldermen plus the mayor would be in a position to ignore African America interests entirely. Ernest Calloway, an African American labor leader, described the 7-7-1 plan as a "legislative 'iron curtain' around the 200,000 or more Negro citizens' living in the city." And to compound the distrust, Tucker had a reputation for "never [having] granted anyone a political favor and [for] his unemotional engineering approach to civic problems."[19] Tucker, in other words, was not a political leader to whom Calloway and other African American leaders could turn to solve problems in their congested and segregated neighborhoods.

On August 6, 1957, some 178,000 voters went to the polls to reject the new charter by a wide margin. African Americans, with an impressive 60

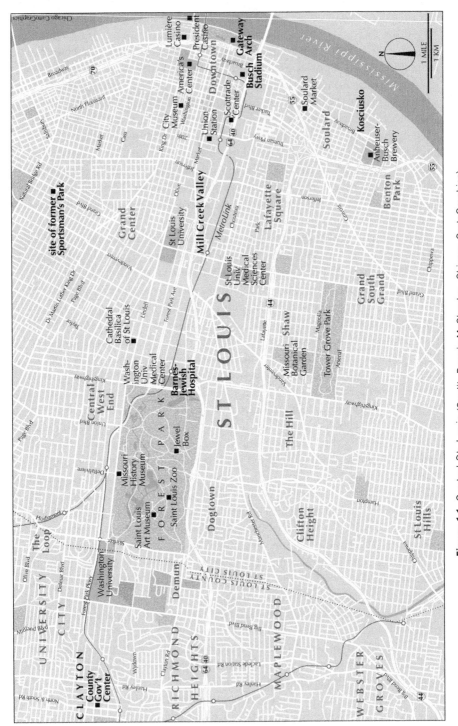

**Figure 1.1** Central St. Louis (Credit: Dennis McClendon, Chicago CartoGraphics)

percent turnout, were vital members of that majority, rejecting the charter by margins of 4 to 1 in one ward and 5 to 1 in another. Leaders of the National Association for the Advancement of Colored People (NAACP) helped galvanize African American voters, a journalist reported. A large number of white residents also voted against the new charter.[20]

Tucker and other Civic Progress leaders judged the massive losses meted out in African American districts to be especially problematic. The city's African American population was increasing in size, and the white population was shrinking. More than dull population statistics were involved. As a result of years of official and unofficial methods of segregation, a large portion of the African American population resided near downtown real estate that remained valuable; and Civic Progress leaders and ordinary white voters saw every African American neighborhood as blighted, or as soon to be headed in that direction. Still more, the negative vote in August 1957 on the proposed charter reinforced the perception among top executives that African American leaders in organizations like the NAACP would never work with them toward common goals. "Mr. Calloway," Edwin M. Clark, the president of Southwestern Bell announced at a meeting about black employment held months after the vote, "you colored people gave us business leaders a hell of a whipping in that Charter fight last August." The charter vote, in other words, had confirmed one of Clark's direst suspicions. Black and white St. Louisans, he feared, were inevitably adversaries more than collaborators in advancing downtown property values and boosting retail patronage. And, almost as inevitably, Civic Progress leaders like Clark intended to clear African Americans from the downtown area and rebuild it for prosperous shoppers and visitors, mostly white. That "whipping" in August reinforced Civic Progress members' determination to eliminate lengthy negotiations with St. Louis's African American leadership and start long-planned redevelopment projects.[21]

## Adding to Racial Distrust: Charles Farris and the "Culture of Clearance"

On February 16, 1959, wrecking balls and bulldozers got to work leveling every structure in Mill Creek Valley. African Americans occupied Mill Creek Valley, a 465-acre tract extending west from 20th Street (near Union Station) to Grand Boulevard. The area was large, crowded, and right in the city's center, starting at the downtown's western edge. In earlier years, legendary entertainers such as Scott Joplin and Josephine Baker had resided in Mill Creek Valley. By the 1950s, planners described the area as "100 blocks of hopeless, rat infested, residential slums." Once underway, Mill Creek Valley was the nation's largest renewal program. Additional bulldozers also leveled Kosciusko, an old industrial area directly south of downtown along the Mississippi River where white people lived and worked. But the Mill Creek project was by far the city's largest and most visible undertaking aimed at protecting downtown retailers and their mostly white shoppers from black neighbors. An expressway and its interchanges eventually posed additional barriers between downtown properties and Mill Creek Valley. In the future, with Mill Creek Valley and Kosciusko cleared, businesses and new residents would fill in the empty space; and, according to optimistic forecasts, the arriving residents would require fewer services, pay taxes, and replenish the city's treasury. Mill Creek Valley would reemerge as a "vast and modern suburb within a city." City officials in the meantime failed to keep tabs on whether the thousands of displaced residents were finding a place to live. Historian Walter Johnson identified an "insistent racial capitalist cleansing . . . including racial removal . . . , and segregated neighborhoods" as routine features in the city's history. A large number of Mill Creek Valley's hard-hit residents moved to Pruitt-Igoe, a gigantic public housing development that opened in 1954 and that the city demolished in 1972. Business and political leaders expected high-income (white) residents to repopulate areas around city hall and other deteriorated sections and "central St. Louis will be reborn," as business authors of an advertisement in the *St. Louis Post-Dispatch* announced on January 3, 1958.[22]

The racial and financial calculations underlying these massive projects blended easily in the minds of Mayor Tucker and his Civic Progress colleagues. Similar redevelopment programs were underway in larger cities, including Chicago and Detroit. And one had only to review any of the reports prepared by trusted business executives about Pittsburgh's heralded renaissance for assurance that all would soon be well. Starting in the late 1940s and extending for the next decade and beyond, Mayor Tucker and his Civic Progress allies ushered into being a politics of racial distrust, massive destruction, and supremely optimistic forecasts of renewed prosperity for downtown property owners.[23] The long-talked-about ballpark for the St. Louis Cardinals was part of those plans for destruction and renewal.

No person mattered more than Charles L. Farris in developing St. Louis's new baseball stadium as part of the city's "culture of clearance." Farris was executive director of the city's Land Clearance for Redevelopment Authority (LCRA), which Mayor Darst had created in 1951. The LCRA directed large undertakings such as Mill Creek Valley and Kosciusko. Farris took charge of the authority in December 1953, on Tucker's recommendation, with the title of executive director. By the early 1960s, the combined LCRA and St. Louis Housing Authority employed more than 350 persons, creating an agency with the ability to plan and develop several projects at one time. Farris remained in that powerful post, for all but three years, until 1989. And Farris, like Mayor Tucker and his Civic Progress sponsors, maintained unshakable convictions that linked downtown's continuing vitality with ideas about race and renewal through large projects such as a new stadium. "I believe we have to use all the tools available to save the biggest shopping center of all—the downtown area," Farris told a reporter in November 1960. In these ways, Farris mirrored Park Martin's ideas as director of Pittsburgh's Allegheny Conference. And, like Martin, Farris never engaged in desultory and unproductive discussions about public as opposed to private authority or Democrats versus Republicans. Farris was, after all, a city employee tied to businesspeople who were mostly Republican yet who lived in a city that was overwhelmingly Democratic. His political expression took the form of bulldozers, expressways, new buildings, and public bond issues that, taken together, were supposed to increase private property values and boost sales for his business sponsors' downtown projects.[24]

Farris brought additional strengths to any project. First, the city's bond monies that voters approved for renewal programs flowed directly to his LCRA. Farris's substantial resources (and federal urban renewal assistance) enabled him to make and carry out large plans, as, for instance, the clearance of Mill Creek Valley. Second, Farris's LCRA possessed unambiguous legal authority to carry out bulldozer projects.[25] And, third, Farris always cultivated close and enthusiastic support from Mayor Tucker and among the city's business leaders. He proceeded only with their approval. During the 1950s and 1960s, decades when Mayor Tucker and business executives like banker David Calhoun and brewery owner August Busch were enthusiastic about the advantages certain to flow from demolition and renewal, Farris never had to make a hard pitch. Farris, in other words, brought clout, cash, and deep connections among local business leaders to any conversation about downtown's renewal. Yet even a powerful figure like Farris needed four years, 1958–1962, to assemble a like-minded coalition around yet another bond issue campaign.

## Stan Musial, Another Bond Drive, and a Downtown Stadium

A new stadium for the St. Louis Cardinals baseball team fit squarely into Farris's ideas about how to bring about downtown renewal. To start, the proposed stadium, if it came into being, would replace an aging structure miles from downtown in an area that city officials had designated as blighted in 1947. Starting in late 1958, after Farris announced the stadium proposal, hopes for downtown's renewal ran high. Supporters figured that as many as fifty thousand spectators would attend each of 77 home games (81 starting in 1962). Such numbers, all concurred, would raise hotel occupancy rates, improve downtown sales, and boost restaurant traffic from early in the day into evening hours. The stadium renewal project, editors of the *St. Louis Post-Dispatch* promptly announced, represented a "chance to build a dream."[26] As with every large project in St. Louis, constructing a new baseball stadium required voter approval for another bond issue, this one to pay $6 million toward the city's expenses for nearby lights, street, and sewer improvements.

On January 23, 1962, St. Louisans approved only one of eleven proposed bond issues. Budget-conscious voters dealt the harshest defeat to bonds for stadium-area improvements. As in earlier years, bond issues required two-thirds approval, and the stadium garnered a lowly 57.9 percent. "Misrepresentation by a small, self-serving group," Mayor Tucker complained, accounted for the stadium bond issue's defeat. That small group consisted of area businesspeople, under the name of the Stadium Relocation Association, who put up billboards and advertised on radio to describe the stadium as a "land grab." Hartley B. Comfort, one of those local businesspeople and the owner of a print and stationery firm, judged the stadium project important for the city's prosperity but resented the imposition of a "crushing financial burden" on firms that would have to relocate. Just like Civic Progress members and property managers such as banker Calhoun, Comfort had downtown property to protect. Banker Calhoun, however, set out to distinguish his bond advocacy as evidence of an unstinting concern for the entire city's well-being. Calhoun and Tucker were quick to label smaller, less visible owners like Comfort as selfishly interested only in their tiny corner of the city. Few paid much attention to the low turnout and the 55 percent favorable vote in the African American wards, areas where St. Louis's racialized environment would almost certainly preclude black people from obtaining union jobs.[27] For Mayor Tucker, a veteran of many bond drives, defeat at the voters' hands was never a reason to abort a project. Tucker and Calhoun turned to Stan "the Man" Musial for assistance in winning voters' support.

Baseball teams often featured outstanding players whom fans idolized. And Musial earned his fans' enthusiasm with stellar baseball performances and with his warmth and accessibility before and after games. Musial was the Cardinal's best-known player. In August 1955, a sportswriter described Musial as "an immigrant's son who achieved fame and fortune by hitting a baseball harder and better than most of the millions of men and boys who've tried." Musial, the writer added, was a "living legend." Cardinal fans adored him as much for his humility and good sportsmanship as for his hitting prowess. In 1963, the forty-two-year-old Musial played his final season and maintained a respectable .255 batting average. That same year, the Cardinals retired his number 6. Musial was not only an outstanding athlete but also a World War II veteran, a tireless ambassador for the sport, and a cornerstone of the Cardinal's franchise.[28] With Musial in the Cardinals' lineup, team owner Busch fielded a franchise player whose impressive statistics and natural rapport with fans helped fill the stadium. During the drive leading to the first bond vote, Musial had been content to endorse the new stadium with a few words. Mostly, however, he had entertained fans on the field with his athletic excellence and off the field with his cheery demeanor. But now city officials needed Musial's help, which he gladly provided.

In the second bond campaign, Musial brought his considerable energy and positive reputation to bear on winning voters' support. Almost certainly, Musial never participated in lengthy budget meetings with Mayor Tucker and planner Farris; and it is equally unlikely that Musial sought to inform himself about the obscure details that surrounded any bond issue worth $6 million. From February 1 on, however, Musial served as chair of a special citizens' committee to promote the upcoming stadium bond issue vote. "St. Louis is my home," he announced, and "I owe it anything I can do to help it go forward." Musial, sounding much like a Civic Progress executive, added that the stadium would serve "millions of visitors who will come here, spend millions of dollars, pay part of our taxes and help to make this a greater and more prosperous city." Whether this special committee actually met and whether Musial wrote any part of his material is not clear. But Musial did make speeches to local political organizations such as the Tenth Ward Democratic Club. And he recruited eight Cardinal players, including such stars as Curt Flood, Red Schoendienst, Ken Boyer, and Bill White to lend support through his newly named "Keep St. Louis Big League" Committee. If the stadium area issue fails, a bond publicist added, "St. Louis cannot hope to refute a growing opinion that it is a second-rate, minor league city." By the early 1960s, Musial, a revered athlete, had joined top business and political leaders to push the idea that their city's tentative hold on a first-tier standing required a new baseball stadium. Musial might not have realized that banker Calhoun and other Civic Progress leaders wanted to fill that stadium and nearby stores with free-spending, mostly white suburbanites and tourists who would replace the African American residents forcibly removed from surrounding areas during the past decade. And perhaps Musial was unaware of or unconcerned about the impending removal of a small area of Chinese businesses and apartments to make way for stadium parking.[29] Regardless, Musial's participation surely heightened the bond campaign's visibility.

On March 6, 1962, St. Louis voters approved seven of the eleven bond issues, including bonds to improve streets and other municipal services around the new stadium. The stadium bonds secured a 67.7 percent favorable vote, carrying it across the two-thirds threshold, if barely. Perhaps the

beloved Musial's endorsement made the difference. In September, appreciative St. Louis aldermen started the process of renaming a street in his honor.
In November, LCRA executive director Farris presided over a ceremony to
launch demolition to make way for the stadium.[30]

By late 1962, Musial was able to fade gracefully from the successful bond
issue drive. His importance in securing passage is not measurable in the
sense of tallying voters who were converted to the stadium cause. Without
doubt, however, Musial's endorsement and carefully prepared speeches mattered in the city's troubled racial history and in its image as a place that
residents and business owners were leaving behind in a rush to the suburbs.
Musial held a unique place in the popular imagination. Fans believed they
knew the Cardinal slugger. An entire generation of St. Louis fans grew up
with Musial, who had joined the team in 1941 and become a civic icon. For
those fans and for ordinary residents who thumbed the sport pages or just
listened to local news on radios and then on televisions, Musial was a central
part of what it meant to be a St. Louisan. And Musial in turn represented
the city shorn of bitter disputes about the multiple ways low-income African
American paid a spectacularly high price to advance downtown redevelopment. Race was at the center of each phase of St. Louis politics, as in cities
like Chicago, Detroit, and Cleveland. Yet the Cardinal players who joined
Musial's eight-member "Keep St. Louis Big League" committee included two
prominent African Americans—all-star outfielder Curt Flood and award-
winning first baseman Bill White. In the early 1960s, Musial was among a
tiny number of the city's residents capable of fielding an interracial group
focused on a common purpose. Musial, White, and Flood's participation in
the bond drive suggested that perhaps the ballpark might serve as conse-
crated ground and in that way as a place free of the hardened politics that
surrounded every other facet of the city's development. In the hands of sports-
writers and the team's talented publicists, the Cardinals and now the stadium
were supposed to symbolize all of St. Louis. In practice, moreover, Musial
had refused to join with teammates in hurling racial insults at visiting black
players, a frequent occurrence as baseball teams integrated in the 1940s and
1950s. And if the apolitical Musial was to be believed, then the proposed stadium, a massive coliseum set in a deteriorated downtown, showed the city's
continuing promise as a place for every person to live and work, or maybe
just visit. For a few months in 1962, Musial's presence altered the narrative
about the city's past and future. (See figure 1.2.)

The new Busch Stadium opened on May 12, 1966. The Cardinals, playing
without the retired Musial, beat the Atlanta Braves. More than forty-six
thousand fans attended that game, some four thousand short of the stadium's capacity. But attendance in 1966 picked up sharply, ending with 1.7
million for the season. The next year, when the Cardinals won the World

**Figure 1.2** President Barack Obama presents the Medal of Freedom (2011) to St. Louis Cardinals' star player Stan Musial, who turned aside the politics of anger. (Photo by Brooks Kraft LLC/Corbis via Getty Images)

Series in seven games against the Boston Red Sox, attendance exceeded two million. By way of contrast, in 1949, Cardinals' attendance at the old ballpark had peaked at 1.4 million.[31]

In 1967, the new St. Louis Gateway Arch officially opened to the public. Together, the Arch and nearby Busch Stadium attracted more than four million visitors to downtown St. Louis. In September 1966, Famous-Barr department store executives, hoping to cash in on the surge in downtown visitors, featured a Scandia exhibition to honor Eero Saarinen, the Arch's Finnish-born designer. Not to be outdone with homages to downtown's success, in January 1967, J. A. Baer II, the president of Stix, Baer and Fuller, reported that the Arch and Busch Stadium "have added immeasurably to the renewed interest in downtown St. Louis."[32]

## Civic Progress and the Politics of Renewal

Those free-spending patrons failed to appear in hoped-for numbers at Famous-Barr or at most of St. Louis's stores and hotels. In 1966, downtown St. Louis hotels had the nation's lowest occupancy rate. In contrast, newer growth centers such as Washington University and Barnes Hospital, both located in the city's west end, attracted visitors in large numbers. Those visitors often stayed at newer, lower-priced, and more convenient hotels in nearby Clayton and other areas beyond the city limits. Wedding guests joined the bride and groom for nuptials and parties at suburban hotels. And each of those visitors, if they chose, could shop in Famous-Barr's Clayton store. Once in a while, St. Louis's growing number of suburban residents ventured downtown to visit the Arch and attend Cardinals games. After the game, those suburbanites joined out-of-town visitors on new and already crowded expressways heading out of St. Louis. The falloff in downtown hotel bookings further limited patronage at nearby retailers. Nor did department store sales improve. Overall, one historian observes, "the stadium served only to underscore the poor condition of the surrounding area." By June 1968, as the dire situation emerged into clearer view, Famous-Barr's downtown store officials explored the idea of having the city declare their block blighted. Famous-Barr was not closing, but a blighted designation would deliver property-tax relief. In 1971, city officials finally declared all of downtown blighted. A decade later, in 1983, the Woolworth store that had opened with much fanfare in 1956 relocated to the city's downtown mall. That store went out of business in 1994 as part of a corporate revamping and another round of capital flight from downtown St. Louis.[33]

Nor had other grand projects delivered on sponsors' promises. The city's wealthier residents, mostly white, continued their march to the suburbs. Just between 1950 and 1970, St. Louis's population declined from 856,000 to 622,000, a 27 percent drop. In 1980, only 453,000 resided in the city. Nor had the city's vast urban renewal projects contributed substantially to the city's financial health. Redevelopment of the sprawling Mill Creek Valley tract took place slowly and in piecemeal fashion. As late as 1970, St. Louis residents and journalists sardonically described the largely vacant area as "Hiroshima Flats." Civic Progress leaders, undeterred by the visible disarray that surrounded them and the negative reports from local and national media, joined new Mayor Alfonso J. Cervantes to endorse construction of a convention center as the city's next big tourist attraction and an indispensable key to bringing about downtown's revival.[34]

For more than two decades after World War II, politicians and business leaders in St. Louis and in every aging city judged the politics of destruction and renewal a vital part of their city's long-term health. Blight removal and rebranding efforts led inexorably to expressways, ballparks, and skyscrapers and also to empty lots now stripped of houses, taxpayers, retirees, and families with young children. And, in a similar fashion, redevelopment in St. Louis during the 1970s unfolded much as it had in previous decades. In June 1976, for example, Charles Farris, still directing the city's renewal projects, proposed construction of a downtown hockey arena. During the 1970s, hockey arenas (and convention centers) emerged among the must-have elements in any business executive's quest to bolster downtown property values, jump-start retail sales, and retain his city's diminished hold on major-league standing. In other words, Civic Progress leaders like Calhoun and Busch and mayors like Tucker and Cervantes spoke and behaved like their counterparts in other cities undergoing massive economic and social change. And again, as in those other cities, hard-nosed executives like Farris drove their redevelopment programs forward, regardless of the hurt suffered mostly by African Americans. Race was embedded in every nook and cranny of postwar urban politics.[35] Still, a small cabal of business leaders had not single-handedly brought about these vast changes in the city's landscape.

In the scramble to restore growth and prestige, St. Louis politicians and business executives labored as members of a policy regime that resided mostly outside their control. Civic Progress, in short, was never a uniform, all-powerful force on the local scene. The Pittsburgh visit in 1953 confirmed what Busch and the others recognized already—that St. Louis business leaders, despite donations of countless hours on behalf of bond issues, were not willing or able to subordinate themselves to Mayor Tucker or to any other executive such as Busch or Calhoun. Each new bond issue required Calhoun or another member to step forward. Under that arrangement, long-range planning was impossible. Civic Progress members, for all their apparent luster and authority, actually lurched from one project and one bond campaign to the next. The voters were not the kings and queens of city politics, but they possessed a veto on bond issues and the contingent growth plans. Those voters, the disdained residents of white neighborhoods and the even more disdained residents of black areas near downtown, had no reason to join the "bankers" in adding to their taxes and rents. As a result, passing those bond issues required Civic Progress leaders to build coalitions of boodling politicians, hard-nosed union and business officials, and an emerging group of African American leaders. Each coalition member asked for a piece of the action in the form of street cash for voters, construction and other contracts for business owners, and the promise of steady union jobs for white workers. Stan Musial did not insist on a side deal in return for endorsing the stadium bond drive. His selflessness set him apart from everyone else in the city and region.

As a plain fact, Civic Progress leaders like Calhoun and Busch never exercised the authority suggested by their tailored suits, attentive corporate staffs, and the flattery of awed journalists. In St. Louis politics, the ability to act decisively lay beyond the hands of mayors and Civic Progress's officialdom. Most basically, Charles Farris held the initiative for massive projects such as Kosciusko, Mill Creek Valley, and the downtown Busch Stadium in one decade and a new hockey arena and convention center in the next. Farris's mandate, as executive director of the LCRA, was to destroy blight and guide hoped-for reinvestment. Long-range plans for downtown could never succeed in the face of such a short-term, project-by-project outlook. Blighting much of downtown in 1971 was by that point a singular act that permitted the city to reduce taxes in yet another gamble to retain firms that might otherwise move to leafy suburbs like Clayton, Ladue, and Creve Coeur. In great measure, Civic Progress leaders such as Calhoun and Busch served as eager participants in a zero-sum political economy that started after World War II and extended into the 1970s and beyond. In turn, the system of bond issues, demolition projects, and rebuilding efforts that Farris dominated possessed a mass and momentum all their own, especially in light of the inability of Civic Progress leaders to agree on another path forward or even to select one leader. And, in addition, precisely as political scientist Barbara Ferman later observed about Pittsburgh, neighborhood groups composed of blue-collar workers, community organizers, or African Americans had few shared interests to make common cause—or at least not enough to challenge Farris and Civic Progress's distinguished leaders on their downtown goals.[36] About all that remained was for Stan "the Man" Musial to add a sunny demeanor and solid handshake to a give-no-ground politics.

Civic Progress also labored in a political economy in which wealth and power increasingly resided beyond city limits. In 1876, St. Louis leaders established the city's boundaries. Those boundaries were narrow, encompassing only a little more than sixty square miles; and, after 1876, those boundaries were unmovable in regional and state politics. During the twentieth century, jobs, businesses, and wealth moved west of the city. Between 1950 and 1970, as St. Louis's population declined, the county's jumped from 406,000 to 951,000. After World War II, moreover, heads of chambers of commerce in newer cities like Clayton behaved like their downtown counterparts. Clayton officials and other suburban executives sought corporate relocations, well-off (white) residents, and hotels and office towers. St. Louis residents were increasingly African American and earning lower incomes. In the unceasing scramble for taxpayers, prestige, affluent shoppers, and rising property values, Clayton officials had no reason to cooperate with St. Louis businesspeople and mayors. Quite the reverse. The grime, destruction, and self-declared blighting that characterized downtown St. Louis stood as an unmistakable advertisement for life in the suburbs. "There is no doubt," the head of Clayton's chamber of commerce boasted in December 1969, "as to the city's continued growth as an Executive City . . . [surrounded by] fine residential areas." St. Louis's seemingly powerful business leaders, including August Busch and Mayor Raymond Tucker, were no match for the combined might of suburban executives and their hometowns' wealthy, fast-growing populations. Altogether, reports historian Colin Gordon, St. Louis "sustained at best a sputtering growth machine."[37]

The political culture in the nation's booming cities replicated Clayton's approach to growth. After World War II, energetic businesspeople and elected leaders in Sun Belt cities like Los Angeles, Phoenix, Charlotte, and Atlanta started to launch intense efforts to lure investors, homeowners, developers, and footloose manufacturers to their towns. Boosters in these fast-growing cities spoke of sunshine, white residents, low taxes, and the absence of demanding unions. And naturally leaders in expanding cities like Phoenix targeted businesses and homeowners in St. Louis, Chicago, Pittsburgh, and similar cities in which racial fissures and economic distress were routine features of daily politics. In the U.S. system, the federal government devolved authority to state governments. State officials in turn dished out authority to cities in which elites clamored for growth or, at least, for a bit of help when the factory closed, and the remaining railroad no longer served their station. Capital and prestige were on the move. In that context, business and political leaders in every city and town had few choices except to look out for their residents' jobs and property values and for new ways to snatch business from the likes of St. Louis.[38]

As the next chapter shows, Chicago found itself in similar straits. After World War II, the Windy City's ambitious business and political leaders started looking for legal devices to protect downtown property values and retailing that were already experiencing sharp declines. Like St. Louis, Chicago's leaders sought to emulate Pittsburgh's model of destruction and racialized renewal to maintain their increasingly shaky hold on a big-league standing. But Chicagoans, like their counterparts in St. Louis, were equally incapable of emulating Pittsburgh's fast redevelopment at the hands of Richard King Mellon, David Lawrence, and Park Martin. Not even Richard J. Daley, Chicago's powerful mayor, or Arthur Rubloff, a celebrated developer of large shopping centers and the city's prestigious North Michigan Avenue, possessed the political skills to forge a successful downtown redevelopment program. Instead, Chicago's downtown renewal politics mirrored the St. Louis experience of white animosities toward black residents, political stultification, and the headfirst loss of jobs and businesses, a story the next chapter tells.

# 2

## Arthur Rubloff and the Grinding Politics of Renewal in Chicago, 1947–1986

I n May 1986, Arthur Rubloff, 83 years of age, died in Chicago. Rubloff's passing created a final opportunity for journalists to lavish praise on his list of business accomplishments. Rubloff was a "colossus of real estate development," observed two newspaper writers. By common agreement, his most remarkable achievement was the redevelopment of North Michigan Avenue, which he launched in 1947. During ensuing decades, as upscale retailers and skyscraping towers appeared one after another on North Michigan, no one could have doubted that Rubloff's redevelopment had brought fabulous increases in property values, rental rates, and worldwide recognition among shoppers and investors. As part of building North Michigan Avenue's brand, Rubloff renamed it the Magnificent Mile, a name that stuck.[1]

The flamboyant Rubloff, resplendent in tuxedo with flowing cape, excelled at self-promotion. Rubloff's penchant for overstatement seemed to pay off in the form of well-regarded properties that earned top rents. But Rubloff never aimed solely to own a portfolio of income-producing buildings. In recognition of his proven ability to build, sell, and rent higher-end properties, Rubloff expected on-demand audiences with bankers, real-estate moguls, influential attorneys, city council members (as did many business leaders like him), and, of course, with Richard J. Daley, Chicago's powerful mayor. And Rubloff, like a small number of prosperous, white male Chicagoans of his age, visualized himself at the center of Chicago's politics and business. His ambition to guide downtown Chicago's redevelopment was seemingly without limits. Yet Rubloff, despite having established a visible presence in

Chicago's real-estate politics, relied on property developers in New York and Pittsburgh to guide his local plans. In November 1949, as his North Michigan Avenue prospered, Rubloff asked an executive active in Pittsburgh's redevelopment to visit Chicago. During that era and later, no one started a large urban project without first learning about how Pittsburgh's post–World War II leaders such as Richard King Mellon had directed their city's downtown from floods and smoke to sparkling skyscrapers.

That 1950 meeting with the Pittsburgh executive was in reality Rubloff's preliminary effort to build financial and political support for his Fort Dearborn project. Rubloff's Fort Dearborn was located north of the Loop, not far from the location of the original nineteenth-century fort built by the U.S. government to support trade and protect white settlers from potential indigenous hostility. But Rubloff's proposed Fort Dearborn project, if it were ever constructed, also threatened property values south of the Chicago River and across a vast swath of the Loop. Raising property values comprised only one aspect of Rubloff's Fort Dearborn project (see figure 2.1). Again, like his Pittsburgh counterparts, Rubloff sought to remove the nearby, lower-income African American population and replace them with more affluent white households whose members would choose to shop nearby in spiffy stores and work in elegant offices. As a plain fact, Rubloff's Fort Dearborn replicated urban renewal projects that racially anxious businesspeople in downtown Pittsburgh, St. Louis, and elsewhere sought for their cities. What set Rubloff's project apart was its ambitious agenda in the midst of extraordinarily expensive Chicago real estate.

Yet not even a skilled operator like Rubloff and members of his large network of business executives possessed the savvy, clout, and resources to bring Fort Dearborn or other projects to a successful conclusion on their own. Politicians like Mayor Daley often determined which proposals would earn a final go-ahead and which were to be set aside, and those politicians, including Daley, could be finicky. To use a term long favored among real-estate developers, Rubloff could not leverage his comparatively modest holdings on North Michigan Avenue (and elsewhere around Chicago) into control of a much larger extent of downtown redevelopment. By 1970, no more than two decades after the Magnificent Mile achieved nationwide attention and its shops regularly logged sales increases, Rubloff's top-tier standing among Chicago's and the nation's developers had run its course. Rubloff lost his membership and his power in the ranks of those who sought to redirect the path of downtown Chicago's real estate from annual losses to uninterrupted growth.[2]

Between the 1940s and the early 1980s, Rubloff's flamboyance, wealth, and reputation as a large developer kept him in the public eye. To be precise, however, Rubloff's most ambitious ventures hit the political and financial

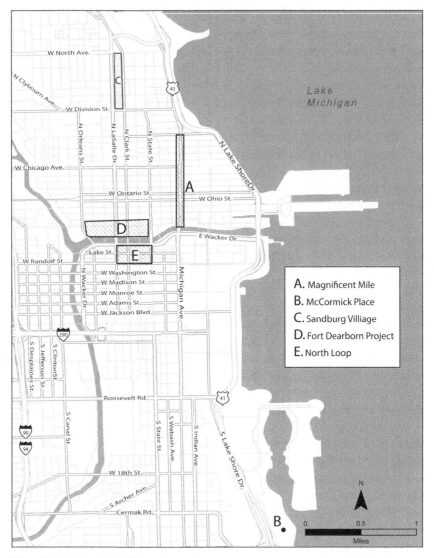

**Figure 2.1** Arthur Rubloff's major projects (Credit: Megan Maher, GeoMaps, Department of Geography and Geology, Illinois State University, Bloomington)

jackpot exactly twice. The first occurred during the 1940s and 1950s, when he ostentatiously presided over the transformation of North Michigan Avenue into the Magnificent Mile. And the second took place during the early 1960s, when he brought (and kept) together an alliance of profit-seekers and city officials bent on converting a deteriorating area north of downtown into a solidly middle-class housing area named Carl Sandburg Village. In every other respect, Rubloff, like similarly influential property owners and, in fact, Mayor Daley, failed to forge a consensus around a renewal program for the city's downtown. Rubloff's soaring success with the Magnificent Mile is an ideal place to begin to acquire an appreciation for his considerable strengths and many limits in navigating the city's tangled politics.

## The Magnificent Mile

On April 9, 1947, Rubloff unveiled his vision for the Magnificent Mile during a luncheon at the Continental Hotel. Rubloff's lengthy guest list included Chicago's dominant business and political leaders with connections to downtown retailing and office space. William Zeckendorf, owner of several tracts along North Michigan Avenue, was among Rubloff's guests. In 1946, Zeckendorf, president and owner of Webb and Knapp, a major real-estate and property-development firm in New York City, had purchased land along New York's East River to construct his X-City as a rival to Rockefeller Center. That project was perhaps beyond Zeckendorf's financial resources, and he sold the land for $8.5 million (including a profit of $2.5 million) to John D. Rockefeller Jr., who in turn donated it to the United Nations to build its headquarters. For several months prior to the Magnificent Mile launch, Zeckendorf undertook tasks such as securing details for Rubloff about how New York City's Fifth Avenue merchants had formed an association that guided property owners and store managers in the creation of a prominent and successful shopping street. Senior executives at Chicago's largest banks, such as the First National, Continental Illinois, and the Harris Trust joined the lunchtime dignitaries at the Continental Hotel. Joseph R. Frey, a Rubloff confidant, a Magnificent Mile promoter, and president of North Michigan Avenue's Lake Shore National Bank, was of course invited to the gala event.[3]

Rubloff's lunchtime guests were not simply well connected and well-to-do. Chicago was among World War II's "arsenals of democracy"—mighty industrial cities whose production of military hardware helped win the war—and the city's postwar population included countless owners and managers of large manufacturing and retail firms, as well as leaders in medicine, law, and architecture. Rubloff's lunch guests were more specialized and focused. They enjoyed decades of experience in the business of assessing, financing, insuring, and developing real estate. For Rubloff and others like him, real estate was not an abstraction studied in college courses, but a matter of profits and losses to be recalculated each day. Every real-estate developer knew his tenants' income with a high degree of certainty; and every realtor and developer knew by heart the occupancy rate and racial composition in each of their buildings. Race was among real estate's constitutive elements.[4]

Holman D. Pettibone's presence at Rubloff's elegant lunch was a case in point. During the late 1940s, Pettibone's firm, Chicago Title and Trust Company, recorded every land sale in the city. After the war, Pettibone took steps to ensure that his firm's balance sheet and Chicago's downtown property values continued together on an upward trajectory. Pettibone served as a member of a small group of business and political leaders who worked with the governor, the mayor, and members of the Illinois General Assembly to establish the legislation that guided Chicago's urban redevelopment program. (The Blighted Areas Redevelopment Act of 1947 and the Urban Community Conservation Act of 1953 paved the way for Chicago's efforts in subsequent years.) Put more generally, Pettibone and many of Rubloff's guests that day had taken a sizable hand over the years in establishing and maintaining the legal and financial networks that set the environments for retail store sales, office rental rates, white/black/brown residential patterns, and property values in the Chicago region.[5]

For several decades, Rubloff was an acknowledged participant in that leadership group, where periods of competition and still other periods of cooperation were among the normal tactics of conducting business. Rubloff's preparations for the lunch announcing his North Michigan Avenue development plans demonstrated his top standing at that moment among the city's foremost real-estate executives and his attention to their customary ways of promoting a new project. To start, he had invited more than 250 leaders of the city's real-estate community and he based his expectation that they would attend on his past dealings with them. "It is going to be important that you be here," Rubloff wrote Zeckendorf in New York on March 14, "and I hope you won't fail me." And, as in any such promotion, Rubloff launched a nationwide publicity blitz that included newspapers in every city with a population of fifty thousand or larger and in high-visibility publications such as *Newsweek* and the *Wall Street Journal*. Future spending plans were an expected feature in any business plan. Rubloff promised to invest $200 million in his Michigan Avenue development. The alternative to his plan, Rubloff told guests, was to allow downtown to continue toward its already "deplorable as well as obsolete state." After the war, developers sometimes used coded words like *deplorable* to describe unwanted racial change near their properties. To put their racial worries in the starkest terms, Rubloff, Pettibone, and others feared Chicago's unrelenting change from a white to a black city. In cities like Chicago, racial animosities, whether in the past or projected into the future, influenced the price of every property transaction and construction project.

Rubloff's announcement also included a biographical sketch with details about his early life that were probably not known except among Chicago-area developers. Born in 1902, Rubloff spent his early years in Duluth, Min-

nesota, but quit school at an early age. He resided as a young man in Cincinnati before settling in Chicago, where in 1930 he established his own firm.
In 1947, Rubloff reported that sixty-three employees worked for him, including seven senior managers. In his time at the firm's head, Rubloff boasted,
he had "been instrumental in developing some of the largest and most visible real-estate transactions in Chicago, involving millions of dollars."[6] Rubloff's widely distributed plan, the promised investment of $200 million, and
his accompanying biographical overview, had a larger purpose. Together,
they served as an invitation to Chicago politicians, bankers, and realtors to
recognize Rubloff's skill at converting ordinary properties throughout the
Chicago region into fancy shops and offices that regularly secured the highest rents and enjoyed sharp increases in value.

The business of converting a snappy street name and a successful lunch
into solid increases in rental rates and retail sales was not easy or automatic.
During the late 1940s, Rubloff's name for North Michigan Avenue, "The
Magnificent Mile" had failed to achieve widespread recognition among shoppers or universal support among nearby building owners. Many Chicago
residents, Rubloff told *Chicago Tribune* publisher Colonel Robert R. McCormick in December 1948, "do not know there is a North Michigan Avenue."
The Magnificent Mile "is a dead duck," argued the president of the association Rubloff had created to foster North Michigan Avenue development.
Even Joseph Frey, Rubloff's confidant and the Lake Shore National Bank president, was uncertain about whether to continue with the Magnificent Mile
term. "The harmony of the group is worth more than the slogan," he told
Rubloff in June 1949. "Jealousy existing in the real estate profession," Rubloff confided to McCormick, threatened "to eliminate the name of the Magnificent Mile."[7]

At this preliminary stage and for years to come, Rubloff never managed
to impose his strong will on allies or on equally strong-willed competitors.
Rubloff, rarely at a loss to explain business and political developments, lacked
the right word to describe a process by which property developers made alliances and just as quickly unmade them. But with the Magnificent Mile still
in its earliest stages, and its precise future uncharted, the perseverant Rubloff launched his Fort Dearborn project. Rubloff depended on the city's lawmakers to call into being what his often-feuding merchants could not.

## The Convoluted Politics of Downtown Renewal: The Fort Dearborn Project, 1949–1957

Two years after launching the Magnificent Mile, Arthur Rubloff began to
plan a massive urban renewal program for downtown Chicago, which he

eventually named the Fort Dearborn project. On November 17, 1949, more than three hundred persons attended a meeting of Rubloff's North Michigan Avenue Association. They had an opportunity to mingle with local architects, members of the Chicago Plan Commission, newspaper executives, and several members of the city council, including president pro tempore Timothy Crowe. Chicago's mayor, Martin J. Kennelly, attended the meeting. The mayor chose not to speak, and yet his presence lent gravity and political approval to these informal deliberations. Gordon Lang, the Greater North Michigan Avenue Association president, provided a hint about the larger agenda. He mentioned "civic leadership" and "civic cooperation," both in short supply along North Michigan Avenue up to that point.[8] A second speaker that evening, the president of Pittsburgh's ACCD, told audience members about efforts to convert his city's grimy and flood-prone downtown into a corporate center that hosted skyscrapers, upscale retailers, and first-class office space for which law firms and corporate executives paid top rents.[9]

Pittsburgh business leaders did not have a new story to tell audience members. Rubloff and every person at the meeting that night would have heard and read extensively about the ACCD's early successes in renovating parts of downtown and about their plans to remove African American neighborhoods located close by. Rubloff's purpose in bringing the ACCD president to the meeting was to provide Chicago's business and political leadership with an opportunity to gather in one place and talk about their shared future with a similar list of large undertakings. Rubloff of course lacked the ability to determine Chicago's future development in detail. But few among the city's business and political leaders could have assembled so many lawyers, bankers, architects, top politicians, and senior executives in one place for an entire evening to talk about downtown redevelopment during the next decade. By calling that meeting, Rubloff linked his planned development to Pittsburgh's recognized success. As well, he showed attendees his determination to exercise a decisive hand in shaping the Fort Dearborn project as a prestigious residential and office area in a remodeled downtown.

Fort Dearborn was embedded in Chicago's history. In 1808, the U.S. Army constructed Fort Dearborn at the junction of the Chicago River and Lake Michigan. In 1839, federal officials ceded 90 percent of the fort's abandoned land to the city. And, of more contemporary value, Chicago's schools continued to teach students about the city's founding, including reports of the fort on the frontier and its strong association with bold entrepreneurs and brave soldiers forging a new continent and a new city. Fort Dearborn, in other words, carried a resonance among ordinary Chicagoans as well as among the lawmakers and investors who would be called on to bring the project to financial, legal, and political fruition. During the next years, as Rubloff worked in secret with architect Nathaniel A. Owings and a few chosen associates, he titled it Project X. The nickname was a hat tip to Rubloff's mentor, William Zeck-endorf, who had also described his project for the area along the East River in Manhattan that became the United Nations Headquarters as Project X.[10]

Rubloff's Fort Dearborn project, formally announced in mid-March 1954, was even more audacious in scale and scope. Rubloff and Owings proposed a major urban renewal program north of the Chicago River and west of the Magnificent Mile that would replace 147 acres of blight with a host of gov-ernment, commercial, and residential buildings. City and county offices would be housed in one massive structure, and the State of Illinois and federal agen-cies would occupy two others nearby. The planned redevelopment site also contained areas for light industry, retail, office space, high-rise housing units for families, an elementary school, a playground park, and a heliport. A Uni-versity of Illinois campus was part of the plan as well. South of the river, the project entailed the demolition of the city hall-county building and several courthouses; a park would take their place. City hall's proposed demolition demonstrated Rubloff's willingness to make bold plans. And, as in similar developments in St. Louis and other cities, Rubloff and Owings included an interstate highway system extension as Fort Dearborn's northern border and underground parking for thousands of automobiles. In April 1954, a favor-ably disposed *Chicago Tribune* writer described the Fort Dearborn site as "largely urban waste-land pocked with decay, [that would emerge] into an architect's dream of what a modern city should be."[11] By any measure, the Fort Dearborn project portended a dramatic rearrangement in downtown property values, office rental rates, and retail sales—indeed, the very trans-formation of Chicago's central business district. Rubloff's Fort Dearborn proj-ect was also supposed to lead to increased sales on North Michigan Avenue.

A portion of the Fort Dearborn project resided only one city block from Rubloff's Magnificent Mile. Rubloff did not own or manage property in the Fort Dearborn area. Yet no one with experience in real-estate development could have doubted that thousands of tenants and a still larger number of employees located one or several blocks away would add to retail sales and property values on North Michigan Avenue. Rubloff, already in his fifties and both wealthy and influential, also perceived Fort Dearborn as an exten-sion of his desire to remake parts of Chicago in the image of the fashionable North Michigan Avenue. In a city where businesspeople had always exer-cised a decisive hand in determining land uses, Rubloff sought to emerge as Chicago's de facto planner. He would hold the ability to arbitrate where the city's wealthy and larger number of poor residents—black, brown, and white—lived and worked.[12] His Magnificent Mile, with its sparkling shops and upscale apartments, was a run-up to the Fort Dearborn project. As a seasoned political operator, moreover, Rubloff knew better than to rely on a prettified street as his ticket to directing the massive Fort Dearborn project.

During the weeks prior to announcing Fort Dearborn, Rubloff had assembled a committee of bankers, major retailers, and other political heavyweights to support his bid. Their active presence, went the reasoning, would help move the project from an architect's design studio to large-scale construction. Rubloff's top backers included Hughston M. McBain, the chair of Marshall Field and Company, the city's largest and most prestigious department store. Chicago Title and Trust's Holman Pettibone was also a member of Rubloff's group. Rubloff had long taken care to ingratiate himself with both men. And together, Pettibone and McBain were longtime activists in promoting urban renewal legislation. As far back as 1945, McBain and Pettibone had agreed to work together to deal with deteriorated properties in and around downtown. In 1947, Mayor Kennelly, newly elected, joined them. McBain at that time had "a very vital interest in trying to remedy conditions in the nearby area." Now, several years later, McBain was prepared to run the risk that a massive revamping of the central business district, with its promise of a larger number of office towers, downtown residents, and additional parking, would restore his gigantic store to a more solid financial footing. Still, the promised apartments and new city hall in Rubloff's plan were proposed to appear north of the river, a lengthy walk from McBain's store in the Loop.[13]

McBain supplied another important element. He assigned Earl Kribben, a Marshall Field vice president, to take overall charge of the Fort Dearborn project. From 1953, Kribben had acquired experience developing urban renewal legislation with McBain and Illinois governor William G. Stratton. Kribben's other assets included McBain's strong backing plus his canny sense for the importance of holding the renewal coalition together to achieve maximum success with public officials. Kribben now applied those talents to the Fort Dearborn project. On July 7, 1954, Rubloff, McBain, Owings, and others gathered in Pettibone's office to assess the state of their project and to outline their next steps. According to Kribben's notes, they argued about Fort Dearborn's boundaries in terms of their need to "qualify the project as a blighted district." The University of Illinois campus proposed for Fort Dearborn, Kribben added, was already "considered dead." About the only topics on which they achieved unanimity that afternoon were the importance of securing state funds, passing favorable state legislation, and creating an "indoctrination program for officials to proceed as opportunity offers." Their Fort Dearborn project "was an enormous and complicated job," Kribben told Rubloff and the others that afternoon, and "success could only be achieved with a maximum of specialized cooperation from those present and from many others."[14] Kribben's recommended program of indoctrination must have reminded Rubloff and their associates of the degree to which the Fort Dearborn project was already tangled in unceasing squabbles among downtown Chicago's rival property owners. And no one at that meeting could have doubted that Kribben rather than Rubloff had taken control of Fort Dearborn's waning fortunes. Richard Daley's election as mayor in April 1955 pushed Rubloff further from the center of downtown renewal politics.

Daley, the boss of Chicago's powerful Democratic machine, was now in charge of downtown renewal planning. And like political and business leaders in many cities, Daley looked toward Pittsburgh and Detroit for answers to downtown Chicago's changing fortunes. In 1956, he had led delegations of influential Chicagoans to the two cities. The ostensible reason for these junkets was to study Detroit's new civic center, built on an urban renewal site, and Pittsburgh's better-known Renaissance area, known as the Golden Triangle. Surely photographs, balance sheets, architects' renderings, and blueprints would have resolved many questions and concerns, especially among officials long accustomed to inspecting, talking about, and buying and selling real-estate parcels. Daley had not led delegations of business executives to two cities to acquire technical information.

Those Pittsburgh and Detroit visits created an opportunity for Daley and his entourage to negotiate among themselves—over lunches, dinners, drinks, cigars, and cigarettes—about how to overcome the political divisions that had stymied the Fort Dearborn project since mid-1954. As well, perhaps Detroit and Pittsburgh's leaders, equally engulfed in local struggles, could suggest a few devices to bridge competing outlooks about location, finances, and the hostility that any project's inevitable opponents would quickly inject into the city's politics. Still more, Daley, alert to the loggerheads at which Chicago's top business executives had arrived about the massive Fort Dearborn project, told a lunchtime audience in Detroit that he hoped guests would soon converge on a set of plans. After the trip, an alert journalist, no doubt eager to drive home Daley's point, described "Chicago's dream" and "Detroit's reality."[15]

Those mid-1956 trips to Detroit and Pittsburgh represented the high-water mark for Daley and other Fort Dearborn enthusiasts. The hopeful talk surrounding Rubloff's new plan and Daley's consensus-building trips to Detroit and Pittsburgh had failed to overcome long-standing rivalries among downtown property owners and executives. Political geography guided many of those disputes. As one example, West Side Loop business managers demanded that new construction take place near their firms rather than north of the Chicago River, as Rubloff planned. A combination of geography and personal animosities informed other complaints. Marshall Field's McBain, for instance, skipped the Pittsburgh meeting that competing store owner John T. Pirie, head of Carson Pirie Scott, chose to attend. And Pirie did not participate in the Detroit confabulation, attended by McBain. Pirie's store, like McBain's, resided in the Loop but was located even farther south of the much-hyped Fort Dearborn project. By early 1957, despite reports about the imminent return of middle-income households to downtown apartments and about the vitality of retailing in the city's central business district, both McBain and Pirie were already investing heavily in new stores in outlying centers such as Evergreen Plaza, another Rubloff development. Meanwhile, in January 1957, Pirie joined twenty-seven downtown business owners and managers to ask Daley to back construction of new buildings in the existing downtown area, near city hall and their properties, and many blocks south of Rubloff's proposed Fort Dearborn.[16] At a moment of considerable uncertainty about downtown Chicago's future development, no property owner was willing to invest cash and political influence solely in Rubloff's Fort Dearborn project.

Members of Rubloff's Greater North Michigan Avenue Association (GN-MAA) joined the revolt. According to March 14, 1957, minutes of the association's executive committee, dissident members opposed the street closings and a portion of the new housing in Rubloff's Fort Dearborn plan. The next day, several of Rubloff's supporters met with one of the opponents. They remained hopeful about bending his insistence that several blocks in Fort Dearborn had to be set aside for commercial or "high-class industrial use." Their entreaties failed, with a Rubloff supporter describing this opponent as "quite obstinate—in fact almost violent at times." Rubloff "had his own private war to fight with some members . . . who were not in favor of Fort Dearborn," a prominent real-estate developer later noted.[17]

Kribben's meeting notes for 1957 chronicled the spreading discord. In years past, Chicago Title and Trust's Pettibone had cooperated with Mayors Kennelly and Daley to promote urban renewal legislation, and he had joined Rubloff's Fort Dearborn committee as one of six sponsors. Those sponsors, all understood, were to take the lead in building a coalition to support the Fort Dearborn project and thwart its opponents. True to his promise, Pettibone had proved an energetic and regular contributor at Fort Dearborn committee meetings; and, in 1956, he was one of those who flew to Detroit and Pittsburgh with Daley and Rubloff.

Now, the previously steadfast Pettibone turned against the Fort Dearborn project. During a meeting held at his request on January 14, 1957, Pettibone expressed concern about Rubloff's plan to locate courthouses north of the river. Such a move, he warned, would affect "judges, lawyers, and owners of Central area building in which lawyers are tenants." Renewal was an undeniable goal among Chicago's downtown property owners, but not when that renewal threatened occupancy rates, rental prices, and property values in which they held stakes. After several years of dead-end discussions, Fort Dearborn just looked increasingly risky. As Pettibone made clear to Rubloff and others that day, downtown property owners were prepared to accept the (seemingly less risky) proposition that additional tenants would abandon older buildings and move to the suburbs, and, for the moment, Pettibone was even willing to discount Fort Dearborn's "protective benefit to properties south of the River." All in all, Pettibone, along with property and shop owners located near city hall judged that a degree of modest decline in the value of current investments outweighed the promise of a greater prosperity at some future time—especially if Rubloff was unable to earmark the fruits of most or all of that growth for them. In contrast, Pittsburgh and Detroit leaders had discovered a formula to resolve comparable differences, or they possessed the political capital to push opponents aside. But that formula and political capital continued to elude Rubloff and his Fort Dearborn sponsors. Pettibone's new proposal was to spread projects throughout the downtown, not just the area north of the river. Pirie's store would secure a nearby renewal project. Chicago "is truly on the march," Pirie declared in August 1957, telling a lunch meeting of five hundred store buyers that "something positive is being done about the proper development of downtown Chicago."[18] Pettibone had thwarted Rubloff's plan to make the Fort Dearborn project emerge as the new downtown.

Pettibone was no city planner. His highest political goals included efforts to accommodate businesspeople's concerns about their real-estate investments and their fears about the city's growing African American population. As part of honoring those commitments, Pettibone agreed to chair the Chicago Central Area Committee (CCAC), a new group of downtown business leaders who sought "a proper balance between rival claims of different portions of the Central area and periphery." Marshall Field's McBain and Carson Pirie Scott's Pirie joined the CCAC as founding members. Membership in the CCAC also included many of the top bankers and major property owners who already served on Rubloff's North Michigan Avenue Association. The differences between the groups centered on which areas most deserved renewal, with CCAC members determined to forge a consensus that included businesspeople and bankers with interests in every part of downtown. A North Michigan Avenue address and focus were inadequate for their purposes. The unity Pittsburgh's business leaders had reportedly achieved was the CCAC's first goal. "The new committee may have to knock some heads together to bring amity," a *Chicago Tribune* reporter noted in announcing the group's formation in January 1956, even before Rubloff and the others took those trips to Pittsburgh and Detroit.[19]

In September 1956, Mayor Daley endorsed the CCAC as the main driver of downtown redevelopment. The mayor's approval set Pettibone and his newly founded committee squarely in the urban renewal driver's seat for downtown. In this reordering of political authority and prestige, Rubloff's already splintering Fort Dearborn group emerged as just one of several claimants for attention and resources. Still other coalitions, such as West Loop business executives and disgruntled property owners in Rubloff's North Michigan Avenue group, also joined the struggle as claimants. More than two years after Rubloff unveiled the Fort Dearborn project, Chicago's real-estate leaders had failed to assemble a consensus about how to finance downtown renewal and where it was to take place. On October 22, Rubloff joined Pettibone and McBain in promising "continuing help to Mayor Daley . . . with carrying out the Central Area Plan."[20] Not even Daley at the head of the mighty Democratic machine had been able to assemble backers for a plan to renew downtown Chicago, but he could certainly block Rubloff or anyone else from launching a rival project. The inexhaustible Rubloff, however, still had other redevelopment projects long in waiting. He succeeded with only one of them.

## The Convention Center and Sandburg Village

During the late 1940s, Rubloff had begun to promote construction of a new convention center. Up to that point, Chicago's convention-goers met at one of the city's three, privately operated halls. Two of those halls were south and west of downtown; and a third operated even farther west, near the stockyards. After World War II, business and political leaders concurred with the appealing prospect that a new and larger center would bring thousands of free-spending business-class visitors straight downtown each day. The convention hall idea had long enjoyed solid support from the city's most influential businesspeople. As early as the 1920s, for instance, the *Chicago Tribune's* Colonel Robert McCormick launched an editorial campaign to "build Chicago the best convention hall in America." During the next decades, however, no one person or group proved able to muster the political resources to get that convention center built. The main obstacles, prosaic enough, included feuds about where that center would be located and who would pay for it.[21]

By the 1950s, convention-hall boosters like McCormick and Rubloff expressed optimism about prospects to secure a new center. In the 1950s, Chicago hosted more conventions and a larger number of convention-goers than any other city. "Some 8,500 bankers and their wives are pouring into . . . [Chicago] for the four-day annual meeting of the American Bankers Association," announced a *New York Times* writer in September 1955. Who could doubt the value of those well-off visitors and their surplus cash for boosting retail sales, restaurant reservations, theater ticket sales, property values, and hotel occupancy rates? Adding to the convention center fever, Rubloff, Daley, and other Chicago leaders perceived themselves engaged in a race with counterparts in other cities to attract visitors. In mid-1956, when business groups like Daley's visited renewal sites in Pittsburgh and Detroit, the convention center, new or proposed, was a mandatory stop on the tour. A convention center was also an essential element in plans to clear those detested and feared areas of blight. Like urban renewal or location of an interstate highway route near their firms, business and political leaders such as Daley, Rubloff, Pirie, and Pettibone judged a new, centrally located convention center to be another must-have item in their efforts to alter the narrative of downtown Chicago's political economy from oncoming decrepitude to unending growth.[22]

Members of Rubloff's North Michigan Avenue Association were unanimous in offering their support to convention-center construction and a future that promised annual increases in downtown spending. In March 1953, Rubloff and his suddenly united North Michigan Avenue executives got about the serious business of rounding up support to spend $15 million to build a new convention center. Naturally, Rubloff and his associates favored a location at the south end of North Michigan Avenue, within walking distance of their shops and office properties, and near the Prudential Insurance Company tower under construction.[23]

Like Rubloff, heads of business groups with substantial investments around downtown had their sights set on a convention hall closer to their properties. John Pirie, the president of Carson Pirie Scott, for example, advanced the case for a convention center south of his store. And just as before, *Tribune* publisher McCormick wanted the convention center located along the city's lakefront, at Twenty-Third Street, several miles south and east of both Pirie's and Rubloff's choices. More threatening to other claimants, McCormick's site was far from top hotels, first-tier offices, and fashionable stores like Marshall Field's that leading businesspeople and style-aware shoppers preferred. Smoky and noisy trains ran alongside the site McCormick was urging. As much as Rubloff, Pirie, and the others detested the Twenty-Third Street location, they were unable to coalesce around an alternative site and identify the funds to pay the much higher costs of clearing space (or buying air rights) to construct a convention center closer to downtown. Mayor Daley, by one account, also wanted a site in or near the Loop, but feared offending *Tribune* executives in case he launched a campaign for governor, and Daley could not crack the lead taken by the *Tribune*'s lobbyists in conjunction with Illinois politicians. In November 1960, McCormick Place, named to honor its sponsor, who had died in March 1955, opened at its Twenty-Third Street location. A few days before, a *Tribune* writer, faithful to the growth script, reported that 1,357 trade shows and conventions would bring $250 million in additional spending to Chicago that year.[24] Once again, Rubloff had little luck assembling a coalition of business leaders and lawmakers who possessed the willingness and capacity to locate and build a project expected to accelerate the arrival of cash and customers in downtown stores. Chicago's renewal politics was always a fluid proposition, one that not even the best-positioned players like Mayor Daley, trust-company president Pettibone, department-store executive Pirie, and developer Rubloff were able to master on each and every project. In his next bid, however, Rubloff assembled a stable coalition built around widely held ideas about race and neighborhood change.

In 1960, Mayor Daley launched another renewal program. He used a $10 million federal grant to pay for building demolition on a large tract near Rubloff's North Michigan Avenue. In his turn, Rubloff and his associates made the winning bid to construct Carl Sandburg Village, a cluster of high-rise apartments and townhouses on the Near North Side. To secure that project required the identical political and cultural work that went into building North Michigan Avenue as a desirable location to construct first-tier offices and to open retail stores aimed at high-end shoppers.

Like many real-estate developments, Sandburg Village fell into place over several years. Key Rubloff associates had already assumed important posts in the Sandburg Village promotion. The first, Newton Farr, was a past president of the Chicago Real Estate Board and chairman of the GNMAA's redevelopment committee, the group Rubloff had organized to promote his Magnificent Mile. The second Rubloff associate, Nelson Forrest, served as the GNMAA's executive director. By one later account, Forrest "fought tooth and nail for businesses on North Michigan Avenue." Carl Sandburg Village was another among Forrest's fights. Starting in 1955, Rubloff, Farr, and Forrest had sought to redevelop the Sandburg Village site. As part of setting the stage, they regularly described the area as blighted. Lower-income white people and Puerto Ricans resided in the area's many older structures. Tearing down those buildings and constructing modern apartment towers for higher-income white residents were supposed "to keep sociological trends to the west contained," Forrest told Farr in November 1955.[25] During this period, Americans sometimes utilized terms like *sociological* when seeking to avoid talking in an explicit fashion about African American or Puerto Rican neighborhoods that loomed nearby.

Rubloff's North Michigan Avenue members had also united around the Sandburg Village proposal. In June 1956, Rubloff reassured them that the site was one of "great value to the entire near north side residential and business community." To maintain forward motion, Forrest and others with an interest in North Michigan Avenue still had to win over public officials charged with approving urban renewal projects. "Implementation of the project," Forrest told a senior official on the city's Land Clearance Commission "will quickly bring about a great increase in confidence on the part of capital in connection with further needed residential and business improvements within the near northside."[26]

The first residents moved into Sandburg Village in April 1963. Sandburg villagers swam in the community's pools and played tennis on the community's courts. And, exactly as planned, historian Lilia Fernandez explains, Sandburg Village worked as "a 'buffer zone' meant to block the blight and deterioration . . . [nearby] from creeping into the Gold Coast" (the historically prestigious, high-rent area directly north of Rubloff's North Michigan Avenue).[27] Still more, several thousand middle-income shoppers would now reside within walking distance of North Michigan Avenue shops. Sandburg Village served as a scaled-down version of Rubloff's Fort Dearborn project. Sandburg Village was also Rubloff's last successful redevelopment project.

During the 1960s and 1970s, Arthur Rubloff remained a visible property owner. His buildings on and near North Michigan Avenue continued to attract expensive shops alongside office tenants willing to pay premium rates. In November 1965, executives of Bergdorf Goodman, an upscale retailer, announced plans to occupy five floors in the new, 100-story John Hancock Center under construction at the north end of Rubloff's Magnificent Mile. Nearly two decades old, Rubloff's innovative development attracted the Hancock's soaring tower, wealthy investors, and affluent shoppers. The Magnificent Mile and Sandburg Village also stood as testimonials to Rubloff's ability to assemble large coalitions of business and political leaders and hold them together from a project's inception to its conclusion.[28] But Rubloff's public visibility stood in decided contrast to his diminished reputation among property developers.

After his death in 1986, Rubloff's partners, employees, and news writers described him as "part huckster" and as the "gruffest, meanest son-of-a-bitch you ever met in your life, but he could charm you to death." No one doubted Rubloff's "ability to see through things," which they labeled his "vision." Curiously, Rubloff's vision and his guiding hand in holding large coalitions together to remodel North Michigan Avenue and develop Sandburg Village failed to extend to his firm's partners. In September 1980, they purchased Rubloff's shares from him and terminated the relationship.[29]

## North Loop Redevelopment

Nor was Rubloff able to complete another major development after Sandburg Village—even though his desire to undertake monumental projects never abated. He failed, for example, to rebuild the North Loop. For decades, the portion of downtown immediately south of the Chicago River's main branch and west of State Street—a six-block tract known as the North Loop—had been steadily declining. Dilapidated buildings and other eyesores had created what Rubloff termed a "central business district slum." Pool halls, coin dealers, and liquor stores had replaced luncheonettes and retail clothiers.

First-run movie theatres had turned to pornographic and blaxploitation films by the early 1970s, attracting a much seedier clientele and driving more respectable businesses out of the area. Most embarrassing to Chicagoans, ramshackle buildings had taken a place alongside elite law offices, and deterioration surrounded city hall, acting as a gloomy backdrop to the municipal command center. Executives of the major department stores and high-end retail establishments farther south along State Street clamored for a major rehabilitation of the shamefully degraded North Loop.[30]

In many ways, Rubloff saw the renewal of the North Loop, which required the razing of several government buildings, as an adjunct to his rejected Fort Dearborn project. Buildings torn down in the Fort Dearborn area would be reborn in the North Loop, or so ran his thinking. Even after the failure of the Fort Dearborn project, Rubloff continued to eye the blocks south of the river as fertile ground for redevelopment. He negotiated with a series of mayors during the 1970s and 1980s in a futile attempt to construct a private-public partnership for salvaging the area. His quest began at the direction of Mayor Daley, who eyed the area as a potential site for a new central library. Daley's successor, Michael J. Bilandic (1976–1979), called North Loop redevelopment his top priority and endorsed Rubloff as sole developer. The city applied for an Urban Development Action Grant (UDAG) from HUD to underwrite the cost of demolition and construction. Rubloff reported an agreement with Hilton Hotels, to build a large convention hotel in the northeast corner of the targeted area and, in conjunction with Illinois Governor James R. Thompson, held a press conference to announce the construction of a new State of Illinois Building at the western edge of the twenty-seven-acre site. Rubloff's plan ran afoul of Chicago's energetic preservation lobby, however, which objected to the destruction of several landmark structures in the heart of the redevelopment district. The preservationists blocked the UDAG grant, which could not be used to raze buildings on the National Register of Historic Places, and the Hilton Corporation withdrew when the city rescinded its offer of a hefty tax abatement. Mayor Jane M. Byrne (1979–1983), while continuing to laud the concept of North Loop reclamation, replaced Rubloff with her own team of developers. They fared no better.[31]

With an aging and infirm Rubloff watching from the sidelines, the North Loop saga crept forward at a snail's pace. In 1983, Mayor Harold Washington (1983–1987) turned the project over to Elizabeth Hollander, the city's imaginative planning commissioner, who secured a new UDAG grant, reached an accord with local preservation interests, wrangled financial contributions from prospective developers, and utilized tax-increment financing for the first time in Chicago history to generate capital for redevelopment. In 1986, the reopening of the beautifully refurbished Chicago Theatre gave hope that

Rubloff's vision would someday be realized. By the time of Washington's death in 1987, however, much remained to be done in the sweeping North Loop reclamation effort.[32]

## Conclusion: The Grinding Politics of Growth in Chicago

A larger-than-life figure in Chicago for more than four decades, Arthur Rubloff never missed an opportunity to trumpet his importance in the city's growth and development. He consorted with Chicago's wealthiest and most influential businesspeople, many of whom were crafting plans about the future shape of downtown, and regularly consulted with mayors and other city hall officials who were making decisions about how and where the Second City would invest its revenue to improve land values. His own overblown rhetoric notwithstanding, Rubloff did indeed involve himself in crucial real-estate activities that helped to reshape Chicago. Yet the impressive completion of the North Michigan Avenue and Sandburg Village projects must be weighed against such decidedly less successful undertakings as Fort Dearborn, the North Loop, and a downtown convention center. Careful consideration of the hits and misses that defined Rubloff's fabled career can be instructive in understanding the uncertain, deeply conflicted nature of urban redevelopment in Chicago and other big cities after World War II.[33]

Rubloff's hard-earned victories and disappointing defeats typically came after years of activity on several fronts. As in the completing of a complex jigsaw puzzle, developers labored to fit pieces together to form a coherent whole. Transformation of urban space downtown depended on coordinated action by the sundry components of an effective urban coalition; mayors, city councils, municipal officials, planners, corporate chief executive officers, successful merchants, federal bureaucrats, and other influential stakeholders participated in a political process that involved considerable give-and-take over substantial periods of time. Even the legendary Mayor Richard J. Daley encountered resistance at every turn as he sought to reconcile his conception of the city's well-being with the self-interests of a disparate commercial elite. Members of the CCAC, when united, exercised considerable influence over downtown projects, but even they lacked autocratic power to dictate the outcome in every real-estate transaction. Rubloff and other opportunistic developers, brimming with moneymaking ideas for the reconfiguration of space in and around downtown, needed to engage in a grinding politics to ensure the support needed from city hall, banks, multinational corporations, local merchants, and other potential investors to actualize their visions.[34] Rubloff never achieved the role of master planner for downtown that he imagined for himself. But his leadership and his many plans, his ubiquity, and his weighty presence in every renewal proposal allow us to discern the deep political and financial divisions that guided every phase of Chicago's downtown renewal from after World War II right up to the 2000s.

The formidable challenge of downtown renewal that Rubloff inherited and engaged in the 1950s and 1960s extended into the following decades. The imperatives that drove Rubloff, Pettibone, Pirie, McBain, and others— the desire to protect the central business district from encroaching blight, declining real-estate values, and the incursion of unwanted racial groups— remained as real in the last decades of the twentieth century as in the immediate post–World War II era. Keenly aware of the need to forge alliances with power brokers in city hall, developers continued to curry favor with each mayoral administration. Downtown redevelopment advocates rued the 1983 election of Harold Washington (1983–1987), the city's first black mayor and a staunch advocate of neighborhood interests, but overall, they found him less resistant to downtown enhancement than they had feared. Washington's grudging recognition of the need for investment downtown contrasted sharply with the views of his successors, Richard M. Daley (1989–2011) and Rahm Emanuel (2011–2019), who enthusiastically embraced the goal of making Chicago a global city—a goal that they felt could not be reached without the gilding of the central business district.[35]

Beginning with Rubloff and continuing in subsequent decades, salvation of the central business district remained a constant theme of city policy. Few among Chicago's political and business leaders doubted the orthodoxy of downtown renewal. The leading entrepreneurs, politicians, and institutions in the ongoing effort changed, of course, even as the fundamental goal remained the same. Members of that next generation of developers supplanted the flamboyant Rubloff, operating with less flair and lacking his insatiable thirst for the spotlight. New investors took center stage. The Continental Illinois National Bank, a leading player in downtown redevelopment during the 1950s and 1960s, filed for bankruptcy in 1984 and faded from prominence. Increasingly, real-estate investment trusts and other financial stalwarts provided the capital for remaking the downtown. The process continued, messy and disjointed, with a number of protagonists struggling to create and maintain the alliances necessary for consummating their schemes. The opportunity to make money and, perhaps most significant, the effort to bolster the downtown as the vital heart of the city attracted as much attention as ever—more so in the postindustrial age when the disappearance of manufacturing made the central business district of Chicago (and other metropolises) more important than ever.[36]

Not every facet of Chicago's renewal politics remained unmovable across the decades. Urban redevelopment enthusiasts such as Chicago Title's Holman Pettibone succeeded in bringing about large projects in targeted areas outside downtown. During the late 1940s, Pettibone had joined with leaders of Michael Reese Hospital and the Illinois Institute of Technology to demolish nearby buildings that housed a portion of the city's surging and largely unorganized African American population. Those low-income householders presented no legal or economic match for the likes of Pettibone and his renewal partners.[37]

In Philadelphia, however, as the next chapter shows, business leaders coalesced with a succession of mayors to demolish portions of downtown. Yet Philadelphia's political and businesses officials were as beset with angry disputes as their Chicago counterparts experienced. Between 1952 and the early 1970s, William L. Rafsky, a largely unknown Philadelphia official, helped untangle the city's politics sufficiently to enable a few of those projects to go forward.

# 3

## William L. Rafsky and the Greater
## Philadelphia Movement, 1951–1985

I n 1992, William L. Rafsky retired from his job with Philadelphia's city government. He had survived more than forty years in and around Philadelphia politics. During the late 1940s, he was active in local politics, seeking
to elect candidates to local offices. In 1952, his first year as a city employee,
Rafsky was an aide to the mayor. Between 1963 and 1970, he served as president of the Old Philadelphia Development Corporation (OPDC), a nonprofit firm that relied on city contracts and connections to build and restore
houses in the increasingly fashionable Society Hill district. Starting in 1972,
he headed the city's 1976 bicentennial efforts, where much of the focus was
on polishing Philadelphia's image as a destination for high-spending tourists, shoppers, and convention-goers.[1] In his final years, Rafsky was back in
important but unheralded city hall jobs. During this entire period, it is doubtful that many Philadelphians recognized Rafsky's name as a key actor in
downtown's redevelopment.

Several factors stand out in explaining Rafsky's ability to succeed in
hard-fought policy arenas. As a start, "Bill" Rafsky possessed an engaging
style and a reputation for uncompromising integrity. And without doubt,
Rafsky brought a record of dedicated service to each position. Yet Rafsky could
not boast a large constituency of avid voters dedicated to the support of his
efforts to advance one or several issues, such as downtown growth, slum clearance, or healing racial discord. The absence of a constituency was actually
one of Rafsky's advantages in policy arenas. Rafsky's inability and unwilling-
ness to threaten mayors, council members, or chamber of commerce leaders

were in fact valuable assets in a political economy undergoing harsh and relentless change. Rafsky's winning personality and his apparent inexhaustibility created opportunities to coordinate among ambitious mayors, large investors, labor union leaders, the city's rapidly increasing African American population, and Edmund N. Bacon, Philadelphia's hard-charging planner. Rafsky's rhetorical style of nonpartisanship allowed him to move from one complex negotiation to the next. And, in every position, Rafsky helped determine which sections of the city and which residents were to prosper and who would soon learn that their homes had been slated for destruction and their jobs for elimination. In this unyielding political environment, Rafsky survived as a policy entrepreneur.[2]

Rafsky's path to policy coordination started at an early age. He was born in Lodz, Poland. In 1919, still an infant, his parents brought him to New York City, and they settled in the Bronx. During his years at New York's City College, Rafsky completed a three-term honors course focused on research in municipal government. Approved topics included housing and transportation problems, industrial migration, and taxation of commercial property owned by nonprofit groups. Rafsky also worked at the school's newspaper, first as a copy editor and later as editor-in-chief. His research and service at the newspaper no doubt alerted him to city government's revenues, programs, and intense partisanship, as well as the value of focused publicity campaigns that won and maintained an audience's attention on unglamorous government topics.[3]

Rafsky held several jobs after college. During World War II, he worked for a U.S. government agency, the War Production Board. At the top level, War Production Board leaders, including the secretaries of war and the navy, directed the conversion of factories from turning out consumer items like automobiles, radios, and clothing to war goods such as bombers, tanks, and uniforms. At the end of the war, Rafsky moved to Philadelphia, where he served as director of research and education for a labor union, the American Federation of Hosiery Workers. In 1920, Philadelphia was the center of hosiery manufacture. During the next two decades, however, hosiery producers engaged in a slow-moving process of relocating operations to the U.S. South, where machines and lower-wage workers replaced skilled union members. By the late 1930s, moreover, U.S. women preferred modestly priced and more durable nylon in their hosiery, further depressing sales figures. During World War II, a temporary enthusiasm for bare legs posed yet another threat to Philadelphia's already beleaguered hosiery manufacturers. After the war, owners of Philadelphia hosiery firms scrambled to install updated machinery, improve color selection, and produce a sheerer stocking. Rafsky also taught a nighttime adult-education class at the Mercantile Library. "Labor must give, management must give," ran the class description. In January 1950, the school's educators elected the ambitious Rafsky to the executive committee. Rafsky's experiences with hosiery workers and nighttime teaching served as part of his own continuing education about rapid changes in manufacturing, labor, and consumer tastes that threatened seemingly immutable ways of organizing production and conducting business in Philadelphia, St. Louis, Chicago, and other cities.[4]

Starting in the late 1940s, Rafsky served as a member of the Citizens Charter Committee, a group sponsored by leaders of the Greater Philadelphia Movement. In April 1951, Philadelphia's voters approved a new city charter by a wide margin. Rafsky's assignments during the charter drive included speaking engagements at area schools. Most fundamentally, the new charter centered authority in the mayor's office; and, like the insurance executives, bankers, and attorneys who populated similar groups in St. Louis, Pittsburgh, Baltimore, and Chicago, the Greater Philadelphia Movement's leaders sought big improvements in their city's downtown. Restoration of the historic Independence Hall area was a coveted improvement. Yet another much-discussed project was construction of express highways around downtown. The presence of those wide roads would in turn create a barrier against noisy and smoky factories and also against the increasing number of low-income African Americans who were streaming north to Philadelphia in search of better lives. As well, years of talk among Greater Philadelphia Movement leaders about eliminating corruption was probably heartfelt and even somewhat accurate. Decades of underhanded dealings at the direction of Republican party bosses posed a worsening threat to the city's reputation and especially to its downtown property values, or so ran the reasoning among the movement's leaders. Altogether, no one who owned downtown buildings, attended Greater Philadelphia Movement gatherings, or just read a daily newspaper could have avoided reports about engineers' and architects' plans to complete the deindustrialization of downtown Philadelphia. Upscale offices, excellent shopping, wide expressways, and fashionable residential areas—housing affluent white households—would take the place of traffic jams, ugly warehouses, and smelly, old-style factories.[5] By the early 1950s, Rafsky's experiences as a college student, federal employee, union organizer, and political activist among downtown-oriented executives had melded into an appreciation for rapid urban change as well as for the city's many interconnected parts, plans, and people.

In November 1951, Philadelphians awarded management of their city's future development to the Greater Philadelphia Movement's ambitious leaders. Voters selected Richardson K. Dilworth as the Philadelphia district attorney and Joseph S. Clark Jr. as mayor. Clark, the scion of Philadelphia investment bankers and a Harvard University–trained corporate attorney, was socially at one with the businesspeople who headed the Greater Philadelphia

Movement. Clark appointed Rafsky to the posts of executive secretary and secretary to the mayoral cabinet. To achieve such prominence so rapidly places a spotlight on Rafsky's obvious willingness to work lengthy days and his adherence to ideas about using government money and authority to remodel downtown in considerable detail. He was thirty-two years old.

In 1952, Rafsky was not the most powerful official in city hall by a long stretch. But he occupied a vital place at a crossroads of government and business. In January 1952, news about each of the mayor's conversations and every one of his decisions and policy recommendations started with Rafsky and from him to cabinet members. "There is no need to point out . . . the harm that could be done if this material went beyond the Cabinet group," a cover memo told cabinet members on January 22, 1952. During February and March, in office only a short time, Clark met with staff to discuss ways to secure additional federal contracts for men's clothing firms, more state funds for road improvements, and a larger number of flights to the city's airport. After World War II, the award of federal contracts, support for local industries, and better air service were among the acknowledged responsibilities of mayors who sought to improve their city's revenues and prestige and stanch the flow of jobs, taxpayers, and investment capital to the suburbs.[6]

Clark and Philadelphia's new leaders sought fresh devices to restore downtown property values and retail sales. The widely recognized success enjoyed by Pittsburgh's Allegheny Conference for Community Development and its director, Park H. Martin, served as a regular point of reference for Clark, Rafsky, and other newly installed Philadelphia leaders. But Philadelphians distinguished their renewal efforts from Pittsburgh's. "We don't intend to have 10 or 12 top brass run our organization," banker and Greater Philadelphia Movement organizer William F. Kurtz had told Allegheny Conference executives during a visit in March 1949. Kurtz, in other words, envisioned an organization operating along the loose lines beer magnate August A. Busch and Mayor Raymond R. Tucker would fashion several years later in St. Louis. A select number of corporate officials would volunteer their time, expertise, and political capital; and one person would serve as the Greater Philadelphia Movement's executive director. (In the early 1970s, Rafsky held that post.) Despite the hoopla surrounding the new charter and Clark's election as mayor, Philadelphia's new leaders soon encountered limits in fostering their big growth plans. The city's business leadership had a history of disputes, and the animosities extended well past 1952. But the absence of a formal hierarchy at city hall and among the Greater Philadelphia Movement's directors also created opportunities for Rafsky and Clark's successors to maneuver among ideas, projects, and partners. Rafsky, according to one historian, was "endowed with superhuman energy and an insatiable appetite for precision and control."[7] Philadelphia differed from St. Louis and Pittsburgh

**Figure 3.1** Center City Philadelphia (Credit: Dennis McClendon, Chicago CartoGraphics)

in two additional ways. Philadelphians knew their downtown by a different name, that of Center City; and the Pennsylvania Railroad's (PRR) stations and tracks stood squarely in the middle of the area's redevelopment plans. (See figure 3.1.)

## Center City Redevelopment: The Chinese Wall, Penn Center, and the "White Noose"

Plans to remove the Pennsylvania Railroad's downtown trains, tracks, and viaduct had a long history in Philadelphia politics. Philadelphians described that massive railroad presence with a local name, the Chinese Wall, a block-wide barrier that split Center City in half. As far back as 1925, the mayor and business leaders reached an agreement with PRR executives to remove the wall, but a disagreement about finances stalled the project. Leaders of the Greater Philadelphia Movement had long advocated for the wall's removal. With Mayor Clark and Bill Rafsky installed in office, conversations with the PRR's top executives turned once again to converting an area described by a newspaper writer as a "blight [of] . . . honky-tonks and beer joints" into an attractive setting for corporate offices and affluent shoppers. This area already had a name. Philadelphia's city planner Edmund N. Bacon and his younger collaborator, Vincent G. Kling, had named it Penn Center, and the name stuck. Now, however, with property values, jobs, investments, and his office's prestige at stake, Mayor Clark wanted city officials to take the lead in accelerating Penn Center's development.[8] The time for railroad executives to act was also at hand. After the war, with trucks taking a larger share of their business and with commuters switching to automobiles, railroad executives' moment as dominant actors in downtown was coming to a close.

Railroad officials acted quickly to make the best deal they could. On February 21, 1952, approximately seven hundred persons attended a luncheon at which PRR executive vice president James M. Symes announced Bacon's Penn Center plan. Planner Bacon also spoke at the lunch, telling audience members about expressways, abundant parking, and a "coordinated center city rebuilding." In Bacon's plan, glitzy office towers would at long last replace smokestacks, skid row, and a noisy railroad. In late February, the publicity-minded Bacon and railroad officers placed his Penn Center model on display at Wanamaker's, an iconic Center City department store several blocks east of Penn Center. Planners and business leaders in every city assumed that shoppers would return downtown in larger numbers once gleaming buildings had replaced aging structures and low-income African Americans. On March 14, Clark spoke with Rafsky and other staff members about the fast-evolving plans. Clark, according to Rafsky's notes of the conversation, had to "make a decision soon." During the next year, rivalries among Center City leaders about building design and selection of a site developer took the place of high-sounding lunchtime rhetoric. Mayor Clark was never able to exercise the decisive hand that Richard King Mellon brought to Pittsburgh's redevelopment.[9] Plans nonetheless lurched ahead. Finally, on April 27, 1952, the Philadelphia Orchestra played, and thousands of sentimental Philadelphians braved a rainstorm to watch the PRR's last train depart Broad Street Station at 9:57 P.M.

During the next decade and beyond, private developers completed Penn Center, which eventually extended across several blocks on city hall's west side. In keeping with Clark and Rafsky's interest in replacing the old with the new, builders started construction with an atomic-age bang. A child waved a Geiger counter above a tiny amount of nuclear material, which in turn helped spark a small explosion. Penn Center was in reality only a group of expensive and prosaic office towers, a below-ground esplanade, parking spaces, an apartment house, a Greyhound bus terminal, and a 21-story Sheraton Hotel. The hotel featured more than nine hundred rooms and a ballroom with a capacity for up to fifteen hundred guests eager to indulge in opulent banquets. As in St. Louis and similar urban centers, developers had not constructed a new hotel in Center City since the mid-1920s. Penn Center will attract more visitors than New York's Rockefeller Center, Clark predicted in April 1955 at a luncheon announcing the start of the hotel's construction. Whether in Chicago or Philadelphia, Rockefeller Center and Pittsburgh's Golden Triangle regularly served as touchstones against which urban leaders calibrated their progress toward bringing a vibrant downtown into being.[10] Ordinary residents who followed urban politics in the mid-1950s would have recognized the booster rhetoric that accompanied a new building's arrival in any city.

Endless talk about renewal and prosperity's return ran alongside fear that racial antagonisms had already clouded Center City's future. "Tons of steel and concrete," a *Time* magazine writer observed early in February 1958 about Penn Center, could not obscure the fact that white households continued their trek to the suburbs. Each month, lower-income African Americans, southerners mostly, took their place. Efforts to relocate those African American households, Rafsky informed that *Time* writer, soon ran up "against discrimination in housing." Joseph Clark's successor as mayor, Richardson Dilworth, described his city's racial geography in more ominous terms. Block after block of white communities, he contended in that *Time* report, had fastened a "white noose" around black communities near Center City.[11]

References to a white noose, suggesting murder by hanging, was a regular part of Philadelphian's angry talk about race. White householders often described nearby African American neighborhoods as "the jungle," a term that put a racist and unyielding exclamation point on Dilworth's description of a noose. Yet few black or white Philadelphians could have learned anything new in Rafsky's and Dilworth's descriptions of their city's hardened black and white relationships. Whites showered African Americans brave enough to rent or purchase outside prescribed areas with bricks and taunts. White residents in other cities such as Detroit and Chicago often displayed equal levels of racialized anger. And like leaders in those other cities, Rafsky worked closely with Mayors Clark and Dilworth to foster massive urban renewal programs, which destroyed African American neighborhoods and put pressure on displaced householders to find new places to live. Public housing in Philadelphia and elsewhere was adequate to take care of most of the displaced families but could never house the steady flow of newcomers seeking to improve their lives in the industrial North. Hardened racial rhetoric and occasional bouts of violence were portions of the indirect price that Rafsky, Clark, and Dilworth paid to shore up Philadelphia's budget and Center City's reputation. James Symes, now the Pennsylvania Railroad's president, offered Rafsky and Dilworth an opportunity to restore another part of Center City along Market Street.[12]

## The Stadium on Stilts

In 1950s America, businesspeople like Symes initiated business deals with sumptuous lunches. On December 22, 1955, he hosted a lunch for Clark, the outgoing mayor, and Richardson Dilworth, the city's incoming mayor, whose term was to start the following month. Dilworth, like Clark, was born into an upper-class family and was also among the Greater Philadelphia Movement's founders. The astute Symes also invited Rafsky to join them for lunch, at which Symes revealed a plan to construct a football and baseball stadium over the railroad's tracks at Thirtieth Street, some twelve blocks west of Penn Center.[13] The stadium's designer, Vincent G. Kling, had served as Bacon's associate on the run-up to their Penn Center proposal. Kling's drawings showed a large stadium supported by beams, a stadium on stilts, above the PRR's tracks.

During the next year, top PRR executives advanced arguments about a Thirtieth Street stadium as part of an emerging redevelopment complex. That complex, if it came into being, would extend east to Penn Center and nearby city hall, the heart of Center City. Symes promoted the stadium to augment the PRR's sagging transportation revenues. The railroad would lease the stadium's space to the city. Naturally, Symes wanted city government to pay the immense construction costs, estimated as high as $21 million for a stadium with seating for up to a hundred thousand fans. Symes could not have believed that city officials would step forward to finance a new stadium principally aimed at propping up his railroad's finances. Instead, Symes and his savvy executives pitched their proposal as a businesslike antidote to Philadelphia's regular loss of population and downtown business. The proposed stadium at Thirtieth Street, stilts and all, resided at the intersection of the PRR's intercity and suburban commuter lines and long-planned expressways. By this reasoning, thousands of commuters, downtown businesspeople, guests at the new Sheraton Hotel, and perhaps even larger numbers of East Coast residents living near rail lines would regularly swarm to Philadelphia to watch live sports and maybe stay over to shop and visit museums. In April, local New York City investors announced plans to construct a stadium on stilts on New York City's West Side, also above railroad tracks. Like Symes, New York's stadium promoters talked about a location at "the crossroads of the world."[14]

The prospect of stadiums on stilts never fired imaginations in either city. In Philadelphia, Dilworth appointed a nine-person committee to consider options. The committee in turn hired a consulting firm to prepare a study, the results of which did nothing to push the project forward. The prospect of building a stadium of any type that required a large city expenditure, added to traffic congestion, or disrupted ongoing renewal programs fell short in local politics. All concurred that Connie Mack Stadium, where the Philadelphia Phillies baseball team and Philadelphia Eagles football team played, was decrepit. Nearby traffic and parking problems in an African American neighborhood added to white sports fans' negative views about the old park. In 1958, the Eagles football team moved across the Schuylkill River to the University of Pennsylvania's Franklin Field, which seated more than sixty thousand fans, a large increase over Connie Mack's thirty-nine thousand seats. During the 1950s, neither the city's feuding politicians nor regular citizens black or white were prepared to sacrifice a favored city program or further dent the city's budget to build a new stadium. Symes's proposal to construct a stadium on stilts nonetheless touched off a multiyear scramble among competitors who sought to identify desirable locations and adequate financing to house the city's sports teams.[15]

## The Dock Street Market, Independence Hall, and Society Hill

Stadium promotion was only one of many activities Rafsky dealt with every day. In matters such as the proposed stadium, Rafsky, representing the mayor, was a prominent voice in a free-for-all scramble to get someone else to finance an expensive project with an unclear future. By the mid-1950s, however, Rafsky had accumulated additional authority. Up to that point, he had served as Mayor Clark's housing coordinator, an important job in a renewing city, but still a posting that was not the first among equals. In 1956, Mayor Dilworth appointed Rafsky as Philadelphia's development coordinator, a new position. His assignment in that position, as Rafsky later described it, was to "harness the combined efforts" of city agencies such as the City Planning Commission with semi-independent agencies such the Housing Authority. Dilworth also appointed Rafsky director of the Redevelopment Authority, which, according to Rafsky, served as "the key agency with the heaviest program."[16] Bill Rafsky was now a key actor in Center City's renewal.

Rafsky's Redevelopment Authority directed large bulldozer projects. Removing the privately owned Dock Street Market from an area near Independence Hall was one of those projects. Philadelphia's leaders harbored big plans for redeveloping the area around Independence Hall. They determined to deal first with the nearby Dock Street Market (where the city's food was delivered in bulk and then redelivered in smaller quantities to grocers and butchers). As early as 1952, an author for *Redbook*, a popular magazine for women, published an article focused on the food markets in Philadelphia and other cities. "No vigorous young American home builder," he contended, "would tolerate the filthy gamut much of the nation's fruit and vegetable produce passes through—if he or she knew the facts." Members of the Greater Philadelphia Movement had long targeted the area for demolition. In 1954, the author of one of the movement's booklets lamented the area's congestion, the nearby skid row, and the "dirt and germs" accumulating on food "heaped on sidewalks." Were those reasons insufficient to advance support for the market's elimination, the booklet's authors included a photograph of a white male lying on the sidewalk clutching a bottle and an African American man standing in weeds next to a food-loading platform and staring vacantly at the camera. "He hasn't much to look forward to in life," the booklet's authors added, but without explaining how a new food center in a distant location would improve his life's chances. In 1955, Rafsky and other top officials joined private agencies to make plans to demolish the Dock Street Market and construct the new Food Distribution Center in South Philadelphia, several miles from Center City. They disliked the Dock Street Market's filth, disheveled appearance, and inefficient food-delivery methods, and they coveted the area for projects that would attract higher-luster occupants and higher property taxes. Rafsky's enthusiasm to relocate their food center echoed the sentiments of business and political leaders in many postwar cities. So eager were Philadelphia officials to bulldoze the Dock Street Market that they even financed the initial demolition expenses. "We believe we can recoup the investment . . . pretty quickly," Rafsky explained to members of the U.S. Senate Committee on Banking and Currency in December 1957. In March 1959, Rafsky invoked a businesslike tone, predicting that the new

Food Distribution Center and similar projects would produce an 8.5 percent return to the city in the form of greater tax revenues. Rafsky even presided as workers prepared to close the Dock Street Market, describing it to a gathering of dignitaries as "a part of living history."[17]

Bill Rafsky had not abolished the Dock Street Market single-handedly. In every Center City project during this period, the mayor assigned Rafsky to coordinate the many public and private officials who handled demolition, finance, and reconstruction. In redeveloping the area around Independence Hall and Society Hill, Rafsky played a more direct role.

In March 1957, Rafsky and Dilworth met at the White House with two of President Dwight D. Eisenhower's top aides. The mayor sought funds to improve Independence National Historical Park, home to the Liberty Bell and Independence Hall, where the nation's founders had written the Declaration of Independence and the U.S. Constitution. In 1948, leaders of Philadelphia's Redevelopment Authority had declared the area around Independence Hall blighted, creating a legal basis to level houses and relocate owners and tenants. That same year, Congress authorized the park project, but the appropriation for 1957 amounted to a miserly $5,800. By way of context, a sympathetic member of the Pennsylvania congressional delegation introduced a bill to authorize $7.2 million to make needed improvements. Up to that point, moreover, the area around the iconic Independence Hall consisted of the as-yet unmoved Dock Street Market, a derelict port district, and aging buildings that housed small manufacturers. Like many parts of Center City, the blocks surrounding Independence Hall were grimy and poorly maintained.[18] Despite the halting progress on redevelopment, regular use of Independence Hall for club meetings, for patriotic speeches, and as a destination point for parades helped to keep the building a part of the popular consciousness.

Dilworth and Rafsky harbored larger goals. The wanted to restore the areas around Independence Hall and nearby Society Hill. (Originally named after the Free Society of Traders, a merchant group that operated in the area before the American Revolution.) The stage for this plan had been set years before. Soon after World War II, reports about Society Hill as a new mecca for upper-income residents began to enjoy regular circulation in the city's newspapers and among downtown business leaders. In 1947, planner Bacon brought solidity to these ideas. He constructed the Better Philadelphia Exhibition, which showed what a restored Philadelphia could look like. Bacon placed the exhibit in Gimbel's Department Store (setting a precedent for showing his Penn Center mockup at Wanamaker's in 1952).

By the end of 1947, in other words, no member of the Greater Philadelphia Movement could have avoided knowing about a big renewal program, including plans for Society Hill. In June 1956, the planning commission invited members of the Chamber of Commerce and the Greater Philadelphia Movement to learn about updated plans for Society Hill. In the mid-1950s, however, the area's aging buildings were unlikely places for executives to reside. Homes lacked plumbing and electricity; Society Hill was another trash-strewn and deteriorated area. Yet Society Hill, only a short walk from Independence Hall, possessed the advantage of a Center City location. Society Hill, with the ghosts of the nation's founders assertedly residing nearby, would be remade into a steppingstone for rising property values and city tax revenues throughout the area. History, in Society Hill anyway, might be converted into a visible, moneymaking enterprise that would launch another section of Center City on its way back to solid, middle-class standing. Society Hill's remodeling was to be a mix of preservation and demolition, in contrast with the emphasis on destruction that characterized the actions of Rafsky's Redevelopment Authority in Dock Street Market and in other sections of the city. In 1957, Mayor Dilworth demonstrated his commitment to the project by purchasing two buildings and launching the costly and time-consuming process of converting them into a single unit. Dilworth made himself a pioneer in a process a *Saturday Evening Post* writer described two years later as "bring[ing] back to town the middle and upper classes that had long ago decamped for the suburbs."[19] The Society Hill idea also had a key sponsor.

Albert M. Greenfield, a prosperous banker and developer, was one of three major actors (along with Rafsky and Dilworth) behind Society Hill's redevelopment. Greenfield owned properties near Society Hill and, like his counterparts in St. Louis, Chicago, and elsewhere, he feared Center City's obsolescence. He had long sought to remodel parts of downtown. Soon after Clark's 1952 swearing in, Greenfield became a regular city-hall visitor. On January 21, 1952, he accepted Rafsky's offer to chair Price Stabilization Week, an honorary post, and Greenfield promised to arrange for Rafsky to be the principal speaker at a Chamber of Commerce dinner scheduled for the following month. Greenfield provided Rafsky with direct access to the city's leading business executives. In talks to corporate executives, the congenial Rafsky explained urban redevelopment using business terms such as "return on investment." In subsequent years, Greenfield met with Rafsky and Clark regularly, often to consider appointments to local offices. "Practically all day on politics, starting with a breakfast meeting in Greenfield's apartment at the Bellevue," Rafsky noted in his entry for February 21, 1955. Rafsky's connection with Greenfield served as a bridge between top executives who populated the Greater Philadelphia Movement and the city's small-business owners. They were tied to the Republican Party officials who had run the city for decades. Dilworth cemented his (and Rafsky's) connection to Greenfield with another key appointment.[20]

In January 1956, Dilworth appointed Greenfield chair of the City Planning Commission. Greenfield, as a major developer and property owner, had a natural interest in streets, highways, and traffic flows and in the politics that governed the organization of factories, apartments, and houses across the urban landscape. After World War II, Greenfield, like major property developers in cities such as Chicago and Pittsburgh, identified Center City's falling property values as a major problem. In particular, Greenfield worried about the downward slope in prices around the historic district, where he was heavily invested. Greenfield was not an easy person with whom to work, many downtown business leaders judged, but Dilworth considered his intimate knowledge of Philadelphia's business and political leaders useful for advancing broad redevelopment plans in Society Hill and elsewhere. And, in Greenfield's hands, Society Hill's and Independence Hall's development shifted from public agencies like the Redevelopment Authority and the planning commission to a nonprofit private company.[21]

In May 1956, Greenfield founded the nonprofit Old Philadelphia Development Corporation (OPDC). Rafsky and Dilworth knew the details months in advance, and they approved. Dilworth served on the corporation's board alongside city officials and more than fifty of Philadelphia's bankers, business executives, and labor leaders. Greenfield lured John P. Robin away from a top post in Pittsburgh's renewal program to head his OPDC. Robin was accustomed to working in Richard King Mellon's successful and carefully organized Pittsburgh Renaissance. As part of Philadelphia's version of that enhanced coordination, Rafsky now included Greenfield's OPDC among the organizations that he "harnessed[ed]" with other city agencies, including his Redevelopment Authority.[22] With Rafsky in charge, public and private were deeply enmeshed in Philadelphia redevelopment planning, much as happened in St. Louis, Pittsburgh, and Chicago. That merging was not an academic fine point, but a conscious effort to deal with the city's racial tensions.

In Philadelphia, race and redevelopment were inseparable. Greenfield's idea was to spend public and private funds to entice well-off white households to Center City. A small number of those homeowners already resided in Center City's Rittenhouse Square, a tony district located south and west of Penn Center. According to a survey conducted in 1960, Rittenhouse Square's residents sought to live near "shopping and cultural activities," exactly as Greenfield predicted.[23] Society Hill, by this thinking, would attract similar white, well-off households who enjoyed theater, museums, and upscale shopping. The presence of those free-spending households would in turn help reverse the slide in Center City tax collections, rental rates, and retail sales.

Despite the publicity surrounding Society Hill's development, Rafsky and Greenfield still needed a developer to assemble funds and manage construction. In November 1958, they selected Webb and Knapp as one of their two developers. In past years, New York City's Webb and Knapp, headed by the flamboyant William Zeckendorf, had participated in several urban renewal projects, including land for the United Nations in New York City, portions of Arthur Rubloff's North Michigan Avenue in Chicago, and another in downtown Denver featuring an office tower and a Hilton Hotel. Society Hill, still another of Zeckendorf's ambitious projects, included executive offices buildings, 30-story apartment towers, a rooftop swimming pool, single-family houses, underground parking, and a shopping center. Society Hill would appeal to households seeking proximity to Center City restaurants and theaters, Greenfield liked to argue. In 1961, Rafsky's Redevelopment Authority established a field office in a refurbished Society Hill building.[24] Rafsky was in the process of making Society Hill his major focus.

In May 1963, Rafsky left his multiple city jobs to accept appointment as the OPDC's executive vice president. In the casual merging of public and private that characterized Philadelphia's redevelopment politics, Rafsky would still attend meetings of the mayor's cabinet and retain access to his Redevelopment Authority office. His secretary remained on the city's payroll. Rafsky was being "deployed," Philadelphia's new mayor, James H. J. Tate, told a lunchtime audience several months earlier, and he "would continue to work with me closely." As part of the job switches, Greenfield had left the planning commission at the end of 1957. But Gustave G. Amsterdam, a top executive at Greenfield's banking firm, served on the OPDC's executive committee and as chair of the Redevelopment Authority. The "deployed" Rafsky would naturally maintain his longtime relationship with Amsterdam, further obscuring distinctions between public and private authorities. As another part of the administrative blur, the Redevelopment Authority signed an agreement to act as the OPDC's agent to recruit a small number of Society Hill purchasers; and, as yet another part, Rafsky secured the OPDC's higher salary and expanded his authority into every phase of Center City redevelopment.[25]

Society Hill, one of the most visible of Rafsky's redevelopments, was no longer an ambitious experiment. In the late 1950s, railroad executive C. Jared Ingersoll and his wife Agnes Ingersoll moved to Society Hill. Other visible executives, such as New York Stock Exchange chairman Henry M. Watts and his wife Anna Watts followed a few years later. Mayor Dilworth and his wife and six children had already moved to the edge of Society Hill. No wonder a *Time* magazine writer described the area as "swank" in 1961. During that same year, Society Hill's growing visibility as a desirable place for high-income families to live and shop encouraged fashionable retailers like Saks Fifth Avenue to open a nearby store. In short order, Gimbel Brothers department store employed experienced buyers in their Bridal Salon and other specialty sections in a store near Society Hill. By 1964, Gimbel Brothers advertised "beautifully feminine" apparel in their maternity department. In another sure sign that well-off young couples were increasingly selecting Society Hill as a desirable place to raise families, Gimbels maintained a full-time buyer in their children's clothing department. Society Hill's expanding prosperity, Rafsky and others hoped, would hasten redevelopment of Market East, a deteriorated area of run-down establishments several blocks away.[26]

But high-income families of every age were not the only ones selecting Society Hill as a desirable place to reside. Several corporate officers made identical choices. During the early 1960s, insurance firms such as John Hancock Mutual Life and Rohm and Haas, a large chemical manufacturing corporation, developed plans to relocate offices to Society Hill. By spring 1965, the mayor and a team of judges studied plans for a new courthouse and federal office building near Independence Hall that would bring attorneys and a larger number of white-collar employees to the area each day.[27] Rafsky, as head of the OPDC, was responsible for maintaining the fast pace set by his predecessors in recruiting wealthy families and top-flight corporations to Society Hill.

## Metropolitan Hospital and Interstate Highways in Society Hill: The Politics of Race and Space

Rafsky also defended Society Hill's upscale brand against lower-income neighbors. Society Hill residents worried about traffic noise, property values, and maintaining an unobstructed view in every direction. A proposal to construct a new building at the nearby Metropolitan Hospital touched each of those nerves. In May 1963, approximately one hundred Society Hill residents gathered to oppose the hospital's application for a zoning variance to construct a 3-story service building next to their 8-story medical building. The hospital provided care to lower-income white people and African Americans, and officials needed the variance to secure a federal grant of $1 million to pay for their new building's construction. By the 1960s, white householders often expressed racial hostility in seemingly neutral language. They cited a shortage of parking places, the hospital's lack of fit with the historical restorations, and the dangers trucks posed to their children's safety. *Eyesore* was another favored term. The activists' attorney, a prominent criminal defense lawyer, questioned whether the hospital was "a good neighbor." Only a week after the meeting, city plan commission members voted to deny the zoning variation. The hospital's expansion had "stir[red] a furor," as the headline in a local newspaper noted.[28]

The fight continued into the fall. In September, members of the city's Zoning Board of Adjustment voted to approve the hospital's request for permits to begin construction. Society Hill homeowners were not prepared to abandon the fight. They cited height restrictions and parking limitations. The president of the OPDC, Rafsky's boss, argued that the hospital "should relocate." In October, moreover, Mayor Tate joined Pennsylvania governor William W. Scranton and the state's U.S. senators to ask federal officials to deny the promised $1 million grant. They would support the grant, provided the hospital relocated. The promise was an empty one, as the federal government had already awarded those special hospital funds to other claimants. In July 1964, hospital officials agreed to construct a new and greatly enlarged facility in the nearby Independence Hall renewal area. Rafsky and his Society Hill supporters, at one point defeated, had mobilized legal and political talent to ward off a threat to their idea of what the area should look like and who should walk and drive there.[29]

Rafsky also protected his Society Hill residents against unsightly expressways and noisy traffic. In the mid-1960s, federal and state road engineers were preparing final plans to construct the Philadelphia segments of Interstate 95, which was to carry trucks and automobiles along the East Coast from Maine to Miami. The road's main route through Philadelphia—directly behind the unimproved Society Hill—had been on engineers' and planners' drawing boards since the late 1930s. In October 1956, only a few months after members of Congress and President Dwight D. Eisenhower approved funding, planner Bacon secured a final route that placed the multilane road below street level at one point and above it at another point. Bacon, Rafsky, and Greenfield, with years of experience dealing with Center City maps and expensive renewal projects like Penn Center, were alert to I-95's location as part of their earliest plans for creating the OPDC and refashioning Society Hill. In other words, the proposed interstate system route contained no surprises among the small group, including Rafsky, who followed such matters in detail. By late 1964, however, Rafsky and his upscale Society Hill residents had determined that a nearby portion of the highway, festooned with lights and rising as high as thirty-five feet at one point, was a development "we simply could not tolerate." The elevated road, he asserted, constituted another Chinese Wall. Rafsky had remained alert to "Chinese Wall" as an evocative term in Center City politics. And now, more than a decade later, state and federal road engineers promptly agreed to eliminate the roadway's elevated portions. In U.S. highway politics, few communities enjoyed such prompt and positive attention to their concerns.[30] But not even Rafsky and his powerfully arrayed allies possessed the resources to keep Interstate 95's noise from their windows and doors.

Society Hill residents continued to judge the ten-lane highway a nuisance. Anxious residents often discussed the idea of relocating the road to another area. Senator Joseph S. Clark, the city's former mayor and Rafsky's first city hall boss, had already urged the head of the U.S. Federal Highway Administration to consider a different route. Federal and state road engineers rarely modified routes, a political fact that increasing numbers of antifreeway protesters in urban and rural districts throughout the United States were beginning to recognize. Alternatively, Rafsky urged road engineers to put a flat roof across the highway where it passed behind their neighborhood. In February 1966, Rafsky met with Mayor Tate and with federal and state officials to look for funds to finance the city's share of the roof's expenses. By mid-1967, the search for funds to cover the freeway in Society Hill threatened to delay I-95's completion in the Delaware-Pennsylvania region. At this point, a task force headed by Vice President Hubert H. Humphrey considered the cost of building the road cover. Rafsky and his state's top leaders had the ability to elevate local issues to the highest political levels. Rafsky remained equally adept at naming the problem. With the Chinese Wall eliminated as a rallying cry, he and the others regularly described the below-ground roadway as an "open ditch."[31]

The covered-road fight had run its course. In 1970, the struggle to locate funds to pay for a roof over I-95 had been a part of Philadelphian and national politics for five years. Federal officials, of course, paid for 90 percent of interstate highway system construction expenses, but not for add-ons like a road cover. The usually determined Rafsky was ready to end the struggle. "The Federal Highway Administration wants to stick to its original formula," he told a city council committee in August 1970. In past years, city and state cost sharing, where needed, was among those intricate and esoteric topics that engineers and politicians dealt with in private. But now, even though federal officials refused to pay for the I-95 cover, cost sharing had emerged as another divisive issue in city politics. Covering I-95, asserted a homeowner in the city's fast-growing northeastern area, was only an "extravagant plan to satisfy a few affluent Society Hill people."[32] Rafsky, in seeking federal funds to cover I-95, had sought not only to protect the area's property values but also to keep the issue outside the city's increasingly harsh class and racial divides.

## Black, White, and Bill Rafsky

By the early 1970s, Philadelphia's racial politics had assumed a starker quality. Society Hill's affluent residents enjoyed talking about their polished neighborhood's connection to the nation's founding. Middle-income white households in the city's fast-growing northeastern neighborhoods lacked a plausible connection to such an enchanted idea. Only a few years earlier, large parts of Northeast Philadelphia consisted of undeveloped land. Modest-income householders in those neighborhoods talked instead about their trim new houses, built solely, they liked to assert, through savings and hard work. One historian describes their ideas as "blue-collar conservatism." Those blue-collar workers, and many who sported white collars, welcomed public spending for roads, parks, schools, and the like in their neighborhoods, and, of course, those white families took advantage of the federal government's mortgage-support programs that allowed low down payments. But Philadelphia's blue-collar conservatives also detested public housing and its many poor and black inhabitants—especially when city officials like Dilworth and Rafsky constructed those units near their neighborhoods. Distrustful white people described public-housing advocates like Dilworth as "do-gooders." Little noticed amid the shouting and anger was the fact that, years earlier, Rafsky and other city officials helped develop Northeast Philadelphia in order to accommodate homeowners who might have left the city for new houses in the suburbs.[33]

Rafsky was also extensively involved in supplying public housing, the place where few white people but many lower-income African Americans ended up residing. African American householders remained poorer than their white counterparts, and they looked to city government to open additional public housing units. At times, the political and social distance separating black and white Philadelphians was unbridgeable; and it widened further as city and federal officials sought to require all-white labor unions to integrate. Lower-income white Philadelphians, including white police officers, harbored additional grievances about the city's politicians. Those blue-collar conservatives profoundly resented what they perceived as city officials' favoritism toward black people who engaged in violence, whatever the immediate or underlying causes. About the only element uniting white and black Philadelphians was their conviction that the city's top officials, such as Mayor Tate, Rafsky, and again Dilworth had bestowed unearned favors on Society Hill's wealthy residents while leaving them to pay the bill. "I've been through too many fiascos . . . [such as] Society Hill," griped civic activist Edna Thomas. "Politicians and bluebloods grow very nervous when they see Thomas," a journalist reported in October 1970. Philadelphians like Thomas, a former high school teacher who regularly attended Redevelopment Authority hearings, increasingly viewed the city's politics as a zero-sum game they were destined to lose. "The poor have welfare, the rich have money," added another woman in Northeast Philadelphia, but "what have we got?"[34]

Philadelphia's politics were not supposed to work that way. In the 1950s, when Clark, Dilworth, Greenfield, and Rafsky launched Society Hill and Penn Center, the implicit promise was that Center City's restored prosperity would extend to neighborhoods near and far. Federal officials, with the support of Rafsky and others who were responsible for making that promise come true, invested $40 million in Society Hill's demolition and site redevelopment. Yet, according to critic Thomas and others like her, money spent in Society Hill to cover I-95 or, in fact, for any Society Hill improvements, left her neighborhood that much poorer. Still more, during the 1960s, leaders of activist organizations such as neighborhood-based white homeowner groups and the National Association for the Advance for Colored People (NAACP) had become adept at mobilizing Philadelphians to stop detested projects judged to benefit others at their expense. From 1952 into the late 1960s, Rafsky had worked for three mayors and for the OPDC in this increasingly strident setting. White and black hostility threatened the Center City strategy on which Rafsky, every mayor, and downtown business executives such as Albert Greenfield had settled. By the early 1970s, leaders of those antidowntown coalitions sometimes coalesced successfully to stop unwelcome developments in favored places like Society Hill."[35]

In 1952, Rafsky, Clark, Dilworth, and Greenfield looked like a political force to be reckoned with. Penn Center, the stadium on stilts, and immense renewal and public-housing programs throughout the city were standard parts of redevelopment that Rafsky and other leaders advanced during those heady years. Yet Penn Center's towers and Society Hill's historic architecture and well-to-do residents possessed virtually no ability to redirect or block the changes taking place all around them. Neither alone nor in tandem could those visible and costly projects fundamentally slow movement to the suburbs, force managers of aging retailers to spend on improvements, reduce job losses, reverse falling tax revenues, mollify racial hatreds, or put cash into the hands of low-income residents of every color. Rafsky and Mayor Tate, by adroitly combining public and private offices, managed to get Society Hill built. Rafsky's move to direct the OPDC signaled the arrival of a narrowed preoccupation with downtown's survival as a taxpaying entity and urban showcase. During the 1960s, Society Hill's completion was one of the few keys still in public hands perhaps able to slow downtown's deterioration. By the early 1970s, even that moment had passed. In 1978, Rafsky's long-planned Gallery at Market East opened, but those stores failed to attract the long-sought upper-income shopper. Among many factors, the federal government's highway and home-mortgage programs had fostered suburban living. Deep racial antagonisms added to the suburbs' lure. U.S. cities such as Philadelphia, observes historian Eric Avila, were white on the outside and brown and black at the center. Yet, for all these limits, Rafsky's (and Greenfield's) efforts during the 1950s and 1960s perhaps helped keep portions of Center City partially alive—at least until members of a succeeding generation of political and business leaders turned to upscale condominiums, tourism, flower shows, ethnic festivals, and other stratagems as growth devices. Undeniably, however, Philadelphia's poverty rate remained at the top of the list among big cities.

In 1992, when Rafsky retired from city hall, he was seventy-three years old. He had reached young adulthood during the Great Depression and World War II. And he was a middle-aged city and nonprofit employee amid Philadelphia's fast-fading economy of textiles, railroads, steel, downtown retailing, and federal spending for big-city renewal. Rafsky's assignment, at its most basic, was to arrest that decline and restart Philadelphia on the path to a new era of growth. Yet those freewheeling days, when Rafsky combined offices, spoke in the mayor's name, and presided over important projects, were an unremembered part of an earlier and brief era. By the mid-1970s, Rafsky held important but anonymous jobs such as deputy finance director and deputy managing director. In those later years, Rafsky's extensive knowledge of the city's budget and neighborhoods would have proven attractive to any mayor dealing with racial strife while still charged to create jobs, boost the tax base, refurbish the city's brand, and compete for investments against mayors and business boosters in Los Angeles and other southwestern cities. In 2001, a *New York Times* obituary writer characterized Rafsky as a "civil servant."[36]

# 4

# Albert E. Cobo's Detroit, Ernest J. Bohn's Cleveland, and Expressway Politics

I n 2014, on the 313th anniversary of Detroit's founding, the *Detroit Free Press* published a list of the five best and five worst mayors in the city's long history. (Detroit celebrated that unusual number of years in existence because 313 also serves as the metropolitan region's telephone area code). The newspaper selected Albert E. Cobo as the city's fourth-worst mayor, attributing the awful ranking to his indelible reputation for racism. According to the prevailing wisdom at that time and since, Cobo's avid defense of segregation impaired the lives of African Americans and hastened the decline of their neighborhoods. Three years later, the *Cleveland Plain Dealer* offered a tribute to native son Ernest J. Bohn as the first director of the nation's first public housing authority. Because of Bohn's many successes as a planner, city official, and legislative draftsman of housing reform measures, he became known as one of the nation's premier progressives. On the surface, these two civic bellwethers seemed to have had very different public policy agendas, but a common thread ran through their distinguished careers. They shared an unshakable commitment to downtown redevelopment after World War II and a firm belief that the revitalization of the central business district began with the massive construction of new expressways. Detroiters knew Cobo first and foremost as a businessperson's mayor consumed with downtown refurbishment, and Clevelanders saw Bohn primarily as a staunch defender of neighborhood interests. Despite that difference in standpoints, the two men concurred that their cities needed to move quickly after World War II to improve access to downtown by automobile.[1]

In response to the critical shortage of affordable housing after World War II, the U.S. Congress passed landmark legislation—the Taft-Ellender-Wagner Housing Act of 1949 and the Housing Act of 1954, most notably—that set ambitious goals for the construction of low- and middle-income housing units and created the urban renewal program designed to redevelop declining downtowns. Before federal agencies inaugurated these national programs, however, progrowth coalitions composed of business elites, mayors, and other city officials initiated programs designed to resuscitate struggling central business districts and lobbied in state capitals for legislation authorizing their redevelopment efforts. Such business-government alliances as the Greater Philadelphia Movement, the CCAC in Chicago, and Civic Progress, Incorporated, in St. Louis acted after the war to shield imperiled downtowns from the threat of encroaching blight. In some instances, pathbreaking measures crafted at the local and state levels served as models for the key national legislation that followed. Hopeful of federal financial assistance but unwilling to wait for slow-moving institutions in Washington, DC, to take action, local policy makers and corporate executives proclaimed the urgency of downtown redevelopment and moved ahead with dispatch.[2]

City leaders identified improved transportation as a vital component of halting decentralization and heartily endorsed the Federal-Aid Highway Act of 1956 that pledged the U.S. government to fund 90 percent of the expansive highway system that was to include urban expressways. Yet, just as in the case of housing and urban redevelopment where local efforts antedated federal involvement, the construction of an extensive network of multilane, high-speed expressways commenced in many cities well before Congress passed the landmark 1956 national legislation. The first mayors and city councils to act encountered challenges that recurred repeatedly in the postwar years and made crucial policy decisions that presaged later developments. Federal aid increasingly expedited downtown redevelopment, but policy makers in Detroit, Cleveland, and elsewhere moved decisively ahead before the U.S. Congress acted in 1956 and accordingly established important precedents for the interstate era.[3]

Federal officials proved supportive in other ways before 1956. Engineers at the U.S. Bureau of Public Roads (BPR) lent their expertise to state and local highway departments, conducting traffic-needs studies and drafting detailed plans that specified proposed routes and the locations of interchanges. In the last years of the war, bureau engineers supervised studies in thirty major metropolitan areas and 135 communities with populations below fifty thousand. Congress then passed the Federal-Aid Highway Act of 1944, which provided funds for highway construction for the three years after the war, with one-fourth of the allocation designated for urban primary roads. By 1948, the BPR had underwritten surveys in sixty cities and detailed preliminary engineering plans in one hundred metropolitan areas. The amount of federal funds allocated for the construction of urban highways rose from $68 million in 1947 to $376 million in 1950, by which time 116 cities had completed plans for new roadways. In 1951, 65 percent of federal urban funds were spent on limited-access highways, and the BPR reported that work on expressway improvements or construction was proceeding in every major U.S. city.[4]

At the forefront of large U.S. cities pursuing extensive expressway construction in the years immediately after World War II stood Detroit, the self-styled "Motor City." Detroit's business elite and city officials began systematic discussions during the war of how to revitalize the ailing central business district, invariably mentioning the need for better roads. In a 1942 report prepared for the Urban Land Institute, a local consulting firm highlighted the city's many problems—including soaring vacancy rates downtown, the spread of slums and blight, population loss, and the proliferation of outlying shopping centers—and devoted considerable attention to worsening traffic congestion and inadequate parking. A section of the report carefully documented the decline in the number of people and vehicles entering and leaving the downtown daily. From 1925 to 1940, while Detroit's population increased from 1,246,044 to 1,623,452, the number of persons leaving the central business district between 5 P.M. and 6 P.M. on typical business days fell from 80,867 to an estimated 67,000. The flight of middle- and upper-class residents from areas adjacent to the city's business core had been accelerating for more than two decades, noted the consultants, and the situation would only worsen unless the city acted immediately. The downtown's accessibility had to be improved for workers, shoppers, tourists, and other commuters. Among its list of recommendations for facilitating the vital flow of automobile traffic in Detroit was the construction of a circumferential beltway to divert trucks and interstate travelers away from the congested core, superhighways funneling commuters into and out of the central business district, and an increase in off-street parking downtown to accommodate the traffic.[5]

Continuing the viability of downtown, according to the 1942 report, depended as much on the availability of adequate parking as on the ability of motorists to negotiate their daily commutes in a timely fashion. Curbside parking on downtown streets provided less than 5 percent of the space needed to accommodate the number of automobiles in use on weekdays, and the dearth of parking lots and garages proved to be a constant irritant for office workers, building owners and operators, merchants, city employees, and well-off shoppers. The untenable situation could be addressed successfully only by adding a large amount of off-street parking. In the short term, suggested the consultants, private companies, downtown merchants' associations, or the municipal government should establish temporary parking facilities on the edge of the central business district with shuttle buses ferrying commuters through downtown streets to and from their destinations. The inconvenience of having to change modes of transportation at peripheral locations would likely annoy commuters, the authors of the report acknowledged, and so a permanent solution would likely entail the construction of terminal off-street parking structures in the heart of the city. Whatever the solution, the provision of ample parking would have to accompany the improvement of roadways in a city tied inextricably to motor vehicles.[6]

Upon approval of the 1944 Federal-Aid Highway Act, planning began in Detroit for the construction of two expressways that would intersect at a right angle just north of downtown. The Edsel B. Ford Expressway would extend eastward across the length of the city, and the John C. Lodge Expressway would connect the central business district with the affluent northern suburbs of Oakland County. In 1945, in a letter to the common council (also known as the city council) on the necessity of urban redevelopment after the war, City Treasurer Albert E. Cobo made the case for multilane expressways as a crucial element in enhancing downtown real-estate values. In turn, members of the common council authorized the Department of Public Works to begin acquiring rights-of-way in 1946, and construction of the two expressways began the following year. The Detroit Plan, a comprehensive design for postwar development issued by the city in 1947, emphasized the importance of downtown revitalization (including the prominent role played by better transportation) through the elimination of African American neighborhoods, which white people invariably judged blighted, in and around the urban core. Endorsing the plan, Mayor Edward J. Jeffries Jr. pledged that the city would devote its own resources to redevelopment regardless of the level of support garnered from the state and federal governments. Glenn C. Richards, general superintendent of the city's Department of Public Works, argued strongly for an increase in federal aid and recommended enhancing the lobbying efforts in Washington, DC, for transportation legislation. In the meantime, however, Richards and other city officials argued that the urgent need for more highways in Detroit dictated that the city should continue its own building program without delay. Work on the two expressways proceeded briskly.[7]

To initiate construction of the Ford and Lodge Expressways, Detroit relied on an innovative funding formula that soon attracted considerable attention among local officials, civil engineers, and urban planners nationwide. The State of Michigan allotted half the revenue collected on gasoline taxes and license fees to counties, which in turn used about half that sum to maintain rural roads and distributed the remaining half to municipalities in each county. Shortly after passage of the Federal-Aid Highway Act of

1944, Detroit entered into a compact with the State Highway Department and the Wayne County Road Commission to construct the two expressways. Under the auspices of the so-called Tri-Party Agreement, each year the city would allocate $1.5 million, the county would contribute $1.5 million, and the state would provide $3.0 million, with the total of $6.0 million to be used to supplement whatever federal funds became available. The annual federal allocation of $4.0 million, along with the dollars from the Tri-Party Fund, initially freed up $10 million a year—an impressive sum in the late 1940s but hardly adequate for the timely completion of twenty-two miles of expressway construction. At that rate, lamented city officials, the road-building project would not be completed until the mid-1960s.[8]

## Albert E. Cobo's Expressways

Such a dilatory pace proved unacceptable to Albert E. Cobo, an impassioned advocate of downtown redevelopment. A native of Detroit, Cobo owned and operated two candy stores while studying accounting in night school at the Detroit Business Institute. After several years of classwork, he sold the candy stores and went to work for the Burroughs Corporation where he rose to an executive position. In 1933, at the nadir of the Great Depression in Detroit, Cobo took a leave from the company and went to work for the municipal government as deputy city treasurer to contribute his expertise during the financial crisis. He won election as city treasurer in 1935 and subsequently served seven consecutive terms as the city's chief financial officer. An unreconstructed conservative, the Republican Cobo believed unquestioningly in government providing strong support for the business community. A devout anticommunist, he vied often with the city's robust trade unions and clashed with African American organizations such as the National Association for the Advancement of Colored People (NAACP) and the National Urban League in his stout opposition to open housing.[9]

In 1949, Cobo ran for mayor promising fiscal responsibility at city hall, more investment in urban redevelopment, and opposition to African American incursions into previously all-white neighborhoods. His Democratic opponent, George Edwards, had served as director of the local housing commission before his election to the common council. Edwards had supported black occupancy of the Sojourner Truth public-housing project, a controversial 1942 initiative that led to forty injuries and 220 arrests in one of the decade's worst race riots. The unions went all out for the Democrat, who had earlier been a United Auto Workers (UAW) activist, but Cobo received strong support from the business community and the uniform backing of community groups on the overwhelmingly white Northeast and Northwest Sides. The Republican won by the lopsided margin of 313,136 to 206,134.

Cobo's resounding triumph over the liberal-labor coalition headed by Edwards allowed him to claim a mandate for his segregationist policies and his probusiness agenda.[10] Because of the decisive vote, Cobo insisted on the force of that mandate throughout his time in office, which extended to September 1957.

An unrelenting champion of downtown refurbishment who became known as "Little Al the Big Builder" during his mayoral tenure, the diminutive Cobo led an ambitious campaign to remake the floundering central business district. Under his guidance, the city built the $112 million Civic Center overlooking the Detroit River, a huge convention center (Cobo Hall) with attached basketball venue (Cobo Arena), a new city-county office building, and the Henry and Edsel Ford Auditorium (home of the Detroit Symphony Orchestra). At the same time, he worked tirelessly to help merchants by improving access for shoppers and workers traveling in and out of downtown. As commuters grumbled about rush-hour traffic that allowed speeds of only fifteen miles per hour, the mayor proposed yet another financial innovation to expedite freeway building. Denouncing the cautious "pay-as-you-go" formula in use at the time, he championed a bill in the state legislature that would allow the state, county, and city to issue thirty-year revenue bonds based on the future collection of gasoline taxes and other user fees paid by motorists. With the additional revenue generated by the bonds, Cobo advised Michigan governor G. Mennen Williams in 1950, the expressways could be completed within four years—a full decade earlier than under the prevailing arrangement. Governor Williams supported the measure, which the state legislature passed later that year.[11]

In 1950, Mayor Cobo also affirmed the city's decision to favor automobile access to the central business district instead of mass transit—that is, to build multilane, limited-access freeways rather than extend and repair the city's modest fixed-rail public transportation system. Five years earlier, outside consultants had recommended to the Mayor's Transportation Committee the inclusion of rapid transit rails in the median strip of the Edsel B. Ford Expressway, but the State Highway Department and municipal government refused to pay the additional right-of-way and construction costs. In 1949, another consulting firm had urged that fixed rails for mass transit be added to the medians of all new expressways, but both the state highway commissioner and the president of the local rapid transit commission refused to endorse the report. In both 1945 and 1949, transportation officials judged the cost of providing mass transit facilities prohibitively expensive. Furthermore, they argued, state law mandated that revenue collected from taxes and fees paid by motor vehicle owners be used only for the construction and maintenance of roads and not diverted for ancillary purposes such as buses or fixed-rail mass transit. The influence of civil engineers and their allies in the trucking industry guaranteed that Detroit would remain a "rubber-tire town."[12]

Mayor Cobo made clear the singular importance of better automobility for the city, asserting that "highways would lure residents of neighboring areas to shop" in Detroit and would "retard the decentralization of business into suburban areas which pay no Detroit taxes." He and other municipal officials confirmed their commitment to better automobile access to the central business district with the release of the Master Plan of 1951. After the city commissioned internationally renowned architect Eliel Saarinen to fashion a blueprint for remaking the urban core, the Detroit City Planning Commission revised the design he and his son Eero submitted to update the Detroit Plan of 1947. Echoing the goal of reviving the downtown commercial sector espoused four years earlier, the Master Plan of 1951 explicitly tied the extensive downtown construction program engineered by Cobo to the need for better transportation. Again forthrightly eschewing the option of mass transit, the city determined to provide commuters, shoppers, and visitors attending special events easier access to the riverfront and surrounding area by building more expressways. Cost considerations and land acquisition disputes later caused city engineers to modify the highway routes drawn in 1951, but the fundamentals of the detailed expressway network sketched by the planning commission that year remained largely unchanged in subsequent decades. The expressway, rather than the trolley or subway, became an immutable fixture of the Motor City's political and social geography.[13]

While local plans crystalized for an elaborate expressway network, Cobo and other Detroit officials lobbied in Washington, DC, for the passage of a new transportation bill that would significantly increase federal funding for highways. In a 1950 letter to Senator Homer S. Ferguson, Cobo detailed the shortcomings of existing federal legislation and reported that Flint, Grand Rapids, Battle Creek, Muskegon, and other Michigan communities sought to join Detroit in building limited-access highways but found it impossible to do so because of inadequate resources. Working in tandem with the American Municipal Association, the Detroit mayor proposed an amendment to a bill under consideration in Congress that would authorize federal largess to be used by local and state governments to reduce bond indebtedness. Mayor Cobo and Glenn C. Richards, who had been named Detroit's expressway coordinator, testified before Congress on behalf of the amendment. The Federal-Aid Highway Act of 1950, passed shortly after President Harry Truman ordered U.S. forces to Korea and requested that Congress curtail spending on such domestic programs as highways, disappointed expressway partisans. By the time that legislators finished trimming the allocations proposed in the original legislation, the final law provided only $125 million for urban projects during the two years beginning on July 1, 1951. As well, the bill's authors refused to increase the federal government's financial role (leaving the federal and state contributions at a 50-50 ratio) and once again disallowed the use of funds for highway maintenance and toll road construction. But the measure still constituted a valuable tool for road building, the mayors and their allies believed, because it included a crucial amendment allowing state and local governments to use federal dollars to retire bonds on new road construction. To the expressway builders and their supporters, the ability to use state and local government bonds in that fashion (per the Cobo proposal) meant much more to them than the future promise of an increase in federal spending.[14]

As additional funding allowed the pace of expressway construction to quicken in the late 1940s and early 1950s, Detroit officials confronted the delicate problems of land acquisition and condemnation. From the outset, the city pledged to select the routes of the new expressways carefully so that minimal disruption of existing neighborhoods would occur. In his 1945 missive to the common council, Treasurer Cobo had outlined a plan whereby "an area should be condemned only when its buildings are actually ready for demolition . . . where some of the buildings have already been removed and where others are actually falling." The section of the 1947 Master Plan of Detroit dealing with expressways went even further: "Whenever possible, the expressways will be routed along belts of industry. Thus, they will avoid carrying heavy traffic through residential neighborhoods, and at the same time serve as buffer strips, separating industrial installations from residential areas." As in many other cities, planners in Detroit prescribed these routes in order to separate factory and residential areas, or what they called noncontinuous land uses. Indeed, promised city officials, the new expressways would actually remove traffic from clogged streets in residential areas, improving the quality of neighborhood life, while at the same time helping to remake downtowns as attractive places where affluent residents could live, shop, and enjoy a variety of entertainment options.[15]

## Expressways in African American Neighborhoods

The reality proved to be much different, however. Site selection for expressways invariably spared middle- and upper-class enclaves, uprooted residents of less affluent neighborhoods, and sparked a series of protests from angry homeowners and businesspersons who had no desire to relocate and who often felt that they were being unfairly compensated for their property. Assaying Detroit's record of achievement in 1955, the Urban Land Institute published a lengthy study that ignored the regrettable effects of displacement on vulnerable residents and awarded the city high marks for achieving its goal of bolstering the downtown. The report concluded that "The routing of the expressways was carried out with consideration for the wishes of the downtown merchants, planners, redevelopers and suburban interests, which in Detroit include both residents and major industries." But outraged residents accused the Urban Land Institute of a whitewash.[16]

Like other cities where bulldozers tore remorselessly through targeted neighborhoods to clear paths for expressways, local officials perfunctorily listened to citizen complaints and then proceeded to implement their original plans. In a letter to Governor Williams, State Highway Commissioner Charles M. Ziegler reported an "organized and concerted effort to resist . . . expressway construction, and particularly the right-of-way acquisitions." To be sure, Ziegler acknowledged that uprooted residents experienced great difficulty finding suitable lodging in the tight Detroit housing market—a situation affecting more people displaced by the Edsel B. Ford Expressway, which destroyed densely populated residential neighborhoods, than by the John C. Lodge Expressway, which cut primarily through commercial areas. Nonetheless, the commissioner maintained, city officials deemed such draconian measures necessary. "It was highly important that right-of-way acquisitions be speeded up in the interest of expediting actual construction on the expressways, as the demand for facilities had become very acute because of greatly increased traffic in Detroit," he concluded. In addition, Ziegler explained to the governor, "On both the John Lodge and Edsel Ford, unforeseen construction difficulties or sequences of operations made necessary the immediate acquisition of certain properties in order to avoid construction delays." In other words, as the displaced residents quickly realized, expediency trumped the earlier assurances given about fairness and due process.[17]

The devastation proved to be especially acute in the densely populated areas near downtown that housed much of the city's African American population. By 1958, the city had destroyed 2,200 buildings (residences, shops, and factories) to build the Lodge Freeway on the Lower West Side and the Ford Expressway on the northernmost edge of the large African American neighborhood of Paradise Valley. The widespread demolition eliminated the bustling Hastings Street business district and many important African American cultural institutions, including a large number of churches, schools, a branch of the YMCA that provided important services and programs to the surrounding area, and several popular jazz clubs.[18]

Because years sometimes elapsed between the announcement of condemnation and demolition of the designated structures, property values often plummeted long before city crews took action. Moreover, once the city proclaimed its intention to exercise eminent domain, demoralized homeowners and merchants lost all incentive to make repairs. As the quality of targeted neighborhoods declined, the remaining residents found it virtually impossible to sell their devalued property and therefore often lacked the wherewithal to purchase homes elsewhere. Renters encountered great difficulty finding affordable lodging in other parts of the city, a situation exacerbated by the refusal of local and state governments to provide financial or logistical assistance to relocated families. Surveying the denuded landscape characteristic of urban renewal sites—what one black businessperson glumly called a "no man's land"—many of the residents and shopkeepers whose land had been spared hurriedly departed and, believing that the area would never regain its former vitality, sold their property at considerable losses.[19]

African Americans in neighborhoods singled out for elimination protested their fate to state and local officials, dispatching petitions to Governor Williams and Mayor Cobo but received no satisfaction. The Detroit Urban League and the local chapter of the NAACP doggedly opposed the local government's callous actions but found no succor at city hall. To document the disastrous effects on the black population caused both by urban renewal projects and by expressway construction, the Urban League interviewed dozens of displaced residents and forwarded the case studies to federal housing officials in Washington, DC. The interview transcripts described how much difficulty uprooted African Americans had finding safe and sanitary lodging, recounting how the local housing commission sometimes failed to seek adequate replacement housing and how the dwellings the city identified for them often proved to be even more dilapidated and hazardous than the structures razed to make way for highways. With their singular focus on speeding up traffic, elected officials and downtown business owners cared only about clearing land for expressway construction.[20]

Racial politics guided these unfortunate developments. Mayor Cobo, who had won election with minimal support from African American voters, offered little sympathy to the aggrieved residents. Widely known as a tireless champion of the city's mercantile elite, Cobo regularly described his landslide 1949 election as a green light to take all necessary actions for the cause of downtown revitalization. Moreover, clearing land for expressways through African American neighborhoods dovetailed with his sturdy opposition to "Negro invasions" of the city's all-white precincts. Ordering bulldozers into African American districts in advance of roadbuilding crews, Cobo brusquely dismissed calls for more humane policies. "Sure there have been some inconveniences in building our expressways and in our slum clearance programs, but in the long run more people benefit," the mayor remarked. "That's the price of progress."[21] And, according to Cobo as well as business and political leaders in cities such as St. Louis and Philadelphia, the urban expressway program would demonstrate its value when white shoppers and businesspeople once again filled downtown offices and stores in large numbers.

In Detroit, Cobo's idea of progress persisted despite the protests of displaced homeowners and merchants. After a new federal highway bill in 1952 appropriated more funds for urban roadways in 1953–1954—and continued to authorize the use of that funding to retire bond indebtedness—Detroit leaders announced plans for the construction of two more expressways. The Oakland-Hastings Freeway (later renamed the Walter P. Chrysler Freeway) would proceed from Jefferson Avenue along the Detroit River northeast to Six Mile Road, and the Vernor Expressway would link the Lodge and Hastings Expressways and extend eastward to Gratiot Avenue. In 1954, testifying before the President's Advisory Committee on a National Highway Program chaired by Lucius D. Clay, Mayor Cobo enthusiastically characterized the new expressways being erected in his city as "a picture of beauty." More important, he asserted that Detroit and other cities could complete their expressway networks without the federal government altering its funding formula with the states, as long as the BPR continued to guarantee all local and state bond issues. Cobo made no plea to the Clay Committee that the federal government assume 90 percent of the cost of highway construction, which the committee eventually recommended and which the 1956 interstate highway law authorized, because Detroit was fully prepared to proceed under less generous conditions. By 1958, the state highway department, city of Detroit, and county board of road commissioners had signed contracts for the building of the Southfield Expressway on the city's West Side, along with extensions of the Vernor, Chrysler, and Lodge Expressways. By the end of the decade, construction crews in Detroit were hard at work pouring concrete for the expressways (collectively known as "Cobo's canyons") that were completed in the 1960s. The businessperson's mayor had bequeathed the city an impressive legacy in concrete and asphalt.[22] Leaders in other cities acted on identical concerns about traffic and the continuing vitality of their downtown.

## Ernest J. Bohn's Plans for Downtown Cleveland's Renewal

Cleveland's leaders were also eager to build expressways. The city's comprehensive 1949 plan attributed maddening delays in traffic flow, interruptions to commerce, and the rising incidence of vehicular accidents to the insufficient number and capacity of limited-access, high-speed expressways—which, the authors of the plan argued, resulted in "several millions of real dollars that . . . Clevelanders [paid] yearly for traffic congestion." In 1949, reported the plan, only a few miles of four-lane divided highway along the lakefront existed as the germ of a citywide freeway system. For the city's planners and elected officials determined to reverse downtown's decline, the economic imperative of highway building seemed undeniable.[23] No one assumed a larger role in securing the crucial expressways for Cleveland than renowned local planning official Ernest J. Bohn.

Bohn brought a diverse background to his planning office. He left his childhood home in Romania and came to the United States with his widowed father in 1911. After graduating from Adelbert College and Western Reserve Law School, Bohn served one term in the Ohio legislature and several terms on the Cleveland City Council as a progressive Republican. The author of the nation's first state housing legislation, which became a model for laws in other states, he organized the National Association for Housing and Redevelopment Officials and participated in the drafting of the landmark U.S. Housing Act of 1937. His years as director of the Cuyahoga (Cleveland) Metropolitan Housing Authority (1933–1968) overlapped with his tenure as chairman of the City Planning Commission (1942–1966). A firm believer in broad metropolitan solutions to urban problems, he served as cofounder and director of the Regional Association of Cleveland, where he sought housing and comprehensive transportation improvements for northeastern Ohio. Leaders of the local Republican party urged Bohn to run for mayor after World War II, but he declined in order to continue his important planning work.[24]

Bohn identified the stagnation of Cleveland's central business district as a crucial factor in the metropolitan area's declining growth and development. The key first step in addressing the desertion of industry and population, the planner believed, needed to be taken in the moribund central business district. He sadly noted the financial and cultural stagnation in downtown, where only four multistory buildings had been completed since 1930, only three department stores survived where once six had thrived, and nightlife had become virtually nonexistent. Noisome discharges from oil refineries and factories located a short distance from downtown combined with the pollution rising from the unsightly Cuyahoga River, which flowed into Lake Erie at the city center to cast a pall over the entire central business district. "One sixth of Cleveland's tax income is derived from the downtown business area," Bohn noted. "One fifth of the employment is centered there. Good transportation and adequate parking facilities are essential to preserve this downtown investment." Like so many other midcentury planners, he judged downtown's revival essential to the city's long-term prospects.[25]

Beginning in the early 1940s, however, Cleveland's highest elected officials had provided scant leadership in conceiving and commencing large-scale urban redevelopment activities. Politicians representing the city's various ethnic groups struggled for control of the municipal government and sat by in city hall as the problems confronting downtown multiplied. Political paralysis continued under a series of "caretaker mayors"—Slovenian

Frank J. Lausche, Irishman Thomas A. Burke, Italian Anthony J. Celebrezze, and Romanian Ralph S. Locher—who capitalized on the city's neighborhood fissures to nurture shifting ethnic alliances and maintained a wary distance from the business elite. In the 1960s, looking back on the immediate postwar period, Mayor Carl Stokes remembered that business and government in that era "eyed each other like strange tomcats."[26]

Filling the leadership void, Bohn led the City Planning Commission in generating a plan for the central business district. In 1959, the planning commission announced with much fanfare the publication of *Downtown Cleveland 1975: The Downtown General Plan*, an appeal for city government to initiate redevelopment of the urban core during the ensuing sixteen years. The document attracted considerable attention nationally because of Bohn's involvement and the contributions of many of the nation's most famous planning consultants, including Philadelphia's Edmund N. Bacon, Detroit's Walter H. Blucher, and Chicago's Harold M. Mayer. The plan concentrated on several glaring problems: Public Square and its soaring Terminal Tower resided at the city's center, serving as a transportation center for buses and as a unifying symbol in an otherwise disjointed city. But Public Square and the nearby mall, a large park surrounded by the city's major public buildings, had grown seedy from lack of regular upkeep. The city's small, antiquated convention center needed to be expanded so that Cleveland could compete with other metropolises for conventions, trade shows, and exhibitions. Relatedly, Bohn and his coauthors asserted, the city needed a "convention-type" hotel nearby the convention center to accommodate the expected increase in event bookings. The number of vacant shops on Euclid Avenue, the locus of the city's principal retail corridor, and the preponderance of drab storefronts throughout the central business district explained the public's perception of downtown Cleveland as an uninviting place to shop. Limited accessibility by automobile and the absence of parking topped off the list of the downtown's many insufficiencies.[27]

In *Downtown Cleveland 1975*, Bohn offered several recommendations for making the central business district a more attractive location. Improving the appearance of commercial streets meant retrofitting aging store facades and establishing reliable new schedules for street cleaning and maintenance. Enhancing the lakefront's economic potential entailed the modernization of port facilities, a necessity to capture the anticipated jump in Great Lakes commerce after the opening of the St. Lawrence Seaway in 1959, and the expansion of Burke Lakefront Airport to accommodate more and larger aircraft. The report suggested additional changes to the Lake Erie shoreline, converting the erstwhile industrial site into a recreation destination, including parkland, piers for excursion craft, a new aquarium, and a sports arena. (The plan devoted considerable attention to lakeside beautification but betrayed no intention of intruding on the industrial activities along the banks of the Cuyahoga River, where oil refineries, steel mills, factories, and stockyards would continue to operate without hindrance.) Finally, the plan reimagined Public Square as a larger transportation hub, the fulcrum of a new subway system.[28]

Beginning during World War II and continuing for several decades thereafter, the city flirted with the construction of a downtown subway as the primary transportation improvement for the regeneration of life in the central business district. The downtown subway would complement the existing twenty-eight miles of east-west rapid transit that culminated in a single station underneath the Terminal Tower adjacent to Public Square. The new subway would make centrally located businesses (such as iconic department stores Halle's and Higbee's) more accessible to suburbanites, alleviate surface traffic on crowded streets, and distribute transit riders around downtown destinations. Local government and the business elite never spoke with one voice in advocating the ambitious undertaking, however. Bohn and the planning staff argued for the project, as did the Citizens League of Greater Cleveland, the Chamber of Commerce, and Mayor Anthony J. Celebrezze. County engineer Albert Porter spoke for suburbanites and the residents of peripheral Cleveland neighborhoods in making the case for new freeway construction instead. Porter injected a racial element into the debate by suggesting that the proposed subway would open the downtown to shoppers from the East Side (principally African Americans), but he ignored the possibility of an increase in patronage by white people living west of the Cuyahoga River. The influx of black shoppers, he suggested, would have a destabilizing effect on the city's race relations. George Gund, the powerful president of the Cleveland Trust Company, one of the largest banks in the Midwest, also parted ways with most of the city's business elite in expressing reservations about a subway's viability. Smaller business groups, such as the Public Square, Euclid Avenue, and Prospect Avenue Associations, quibbled about where subway stops should be situated in order to benefit their merchants.[29]

In 1953, ignoring the divisions among the city's leaders, voters approved a $35 million county bond issue to build the subway, but support for the venture ebbed in the following years. In 1957, two of three county commissioners voted not to fund the subway's construction. *Downtown Cleveland 1975* included plans for a smaller, less expensive subway in 1959, but Porter's warnings of the need for additional tax levies and predictions of unsustainable construction cost overruns convinced many Clevelanders that a subway would simply be too costly to construct and operate. In 1959, two of three county commissioners again voted against project outlays endorsed by the electorate six years earlier. The city never built the subway.[30]

## Expressways to Speed Traffic and Demolish African American Neighborhoods

While the discussion about the downtown subway dragged on and on, Cleveland followed the path chosen by Detroit and countless other metropolises by pursuing massive expressway construction. A master plan for a freeway network, issued in 1944 by the Express Highway Subcommittee of the Regional Association of Cleveland, reflected Bohn's insistence on a sweeping design that would serve the needs of the entire metropolitan region. The plan recommended construction of an integrated expressway system at an estimated cost of $240 million, which would combine Cleveland and its suburbs into a seamless netting of high-speed highways. The net would include a circumferential inner beltway, with an immense bridge over the Cuyahoga River, as the main thoroughfare funneling automobiles downtown, and an outer beltway farther south to handle suburban and interstate traffic in northeastern Ohio. The plan also included an expressway linking downtown with Hopkins International Airport twelve miles to the southwest. Seven radial freeways connecting the inner beltway both with the outer beltway and with interstate highways projected to be completed at a later date would allow residents of northeastern Cuyahoga and Lake Counties to commute more easily to downtown Cleveland. One delay followed another as city planners and engineers modified the plans, altered routes, acquired more than 1,250 parcels of land, and negotiated with state authorities over roadbuilding costs. As a result, construction did not begin on the highways designated in the 1944 plan until 1954 and did not conclude until the mid-1960s.[31]

Completion of an extensive highway system meant the displacement of thousands of homeowners, renters, and shopkeepers, of course, and the years-long process generated considerable controversy. The contentiousness in Cleveland became especially virulent because the obliteration of neighborhoods for expressways occurred simultaneously with the extensive land clearance necessary to build Erieview, the nation's largest urban renewal project to that date. Completion of the inner beltway spanning the length of the city resulted in hardships for people living on both sides of the Cuyahoga River—for the many white ethnic communities nestled on the west side of it and the large African American population on its east side. Construction of the expressways necessitated the razing of houses, churches, synagogues, warehouses, factories, retailing, and wholesaling businesses, including several municipal parks and a cluster of commercial greenhouses. Consequently, it seemed that the highways were sprouting up throughout the city at the expense of precious greenery, an affront to the ecology as well as to aesthetics.[32]

Embattled residents and shopkeepers threatened with eviction at last found a friendly face in local government when Carl Stokes, the city's first

African American mayor, took office on January 1, 1968. Like his predecessors in city hall, Stokes believed in the importance of improving automobile access as a precursor to downtown rehabilitation, but he also sympathized with the plight of the uprooted Clevelanders. The mayor said that expressway construction in the city had already claimed more than 6,000 housing units and displaced an estimated 19,000 residents, while future excavations for highways would destroy an additional 3,500 units and dislodge another 11,000 people. He proposed leaving parkland and vibrant neighborhoods untouched, instead erecting elevated highways that would carry vehicular traffic far above ground level. His attempt at compromise engendered fierce opposition from Cuyahoga County Engineer Albert Porter and his allies, who cited excessive costs and logistical challenges as sound reasons to reject elevated roadways. A blunt critic of Stokes's proposal said, "It is a joke for City Hall to come up with some impractical, unachievable, elevated expressways which will not serve present or future auto truck and bus traffic flows." The mayor's plan appeared to the critic as an open invitation for more office buildings and factories to flee the city.[33]

His concerns about neighborhood destruction having gained little traction throughout city government, Stokes failed to change the engineering designs for the expressway being built. The federal government's offer to pay 90 percent of the cost of construction proved too tempting for progress-minded boosters to alter the city's course. New routes and spurs opened for use in the 1970s and 1980s, spinning together a complex web of roads that allowed people living on one side of Cuyahoga County to work on the other side. Enhanced automobility allowed Clevelanders to move across municipal boundaries to contiguous suburbs, sending the residents and businesses of the older inner suburbs to distant outer suburbs recently brought into the orbit of the expanding metropolitan region. Ironically, the high-speed expressways designed to whisk commuters more efficiently into and out of downtown did so—but at the same time made possible the exodus of Clevelanders to sprawling suburbs, thereby leaching the inner city of human and financial resources and further increasing metropolitan decentralization.[34]

## Expressways and Downtown Redevelopment in Other Cities

As Bohn avidly supervised the expressway bonanza in Cleveland, city elites, mayors, and planners launched expressway construction in other large cities for similar reasons and with comparable results. In each case, preliminary plans surfaced during or even before World War II, with cities acting quickly during the return of prosperity in the late 1940s and continuing in the

1950s and 1960s. Mayors and other elected officials scoured city coffers, exploited available state and federal resources, innovated to uncover new funding sources, and borrowed money to take what they considered a vital step in resuscitating their downtowns. Accepting the primacy of the automobile, they rejected the option of mass transit or made minimal investments in fixed-rail public transportation that supplemented highway networks. Even in Chicago, where a robust mix of subways and elevated trains served a significant number of daily riders, city hall embraced the automobile as the key to sustaining the vibrancy of the central business district.

In 1939, Chicago's Department of Subways and Superhighways laid out a grandiose plan for blanketing the city and region with freeways. Construction commenced in the late 1940s. After Richard J. Daley became mayor in 1955, the pace quickened. Daley unashamedly worshipped at the altar of automobility and, during the first few years of his administration, construction crews worked around the clock to complete a five-hundred-mile freeway system. The injection of federal funding after 1956 shifted the work into overdrive. In 1957, the city completed the Congress Expressway (renamed the Dwight D. Eisenhower Expressway in 1964), an east-west multilane roadway that connected the city's western suburbs to the Loop as originally posited in the iconic Burnham Plan of 1909. In short order, other expressways opened for business—the John F. Kennedy to the north in 1960, the Dan Ryan to the south in 1962, and the Adlai E. Stevenson to the southwest in 1964. Chicago broke new ground by inserting mass-transit lines into the medians of the Eisenhower, Ryan, and Kennedy Expressways. Additions to the sprawling system continued throughout the 1970s. Nothing interrupted the relentless advance of concrete, despite growing citizen protest at the loss of homes and businesses, until the final defeat of the proposed Crosstown Expressway in 1979. By that time, three years after Daley's death, a complex of expressway radials funneled the traffic of the metropolis into the gargantuan circle interchange a few blocks west of the Loop.[35]

At considerably less than Chicago's frenetic pace, Philadelphia made plans to build a system of arterial highways that would link Center City to the metropolitan region encompassing southeastern Pennsylvania and southern New Jersey. In 1953, the state initiated the building of the Schuylkill Expressway, the first of the spokes emanating from the central business district hub, which improved access to the northwestern and southeastern parts of the city. The building of Interstate 95, which skirted Philadelphia's eastern edge and angled alongside the airport, brought residents in the northeastern quadrant of the city speedier access to Center City. The opening of the Walt Whitman Bridge in 1959 tied residents of the southeastern portion of the city to New Jersey. As a result of such concentrated building, observed planning historian Robert A. Beauregard, the southern area of Philadelphia became "a virtual tangle of interstate highways, access roads, and bridge ramps." Philadelphia also expanded its existing public transit, opening the Lindenwold Line into southern New Jersey and extending the Broad Street subway south to provide greater access to two new professional sports facilities, Veterans Stadium for baseball and football and the Spectrum for basketball and hockey. The cost of the city's wholesale assault on existing neighborhoods and landmarks to build expressways included a portion of Fairmont Park, Philadelphia's largest municipal park and the site of the 1876 Centennial Exposition.[36]

The relentless drive to improve transportation to and from downtown prevailed in St. Louis as well, where the business community's campaign for freeway construction dated back to a 1920s proposal for a limited-access highway alongside the Mississippi River. In its emphasis on downtown reclamation, Harland Bartholomew's 1947 Comprehensive City Plan for St. Louis emphasized the need to bring such earlier freeway plans to fruition. The metropolitan area's first expressway, built with a modicum of federal funds in addition to state and local dollars, opened in stages during the late 1930s. Known as the Daniel Boone Expressway, the road extended from the riverfront downtown to the city's western border by the time of its completion in 1959. Two additional radials originating from downtown, the Mark Twain Expressway and the Ozark Expressway, cut diagonally across the city northwest and southwest respectively. The trio of freeways, along with a proposed loop around the central business district that the city never completed, formed the basic structure of the expressway network outlined in the Comprehensive City Plan of 1947 and (with a few minor differences) the Comprehensive Plan for Redevelopment of the Central City Area (1953). In 1960, Mayor Raymond R. Tucker warned the Board of Aldermen against total reliance on the automobile and urged a more balanced approach that included mass transit. In 1963, in addition to the expansion of bus and streetcar service, he recommended the construction of a fixed-rail rapid transit system serving downtown. His admonitions notwithstanding, St. Louis's construction of freeways continued unabated through the 1970s. An influx of federal funds accelerated the pace of building in the 1960s and 1970s.[37]

In step with their counterparts elsewhere, Albert Cobo in Detroit and Ernest Bohn in Cleveland welcomed the cornucopia of federal dollars allocated for expressway construction by the seminal 1956 highway act because the financial windfall allowed much quicker completion of the costly construction projects they had launched a decade earlier. Despite their differences, Cobo (an unabashed salesman for business interests) and Bohn (a famous city planner and public housing advocate) agreed on a fundamental premise: the need to salvage downtown for the good of the city. Dedicated to providing easier access to their central business districts, a vital part of the downtown redevelopment strategy they pursued after World War II, city officials in Detroit and Cleveland, as elsewhere, began work principally with state and local funding, a modicum of federal resources, and the hope of acquiring more dollars from Washington, DC, in the future. In the late 1940s and 1950s, municipal governments spent their own tax dollars and incurred substantial debt on behalf of a program they deemed essential to their cities' reclamation. Convinced of the importance of highway improvement, local officials initiated ambitious roadbuilding programs without iron-clad assurances of federal funding; they accepted the need to rely on local and state revenue streams as the necessary price of central business district refurbishment. At the same time, they unhesitatingly uprooted residents and small businesses to make way for highways and interchanges in a manner that became familiar throughout the postwar decades—and, as in so many other cities, minority neighborhoods poorly equipped politically to oppose the march of progress paid the heaviest price. A series of citizen revolts against freeway construction erupted in countless communities in later years but, as the cases of Detroit and Cleveland illustrate, the contours of the post-1956 expressway construction frenzy became clear shortly after the war. The postwar expressway boom served as a testament to the effort of urban growth machines, prominently led by the always-influential business community and energetic city officials like Ernest Bohn and Albert Cobo, to improve the flagging fortunes of their declining downtowns.[38]

# II

# Refashioning the American City,
# 1970–2000

The golden age of urban renewal concluded by the 1970s. Generously aided by federal grants and loans, city officials in St. Louis, Chicago, Philadelphia, and other cities launched a host of redevelopment projects in the 1950s and 1960s. They came up short in their search for a panacea. Physical deterioration continued, slums worsened, urban populations dwindled, and central business district retailers lost customers to suburban locations. Investors shunned downtowns, and racial conflagrations in the late 1960s enhanced the image of cities as being unsafe and unwelcoming places in which to work and raise a family. Higher-income white residents abandoned major cities in search of suburban settings that remained in the hands of people like themselves. That exodus piled another problem on leaders of beleaguered cities like Philadelphia and Detroit. As urban scholar Robert Beauregard concluded, "The promise of government renewal had become tarnished by the formidable scale of the task." And then the federal government took a conservative turn that sharply reduced aid to the cities. President Richard M. Nixon imposed a "new federalism" that largely left cities to fend for themselves, a policy replicated by his successors in the White House. Forlorn mayors such as Cleveland's George Voinovich and other local officials including Philadelphia's Bill Rafsky discovered that the spirit of Nixon's new federalism infused all the presidencies that followed in the twentieth century. Both Republicans and Democrats invoked decentralization and devolution to defend the repeated funding reductions for urban America. In an era of rising defense appropriations and escalating costs for such domestic programs as Social Security and Medicare, one presidential administration after another found budgetary relief by cutting funds to cities and trumpeting public-private partnerships. In the last twenty-five years of the twentieth century, federal aid to cities fell from 15 percent of municipal revenue to less than 5 percent. No longer able to rely on aid from Washington, DC, city halls and commercial-civic elites opted by necessity for alternative funding sources to fight the war against falling sales and declining property values. These guardians of the downtown also sought to deflect unwanted incursions from low-income populations in general and African Americans, Latinos, and other people of color in particular.[1]

In the 1960s, urban leaders began to abandon traditional conceptions of the central business district in favor of a new vision of downtown growth. Reflecting the national transformation from an industrial to a postindustrial economy, city leaders such as Detroit's Coleman Young placed a new emphasis on services. Accordingly, municipal leaders began appealing to tourists, sports fans, conventioneers, and others with disposable income to spend on entertainment and leisure activities. As factories continued to shutter their doors, universities and hospitals ("eds and meds") consumed huge chunks of urban land and became indispensable sources of employment for skilled and unskilled workers. Just as elected officials remained devoted to the idea of the downtown's centrality in urban redevelopment, they also foresaw the need to alter the form and composition of the city center. The new downtown would be a cultural as well as an economic and administrative hub.[2]

## Pittsburgh's Continuing Relevance in Other Cities

Again, policy makers in other communities looked at Pittsburgh as a model of how to manage these important transitions. Outsiders observed closely as the election of Mayor Peter F. ("Pete") Flaherty in 1970 brought the Pittsburgh Renaissance to an abrupt close. Flaherty had campaigned that year against both the ACCD for elitism and the municipal government for its single-minded devotion to downtown redevelopment to the total exclusion of neighborhood improvements. As mayor, he dissolved the heralded public-private partnership, imposed budgetary austerity, and diverted earmarks for downtown projects to neighborhood rehabilitation. His administration created the Community Planning Division to connect with neighborhood development organizations. After Flaherty left city hall in 1977 to become the deputy attorney general in the Jimmy Carter administration, the frosty relationship between city hall and corporate boardrooms began to thaw. Repudiating his predecessor's flinty independence and tight-fisted fiscal policies, incoming Mayor Richard S. Caliguiri brought a conciliatory posture to municipal governance. The new mayor, said *Time* magazine, appeared to be an "unobtrusive" person with the "muzzy charm of a maître d'." He quickly resumed downtown redevelopment (with the promise of maintaining attention to neighborhood concerns) based on the prompt renewal of the public-private partnership. With a concerned eye on the steel industry's precipitous decline and the city's accelerating population losses, Caliguiri loosened the city's purse strings. Pittsburgh unleashed Renaissance II.[3]

Years earlier, during Renaissance I, Mayor David Lawrence and business tycoon Richard King Mellon had achieved notable successes in air-pollution abatement, flood control, rebuilding the central business district, and improving infrastructure. In Renaissance II, Caliguiri and the city's business executives broadened the scope of redevelopment to include abandoned warehouses, docks, and the like on both sides of the Golden Triangle. The city helped developers by assembling parcels of land for purchase, relocating uprooted businesses, offering tax incentives, granting low-interest loans, improving municipal infrastructure, and awarding other inducements. The expanding research universities and medical complexes (especially the University of Pittsburgh Medical Center) assumed new roles as economic development engines and job creators. Most striking to visitors, of course, was the sprouting of magnificent skyscrapers in the Golden Triangle under Caliguiri's leadership. Eight office towers, which included a new luxury hotel and prestigious ground-level retail establishments, rose downtown within a few years. The most impressive high-rise complexes included the 54-story One Mellon Bank Center; PPG Place, a plaza surrounded by a 40-story tower and six low-rise buildings covering six city blocks; and Liberty Center, which contained a 27-story office tower and a 28-story, 615-room hotel. Seeking to elide the community's reputation as the gritty home of the steel industry, Caliguiri envisioned the future Pittsburgh as a headquarters city where corporate executives, bankers, and lawyers bustled throughout a gleaming downtown. Between 1980 and 1987, investors spent an estimated $2.3 billion on commercial projects in and around the Golden Triangle.[4]

Pittsburgh's second renaissance was focused on more than building additional skyscrapers. Mayor Caliguiri and other authors of Renaissance II assigned a new importance to cultural development as a means of economic revitalization. Members of the growth coalition believed that cultural institutions would especially appeal to such desirable groups as suburbanites and tourists, whose frequent visits would enrich downtown restaurants and shops. The new emphasis became evident in the planning of a cultural district in the shadow of the emerging skyscrapers. Planners and politicians sought to shift the city's cultural center from the University of Pittsburgh campus in the distant Oakland neighborhood to an area adjacent to the central business district more convenient for tourists and patrons of high culture. In 1984, the ACCD incorporated the nonprofit Pittsburgh Cultural Trust to monitor the fourteen-block cultural district, which included Heinz Hall (an old movie theater converted into a concert hall for the Pittsburgh Symphony), the Frick Museum of Art, the Mattress Factory (a contemporary art museum), and the Benedum Center for Performing Arts (another re-modeled movie theater). In response to the decades-old cry from the business community for a facility to host conventions and trade shows, the city cooperated with the ACCD to build the David L. Lawrence Convention Center on a scenic spot alongside the Allegheny River at the northern edge of the cultural center.[5]

Pittsburgh's plan to entice crowds to a refurbished downtown also included a new stadium for the city's professional baseball (Pirates) and football (Steelers) teams. Years earlier, local officials had warned about the disastrous consequences if either franchise departed the city because of a substandard venue. "Pittsburgh's prestige—its standing among cities—would decline sharply," former Mayor David L. Lawrence had asserted. "And this city," Lawrence added, "would be substantially less attractive to industry, science, and other enterprise in search of a proper setting in which to operate." In 1958, the University of Pittsburgh purchased privately owned Forbes Field, where the Pirates continued to play until Three Rivers Stadium opened just across the Allegheny River from downtown in 1970. The decision to provide professional sports teams a new stadium built entirely with public funds stirred controversy in some quarters, but civic boosterism prevailed. In 1966, the Pirates and Steelers each signed forty-year leases to play in Three Rivers Stadium, which opened in July 1970 and eventually cost the city more than $40 million to build. The teams provided an immediate payoff for the city through their unprecedented success on the field—the Pirates won the World Series in 1971 and 1979, and the Steelers took home Super Bowl trophies in 1975, 1976, 1979, and 1980. Spillover crowds from the stadium spent freely downtown before and after games and, as local boosters had maintained, the surge in civic pride proved incalculable. In contrast, St. Louis sports fans headed for the exits and expressways after games. In Pittsburgh, civic leaders and committed sports fans boasted that they hailed from the city of champions.[6] In both Renaissance I and Renaissance II, professional sports were an important part of maintaining and enhancing Pittsburgh's image as a corporate center and as a fun place for higher-income households to visit.

After the construction of Three Rivers Stadium, civic leaders supported additional development on the north shore of the Allegheny River. Flanked by the Carnegie Science Center and the Heinz corporate complex, the area around the ballpark soon included Alcoa's new corporate headquarters, the Andy Warhol Museum, and dozens of business offices wedged into rehabilitated warehouses. The termination of industrial pollution and the cleanup of the river restored the natural beauty of the downtown site and made possible such riverine pastimes as recreational boating, rowing, and fishing, all of which lured more people downtown.[7]

Even with all the attention on downtown redevelopment during Renaissance II, Caliguiri insisted that his administration was not neglecting the neighborhoods. He claimed to reporters that "[I work] a lot closer with . . . community organizations than I do with the business organizations." In 1979, his administration combined with community groups to create the North Side Revitalization Program and, in 1983, founded the Pittsburgh Partnership for Neighborhood Development with funding from the Howard Heinz Endowment, Mellon Bank, Ford Foundation, and City of Pittsburgh. Moreover, he pointed proudly to the many infrastructure upgrades completed throughout the city.[8]

## Pittsburgh's Business and Political Leaders and Downtown's Continual Relevance

Still, no one could deny that the focus of Renaissance II remained on the central business district. Caliguiri's death in office in 1988 supposedly brought the second round of downtown redevelopment to a close, but the election of Thomas J. "Tom" Murphy Jr. six years later revived the effort. A self-proclaimed public entrepreneur, Murphy vowed to continue the city's makeover from blue-collar manufacturing center to white-collar showplace. Indeed, the list of proposed and completed projects downtown during his three-term mayoralty led Pittsburghers to speak of a third renaissance. The mayor sought to establish Pittsburgh's reputation as a twenty-four-hour city—the ideal destination for young middle-class professionals, as prescribed by former Carnegie Mellon University professor Richard L. Florida in an influential book that lionized what he termed the "creative class." (According to Florida, the creative class included such people as forward-thinking academics, artists, technology workers, attorneys, financiers, entrepreneurs, and other innovators.) Murphy spearheaded the successful effort in the state legislature to negotiate the $332 million necessary for remodeling the convention center, led the city's effort to acquire vacated steel mills along the waterfront for conversion to mixed-use commercial and residential developments, and retooled abandoned railroad lines into bicycle paths and recreational trails. The hard-charging mayor promoted the changeover to advanced technology and research and reveled in the city's growing reputation for computer programming, robotics, and health care. He praised the increased economic importance of universities and hospitals. In his words, eds and meds had become "anchor institutions" in an "innovative economy [that] is sweeping away the old rules of city building."[9]

## Life outside Downtown

Pittsburgh's transformation was in many ways remarkable. In plain fact, however, those anchor institutions, in the hands of creative-class leaders, had fostered prosperity among only a narrow segment of Pittsburgh's population. Residents of the city's less-favored neighborhoods found themselves shortchanged in the headlong rush to improve the downtown. Those residents protested that the capital reallocation necessary to effect the heralded renaissance consistently bypassed the city's beleaguered working class. Murphy was diverting $7 million annually from the city's operating budget into the Pittsburgh Development Fund to underwrite his ambitious projects, for example, and the public routinely suffered from shortfalls in service provision. The disappearance of unionized jobs that paid living wages—Pittsburgh lost 120,000 manufacturing jobs in the 1980s alone—took a terrible toll on working men and women. Community activists wondered out loud whether elected officials, in their single-minded quest to attract more members of the coveted creative class, were paying enough attention to the plight of local workers suffering from the ravages of deindustrialization.[10]

Consigned to the lowest-paying, most dangerous jobs in factories and barred from access to more desirable service occupations, African Americans suffered disproportionately when manufacturing jobs disappeared. Tragically, they profited little from the city's devotion to the redevelopment blueprint. Blacks in Pittsburgh initially hoped to benefit from the Renaissance, especially in the provision of better housing for low-income residents in the Hill District and other impoverished neighborhoods, where a modicum of new public housing barely addressed the desperate need for decent lodging. The operation of the city's nonprofit ACTION-Housing program, launched with much fanfare in 1957, dashed their expectations in short order. Community leaders protested when wrecking crews leveled houses occupied by African Americans to build luxury apartments and townhouses; city hall took no action to curtail real-estate agents from practicing discrimination and, kept from moving into all-white areas, displaced black homeowners were left to buy or rent in the least desirable neighborhoods. Instead of desegregating Pittsburgh, the Renaissance expanded racialized ghettos.[11]

The pattern that played out in the erstwhile Steel City appeared as well in other Rustbelt cities in the waning decades of the twentieth century. The desperate need to replace manufacturing resonated everywhere, and urban leaders pursued economic salvation through tourism, entertainment, and other service industries. Just as Richard Caliguiri and Tom Murphy courted the middle class in Pittsburgh, so did Richard J. Daley in Chicago, Richardson Dilworth in Philadelphia, and the mayors of countless additional cities. Civic leaders fought hard to keep the Pittsburgh Pirates, Cleveland Indians, Detroit Tigers, and other professional sports teams from pulling up stakes, departing for more remunerative stadium, parking, and concession deals in distant urban centers, and endangering their diminished cities' claim to major-league standing. The University of Pittsburgh and Carnegie Mellon University performed the same vital functions in a changing city as did Wayne State University in Detroit, Cleveland State University in Cleveland, and Temple University in Philadelphia—and also as did sprawling medical complexes such as Barnes-Jewish Hospital in St. Louis, Cleveland Clinic, and the Hospital of University of Pennsylvania in Philadelphia. And in all these large cities, residents of collapsing neighborhoods fought to stay afloat until the benefits of downtown revitalization materialized closer to their homes. In 1984, Pittsburgh officials proclaimed that they sought to attract one hundred thousand new business executives to the city within the next decade, a goal likely to have been cited in other postindustrial places, with scant mention of making the community more livable for the people who already resided there.[12]

# 5

## George V. Voinovich and the Pursuit
## of Business in Cleveland

No U.S. community surpassed Cleveland in coining slogans to advance its reputation. In 1944, the Cleveland Electric Illuminating Company contributed "Best Location in the Nation" with an eye toward maintaining prosperity in the postwar years. In 1962, the Cleveland Development Foundation, which had been created in 1954 to foster urban renewal, premiered a half-hour promotional film, "Cleveland: City on Schedule," that celebrated the progress achieved in the city. The Greater Cleveland Growth Board, an industrial promotion and retention arm of the Chamber of Commerce, trumpeted the potential for international trade on the "North Coast" of the United States, which later morphed into a new slogan for promoting the city. In 1968, Mayor Carl Stokes introduced his own plan for a civic rebirth, "Cleveland: NOW!" After the polluted Cuyahoga River caught on fire in 1969, ridicule of the Lake Erie port city intensified. When wags mocked Cleveland as "the mistake by the lake," local boosters countered with more catchy taglines to improve public perceptions of their city. In 1974, the Greater Cleveland Growth Association, as the Chamber of Commerce was renamed seven years earlier, launched a new advertising campaign, "The Best Things in Life Are Here." In 1981, the *Cleveland Plain Dealer* supplied subscribers with purple bumper stickers reading "New York may be the Big Apple, but Cleveland's a Plum." (That summer, Mayor George V. Voinovich delivered the ceremonial first pitch at an Indians-Yankees game with a plum instead of a baseball.) Voinovich's relentless public-relations efforts during the 1980s avidly made the case for Cleveland's economic recovery and the legitimacy of its claim to be "Comeback City." In 2005, the *Plain Dealer* weighed in with "Believe in Cleveland," replete with billboard signs and bumper stickers, as well as newspaper, television, and radio advertisements. Regardless of whether their praise accurately reflected changing conditions, members of the city's business and political elite also did their best to improve Cleveland's image.[1]

In burnishing the city's reputation, Cleveland's leading citizens basked in the knowledge that they were upholding a rich tradition of civic responsibility that had served the city well for generations. The widely known business tycoons, men who relaxed at the same exclusive clubs, worshipped at the same churches, and belonged to the same overlapping boards of directors, contributed sizable sums of money to the same charitable enterprises. Altruistic members of the establishment usually made their philanthropic donations to the Cleveland Foundation or the Gund Foundation. (George Gund was president of the Cleveland Trust Company, the largest bank in Ohio, and majority owner of the *Cleveland Plain Dealer*.) As one member of the close-knit corporate community remarked, "Of course, we're all on the banks. . . . We all know each other. We all belong to the Union Club." Another proud member of the select group boasted, "You can beat our Browns and our Indians, but it's tough to beat our Union Club." Boastful sloganeering was only a first step in politically driven efforts to revitalize Cleveland and especially the downtown economy.[2]

## Cleveland Leaders' Search for Devices to Rescue the City

As early as the 1950s, while Cleveland's businesses encountered hard times, members of the local elite were working closely with elected officials who unquestioningly endorsed downtown improvement as the key to economic revival. Bankers, corporate executives, and major retailers had invested heavily in the central business district, an indispensable contributor to the city's tax base and the epicenter of commerce for northeastern Ohio. These wealthy entrepreneurs enjoyed the wholehearted support of one business-friendly mayor after another in the postwar years—Thomas A. Burke, Anthony J. Celebrezze, Ralph S. Locher, Carl B. Stokes, and Ralph J. Perk, in order. The first major attempt at reinvigorating the central business district came with Erieview, the largest urban renewal project in the nation at the time of its launching in 1960 under Mayor Celebrezze. (See figure 5.1.) Internationally renowned architect I. M. Pei designed a mix of towers and low-rise buildings on 163 acres in the declining area just northeast of downtown. The portion

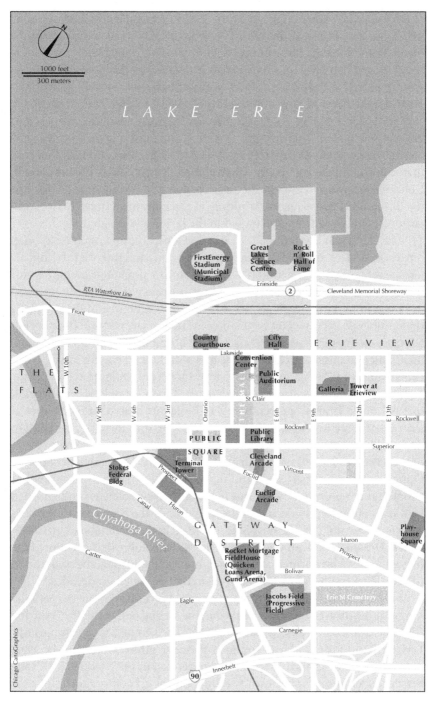

**Figure 5.1** Downtown Cleveland (Credit: Dennis McClendon, Chicago CartoGraphics)

of the elaborate plan completed by the 1980s included a new federal building, commercial offices, and multifamily housing. Upscale retail establishments abandoned Euclid Avenue, the city's most fashionable shopping destination, and their elegant shops gave way to discount pharmacies, costume jewelry marts, fast-food joints, and empty storefronts. As well, many businesses in the heart of downtown seeking new office space joined the move to the new development. As a result, warned distraught building owners and property managers, the siting of Erieview some distance from the established central business district threatened to create a second business core that would compete with (rather than complement) the existing urban hub. Conceived as the first step in the resurrection of downtown, Erieview had the unintended consequence of adding to the movement of businesses and customers outward from downtown to the fast-growing suburbs.[3]

Cleveland's slide continued. At its most basic, the city often postponed repairs to underground leaks, leaving pedestrians and motorists to find alternate routes to downtown stores. And optimistic pronouncements heralding a downtown revival notwithstanding, upscale retail outlets continued to vanish from the increasingly desolate urban core. Between 1985 and 2005, the number of Fortune 500 companies located in the metropolitan region fell from twelve to seven. The expansion of hospital and university employment failed to offset the catastrophic loss of industrial employment, which ebbed rapidly in Cleveland and the nearby industrial communities of northeastern Ohio. Manufacturing provided just 27 percent of jobs in the region in 1987, down from 47 percent in 1970. Residents deserted their homes at the rate of three units per day during the 1970s, and the city's population declined by more than ninety-five thousand during the "comeback" years of the 1980s and 1990s. Also during the 1980s, the Council for Economic Opportunity in Greater Cleveland reported a sharp rise in the number of people living below the poverty line in the city. Television news footage often showed boarded-up buildings and empty lots as the backdrop to the fires frequently burning on the East Side, the principal area inhabited by Cleveland's African American population. The violent outbreak that claimed the lives of four African Americans in the impoverished Hough neighborhood in 1966 left a residue of racial antagonism that persisted for decades.[4]

Public dissatisfaction with the unfulfilled promises of the perpetually sanguine business community peaked in the second half of the 1970s during the disastrous mayoralty of Ralph J. Perk. The son of Czech immigrants, Perk parlayed his popularity in the city's white ethnic wards on the West Side into election as mayor in 1971 and reelection in 1973 and 1975. Despite his close identification with white ethnic neighborhood organizations, he became so solicitous of downtown financial interests that his disgruntled constituents called him a patsy for the business community. Perk's administration made liberal use of tax abatements to attract businesses from other localities and especially concentrated on the retention of firms already located in Cleveland, exercising what the city's commissioner of economic development called the "bird in the hand" approach. Forced to deal with a national recession, rising inflation, and a 30 percent increase in the cost-of-services, Perk spent freely and presided over a mounting financial deficit that led local bankers to speak ominously about the possibility of bankruptcy. Unalterably opposed to tax increases, the mayor relied on several stopgap measures to balance the books and traded long-term solvency for immediate relief. He received copious revenue-sharing funds from the Richard Nixon administration, so that federal dollars accounted for fully one-third of city revenue by 1977; another 29 percent of municipal funds came from short-term borrowing. He initiated the sale of the sewer and transit systems to regional authorities, leased Cleveland Municipal Stadium to private entities, and made ill-advised withdrawals from restricted municipal accounts. Perk's financial sleight-of-hand only managed to forestall a looming financial crisis.[5]

Perk collaborated eagerly with the Cleveland Foundation to revive the city's ailing central business district. The foundation hired Lawrence Halprin and Associates of California, the designer of San Francisco's celebrated Ghirardelli Square, to create a roadmap for the rehabilitation of the Cleveland downtown. In 1975, Halprin announced "Concept for Cleveland," a comprehensive plan that called for a sweeping rearrangement of the cityscape from the Cuyahoga River's eastern bank to Playhouse Square (a collection of theaters on the eastern edge of downtown). The most striking aspect of the proposal called for the conversion of Euclid Avenue, the city's principal retail corridor, into a pedestrian mall lined by high-end shopping outlets and upscale apartments—and specifically excluded Section 8 (low-income) housing. The design also featured a Euclid Avenue trolley line, a highway loop encircling the central business district, the renovation of Playhouse Square, and a refurbishment of Public Square at the heart of the downtown. Local government, the Cleveland Foundation, and the Greater Cleveland Growth Association pledged a combined $100,000 to create the Downtown Cleveland Corporation, a nonprofit group tasked with implementing "Concept for Cleveland" and underwriting its first year of operation. The enthusiasm for the Halprin plan soon waned, however, because of the proposal's expensive price tag and insufficient commitment by downtown stakeholders. Critics also complained that, at the same time that city planning director Norman Krumholz was touting social equity planning with a new injunction to address citywide problems, the Halprin plan focused entirely on the domain of corporate interests. Perk's endorsement of "Concept for Cleveland" and his frequent use of tax incentives to attract businesses to the city provided much of the fuel for Dennis Kucinich's mayoral candidacy in 1977, which the challenger based on a platform of "urban populism."[6]

## Dennis Kucinich's "Urban Populism"

Kucinich's insurgent mayoral candidacy in 1977, as he explained repeatedly on the stump, constituted a full-blown populist challenge to an entrenched plutocracy that had ruled Cleveland for more than a century. The precocious son of a Croatian father and an Irish mother, Kucinich grew up in poverty and held several low-paying jobs before entering politics. Elected to the city council at the age of twenty-three, he became a pugnacious champion of blue-collar Clevelanders and survived three recall attempts. While serving on the city council, he received BA and MA degrees in speech communications from Case Western Reserve University. Having lost races for the U.S. Congress in 1973 and 1974, the ambitious Kucinich won election as clerk of municipal court in 1975 and ran for mayor two years later as an independent Democrat. His disparagement of tax abatements and other incentives for corporations characterized a campaign rich in antibusiness rhetoric; he defended the working class at every turn, vowed to pay more attention to neighborhood concerns, and promised to level the economic playing field to the benefit of Cleveland's have-nots. He defeated the regular Democratic candidate, state representative Edward F. Feighan, in a run-off election after Perk had been eliminated in the nonpartisan primary. At thirty-one years of age, Kucinich became the nation's youngest big-city mayor.[7]

When Kucinich took office, Cleveland teetered on the brink of insolvency in large measure because of the fiscal legerdemain of the Perk years. The practice of short-term borrowing to meet impending financial deadlines had kept the city afloat for years, but local financial institutions announced a halt to the practice under the new administration. After an initial standoff, the banks agreed to extend the embattled city additional credit on one condition—that the mayor privatize the publicly owned Municipal Light Company (Muny Light), one of the city's two electricity providers. Kucinich had opposed the sale of Muny Light to Cleveland Electric Illuminating Company during the 1977 campaign, a move that Perk had endorsed as a means of reducing city debt. Kucinich called the proposal a thinly disguised attempt by the private sector to eliminate competition and thereby exploit powerless consumers. His absolute refusal to consider the sale of Muny Light became the symbolic centerpiece of his unsparing war against big business on behalf of "the little people." By the same token, Cleveland's elite businesspeople pointed to the Muny Light imbroglio as evidence of how Kucinich's "wild-eyed, publicity-hungry, populist style of government" would ruin the city.[8]

Constantly clashing with Cleveland's financial leaders, the Boy Mayor conducted the city's affairs with a cavalier disregard for the ways government and business had often worked together. Kucinich's practices made for colorful newspaper copy but created the image of rampant dysfunction in city hall. The city council routinely passed measures opposed by the mayor and then overrode his vetoes by substantial margins. Three months after hiring Police Chief Richard Hongisto, a progressive law-enforcement officer from San Francisco, the mayor fired him on prime-time television citing unspecified policy differences. The mayor also engaged in bitter contract negotiations with the police union, the members of which he sneeringly dismissed as "crybabies." Kucinich and his few allies on the city council theatrically withdrew from a council meeting—and threatened to boycott future meetings—to underscore their opposition to the city building an ore dock at the mouth of the Cuyahoga River for the Republic Steel Corporation. Cleveland-based Republic Steel hinted that further expansion of its facilities hinged on the provision of a new loading dock, a step supported by the United Steelworkers union, the city council, and the local business community, but Kucinich stubbornly held his ground. Republic Steel opted to build its ore dock in Lorain, a steel-mill community thirty miles farther west on Lake Erie, a decision that company spokespeople attributed to antagonistic leadership in Cleveland.[9]

In March 1978, citing the mayor's refusal to compromise and his open pursuit of dictatorial powers, the Recall Committee to Save Cleveland began circulating a petition to hold a recall election. Thomas F. Campbell, a history professor at Cleveland State University and one of the architects of the recall effort, wrote in a Cleveland Plain Dealer op-ed that Kucinich had made Cleveland the "crisis center of the nation." The petition drive secured the necessary number of signatures, and the city scheduled the recall election for Sunday, August 13. The mayor survived by 236 votes out of 120,264 cast, the percentage margin being 50.10 percent to 49.90 percent. According to a study by the Plain Dealer, most of the funding for the recall campaign came not from within the city but rather from the suburbs. Kucinich retained office despite the efforts of the economic elite, the group he had singled out as his principal adversaries.[10]

The attempt to remove Kucinich having failed, the stalemate between the mayor and the city's banks hardened. Cleveland's cash-strapped municipal government limped along from month to month struggling to pay its debts. In 1978, the Ohio auditor found the municipality's accounts indecipherable, declaring himself unable to make any sense of the "bookkeeping chaos." The accounting firm of Ernst and Ernst discovered that city hall had illegally spent $52 million in bond receipts on operating costs that had been designated for capital improvements. The municipal-bond-rating agencies took extraordinary disciplinary action against the city. After Moody's municipal division chief said, "It looks to me like the people in charge of managing [Cleveland's finances] don't have the foggiest idea of what they are doing," the rating agency drastically downgraded the city's bond rating twice within a month. Standard and Poor's suspended Cleveland's rating altogether. Frozen out of the money market, the city could no longer raise funds by selling bonds or short-term notes. Borrowing money from local banks became the only remaining option.[11]

The fiscal crisis peaked in December 1978 when Cleveland proved unable to pay off $15 million in short-term bond anticipation notes and the banks refused to come to the city's aid. Implored by business leaders to make peace with the local banks for the good of the city, Kucinich defiantly responded, "I'm not going to give in on Muny Light. I'll go to hell first." Equally intransigent, Cleveland's lending institutions refused to rollover the municipality's notes. An investigation by a U.S. House of Representatives subcommittee concluded that local business leaders took a hard line in order to discredit Kucinich's brand of urban populism. On December 16, the city defaulted, becoming the first major U.S. city to do so since the Great Depression. In February 1979, the local electorate approved a 50 percent increase in the city income tax, which restored financial equilibrium—at least for the moment. Wary of future financial catastrophes, business analysts continued to question Cleveland's ability to steer a steady financial course in the midst of such a toxic political environment.[12]

## George Voinovich and Downtown Redevelopment

Cleveland's civic elite believed that the broken city government had to be repaired before economic recovery could begin. The tumultuous reign of the Boy Mayor had to be terminated in order to overcome the city's reputation for open hostility to business. Searching for a candidate to unseat Kucinich in the 1979 election, a coterie of executives and entrepreneurs decided on Lieutenant Governor George V. Voinovich. A native Clevelander of Slovenian descent, Voinovich had graduated from Collinwood High School, Ohio University, and Ohio State University Law School. After practicing law with a Cleveland law firm, he held a series of appointive and elective offices in state and local governments. His posts included, in chronological order, assistant to the Ohio attorney general, two-term state legislator, Cuyahoga County auditor, county commissioner, and lieutenant governor. Though a Republican in a predominantly Democratic city, Voinovich had demonstrated in earlier victorious campaigns the ability to attract votes from African Americans as well as white ethnics. His calm demeanor and reverence for rational discourse provided a perfect counterpoint to Kucinich's frenetic, belligerent populism.[13]

The business cabal sent an emissary to the lieutenant governor, promising to fund his campaign and continue their support after the election to resolve the city's financial crisis. "All they wanted was somebody to bring some saneness and just establish a C+ city administration, so the city would function," remembered Voinovich. He vowed to put Cleveland on a sound business footing by running the municipality like a corporation. Voinovich enjoyed the wholehearted backing of the Cleveland Foundation, which he promised to make a key component of the public-private partnership that would operate at the heart of his administration. More than anything else, he campaigned in 1979 on the promise of comity and an end to the confrontational politics that had forced city government into gridlock. He opened his campaign in front of the Muny Light plant, which he pledged to retain for the city, thereby defusing one of his opponent's leading issues. In stark contrast to Kucinich's slogan, "One Man Can Make a Difference," Voinovich tellingly offered the much more conciliatory "Together We Can Do It." Voinovich prevailed in the acrid contest with 56.2 percent of the vote.[14]

Having inherited the mayoralty of a city with a $111 million debt and disreputable credit, Voinovich acted quickly to confirm his probusiness bona fides. Only days after taking office, he instructed the vice president of the Greater Cleveland Growth Association to schedule a meeting in Detroit with Mayor Coleman Young and Henry Ford II to discuss the primary engine for that city's public-private partnership, New Detroit, Incorporated. The mayor conscripted executives from Cleveland's major corporations to serve on an ad hoc committee, the Operations Improvement Task Force, which would examine the day-to-day operations of municipal departments with the goal of bringing city government out of "the Dark Ages of management." The task force made 650 recommendations, including consolidating operations, reorganizing city agencies, and improving accounting procedures. Voinovich believed that his relentless salesmanship—he spent an inordinate amount of time telephoning, writing letters, sending follow-up missives, lunching with potential investors, and waylaying influential persons at cocktail parties—produced real dividends for the city. Under his direction and with the unwavering encouragement of the growth coalition, the local government purchased and cleared land, concluded sweetheart deals to attract downtown tenants, and cut ribbons at the grand openings of new corporate headquarters, sports venues, and lakefront tourist attractions. Voinovich's diligence seemed to pay off, and the powerful members of the business community breathed a collective sigh of relief at the passing of Kucinich's "political vaudeville."[15]

Within two years, the mayor later reported, the city had implemented three-fourths of the task force's recommendations and had accrued considerable savings. More good news vindicated Voinovich's collaborative leadership style as relations between the mayor's office and the city council improved, just as lines of communication between city hall and the business community reopened. Within a year, local banks refinanced $36 million of the city's short-term debt. In 1981, embracing the mayor's call for sacrifice, the voters approved a 33 percent city income tax increase. In 1983, Moody's and Standard and Poor's restored the municipality's bond ratings to investment grade, allowing reentry into the national bond market. Clevelanders of all stripes welcomed Voinovich's deft touch after the ill will created by Kucinich's stridency. The mayor's popularity soared, as evidenced by his landslide reelections in 1981 and 1985.[16]

## Government-Business Partnerships

Yet, for all of Voinovich's success in eradicating the gloom that hung over city hall, Cleveland's fundamental economic problems remained as grave as before. Despite encouraging progress in relieving the debt burden, the State of Ohio insisted on maintaining close supervision of all fiscal matters in the municipality. The city's population continued to decline in the 1980s, reducing receipts from the local payroll tax. The landmark 109-year-old Sherwin-Williams paint plant closed its doors in 1982. In the mid-1980s, as manufacturing jobs vanished, the city's unemployment rate stood at twice the national average. One by one, beginning in the 1960s, most department stores closed their flagships downtown. Shoppers were taking their business to suburban stores, reducing employment and tax revenues needed to support important services such as schools. As a result, the city's public-education system remained a disaster. Financial distress—public education was operating $40 million in the red by 1982—forced the schools into receivership. While class sizes barely stayed under the maximums allowed by the state, the buildings and equipment fell short of acceptable standards. With more than half of the system's eighty thousand students coming from families receiving public aid, federal cuts in welfare during the Ronald Reagan administration increased the pressure on city government to make up the difference.[17]

Voinovich and his corporate allies never wavered in the face of discouraging news, however. They staked Cleveland's future on strengthening the partnership with business to attract investment, jobs, people, and retail back to the urban core. To formalize the unofficial alliance that had drafted a suitable mayoral candidate in 1979, eight chief executive officers of the city's leading corporations created Cleveland Tomorrow in 1982. (The eight charter members included the head of the Federal Reserve Bank of Cleveland;

the publisher of the Cleveland Plain Dealer, the city's lone daily newspaper; the senior partner at Jones Day, one of the city's leading law firms; and five chief executive officers of major corporations.) Soon membership of the organization expanded to thirty-seven and finally to fifty. In their version of Pittsburgh's ACCD, the founders of the new consortium limited membership to top corporate leaders and purposely excluded lesser executives, politicians, religious leaders, and other civic notables. Whereas the Cleveland Foundation's broad mandate included the enrichment of civic life in all its aspects—economic, cultural, charitable, and political—Cleveland Tomorrow existed for the sole purpose of restoring economic prosperity to the city. For Voinovich and Ohio governor Richard F. Celeste, both of whom endorsed the new organization's raison d'être, the path out of the financial wilderness led to the recruitment and retention of business firms for the city.[18]

## Selling Cleveland at a Discounted Price

Voinovich reveled in his role as super salesman and chief cheerleader for Cleveland. A gregarious, easygoing politician with superb interpersonal skills that charmed audiences in the corporate boardroom, the union hall, and the ethnic lodge, he determined to improve Cleveland's reputation as a business-friendly city. More than anything, Voinovich fretted to Bradley Jones, chairman of the Republic Steel Corporation, he feared presenting "an image to the rest of the country that Cleveland is a bad place to do business and that outsiders are not welcome." He exhaustively made the case for a downtown revival spearheading a citywide rejuvenation. The mayor's plan for recovery, based on a public-private partnership of unprecedented scope, entailed the restoration of Cleveland as a major regional business center. His prospectus for Cleveland's return to greatness featured the construction of new skyscrapers housing corporate headquarters and banks. Society National Bank, Standard Oil of Ohio, National City Bank, Ohio Bell, Medical Mutual of Ohio, and the Eaton Corporation built large corporate headquarters in the central business district during the 1980s; the Key Tower, home of financial-services megalith KeyCorp and the tallest building in Ohio, opened in 1992. Locally owned Forest City Enterprises, one of the largest commercial real-estate concerns in the nation, invested $400 million to convert Cleveland Union Terminal into a mixed-use tower containing stylish shops, business offices, and a swank hotel, as well as a rapid transit station. He initially foreswore use of tax incentives but reversed his stance in awarding abatements worth $250 million for the construction of AmeriTrust Center and Society Center on Public Square.[19]

Voinovich's increasing use of tax abatements notwithstanding, Urban Development Action Grants (UDAGs) quickly became his preferred financial mechanism for underwriting downtown redevelopment projects. (The UDAG program, created during the Jimmy Carter presidency, provided federal funding for large redevelopment projects and was contingent on proof of private financial contributions.) Voinovich leveraged his status as one of the few Republican mayors among the nation's big cities to acquire a windfall of UDAG money during the years of the Reagan administration. The mayor's deft lobbying efforts yielded more than $100 million between 1981 and 1988, 70 percent or more of which went toward funding sixteen downtown commercial projects. Neighborhood rehabilitation efforts received only $16.9 million, and the Voinovich administration initiated public-private partnerships for just two low- and moderate-income housing projects, both at Lexington Village in Hough, totaling a commitment of $4 million. The critical importance of UDAG dollars for downtown redevelopment explained why Voinovich wrote such forceful letters to Reagan administration officials when rumors of the federal program's demise swirled around the country in the mid-1980s. He pleaded with White House aides to spare UDAG if cuts in urban programs became necessary and wrote President Reagan that "elimination of UDAG will cost Cleveland $75 million in private investment and 3,300 job opportunities annually" (emphasis in original). His ardent pleas failed as the administration terminated the program in 1988. Republicans in Washington DC also severely cut allocation for Community Development Block Grants and revenue sharing, and Voinovich and his peers in other large cities scrambled to find other funding sources for their downtown redevelopment plans.[20]

## Go Downtown and Have Fun

Voinovich sought a fundamental makeover for downtown. Instead of just a bland assortment of government centers, banks, and soaring office buildings scattered across a few major streets that emptied out at the end of the business day, the makeover also needed to make the area a magnet for suburbanites and out-of-towners looking for entertainment after 5:00 P.M. and on weekends. The mayor intended to put Cleveland on the map as a destination for sports fans, conventioneers, and tourists. To engineer the necessary transformation in the central business district, Voinovich and his business allies drew heavily on the discarded Halprin plan in composing a detailed blueprint for redevelopment that contained a laundry list of the seven most important endeavors ahead for the city: the construction of new venues for the city's professional sports teams, refurbishment of Playhouse Square, expansion of the outdated convention center, creation of a lively restaurant and bar district along the river, provision of middle-class housing downtown, redevelopment of the lakefront, and attraction of major hotels to accommo-date the expected crush of visitors. With these improvements, Voinovich contended, high culture and prospering entertainment zones would take the place of drab and rusting manufacturing plants and deserted buildings. Still more, those new firms and the many tourists would pay taxes. In Voinov-ich's rearrangement of downtown priorities, stadiums were among the city's most visible institutions.[21]

Nothing reinforced Cleveland's image as a dreary postindustrial grave-yard more than the tired old structures in which the professional sports teams competed. The Indians (baseball) and the Browns (football) shared cavernous, eighty-thousand-seat Municipal Stadium, a dank, blustery edi-fice completed in 1931 on reclaimed land abutting Lake Erie. Team owners lamented the advancing age and deterioration of Municipal Stadium, which necessitated frequent and expensive upkeep, while players and spectators complained about the inclement weather they regularly had to endure. Har-dy football fans withstood the icy winds and snow showers knifing off the lake, circumstances mitigated somewhat by the small number of home games each year, but baseball fans shivered during night games (and some day games) throughout the much longer season. Both the Indians and the Browns clamored for the construction of a new ballpark. The situation for the city's professional basketball team may indeed have been worse. After their ad-mission to the National Basketball Association (NBA) as an expansion team in 1970, the Cavaliers played their first four seasons in the Cleveland Arena on Euclid Avenue some twenty blocks from the edge of downtown. Origi-nally built in 1937 for ice hockey, the multipurpose Arena juggled as many as 330 events a year, including the ice follies, circuses, rodeos, wrestling and boxing matches, midget automobile races, and six-day bicycle races. Bedev-iled by scheduling mix-ups, inadequate parking, and substandard playing conditions, the Cavaliers moved to suburban Richfield in 1974.[22]

Voinovich sought to bring the Cavaliers back to Cleveland, ideally in a new downtown arena, while pursuing the construction of a new stadium or stadiums for the Indians and Browns. The city conducted feasibility studies on the construction of an "all-weather domed stadium with a seating capac-ity in the range of 35,000 to 50,000 seats." (Original discussions included the possibility of Cleveland State University sharing in the cost of constructing the stadium, which it would use as a convocation center.) In 1984, county voters defeated a referendum by a 65-to-35-percent margin to raise prop-erty taxes for the building of a domed stadium. The idea of the two teams sharing a new venue perished in 1986 when local developers Richard and David Jacobs purchased the Indians and announced that they wanted a new stadium for baseball only. Browns owner Art Modell said that he had no interest in sharing a stadium either, but he would be willing to have his team remain in Municipal Stadium if the city assumed the entire cost of a $90 million renovation.[23]

When the Jacobs brothers threatened to move the Indians to another city, Voinovich pledged to retain the team at all costs. "It's vital to our image and to our economy to show our support and keep the Tribe here," he intoned, promising to join the Greater Cleveland Growth Association in a campaign to sell five thousand season tickets to local businesses. Major League Baseball Commissioner Fay Vincent told the Cleveland City Council that he would support the Indians' departure if a new stadium were not built. The mayor selected the historic Central Market site south of the central business district, at that time filled with old warehouses, abandoned buildings, and surface parking lots, for the baseball stadium as part of the Gateway Project (south of downtown). In addition to the new ballpark, the redevelopment project would include a new basketball arena for the Cavaliers, parking garages, retail outlets, restaurants, and bars. Boosters claimed that Gateway, an economic development undertaking to be paid for by sin taxes on alcohol and tobacco products, would create twenty thousand new jobs and generate $344 million of new investment. Skeptics questioned the appropriateness of the city's $425 million outlay at a time when the public schools stood $150 million in debt and only 8 percent of Cleveland residents had earned a college degree. In 1990, county voters narrowly approved the expenditure, 197,044 to 185,209, with the referendum failing in twenty-one of the city's twenty-two wards but passing comfortably in the suburbs. Groundbreaking on the project began in 1992.[24]

Just as bringing crowds to the Gateway for a ballgame would help to revitalize the lifeless downtown, Voinovich believed, so too would luring people to Playhouse Square. Just as baseball fans would spend money at hot-dog stands, taverns, and souvenir shops near the ballpark, so too theater patrons would frequent restaurants, nightclubs, and coffee shops before and after performances at Playhouse Square. The mayor admitted harboring a sentimental attachment to Playhouse Square, recalling how years before he had taken his wife there on their first date. To Voinovich, an evening in such a refined setting should remain an essential part of the Cleveland cultural experience— a tradition established in the 1920s with the opening of the Allen, Hanna, Ohio, Palace, and State Theaters on Euclid Avenue between East Fourteenth and East Seventeenth Streets. Once one of the nation's largest concentrations of motion-picture palaces, Playhouse Square had fallen on hard times after World War II because of competition from suburban theaters, drive-ins, and television. The theaters closed in the late 1960s, and upscale stores nearby decamped or reopened as discount clothing outlets. Beginning in the 1970s, the fledgling Playhouse Square Association began the preservation of the deserted theaters; grants from the National Endowment for the Arts, the Cleveland Foundation, and other local nonprofit organizations, along with aid from city government, underwrote what became the nation's largest such restoration project. Arguing that Playhouse Square provided an anchor to the eastern edge of the Euclid Avenue retail strip, Voinovich pledged city hall support for the reclamation project. He specifically urged funding for phase I of the project, which entailed renovation of the Ohio, Palace, and State Theatres and the addition of parking to the surrounding area.[25]

## A Good Place to Hold a Convention

Voinovich also favored upgrading the downtown convention center, which had been the subject of intense criticism for decades. Considered a state-of-the-art facility when it opened in 1922, the convention hall had lost ground over time to its many competitors around the nation. Saddled with the ninth-largest convention center in the nation in the early 1980s, the Greater Cleveland Convention and Visitors Bureau consistently lagged in attracting exhibits and trade shows. Bureau officials blamed the paltry numbers on the unattractive appearance of downtown, the dearth of nighttime activities in the area, the stagnant national economy, poor airline service to Cleveland, and especially the shortage of first-class hotel rooms nearby. A representative of Conferon, Inc., the country's largest meeting-management firm, placed the lion's share of the blame for poor attendance on the low ceilings and numerous columns in the antiquated building that obstructed views and induced claustrophobia among visitors. Without consulting voters, Voinovich spent $28 million in hotel tax receipts to renovate the shabby structure. Attendance figures continued to lag after the renovation, however, and many boosters argued against additional piecemeal improvements to what they summarily dismissed as a hopelessly inadequate facility. In 2007, Cuyahoga County built a convention center and Medical Mart (later renamed the Global Center for Health Innovation), to take advantage of Cleveland's standing as a regional, national, and international hospital center.[26]

## Bringing the Flats Back to Life

Beginning in the late 1960s and early 1970s, mindful that a lively nightlife provided conventioneers an enjoyable escape from the daytime drudgery of meetings and presentations, city hall planners had encouraged the creation of an entertainment district downtown. Seeking to create a setting comparable to Chicago's Old Town or St. Louis's Gaslight Square, they eyed the Flats, an aggregation of docks and wharves alongside the Cuyahoga River. Voinovich and his top aides also realized that, the appeal of authenticity notwithstanding, investors would need to improve the seedy area of dive bars, greasy spoon eateries, and tattoo parlors that had historically served a ribald clientele of sailors, stevedores, and steelworkers. Boosters hoped that the Flats, newly respectable in its sanitized incarnation, would emerge as a favored destination for dining, drinking, and listening to live music in a rustic historical setting. The city trumpeted the Sohio RiverFest as the perfect example of how the Flats was coming alive after decades of repose. The three-day celebration drew more than a half million people in 1987, boasted the New Cleveland Campaign in a *Wall Street Journal* advertisement, hitting a "high-water mark in fun and excitement."[27]

The centerpiece of the refashioned Flats would be Settlers' Landing, an amalgam of new and renovated buildings that included apartments, a hotel, shops, and restaurants scattered around a small city park. Fittingly, the redevelopment would occur at the spot where the city's founder, surveyor Moses Cleaveland, had laid out the first town lots in 1796. Herbert E. Strawbridge, president of Higbee's Department Store, took the lead in honoring the city's "Plymouth Rock" with a business venture linked to its future prosperity. According to Strawbridge, department stores in the central business district such as Higbee's could not survive unless entertainment and leisure brought more people downtown. Because suburban malls provided consumers with abundant free parking and ample opportunity for evening and weekend excursions, downtown stores could no longer rely on quick lunchtime shopping trips by office workers. Strawbridge believed that Settlers' Landing could become Cleveland's version of such successful tourist meccas as Underground Atlanta or San Francisco's Ghirardelli Square. Despite Higbee's multimillion-dollar investment, neither Settlers' Landing nor the Flats became the tourist magnet city hall hoped for during the 1980s.[28]

While businesspeople and members of the Voinovich administration envisioned the construction of apartment buildings in the Flats, they looked at another riverfront area—the warehouse district—as the principal site for new downtown housing. The mayor saw the perfect opportunity there for a robust public-private partnership, wherein the municipality would alter building codes and make other zoning changes to encourage the conversion of deserted warehouses into lofts and other trendy housing units. He suggested that business firms create a nonprofit corporation to pursue investment opportunities in the prime location. He also indicated the city's intention to lobby Governor Richard F. Celeste and influential Ohio legislators to revise state laws and practices relevant to housing standards. Voinovich's keen interest even extended to recommending which warehouses would be good choices for sale and remodeling. Concerns arose that the air pollution generated by the area's remaining steel mills would discourage potential tenants in the warehouse area, but gradual progress in reducing harmful emissions by Republic Steel and Jones and Laughlin Steel encouraged city officials to believe that the problem could be solved. Voinovich called for the adoption of specific plans for the Flats and the warehouse district to maximize private redevelopment efforts along the river.[29]

In contrast to his intense interest in shifting the primary economic function of the Cuyahoga River from manufacturing to entertainment, Voinovich assigned a lower priority to lakefront redevelopment. He candidly admitted to being pessimistic about the prospects for significant improvement of the landscape along Lake Erie any time soon, especially with the need for prompt action to address other items on his downtown improvement agenda. He opposed the closing of Burke Lakefront Airport, a municipally operated terminal built on landfill that relieved Hopkins International Airport of handling smaller airplanes, and the redevelopment of the site for nonaviation use. In a modest concession to developers eyeing the lakefront, the administration allowed the creation of an inner harbor for recreational craft to moor. Voinovich alluded to the possibility of adding an aquarium, placing a small vest-pocket park on Pier 34, and attending to other minor housecleaning tasks to "spiff up" the area, all as a means of "utilizing the lake as a development tool," but he saw such measures as long-term goals of lesser moment.[30]

## Hotel Rooms for the Visitors Who Would Soon Arrive

Finally, Voinovich and downtown businesspeople angled for the addition of four thousand hotel rooms to a central business district strikingly devoid of overnight options for the well-heeled traveler. In doing so, they were echoing a complaint that had been voiced by their forebears for decades. The perennial cry for more hotel rooms to accommodate the convention industry assumed greater urgency with the intention of transforming downtown into a destination for tourists and other pleasure-seekers. A breakthrough had seemed imminent in 1959 when the Hilton Corporation announced its intention to build a 25-story, thousand-room hotel, underwritten by $6 million in public funding, in a downtown location. The plan unraveled, however, when the electorate voted no to the subsidy in a public referendum that year. Despite Voinovich's best salesmanship efforts, including the offer of tax abatements, no major hotel chains (Marriott, Hyatt, Hilton, or Westin) agreed to build downtown during his mayoralty. In 1987, the owner of two of the city's four downtown hotels claimed that the occupancy rates of his inns averaged only 35 to 40 percent and that he had lost $3 million in the preceding four years. By 1989, with the closing of the venerable Hollenden

House Hotel, the number of available rooms downtown had fallen to 1,400. Hoteliers apparently were waiting for evidence of enhanced activity in the central business district before assuming risky investments in an area with a poor history of profitability.[31]

## Restoring Euclid Avenue and Connecting the City's Parts

In addition to the seven projects identified by Voinovich and his cohorts as essential to the central business district's rebirth, the mayor designated the Euclid Avenue corridor from downtown to University Circle as "the City's best opportunity for future development." Euclid Avenue had once sparkled as the city's most coveted address, the storied "Millionaires' Row" where oil tycoon John D. Rockefeller; Henry Sherwin of Sherwin-Williams Paints; Jeptha Wade, president of Western Union; and other captains of industry resided in palatial splendor. By the middle of the twentieth century, real-estate interests had converted the weathered mansions that remained into cheap rooming houses. The unsightly Euclid Avenue corridor linked the central business district to University Circle, a 488-acre enclave that included Case Western Reserve University, Cleveland Clinic, University Hospitals, various museums, botanical gardens, and the local symphony hall, creating what became known as Cleveland's Dual Hub. In seeking to insulate its lush grounds from Hough, an African American neighborhood to the west, the University Circle Development Foundation had launched an urban renewal project in the 1960s. The University-Euclid Plan aimed to replace decaying housing with new units within University Circle and in the neighboring slum. University Circle successfully resisted decline, largely thanks to the success of the 1,000 New Homes project, but the drive to rehabilitate Hough and Euclid Avenue came up short.[32]

In Voinovich's thinking, the central business district, University Circle, and the four-mile corridor between them would contain Cleveland's high-end commercial and residential development in the shape of a barbell. Voinovich sought bustling financial activity on downtown streets, along Euclid Avenue, and amid the city's medical and cultural institutions as a new economic geography for the city. The phenomenal expansion of the Cleveland Clinic and University Hospitals revitalized the "Bring Back Euclid Avenue" effort in the 1990s. (Cleveland Clinic had earned an international reputation for excellence in certain medical specialties, its reputation enhanced by the striking number of wealthy Middle Easterners traveling there for cardiac care). By 1986, Cleveland Clinic and University Hospitals had become the third- and eleventh-largest employers in the city, respectively. To connect the city's dual commercial hubs, local officials devised plans for a fixed-rail rapid-transit system operating on designated lines along Euclid Avenue. Cost overruns led the city to discard the light-rail plan for a bus rapid-transit alternative that became known as the Healthline. Taking advantage of $82.2 million in funding from the federal government's Intermodal Surface Transportation Efficiency Act (ISTEA) of 1991, the $200 million project commenced operation in 2008. Within ten years, the city claimed that $5 billion in real-estate development along the corridor could be tied directly to the introduction of the Healthline.[33]

Encouraging news from the Euclid corridor seemed to validate the Dual Hub strategy, creating a sense of optimism in Cleveland by the late 1980s. The Voinovich administration proudly pointed to the addition of more than 6 million square feet of office space downtown during the decade. In 1988, the city's planning commission issued Civic Vision 2000, a design for the continued buoyancy of downtown that essentially recommended adherence to the path followed by the business-friendly Voinovich in the preceding years. In 1989, expressing gratification at his administration's success in reversing Cleveland's plummeting fortunes, Voinovich announced his decision to vacate the mayor's office and run for governor of Ohio the following year. The mayor had spurned entreaties from the state's leading Republicans to run for the governorship in 1986, he explained, "because we had not finished our work to make Cleveland an asset." By 1989, his sense of accomplishment felt complete. More than satisfied with the man they had selected to restore political normality after the contentious Kucinich interlude, members of the business community only hoped that the next mayor would be as accommodating to their views.[34]

## The Voinovich Legacy

Dining or socializing over drinks at the Union Club in 1989, Cleveland's most accomplished businesspeople would likely never have selected Democrat Michael R. White to succeed Voinovich in city hall. An African American from the run-down Glenville neighborhood north of plush University Circle and a resolute city councilman and state senator who had vigorously advanced his constituents' needs, White hardly seemed to possess the pliability the civic elite sought in a mayor. Nor did they assume that he would share their views on the supreme importance of downtown refurbishment. During the mayoral campaign, however, White repeatedly spoke of the need for balanced development; he asserted that he would attend both to the needs of the central business district and to the impoverished neighborhoods. He promised to assuage racial tensions and to provide a "new leadership" characterized by nonpartisanship and businesslike efficiency. After

finishing second in the open primary to another African American Democrat, city council chairman George Forbes, White beat Forbes in the general election by a margin of 56 to 44 percent. The press attributed the new
mayor's dramatic turnaround victory to his ability to sell white West Side
voters on his promise of "new leadership." Perhaps most important, his
soothing comments about the indispensability of public-private partnerships put the concerns of Cleveland's commercial elite to rest. The fundamental precepts of Civic Vision 2000 would go forward.[35]

White demonstrated that he planned no abrupt changes in the policies
established by the previous administration. The mayor's intentions became
clear when he retained many of Voinovich's officials and advisers. Downtown redevelopment remained paramount. White completed the Gateway
Project, which in 1994 added a new stadium for the Indians (Jacobs Field)
and a new home for the Cavaliers (Gund Arena). Surpassing Voinovich's
vision for limited lakefront development, he presided over the opening of
the Rock and Roll Hall of Fame in 1995, the Great Lakes Science Center in
1996, and a new stadium for the Browns in 1999. White crafted arrangements
among local, county, state, and private entities to create the funding for the
projects, never hesitating to offer tax abatements and other inducements to
corporate interests. Deflecting grassroots criticism of his chummy relations
with the corporate sector while harking back to his campaign call for balanced growth, he routed roughly half of a tax-incentive package approved
by the state legislature to Cleveland's public school system. Despite a periodic
nod to neighborhood concerns, however, his first priority remained downtown revitalization. Local businesspeople breathed a sigh of relief as the transition between the Voinovich and White administrations unfolded in a seam-
less fashion.[36]

The focus on tourism and entertainment would continue in the twenty-
first century as the city sought to become "the pre-eminent visitors' destination between New York and Chicago." With the support of Mayor Frank G.
Jackson (2006–2022), for example, gambling came to downtown Cleveland.
After four unsuccessful proposals in the preceding two decades, Ohio voters
in 2009 approved gambling in four cities (Cleveland, Cincinnati, Columbus,
and Toledo) as an economic boost in a sagging national economy. Permission to build a $600 million casino downtown went to Daniel Gilbert, the
majority owner of the Cavaliers, in partnership with Caesars Horseshoe of
Las Vegas, Nevada. Gilbert's original design called for construction of the
casino in the Flats across from Quicken Loans Arena, formerly Gund Arena,
but the plan finally situated the gaming establishment on the three lower
floors and basement of the partially vacant Higbee Building on Public Square.
Gilbert's Rock Ohio Caesars converted Higbee's Department Store into the

Horseshoe Casino, which opened as the first casino in Ohio in 2012. The following year, after decades of complaints about inadequate facilities for conventions and trade shows, the Huntington Convention Center and attached Hilton Hotel opened thanks to funding from Cuyahoga County. A glitzy gambling casino, a spacious convention center, the Medical Mart, new sports arenas, and lakeside tourist meccas provided several new magnets to attract suburbanites and other out-of-towners.[37]

Yet, despite more than three decades of investment in downtown, the anticipated comeback remained stalled. The Gateway Project, the crown jewel of the redevelopment effort, produced mixed results. Local taxpayers spent $9 million annually for several years to settle construction loans on the sporting venues and found themselves obligated to pay $125 million in cost overruns. Originally projected to liquidate half of the proposed $344 million cost, the public ended up paying 70 percent of the final $470 million. The streets around Progressive Field (previously Jacobs Field) and Quicken Loans Arena thrummed with activity on game days but stayed eerily quiet on nights when no sporting events filled the calendar. In the face of stalled development, Clevelanders grumbled that Gateway partisans had promised jingling cash registers throughout the reconstructed area along with homeruns and slam dunks. The Rock and Roll Hall of Fame, an attempt to "lift Cleveland beyond the old age of steel and into the age of Steely Dan," proved to be a popular attraction but failed to add luster to Cleveland's stodgy image. New restaurants, hotels, and bars made downtown a more inviting place for visitors but stopped well short of transforming the city into the preferred destination for tourists in the Rustbelt. Few Cleveland residents attended the expensive sporting events, which mostly attracted well-heeled suburbanites able to pay the exorbitant ticket prices. Without doubt, redevelopment had made downtown a much more attractive place, but at what cost? And who benefited?[38]

Mayor Voinovich and his Union Club cronies proudly extolled the results of their remedial work in the 1980s, efforts brought to fruition by Mayor White in the 1990s. But residents of the city's neighborhoods still awaited the promised rewards that were supposed to follow promptly after downtown's renewal. In 2000, pondering the lack of economic recovery outside the central business district, the city council president called Cleveland "a major league city with minor league schools and minor league infrastructure." Poverty, housing abandonment, homelessness, crime, and drug addiction remained problems, especially among the city's African American population. Little wonder that the city's black population often judged downtown improvements remote from or even foreign to their work and home lives. All the while, racial antagonisms remained a corrosive reality for the city's white and black residents. The plight of Cleveland's poor and power-less, a disadvantaged population untouched by downtown renewal, remained a blind spot in Civic Vision 2000. In nearby Detroit, a city reeling with di-sastrous economic and social problems, Mayor Coleman Young succumbed to an identical myopia, as the next chapter investigates.[39]

# 6

# Coleman Young and Gambling on Detroit

"On election day I became godamn mayor of Detroit," recalled Coleman Young, the city's first African American mayor. After his election in November 1974, Young observed, "I was taking over the administration of Detroit because the white people didn't want the damn thing anymore." Young, after years of experience dealing with a segregated nation and an intensely segregated city, was a perceptive observer of Detroit's racialized politics. White residents were leaving Detroit as large numbers of African Americans moved in. The white population of the city, which had been falling since the 1950s, accelerated its decline after a 1967 racial disturbance that resulted in 43 deaths, 700 injuries, thousands of arrests, and $50 million in property damage. Whites indeed composed the overwhelming majority of the roughly four hundred thousand Detroit residents who deserted the ailing metropolis during the mayor's twenty years in office. Meanwhile, the percentage of black residents increased from 44.5 to 78.4 percent between 1970 and 1990, giving Detroit one of the largest African American populations among northern cities.[1]

Many of the white women and men who fled the inner city for suburban havens such as Warren, Livonia, and Dearborn explicitly cited the new mayor as the reason for their headlong departure. Pointing to Young's fiery campaign rhetoric and his reputation as a dangerous revolutionary, the suburbanites expected that his arrival in city hall would consign them to second-class citizenship had they remained in Detroit. By this thinking, white people feared that Detroit would belong to "them" rather than people like "us." And disgruntled white people charged that Young cared more about retribution than rehabilitation. The mayor seemed to confirm their fears after his election, disdainfully dismissing "bleeding heart, pansy-ass" liberals and warning that "the change I seek for the world around me is a radical one." During the ensuing two decades, Young remained a coarse and uninhibited defender of Detroit who never hesitated to criticize the state and federal governments for reducing aid to cities, white people who fled to the suburbs to avoid busing their children to integrated schools, and corporate executives responsible for accelerating the exodus of taxpaying businesses from the city. For their part, white people blamed Young's misrule for the city's drastic plight.[2]

Coleman Young was undeniably a confrontational and profane defender of Detroit's beleaguered population. Young was at the same time not a revolutionary bent on taking private property from the wealthy and handing it to his city's poorest residents. Instead, he unquestioningly accepted the prevailing wisdom that downtown rehabilitation had to take precedence in any effort to improve the city. Young needed wealthy Detroiters to remain attached to the city and especially to the downtown. "The reality," he contended, "is that if you have a billion dollars to spend in the city and spend every penny of it rebuilding the neighborhoods—giving people brand-new or refurbished houses—and *they don't have jobs*, within five years the goddamn place will be a slum again." Although he regularly warred with suburban politicians, state legislators, Republican presidents, and the media, Young worked hard to ingratiate himself with the local lions of industry whose support he judged essential for turning the city around. In deference to the key economic role played by the automobile industry in Detroit, he especially cultivated good relations with the leading executives of the Big Three car manufacturers—Ford, General Motors, and Chrysler—whose well-being he deemed essential to the city's financial health. (Young enjoyed a particularly cordial relationship with Henry Ford II, whom he fondly referred to as "Hank the Deuce.") Contrary to the mayor's popular image as a dangerous radical, he proved to be anything but antibusiness. "I don't give a goddamn about them making money," he said of Detroit's economic elite, "so long as it's not excessive and as long as they have the city's interest at heart."[3]

Young followed the familiar path charted by mayors in other shell-shocked Rust Belt cities, seeking to offset declining manufacturing output with greater emphasis on service industries in central business districts. Like so many of his peers around the country, such as Alfonso J. Cervantes in St. Louis and George V. Voinovich in Cleveland, Young embraced tourism and entertainment as necessary elements for improving the city's future. The mayor wanted to persuade hunters, fishers, and other vacationers bound for the sportsman's paradise of upstate Michigan, as well as tourists headed for the Ford Museum and Greenfield Village in nearby Dearborn, to include a detour to Detroit in their itineraries. Young chose the legalization of gambling in the Motor City as his signature issue. Convinced that casinos would bring fabulous sums of money into the city's coffers to offset the catastrophic loss of manufacturing jobs, the mayor struggled unsuccessfully throughout his administration before his successor persuaded Michigan lawmakers to allow gaming on the U.S. side of the U.S.-Canadian border. Although subsequent developments confirmed Young's judgment that gambling would serve as a reliable revenue stream for the cash-strapped metropolis, Detroit continued to decline even after the opening of casinos and eventually became the nation's premier example of urban ruin.[4]

## Young's Early Years

Young's efforts as mayor to pull Detroit out of its dramatic tailspin came as the culmination of a lifelong commitment to fomenting change. A native of Alabama, he moved to Detroit with his family in 1923 and grew up in the city's hardscrabble Black Bottom community. Young and his peers, many recent arrivals from the U.S. South, hoped to find employment in one of the city's many factories. After graduating from Eastern High School, he went to work on the assembly line for the Ford Motor Company. Young became a United Auto Workers (UAW) organizer, civil-rights activist, open-housing advocate, and a critic of the city's overwhelmingly white police force. During World War II, he underwent pilot training with the elite Tuskegee Airmen but never flew in combat. He helped found the National Negro Labor Council in 1951. Subpoenaed the following year to testify before the U.S. House Committee on Un-American Activities about his alleged communist sympathies, Young sparred verbally with committee members in defending his constitutional rights. He became a hero in the city's African American neighborhoods when a purloined recording of his combative congressional testimony, marketed by a Detroit music executive, became a hit record locally. Blacklisted by the automobile companies as a dangerous subversive, he made ends meet as an insurance salesman, dry cleaner, butcher, and taxi driver before entering politics. He served as a delegate to Michigan's constitutional convention in 1960 and as a state senator from 1964 to 1973. Young became the first African American to serve on the Democratic National Committee and eventually rose to the position of vice chairman of the party. In 1973, he narrowly won election as mayor in the racially divided city, garnering 92 percent of the African American vote while his white opponent, Police Commissioner John Nichols, collected 91 percent of ballots cast by white voters.[5]

Widely characterized by conservative white people as a divisive figure more given to confrontation than conciliation, Young entered city hall at a precarious time for a city already in the throes of catastrophic population and job losses. Added to the nightmare of racial violence in 1967, the lingering bitterness from the rancorous 1973 election left white and black people in the city eyeing each other warily. Intended or not, his first inaugural address fanned the flames. Young said, "I issue a forward warning to all those pushers, to all rip-off artists, to all muggers: It's time to hit Eight Mile Road [the city's northern border]! And I don't give a damn if they are black or white, or if they wear Superfly suits or blue uniforms with silver badges. Hit the road!" The press complained that the statement he considered a generic admonition to all wrongdoers escalated tensions and unfairly implicated the police in the city's rampant lawlessness. A worsening economic climate exacerbated the situation. Businesses continued to depart Detroit, and the loss of their tax dollars forced the city to lay off more than four thousand employees in 1975 alone. The immediate onset of an economic recession triggered by a severe oil shortage sent the Motor City, a one-industry town dependent on the vagaries of domestic automobile sales, into its worst financial crisis since the Great Depression. As Joseph Hudson, scion of Detroit's leading department store and one of the city's foremost civic leaders, observed, "The black man has the feeling he is about to take power in the city, but he is going to be left with an empty bag."[6]

## Young and Downtown Redevelopment

Even as Detroit's fortunes spiraled downward, the black community remained firmly entrenched in the new mayor's camp and applauded his formula for an urban renaissance. A smaller number of white people, committed to building a prosperous, racially integrated city, joined their African American counterparts in support of the mayor's key idea. "Revitalize the riverfront," Young had repeated often during the 1973 campaign, "and I guarantee you'll revitalize the whole city." When Young became mayor, most of the land adjacent to the Detroit River remained undeveloped and unsightly—a disastrous situation that he felt should have been addressed decades earlier. His goal of upgrading the neglected riverfront put him squarely within a national movement to reclaim urban waterfronts for leisure and residential land use as pioneered in Pittsburgh, Baltimore, and other places. The president of New Detroit, Inc., a businessperson's organization created after the 1967 conflagration to facilitate the city's reconstruction, recalled that all Young could see looking south from his office window on Jefferson Avenue was a depressing pastiche of unused railroad tracks and deserted boxcars. Something had to be done to improve the city's forlorn front yard.[7]

To provide the wherewithal for downtown redevelopment, Young turned first to the federal government. In 1975, he headed a delegation of the city's leading businesspeople to meet with Republican president Gerald R. Ford in the White House. The Detroit deputation submitted an unrealistically ambitious proposal, "Moving Detroit Forward: A Plan for Urban Economic Revitalization," that requested $2.5 billion in federal funding over five years for municipal improvements. (He asked the State of Michigan for an additional $328 million.) Detroit requested a generous package of direct grants-in-aid, interest-free loans, low-interest public facility loans, and debt guarantees. At a time when the Department of Housing and Urban Development (HUD) allocated $2.2 billion for its entire Community Development Block Grant program, the audacity of Young's request staggered HUD administrators and White House officials. The mayor sought a massive infusion of dollars at a time when President Ford, a staunch fiscal conservative, was poring over the federal budget line by line in search of places to cut funding for urban America. Causing no surprise, the frugal Republican administration declined to move Detroit forward.[8]

Young had limited success appealing for federal aid even after Democrat Jimmy Carter took the presidential oath of office in 1977. The mayor immediately returned to the White House for a meeting with the new president, armed with an updated version of "Moving Detroit Forward" that solicited $2.8 billion in federal funding over five years. He argued that, despite the unresponsiveness of the Ford administration and the challenges presented by a worsening recession, the city had achieved demonstrable progress during the previous years in curtailing unemployment, reducing crime, and attracting private investment. Young pleaded with Carter and his aides to help the proud city that "put the world on wheels and became known as the Arsenal of Democracy." Like their predecessors in the Ford administration, the president, his aides, and HUD officials rejected the unrealistic financial request. They did, however, authorize funds for an important initiative that helped set Young and future mayors on a course of replacing shuttered factories with sports and other entertainment venues.[9]

## Sports and Spectacle as the Answer
## to Downtown's Problems

The Carter administration provided a crucial piece of the funding to build a new riverfront arena. After the Detroit Lions of the National Football League departed the city in 1975 for a new stadium in suburban Pontiac, the mayor resolved to keep the Red Wings, the National Hockey League franchise, from following the same path. The hockey team's owner had announced his intention to leave Olympia Stadium north of downtown for a new home in Pontiac until Young persuaded the Carter administration to provide a

$38 million loan for the construction of a new $58 million riverfront facility for hockey (Joe Louis Arena). With a bravado that exemplified his willingness to take enormous risks, Young used a $5 million public-works grant from the U.S. Department of Commerce to begin clearing the site in 1976, long before the hockey team agreed to the deal. Accused of recklessness, Young defiantly replied, "Look, I've got five million dollars to dig with, and if nothing else, we'll have the biggest fucking hole in the state of Michigan!" The Red Wings began to play at Joe Louis Arena in December 1979, three months before HUD finalized approval of the financing. Construction crews toiled day and night in 1978–1979 to ready the arena for two events the confident mayor had scheduled for 1980—the National Hockey League All-Star Game in February and the Republican party's presidential nominating convention in July. Fortunately for the mayor, both came off without a hitch. Young later boasted that Detroit had received the largest loan ever given for downtown redevelopment and the only one awarded for the building of a sports venue.[10]

The $38 million loan granted by the Carter administration proved to be an anomaly in an age of retrenchment, however, and the federal government repeatedly cut appropriations to cities during Young's years in city hall. Aid from the federal government declined drastically during the two-term presidency of Republican Ronald Reagan, whom Young contemptuously referred to as "Old Pruneface," forcing big-city mayors to look elsewhere for capital. HUD officials saw their budgets cut more than 50 percent during Reagan's presidency, as the Republican administration practiced its New Federalism designed to impose an embargo on federal funds to big cities. Communities often issued municipal bonds to raise funds for improvement projects, but the principal bond rating agencies (Moody's, Standard and Poor's, and Fitch) increased the difficulty for Detroit's mayor by lowering the city's bond ratings from investment grade to speculative grade in 1980. The devaluation of a city's bonds both raised the interest rates, thereby increasing borrowing costs by millions of dollars, and limited the attractiveness of the venture for wary investors. Young protested bitterly—at the same time, he negotiated wage concessions from municipal unions and successfully pushed for an increase in the city income tax—but his stringent economy measures received no credit from the Wall Street arbiters. He reluctantly had to accept the fait accompli. "After all," asked Detroit's financial director fatalistically, "who is going to brawl with the ratings agencies?" Deprived of such rich sources of funding, Young turned elsewhere to underwrite his plans for riverfront development.[11]

Young believed that the creation of a vibrant riverfront, home to profitable businesses and a desirable gathering point for festivals and other public events, would be instrumental not only in burnishing the city's image but also in revitalizing the adjacent central business district. Levying new taxes, passing zoning ordinances, issuing building permits, and offering a variety of financial incentives, city government replaced railroad yards and boxcars with new buildings and attractive outdoor spaces. Young engineered a $180 million enlargement of the convention center, Cobo Hall, doubling main-floor exhibition space and elevating the facility from the twelfth- to the seventh-largest convention center in the nation. The changes to Cobo Hall allowed for the expansion of the North American International Auto Show—or the Detroit Auto Show, for short—at which each car company introduced its new models for the coming year. The annual extravaganza had served as the highlight of the city's social scene since its inception in 1899. The mayor also completed a series of improvements to the Civic Center, including Hart Plaza, which became a popular site for outdoor concerts and ethnic group celebrations at the historic site where French explorers had founded Detroit centuries earlier.[12]

Professional sports were also an important element in Young's plans for downtown revival. The mayor's dreams for a complete makeover of the riverfront included a new ballpark for the Detroit Tigers, the city's major league baseball franchise. The Tigers had played since 1912 at the intersection of Michigan Avenue and Trumbull Avenue—"the Corner," as it was known locally—about 1.5 miles west of downtown. By the time that Young became mayor, the team was handling one structural problem after another at the superannuated stadium and laying out $500,000 annually in maintenance. The team's owner, broadcasting tycoon John E. Fetzer, stopped short of threatening to follow the Lions to the suburbs but felt that something would have to be done about the deteriorating Tiger Stadium. In the long run, Fetzer favored construction of a new downtown ballpark; in the short run, the owner sought a $15 million renovation that he expected the city to finance. Instead, Young countered with a plan whereby Fetzer would sell the ballpark to Detroit for one dollar and sign a lease for thirty years with options for renewal; the city, which issued bonds for $10 million and received a $5 million grant from the federal government, would assume all responsibility for repairs and maintenance during the life of the lease. The two parties finalized the agreement in 1978. A jubilant Young boasted that his deal "ensures the Tigers will remain in the city for an entire generation."[13]

Young's resolve to keep the baseball team in Detroit did not include remaining at antiquated Tiger Stadium, though, especially with riverfront development beckoning. Unlike nostalgic Tiger fans who viewed the venerable old stadium as an irreplaceable link to the team's storied past, the mayor saw an unsightly rattletrap constantly draining municipal resources and nestled in a residential neighborhood with inadequate parking. Young's secret desire to vacate the decrepit stadium and relocate to the riverfront became public after Fetzer sold the team to Tom Monaghan, the owner of Domino's Pizza. Monaghan soon began to voice his dissatisfaction with the ballpark, and rumors circulated that he would move the team to suburban Ann Arbor, Dearborn, or Novi. By 1988, Young was no longer using diplomatic language to appease Tiger fans and historic preservationists who hoped to save Tiger Stadium. "It's obvious the damned thing is falling down," he complained in arguing that both the team and the city would be better served by erecting a multipurpose stadium with a retractable dome and attached hotel on the riverfront. Clearly, Young proclaimed, the city must work with the Tiger owner to build a new ballpark as the price of keeping the team in Detroit.[14]

In 1991, Young and Wayne County executive Edward H. "Ed" McNamara jointly announced the formation of a city-county stadium authority tasked with choosing a Detroit location for a new baseball park. Several members of the authority preferred to build on the grounds of the Michigan State Fairgrounds at Eight Mile Road far from the central business district, which would improve access for suburbanites living in Oakland and Macomb Counties. Young continued to lobby for a location west of Cobo Hall in keeping with his riverfront development plan. The lack of agreement on a site between city and county officials, combined with the exertions of grassroots activists organized to save Tiger Stadium, brought discussions to a standstill. The Tiger Stadium Fan Club, an eclectic mix of preservationists and loyal baseball fans, elevated the local issue into a national cause célèbre and turned public opinion against the move. In 1992, a frustrated Monaghan sold the team to another pizza tycoon, Little Caesars owner Michael "Mike" Ilitch, who quickly began scheming for construction of a new ballpark. The Tigers continued to play at Tiger Stadium until the opening of a new stadium in 2000, years after Young had left the mayor's office.[15]

## The Renaissance Center and Bringing Suburbanites Back Downtown

Young wanted upscale riverfront housing as well, part of his effort to encourage young, well-educated suburbanites to resettle in downtown Detroit. He targeted members of the middle class who sought proximity to bustling restaurants, professional sports, and a variety of entertainment options. He twisted arms on the city council to approve a tax abatement and brokered a deal to acquire riverfront property just west of the Joe Louis Arena for construction of the luxurious Riverfront Towers, the brainchild of Marathon Oil magnate Max Fisher and real-estate baron A. Alfred Taubman. Young interceded with HUD leadership in Washington, DC, to obtain a federally insured mortgage for the project and, at his direction, the Detroit delegation to the state legislature pushed a bill through that provided the owners of the residential structures with a twelve-year property-tax abatement. Riverfront Towers opened in 1984 with two 29-story buildings—developers added a third high-rise in the 1990s—complete with apartments, condominiums, townhouses, and a marina with space for seventy-seven boats.[16]

Riverfront Towers marked the western end of the redeveloping downtown, and Young avidly supported Henry Ford II's plan to construct a monumental edifice at the eastern end to bookend the upgraded riverfront real estate. After the devastating 1967 racial upheaval, Ford had assembled a coalition of the city's leading businesspeople, called Detroit Renaissance, Inc., to oversee the community's physical and emotional recovery. (Several civic groups led by the monied elite, including Detroit Renaissance, Inc., New Detroit, Inc., and the Detroit Economic Development Corporation, formed after the 1967 outbreak to help the city recover from the devastation.) As a potent symbol of the reconstruction effort, which the business community naturally believed began with the refurbishment of downtown, Ford called for the creation of Renaissance Center on the riverfront. He spearheaded the drive to launch construction of a multiuse structure underwritten entirely with private money, personally enlisting the financial support of the fifty-one executives whose corporations pledged to invest in the largest urban real-estate venture in the nation's history. Rumors at the time suggested that the hard-driving automobile executive strong-armed contributions from local business luminaries who relied on their financial connections to the Ford Motor Company. Like Richard King Mellon in Pittsburgh, Hank the Deuce occupied a singularly influential position in Detroit and compelled the city's lower-rank power brokers to follow his lead. The first phase of the Renaissance Center, which soon came to be called the RenCen, opened in May 1976, with the official dedication following on April 15, 1977. In 1981, the Ford Motor Land Development Corporation and New York City's Rockefeller Center partnered in adding two additional 21-story towers on the east side of the complex. The glass-encased RenCen, enthused Detroiters, loomed over their city much as the Eiffel Tower rose above Paris.[17]

The modernistic RenCen, designed by architect John C. Portman Jr. and built at an eventual cost exceeding $500 million, gained international recognition for its monumentality if nothing else. The building sprawled over 14 acres and contained 5.5 million square feet of space, extending 727 feet into the air at its highest point. A Westin Hotel with 1,456 guest rooms occupied one 73-story tower surrounded by four 39-story towers that housed corporate offices (including the headquarters of Ford Motor Company's Ford and Lincoln-Mercury Divisions). The lower floors in the soaring towers contained conference rooms, retail shops, restaurants, a bakery, four movie theaters, a dry cleaner, and a post office—in short, virtually every amenity

**Figure 6.1** Coleman Young (*left*), who worked with corporate leaders like Henry Ford (*right*) to redevelop downtown, including the Renaissance Center (pictured) (Credit: Walter P. Reuther Library, Archives of Labor and Urban Affairs, Wayne State University)

a vacationing guest, a top executive, or a well-off shopper could want under one roof. Having parked their cars in the attached garage, visitors could indeed spend an entire day, or longer, in the RenCen. Much like a suburban mall, visitors roamed an indoor universe devoid of the bustle, clamor, unemployment, and palpable racial tensions that enveloped less-well-paid Detroiters each day.[18]

Such self-sufficiency proved to be a fundamental drawback, however. Rather than stand apart from downtown, the RenCen was supposed to act as a beacon, welcoming tourists to the heart of Detroit. Viewed from afar, the building's glass facades sparkled alongside the river. At street level, however, the opaque towers appeared impenetrable rather than inviting. The RenCen seemed to be an impregnable fortress, separated from the central business district by two 30-foot-high concrete berms that obscured the main entrance. Jefferson Avenue, a busy ten-lane speedway that served as the main vehicular artery along the river, discouraged pedestrians from venturing into the city core and further isolated the building. Viewed in the context of the recent racial strife, architect Portman noted, the imposing RenCen would provide a safe refuge for business in an otherwise threatening cityscape. Inside, the dearth of clear signage and a lack of visible landmarks left visitors with the impression of being trapped within a self-contained, hermetically sealed bubble. "People told us you could eat, sleep, work, and shop in Renaissance Center," observed a bewildered couple from Kalamazoo, Michigan. "We didn't realize they meant we would *have* to spend our whole lives in Renaissance Center."[19]

Opponents of the RenCen sounded off immediately, citing everything from its poor location and design flaws to its misguided conceptualization and harmful economic impact on established retail outlets just blocks away in the central business district. The press charged that the failure to integrate the gigantic edifice into the fabric of downtown constituted a fatal and irreversible error. The dream of luring shoppers from suburban malls to the project's riverfront location and then to the stores remaining in the desiccated downtown never materialized. Whatever success RenCen retailers enjoyed—and optimistic projections went unrealized—failed to benefit its neighbors. If anything, reported business analysts, the sales posted by RenCen tenants took business away from shops in the central business district. Almost immediately, the notion that the civic elite had foisted a white elephant on the struggling city took hold. Criticism intensified in the early 1980s as downtown merchants saw no sales increases, and the Westin Hotel reported wholesale vacancies. Most of the RenCen's high-end retail establishments closed for lack of business, and rumors of foreclosure soon circulated. Awash in red ink, many of the original investors in the project sold their ownership to forestall further losses.[20]

In 1984, the RenCen's owners hired Rubloff, Inc., a respected real-estate brokerage and property-management company from Chicago, to assess the damage and prepare a salvage operation. Members of the Detroit civic elite hoped that the expert tutelage provided by the heralded Chicago firm could help their venture replicate the glamorous success of the Magnificent Mile. The Rubloff inquiry identified a host of problems and proposed numerous alterations, the sum of which called for an additional $27 million investment. The RenCen's executives approved the recommendations and subsequently hired the Chicago firm to market and manage the operation. Tenants and visitors generally reacted favorably to the modifications introduced in the next few years, most of which dealt with the rearrangement of functions within the complex that resulted in a more efficient use of space, but the Rubloff management team could do nothing to change the location of the forbidding towers. The problem of integrating the RenCen into the rest of the downtown remained unsolved. Architect Bruce N. Wright likened its isolation to a "snobby, rich kid shying away from low-class neighbors."[21]

## The People Mover and Grand Prix Racing

Mayor Young sought devices to bolster the RenCen's finances. For one, Young hoped that the provision of public transit, underwritten primarily by federal transportation dollars, would help in that regard. The People Mover, an automated monorail circling the downtown in a 2.9-mile, one-way loop, included a stop at the RenCen that allowed pedestrians to avoid having to dodge automobile traffic on Jefferson Avenue. (The city also built a bridge over the busy thoroughfare connecting the RenCen with the new Robert L. Millender Center, a hotel, apartment, and retail complex on the north side of Jefferson Avenue designed to bring more visitors to the southern end of downtown.) Burdened by construction delays and cost overruns, for years the People Mover stumbled unsurely toward completion. When responsibility for the project passed from the Southeastern Michigan Transportation Authority (SEMTA) to the city in 1985, Young eagerly accepted the responsibility—including a portion of the hefty price tag. Originally budgeted at $137.5 million, the elevated railway ended up costing approximately $215 million. The head of the Urban Mass Transportation Agency, the federal unit that contributed $110 million to the project, called it "a pork-barrel project gone wild." The People Mover finally commenced operation in 1987. Although Young had originally predicted a daily ridership of sixty-seven thousand people, city officials revised the number down to fifteen thousand shortly before the beginning of service. After an initial burst of activity, the number of passengers fell to a few thousand per day. With the inflated expectations nurtured during the protracted construction phase, the expense of operation, and the limited usage, naysayers unsurprisingly labeled the People Mover yet another costly boondoggle of the Young administration that failed to resuscitate the dreary downtown.[22]

Nor did the public acclaim another of the mayor's creative attempts to attract more people to downtown Detroit, the introduction of Grand Prix automobile racing to the riverfront. In 1982, the city became an official part of the World Championship Series for Formula One racecars, one of only four events in the United States sanctioned by the international racing authority. To the chagrin of many Detroiters, particularly environmentalists, hosting the event each summer meant tolerating the disruption of local traffic, the deafening roar of turbocharged engines, unsightly plumes of smoke rising above downtown streets, and the odor of burned rubber—as well as tending to a multitude of potholes and oil slicks after the competition concluded. Drivers quickly declared the 2.5-mile course their least favorite on the Formula One circuit, criticizing the poor sightlines, dangerous hairpin turns, and inconvenient fueling stations. The Grand Prix governing board moved the race to Phoenix, Arizona, in 1989, after which Championship Auto Racing Teams negotiated a new deal with the city and moved the race to Belle Isle Park, east of downtown. Young continued to defend the annoying logistical modifications necessary to accommodate high-speed automobile racing in the heart of a big city as a temporary inconvenience fully justified by the priceless publicity.[23]

## Casinos and Another Bet on Detroit's Recovery

Undeterred by the rising tide of censure flowing his way, Young blithely dismissed the setbacks he suffered and continued to seek public-private partnerships as the only means of stemming Detroit's ongoing deterioration. Determined to acquire the capital his redevelopment projects required and contemptuous of moralistic politicians and interest groups opposing his call for legalized gambling, the mayor repeatedly returned to casino revenue as the only financial panacea for the insolvent city. He pointed to the increasing respectability of gaming nationally and to the profitability of numerous gambling establishments operated by Native American tribes in Michigan. His original design called for the placement of thirteen casinos scattered throughout the downtown and surrounding neighborhoods. Not only would business taxes enrich the city, Young claimed, but the casinos would provide good wages for unemployed Detroiters. "I don't believe that any enterprise that offers the prospect of 50,000 jobs can be cavalierly dismissed," he said. The mayor unrelentingly asserted that the potential financial benefit offset the moral reservations voiced by many African American clergymen, an important political force in the city, who advised their parishioners to spurn legalized gambling. The influential black ministers, Young tartly observed, seemed indifferent to the existence of a state lottery and turned a blind eye to the bingo games regularly held in their own church basements. Detroit voters remained unpersuaded by the mayor, however, rejecting referendums in 1977 and 1981 that would have legalized casino gambling.[24]

Still other casino opponents focused on the probable economic and social consequences of organized gambling for the city, especially for its poorest residents. Leading the opposition in municipal government, city council member Melvin Ravitz considered the attraction of casinos a chimera that would do citizens more harm than good. A professor of sociology at Wayne State University and a consistently progressive voice on the city council, Ravitz systematically outlined his opposition to Young's proposal in a 1987 statement to the state senate during public hearings on two pending gaming bills. In that statement, Ravitz indicated that a thorough evaluation of gambling could be completed in only one place, Atlantic City, New Jersey, and that the evidence from that community pointed to disastrous outcomes. (Oddly, Ravitz ignored Las Vegas, Nevada.) Crime rates had soared in and around Atlantic City, Ravitz contended, especially in neighboring suburbs, where greater affluence provided more inviting robbery targets to unlucky gamblers just relieved of their bankrolls. Because casinos offered such complementary perquisites as free parking, inexpensive lodging, cheap or free food, and other forms of entertainment, small businesses in the surrounding areas suffered. The population of Atlantic City declined significantly as inflated property values drove low- and fixed-income populations to poor communities nearby in search of affordable housing—a disastrous possibility for Detroit, which was already suffering catastrophic population loss. Of the forty-six thousand jobs created by the gambling establishments in Atlantic City, only 10 percent went to local residents. "In Detroit," Ravitz insisted, "we should not expect laid-off automobile workers to be retrained as blackjack dealers or croupiers."[25]

Having carefully detailed the harmful influence of the casinos in Atlantic City, Ravitz made clear his principal objection to the bills legalizing the gaming industry in Detroit. The proposed legislation authorized gambling only in Michigan's largest city—a "calculated" decision, according to Ravitz, owing to Detroit's status as a "throw-away" city. In other words, the disproportionate numbers of low-income, minority, elderly, and dependent people made the Motor City expendable to many Michiganders outside the southeastern portion of the state. Gambling preyed on society's most defenseless people, in the Detroit case "a vulnerable population made desperate by corporate plant closings, layoffs and over-extended public financial support to big business." Authorizing legalized gambling in Detroit, charged the outraged city council member, amounted to a cynical means of dealing with a crippled city's financial problems so that others in the state could shirk their responsibility. Such a tradeoff amounted to what historian Hal K. Rothman's termed a "devil's bargain."[26]

The city council followed Ravitz's lead and twice passed ordinances in 1987 prohibiting casino gambling in Detroit. The mayor vetoed both. In 1988, Young appointed the City of Detroit Gaming Study Commission—a sixty-four-member blue-ribbon panel composed of corporate executives, labor leaders, clergymen, government officials, and community representatives— to prepare a feasibility study for casinos. Ostensibly to ensure that the committee would not simply serve as a rubber stamp for the mayor, whose advocacy of legalized wagering had been firmly established, he also created an eleven-member oversight committee of print and broadcast journalism executives with full access to all deliberations. While pledging to give members of the commission free rein in pursuing their charge, Young frequently reminded them of the urgent need to expand Detroit's tourism industry and again noted the potential of casinos to create an estimated fifty thousand jobs. In its final report issued later that year, the commission recommended building from three to six casinos in the central business district during a first stage of implementation with perhaps as many as twelve slated for construction at a later time. Young applauded the final report but recognized that a crucial legal hurdle remained in the form of an impending local referendum.[27]

In 1988, rather than waiting for the city to initiate another referendum, opponents of legalized gambling in Detroit introduced a ballot measure that specifically banned casinos within the city. Young responded with an extensive public-relations campaign that argued the need for the revenue generated by the gaming industry. Once again, the city's voters rejected the casino proposal. The despondent mayor saw the third rejection of his plan by the public in twelve years as a decisive verdict. He still advocated casino gambling after the 1988 loss but stopped short of engineering a full-scale campaign to persuade residents. After leaving office in 1994, Young formed a group of investors (Paradise Valley/Rio Casinos) intent on operating a casino in Detroit, but he died before the city began issuing licenses.[28]

Young's mayoral successor, Dennis W. Archer, eventually presided over the introduction of legalized gambling to the city. In 1996, the local electorate approved a ballot initiative allowing the construction of no more than three gambling venues within city limits, and Governor John M. Engler signed the enabling legislation (the Michigan Gaming Control and Revenue Act) in 1997. As a further impetus, a casino opened across the Detroit River in Windsor, Ontario. The potential loss of millions of dollars in revenue annually to the Canadian gaming establishment, conveniently situated only a ten-minute drive from Detroit via bridge or tunnel, persuaded Archer to take action at a time of still more crippling job loss and ever-mounting financial disaster. As he put it, "Detroiters looked across the river and concluded that if Michigan money was going to be spent on casino gambling, it might be better done in Detroit than in Windsor." Archer issued the inaugural license to the MGM Grand Detroit Casino in 1999, making Detroit the largest U.S. city with casino gambling. He granted licenses to two others—the Greektown Casino and the Motor City Casino—later that year. In doing so, the mayor rejected the top choice as determined by a *Detroit Free Press* public opinion poll. Popular sentiment favored the bid submitted for a casino and accompanying 800-room hotel by Donald J. Trump, owner of several Atlantic City gaming establishments and a riverboat casino in Gary, Indiana. The committee formed to advise the mayor found Trump's submission intriguing, flamboyantly packaged but financially vague. Trump promised to crown his hotel with a rotating sphere (in the shape of an automobile hood ornament) and to bring his Miss Universe pageant to Detroit every three years, but the advisory committee deemed the foundation of his business empire to be unstable.[29]

Subsequent events proved Young correct in predicting that casinos would create a reliable revenue stream for the cash-strapped metropolis. Within the first five years, Detroit was collecting more than $100 million annually in gaming taxes. Moreover, in a list of the city's twenty-five leading employers, the three casinos ranked seventeenth, eighteenth, and nineteenth—or sixth, if all three are counted together as a single source of employment. Downtown bars and restaurants reported an increase in business from the patronage of workers on three shifts, twenty-four hours a day. Legalized gambling provided a modest income stream for Detroit, but never enough to overcome the harrowing financial problems nudging the municipality ever closer to bankruptcy. The city continued to founder in its search for economic stability in the postindustrial age.[30]

## Keeping Automobile Manufacturers in the City

Even though his devotion to downtown revitalization remained unshaken, Young recognized the transcendence of Detroit's metal-bending history and refused to accept the demise of manufacturing in the city. Indeed, two of his most ambitious projects entailed industrial redevelopment. The mayor's sponsorship of the Central Industrial Park Project, arguably the most controversial undertaking during his twenty years in office, occurred at a time of rampant automobile plant closings in the city. Jobs in local automobile factories were hemorrhaging at an alarming pace. Just between 1978 and 1980, the number of workers employed in the industry declined from 253,000 to 191,000. Detroit's unemployment rate increased to 18.3 percent in June 1980, at which time General Motors (GM) announced the imminent closing of two more plants. The same year, the Chrysler Corporation shuttered its Dodge Main factory complex, which consisted of thirty-five buildings spread across sixty-seven acres. (The factories were just outside Detroit city limits, in Hamtramck, a municipality surrounded by the Motor City.) The demise of Dodge Main, at one time the largest automobile production facility in the world and the employer of forty thousand workers, idled nearly five thousand autoworkers and thirty-seven miles of conveyor belts in 1980. The plant closing led to another round of small business failures and emptied houses in Detroit and Hamtramck.[31]

The top executives of the Big Three automakers had promised Young that if their plans included the construction of new factories in the region, they would give Detroit the first opportunity to bid on the project. On June 23, 1980, GM announced its intention to build a gigantic state-of-the-industry Cadillac plant, a $1.2 billion facility that would employ approximately six thousand full-time workers. Detroit officials worked frantically to identify a site within the municipal limits that would offer the enormous size (at least five hundred acres), freeway access, and railroad connections that GM requested. The automobile firm also imposed a stringent timeline, insisting that the site be cleared within a year to ensure the completion of all work by 1983. A joint proposal by the Detroit and Hamtramck economic development corporations offered a 465-acre parcel of land straddling the two cities, including the vacant Dodge Main factory, along with tax abatements and other economic incentives. City officials estimated that the project would provide 4,200 temporary jobs for site clearance and construction during the next three years, in addition to the six thousand permanent jobs for autoworkers, and they hoped that the new GM plant would revitalize an area left devastated by Chrysler's exit.[32]

The 319 acres of the site within Detroit included 1,176 homes, commercial establishments, and industrial structures, along with several important community institutions such as schools, churches, and a hospital. Altogether, the city acquired nearly two thousand property parcels and faced the task of relocating more than four thousand people. The media referred to the area as Poletown, an allusion to the preponderance of Polish immigrants who resided there several generations earlier, but African Americans composed more than half the population in the diverse area by the early 1980s. A substantial number of Poles, Albanians, Yemenis, and Filipinos also resided within the heterogeneous neighborhood. Young immediately invoked the city's power of eminent domain to acquire and clear the land, aided by a state law signed just two months earlier that substantially streamlined the acquisition process. Owing to the "quick-take" provision of Michigan's 1980 Uniform Condemnation Act, cities could seize land immediately rather than wait for the resolution of legal issues in the courts and before determination of the condemnation award. The mayor encountered determined opposition from neighborhood residents, who formed the Poletown Neighborhood Council to spearhead their resistance. Several members of the city council balked as well, decrying the destruction of a viable working-class neighborhood and objecting to the twelve-year, 50 percent tax abatement requested by GM. Ralph Nader, the renowned consumer-rights advocate, came to Detroit and spoke on behalf of the embattled Poletown residents. Young contemptuously dismissed him as a "carpetbagger." He said, "Nader doesn't live here. He comes in, he sues, he leaves." Nader left town, and the mayor prevailed.[33]

Dramatic photographs of police dragging elderly female residents wearing black dresses and babushkas out of a church designated for destruction engendered sympathy for the scrappy Poletown resisters in local and national media. Nevertheless, Young and Hamtramck mayor Robert Kozaren successfully concluded their deal with GM. The excruciatingly detailed agreement required the cities not only to acquire land and demolish buildings, but also to reroute roads, install utilities, and straighten railroad tracks. With Hamtramck perched precariously on the verge of bankruptcy, the Detroit mayor unilaterally pieced together an intricate financial package that included grants from two federal programs (Community Development Block Grants and Urban Development Action Grants) and two state agencies, a U.S. Department of Housing and Urban Development (HUD) Section 8 loan, a loan from the private Detroit Economic Growth Corporation, and the proceeds from the city's tax-increment financing initiative. In the process, the project survived several challenges in state and federal courts. In 1985, two years after the projected opening date, workers drove Cadillac Sevilles and Eldorados, Buick Rivieras, and Oldsmobile Toronados off the production line at Poletown.[34]

Such uncommon efforts by the city yielded a disappointing outcome to supporters of the endeavor, who had expected a much bigger payoff. Despite GM's pressure to clear the land as quickly as possible, the corporation dawdled in fulfilling its responsibilities and opened the new facility two years behind schedule. The expected creation of ancillary supply plants, projected to create as many as 15,000 additional jobs, never materialized in the undeveloped blocks adjacent to the new factory. More disillusioning, the number of jobs at the Cadillac facility eventually amounted to about 3,400—a far cry from the 6,000 bandied about by GM—and the plant closed sporadically in subsequent years because of sales fluctuations and model changeovers. The financial estimates allowed no room for error, as Detroit had pledged all future revenue from tax increments, property taxes, and income taxes toward the repayment of debts incurred in meeting project deadlines. In 1987, GM unexpectedly closed two assembly plants elsewhere in Detroit, resulting in a loss of 6,000 jobs. So many setbacks juxtaposed against the opening of a single new plant exasperated many of the Detroiters who had initially praised the mayor's intrepid leadership. Even so, Young said he would have seized the lifeline extended by GM for as few as 2,000 jobs. Looking back at the episode several years later, he called the construction of the GM plant his "most significant accomplishment." Young's eagerness to scoop up whatever scraps fell from the Big Three's table, regardless of his uncompromising rhetoric just a few years earlier, revealed the hard survival lessons grudgingly learned by a mayor desperate for any good news about job growth.[35]

Young thought that Poletown demonstrated the importance of city hall working in tandem with the automobile industry to cultivate a mutually beneficial relationship. He believed in the adage "when the auto industry catches a cold, Detroit develops pneumonia." Concerned about the financial health of the Chrysler Corporation, the largest employer in Detroit, he turned next to the fate of the company's seventy-eight-year-old Jefferson Avenue assembly plant for his second major industrial redevelopment project. Young had lobbied with President Jimmy Carter and the U.S. Senate on behalf of a federal bailout of the frail automaker, brokered a deal between Chrysler and the UAW, and awarded the corporation six tax abatements in the 1970s and 1980s in an effort to keep the failing patient on life support. In 1986, the city purchased 380 acres adjacent to the aging Jefferson Avenue facility, the employer of 3,600 workers, and began relocating residents in anticipation of the existing plant's expansion. In contrast with the situation in Poletown, the city encountered no protracted resistance from a galvanized population near the factory. Deterioration of the housing stock in the blocks surrounding the factory had already led to widespread abandonment. In 1990, the Jefferson Avenue plant closed, leaving GM's Poletown complex the only automobile-assembly plant in the city. Chrysler chief executive officer Lee Iacocca then announced his intention to raze the old factory and build a new plant on the adjacent site. Expansion had become replacement. Chrysler predicted a future labor force of 15,000 at the new plant, but human resources personnel hired only 2,500 autoworkers at the time of its opening in 1992.[36]

Young avoided a repetition of the criticism suffered in the Poletown episode for destroying a vibrant neighborhood, but the Jefferson Avenue project generated no shortage of harsh commentary from the media and others. Chrysler failed to keep its promise to continue production at the old factory until the new facility commenced operations, banishing thousands of autoworkers to the unemployment rolls for nearly two years. Evidence surfaced, as Young admitted, that a series of expensive mistakes had plagued the project from the start. The city overpaid for land and needlessly purchased several real-estate plots in the vicinity. Unscrupulous businesspeople, some allegedly linked to organized crime, overcharged the city for warehouses filled with used machinery and made windfall profits at public expense. A tabulation of all the inflated purchase prices showed that the city overpaid by approximately $25 million. A grand jury investigated but returned no indictments. The press chided the mayor's office for indifferent management and the city council for inadequate oversight. Young survived the scandal, but his community and economic director resigned because of the negative publicity. As with the Poletown episode, however, the mayor expressed no regrets. He firmly believed that the symbolic importance of opening the two new automobile plants was paramount. "There can be no dispute," he asserted in 1994, "that the parlaying of Poletown and Chrysler Jefferson has grandly preserved Detroit's tradition as the Motor City."[37]

## Coleman Young and the Failure of Redevelopment

The preservation of Detroit's tradition as the Motor City did nothing to stem the flow of people and money from the municipality during Young's twenty years as mayor. By the mid-1990s, as the city's population continued to plummet, approximately half the city's business owners had packed up inventories, boarded over storefronts, and headed for the suburbs during those two decades. With the payment of fewer tax dollars came the unavoidable reduction of vital city services. Garbage trucks operated sporadically and left putrid mounds of refuse on sidewalks, buses broke down often and no longer ran on schedule, city workers distributed surplus food irregularly, and demolition of the growing number of abandoned houses occurred less frequently. Glacially slow response times by the underfunded and ill-equipped police and fire departments made the city unsafe for the roughly one million hardy residents who remained within the municipality's jurisdiction. Skyrocketing homicide rates, a crack cocaine epidemic, and an increasing incidence of arson added to Young's growing list of intractable problems. As Detroit's plight worsened and the mayor proved incapable of stemming the decline, he replied in typically florid fashion to those who held him singularly responsible. Young asserted that cities such as Detroit had been cut adrift by the nation's policy makers and forced to confront deindustrialization and automation on their own.[38] To charges that the city had continued to lose ground during his administration, the mayor responded,

> Hell no, I don't think Detroit is better off now than it was when I became mayor. The auto industry certainly isn't better off than it was then. How the hell could Detroit be better off? But I damn sure think it's better off for me *becoming* mayor. I'd hate to think of the shape my city would be in right now without the Poletown plant and without the Chrysler plant and without Joe Louis [Arena] and without a

bigger Cobo Hall and without the highest income tax in the state and without a mayor who will take on any motherfucker who tries to mess with Detroit.[39]

Young's most virulent critics ignored his disclaimers, finding abundant fodder for their displeasure in the recurring rumors of lawlessness swirling around the mayor. The Federal Bureau of Investigation (FBI) examined Young's public and private conduct for decades, beginning with his time as a UAW organizer and throughout his years in city hall. In the course of their extensive probe, government agents covertly wiretapped the mayor's townhouse, eavesdropped on his conversations with other municipal officials, and scrutinized his finances. The FBI dragnet apprehended members of Young's family and high-level members of his administration, including most notably the police chief, but the Justice Department never indicted the mayor. Members of the press detailed the persistent appearance of impropriety in city hall, but the mayor steadfastly ignored their charges.[40]

Unable to pinpoint any links between Young and the improbity surrounding him, a legion of critics downplayed the subject of corruption and instead intensified their criticism of the mayor's policy choices. In particular, they questioned his repeated reliance on complicated funding arrangements to underwrite imposing brick-and-mortar projects—mostly downtown and in partnership with the city's economic elite—while ignoring the ghastly plight of the neighborhoods. The reconstructed riverfront in 1994 undeniably looked much more alluring to outsiders gazing at Detroit than it had in 1974, but the promised benefits failed to accrue for residents in the rest of the city. The gala openings of the new Poletown and Chrysler Jefferson factories provided work for a few thousand rank-and-file UAW members but did little to curtail the mammoth loss of jobs in the automobile industry. The eventual licensing of casinos yielded impressive sums of money for the city in the form of gaming taxes, much as Young had consistently predicted, but the Motor City's alarming fiscal deficits still shot skyward as population, retail, and industry emigrated rapidly. For two decades, Young remained a true believer in his strategy for saving Detroit and disdainfully likened the approach that emphasized neighborhood rehabilitation to "coaxing the tail to wag the dog." Despised throughout much of Michigan as a vituperative bully who nurtured racial discord and at the same time lionized in Detroit as the proud defender of an emasculated black metropolis surrounded by a hostile white suburbia, the mayor wagered the city's future on a downtown renaissance completed in concert with the corporate elite. His abrasive style notwithstanding, Young traveled the same path taken by his peers elsewhere in the last decades of the twentieth century. Seeking to transform their cities from manufacturing to service centers, these mayors built huge structures such as stadiums, convention centers, casinos, and universities.[41] In the mad scramble for a place in the urban hierarchy, big-city mayors regularly neglected residents who lost homes and livelihoods to make way for gigantic redevelopment programs. African Americans, Puerto Ricans, and working-class white households suffered disproportionate losses. Florence Giovangelo Scala, an activist, and Melvin J. Ravitz, a college professor and city council member, determined to stop the onrushing bulldozers, as the next chapter shows.

# 7

## Florence Scala, Mel Ravitz, and the People
## Left Behind in Five U.S. Cities

The privileging of the central business district to reinvigorate fading industrial cities played out with only varying degrees of success. Yet the conventional wisdom that saw revitalizing the business hub as the essential element remained an unassailable article of faith among elected officials and their business allies. In Chicago, St. Louis, Detroit, Cleveland, and Philadelphia, the downtown-first approach left great numbers of residents isolated from whatever prosperity was being generated by the public-private partnerships guiding the reclamation efforts as fashioned by mayors such as Richard M. Daley in Chicago. Disgruntled citizens (black and white) identified glaring inequities in the redevelopment strategies of commercial-civic elites and municipal policy makers, noting that the predicted economic benefits were not trickling down to working-class precincts. Furthermore, dissidents claimed, minority populations inevitably suffered the most when promised improvements such as those engineered by Mayor Coleman A. Young in Detroit failed to reach the disadvantaged in foundering ghettos and barrios. While real-estate moguls and other well-heeled investors such as Arthur Rubloff in Chicago praised the sustained emphasis on downtown uplift, neighborhood activists labored to mount grassroots opposition to initiatives conceived in corporate boardrooms and city halls. Challenging the economic and political power mobilized in favor of enriching the central business district, community organizers fought the good fight for a more balanced and just approach to urban redevelopment. The unevenness of the contest between the monied establishment and neighborhood dissenters recurred in all Rustbelt cities but appeared nowhere more evident than in Chicago, where the potent local government advanced downtown interests with extraordinary zeal.[1]

## Demolishing the Valley

The gilding of the Loop at the expense of modest working-class enclaves resulted in several highly publicized David-versus-Goliath struggles, beginning with the confrontation on the Near West Side. An area a few blocks from the Loop also known as "the Valley," the Near West Side consisted of tiny bungalows, rooming houses, restaurants, and a hodgepodge of small businesses around the intersection of Harrison and Halsted Streets. High population densities created a lively street life with peddlers, grocers, butchers, and others hawking their wares from street carts and makeshift stalls. The neighborhood had become notorious because many of the city's *mafiosi* had congregated there in the early decades of the twentieth century. In 1889, Jane Addams and Ellen Gates Starr had founded Hull House in the Valley to serve the needs of a poor immigrant population scrambling to establish an economic foothold and assimilate into American society.

By the mid-twentieth century, the inhabitants of one of the historically most polyglot neighborhoods in Chicago included mostly working-class Italians, Greeks, Mexicans, and African Americans. Just as the neighborhood had served as a launching pad for their upwardly mobile forebears, residents in the 1950s and 1960s worked hard, lived frugally, and saved to purchase property in the vicinity or move to a more inviting location elsewhere in the city. Though viewed as crowded, dirty, unhealthy, and unsafe by outsiders, the vital community offered security and stability to hardworking Chicagoans striving to better their circumstances—that is, until the city determined to safeguard downtown property values by completely reconfiguring the Near West Side.[2]

The sacrifice of Near West Side homes and businesses became an essential part of Democratic Mayor Richard J. Daley's grand strategy to protect the Loop from threats to commerce originating in the surrounding blocks. At the same time that he poured money into Loop redevelopment, the mayor strove to expand the downtown perimeter in all directions by eliminating the blight that loomed on the fringes. An influential partisan with strong ties to Democratic presidents John F. Kennedy and Lyndon B. Johnson, Daley obtained a cornucopia of federal funding designated for urban improvement. Near West Side residents panicked when they heard rumors that the mayor intended to employ some of those urban renewal dollars to raze their neighborhood.[3]

Chicago designated a fifty-five-acre urban renewal site in the Valley as a bulwark against the declining housing stock and overcrowding rampant on the Near West Side. Fortuitously for Loop merchants, they thought, the federal program in this case also provided the opportunity to erect a racial barrier. Just a few blocks away from the Harrison-Halsted site rose a foreboding sight to downtown's defenders: roughly three thousand units of public housing in the Jane Addams Houses, Grace Abbott Homes, and Robert Brooks Homes that contained mostly African American tenants. Urban renewal in the Valley would keep that undesirable population at bay, a vital consideration for merchants fearful that an increasing number of black shoppers from a nearby ghetto would scare off their affluent white customers. As city bulldozers began tearing down some of the worst eyesores on the Near West Side, Daley vowed that urban renewal would be used constructively to stabilize the community. City officials spoke about replacing decrepitude with generous amounts of moderate-income housing. The mayor encouraged Near West Side residents to improve their homes and businesses, issuing reassurances that seemed all the more authentic when the Roman Catholic archdiocese built a new school within the parish. At first, the city's intention to protect the Loop by improving the Valley through "partial renewal" promised to be only mildly unsettling to the people who lived and worked there.[4]

## A New University for Downtown Chicago

To the dismay of Valley residents, however, a more disruptive use for the urban renewal site soon surfaced. Daley had secretly decided against piecemeal development of the Harrison-Halsted neighborhood, instead reserving the area as the location of a new University of Illinois campus. Half the students attending the state university's flagship campus in downstate Champaign-Urbana were from Cook County, and Chicago taxpayers wanted a local branch as an alternative to sending their children 125 miles south to the twin cities. Years passed without action as politically powerful university administration and alumni blocked legislation in Springfield, the state capital. Meanwhile, Chicago-area students matriculated at a temporary facility on Navy Pier, which became glaringly inadequate as post–World War II college enrollments increased significantly. In 1959, university trustees announced that a permanent campus would be built in Riverside, twelve miles west of Chicago. Daley objected strenuously, fearing that the university's placement in the suburbs would accelerate the metropolitan decentralization he opposed in all instances. He proposed that Chicago pay the difference in land costs to the university so that officials would have no reason to accept a more attractive offer from another locality (such as Riverside).

The chauvinistic mayor was determined that the metropolitan area's public university would be within his beloved Chicago.[5]

Several potential inner-city sites emerged, with University of Illinois officials favoring one in Garfield Park four miles west of the Loop and another next to Meigs Field on Northerly Island. Daley had a different vision. In keeping with his goal of protecting the Loop, he preferred a location nearby the central business district. So did the Metropolitan Housing and Planning Council, the Chicago Central Area Committee (CCAC), and the State Street Council, as well as other influential civic organizations with strong ties to city hall. Many of the city's most influential businesspeople, including Hughston M. McBain of Marshall Field and Company and Holman D. Pettibone of the Chicago Title and Trust Company, aligned with the mayor. Loop merchants and developers argued for the reclamation of seedy railroad terminals just south of downtown, but negotiations with the railroads bogged down over an acceptable purchase price. As speculation about site selection increased in the summer of 1960, the mayor assured members of the Near West Side Planning Board (NWSPB) that their neighborhood was not under consideration. On September 27, 1960, however, Daley formally proposed a site several blocks east of the University of Illinois Medical District, the nation's largest medical complex, and west of the Loop, firmly in the middle of the Valley. Because the Harrison-Halsted area had already been designated as an urban renewal site, construction could begin without delay and federal dollars could be used to defray construction costs. Although loop businesspeople preferred the parcel of land with the vacated railroad terminals south of downtown, they accepted the mayor's alternative. The solution seemed perfect, except for the refusal of the Harrison-Halsted residents to go along quietly.[6]

Having been led to believe that the city's urban renewal plan would spare much of the Valley and then suddenly discovering that creation of the university would require leveling almost all of the Harrison-Halsted district, neighborhood residents felt angry and betrayed. They thought that the city would pursue a renovation program, rather than wholesale clearance, and concluded that Daley had been disingenuous in urging them to invest anew in their homes and businesses when he secretly harbored plans to obliterate the buildings all along. They further objected to the city's characterization of the blocks targeted for demolition as "slum and blighted areas," arguing that a healthy, resilient community existed there. In the weeks following the mayor's proposal, the residents suspected, the lack of responsiveness from their elected officials and the archdiocese indicated that they had been overrun by the Democratic machine. Even leaders of Hull House, which stood squarely in the projected path of the wrecking ball, remained silent after Daley's shameful about-face. Neighborhood residents accepted what they saw as a fait accompli, until Florence Scala urged resistance.[7]

# Florence Scala and the Exhausting Battle
# for Chicago's Near West Side

After the University of Illinois approved the Harrison-Halsted site on February 10, 1961, the muted reaction in the Valley abruptly gave way to defiance. The local parish priest held a meeting on February 13 at Holy Guardian Angel Church, which had relocated in 1959 to make way for the Dan Ryan Expressway and which was destined to become another casualty of the redevelopment project, to organize resistance to the neighborhood's destruction. With reporters from the daily newspapers in attendance, a standing-room-only crowd at the church vowed to organize in opposition. Attendees prevailed on Florence Scala, a young Italian American housewife who had attended simply out of curiosity, to chair the meeting. At a second gathering a week later at Hull House, at which Scala again presided, the more than five hundred people in attendance agreed to form the Harrison-Halsted Community Group (HHCG) as the vehicle for protest. They also selected Scala and Jesse Binford, a legendary Hull House resident and retired director of the Juvenile Protective Association, to cochair the organization.[8]

In the ensuing months, as the aged and infirm Binford became less engaged in HHCG activities, Florence Scala emerged as the driving force and public face of the protest movement. The daughter of Italian immigrants who had settled in Chicago, Scala was born in 1918 and grew up on the Near West Side. Her father owned a tailor shop where her mother worked as a seamstress. The family lived above the store. While attending McKinley High School, Scala participated in acting and dance programs at Hull House. She found a job after graduation with the Federal Theatre Project, a New Deal agency established to provide employment during the Great Depression for men and women interested in the performing arts. After World War II, during which she performed clerical work at the local draft board, Scala married and settled into the role of homemaker. She and her husband lived with her parents on the second floor of the tailor shop. In 1947, she began serving as the only woman on the NWSPB. Because of her interest in municipal housekeeping, Scala became well known in the Valley as a persistent advocate for neighborhood improvement. Outspoken and unafraid to voice disagreements with more learned members of the NWSPB from Hull House, she emerged as the plainspoken voice of the Valley's common folk (see figure 7.1).[9]

Scala and an HHCG delegation spoke with the mayor in his office to plead their case for sparing the Near West Side. She remembered Daley as having been friendly and gracious at the meeting for the most part, attempting to assuage the fears of the women and promising to build copious amounts of new housing for the displaced residents. The mayor remained

**Figure 7.1** Florence Scala (*left center*) at a meeting to protect homes in the future site of the University of Illinois at Chicago (Credit: "Florence Scala seated with men; UIC construction," FLSC_0002_0046_0097. Florence Scala collection, box 2, folder 26, Special Collections and University Archives, University of Illinois at Chicago)

firm in his commitment to execute the plan, however. Scala concluded the meeting by saying, "I'm going to fight you on this," and she recalled that "his face got so cold and the smile just disappeared."[10]

With the intrepid Scala leading the way, the HHCG wasted no time lodging protests at locations around the city and the state. Day after day, dozens of women picketed noisily outside city hall. In the spring of 1961, the group's representatives appeared before the Chicago City Council, the City Council's Planning and Housing Committee, the Illinois State Legislature, the University of Illinois Board of Trustees, the Illinois Housing Board, and the U.S. Housing and Home Finance Agency; its entreaties went unanswered by each government entity. Attempts to recruit backing from such influential Illinois politicians as U.S. senator Paul Douglas and former governor Adlai E. Stevenson likewise proved fruitless. In the absence of external aid, the battle to preserve the Valley fell to its inhabitants. The grassroots campaign relied mostly on the voluntary efforts of women, especially during daytime hours when husbands, brothers, and sons worked outside the home. Scala embraced the tactic of direct action, a decision designed to attract widespread media coverage and highlight the theme of an arrogant city hall exploiting a vulnerable citizenry. The picture of the plucky underdogs standing up to city hall won sympathetic treatment in the news media, which emphasized that housewives and mothers stood in the forefront of the protests.[11]

Scala's approach owed much to the strategy championed by famed organizer Saul Alinsky, whom she unsuccessfully tried to enlist in the fight against city hall. The son of Russian-Jewish immigrant parents, Alinsky grew up on Chicago's West Side and in 1930 earned a B.A. degree from the University of Chicago, majoring in archaeology. He commenced his community organizing career in the area adjacent to the Union Stock Yards, where thousands of immigrant workers resided in unspeakable squalor. He and park supervisor Joseph B. Meegan forged an alliance in 1939 that included organized labor, the Roman Catholic Church, and various ethnic organizations; they subsequently cofounded the Back of the Yards Neighborhood Council to empower all area residents regardless of nationality, race, or religion. Alinsky hoped to gain agency for working-class people, urging them to pool their efforts in common cause and employ provocative confrontational tactics to achieve their goals. He later transplanted his methods to Woodlawn, an African American neighborhood on the South Side that was seeking to deflect incursions from the neighboring University of Chicago backed by city government. Under Alinsky's tutelage, black clergymen organized the Woodlawn Organization (TWO) in 1961 to protect homes and businesses from the university's expansion and to promote black self-determination. TWO conducted rent strikes, led boycotts of local stores that overcharged customers, and protested the neighborhood's overcrowded and segregated public schools, all the while challenging city hall's penchant for riding roughshod over society's less fortunate citizens. Scala had become an avid admirer of Alinsky's work in the Stock Yards and Woodlawn and thought his assistance would provide her organizing efforts additional publicity and an infusion of energy. Alinsky informed her, however, that the press of TWO activities precluded his participation in the Near West Side fight.[12]

On March 20, Scala led one thousand protesters, mostly women, from St. Francis of Assisi Church to Hull House to publicize their plight. Demonstrators held signs reading "Haven't We Had Enough Daleyism?" and "Daley Is a Dictator—He Won't Get any More Democratic Votes from Us." Shortly thereafter, someone tossed an effigy drenched in ketchup with what appeared to be a bullet hole onto the mayor's front yard. Scala told Daley that the HHCG had nothing to do with the incident, and he privately accepted her assurances. Publicly, he reacted very differently. He made no mention of HHCG's denials and, Scala felt, left the impression with the press that the Near West Side protesters had been responsible. "No one is going to threaten me as mayor of Chicago," he bellowed. "I don't fear death either." Tensions rose, and the mayor doubled the number of police officers guarding his house.[13]

On March 30, the Chicago City Council Housing and Planning Committee considered the mayor's proposal to build the new university campus on 155 acres in the Valley. Speaking in front of an overflow crowd of four hundred persons in city council chambers, Daley called it "unfortunate that in the selection of sites for public improvement some must suffer." He nevertheless defended the plan as essential "to give the young people of Chicago and Cook County an accessible university." As a sop to dissenters, he promised that the university's School of Social Work would be named in honor of Hull House's founder, Jane Addams. As expected, the city council dutifully rubber-stamped the proposal. After the vote, an estimated two hundred HHCG members angrily stormed the mayor's office and left only when promised a meeting between Daley and their representatives. At that gathering, attended by Scala and two other women, the mayor blamed the university trustees for choosing the Near West Side location. He told the delegation, "This has been misrepresented and twisted as though the city had selected the site." Scala then hurriedly met with the university trustees, who deflected responsibility back to the mayor—but also affirmed the choice of the Near West Side location. The university and the city's power brokers had finalized their deal.[14]

Scala and her passionate followers continued nevertheless to conduct sit-ins in city hall corridors and picket on sidewalks outside, gradually gathering endorsements from other community groups around the city. Such organizations as the Citizens' Housing Committee and the Illinois Federation of Mexican Americans joined in the battle for neighborhood empowerment. Still, clearance of the major administrative hurdles in Chicago, Springfield, and Washington, DC, proceeded apace. In May 1961, the entire city council passed the requisite ordinances, and in August the state housing board approved the redevelopment project. In March 1962, the federal Housing and Home Finance Agency allocated the necessary funding for the first phase of construction. The Illinois General Assembly chipped in with a law, which amended existing legislation, allowing Chicago to engage in urban redevelopment by building schools; the state legislature also approved a higher education budget that granted the University of Illinois $4.6 million to purchase land for the new campus on the Near West Side.[15]

As a last resort in the attempt to alter the apparently unavoidable outcome, Scala and her energetic HHCG members looked to state and federal courts. In a flurry of lawsuits, they contested the city's actions on several grounds—that the local government had not held good-faith public hearings prior to making a decision to condemn the land, that municipal authorities had misrepresented the Near West Side as a "slum and blighted" area, and that the actions taken by the city council contradicted existing municipal statutes. (Voluntary financial contributions from the community and sympathetic outsiders, as well as a portion of Jessie Binford's savings, paid the HHCG's considerable legal fees.) Multiple court filings and appeals delayed work on the project for months before the U.S. Supreme Court's refusal on May 13, 1963, to review lower court decisions on the project's legality, effectively terminating legal proceedings. "We know now the thing is pretty much over," acknowledged Scala, who had moved into Hull House along with her husband approximately six months earlier after two bombs exploded at her home. (The explosive devices damaged parts of the house, but Scala and other family members escaped serious injury.) The end of the prolonged court battles relaxed tensions in the Valley, allowing Scala and her husband to return home.[16]

## Scala's Losing Fight to Save the Valley

The evident futility of the long and costly struggle dispirited many Harrison-Halsted residents, but Scala emerged emboldened from the crushing defeat at the hands of city hall—at least temporarily. She ran for alderman of the First Ward in 1963 as an independent write-in candidate, vowing to represent neighborhood interests and democratize city government, and she secured the endorsement of the Independent Voters of Illinois (IVI) and other reform organizations. The Democratic machine apparently perceived Scala as enough of a threat, she charged, to offer her a bribe to withdraw from the race. She lost to incumbent John D'Arco, who had frequently in the past run unopposed, receiving approximately one-third of the vote. After that defeat, Scala retired from political activism and disappeared from public life. The University of Illinois at Chicago Circle, which later became known simply as the University of Illinois at Chicago, opened in 1965. She grudgingly made peace with the gigantic institution that arose virtually on her doorstep. But occasionally the bitterness came flooding back, as it did one night when she was returning home from a community event. "There was all of downtown lit up in front of me and for the first time in many years I felt teary-eyed," she remembered. "I thought, you bastards, you took it all, we don't have anything. I'm an alien person here."[17]

Scala lived unobtrusively during the last years of her life in a sliver of the Valley spared from demolition. When she died in 2007, the local media recalled her fight against city hall in the early 1960s as a hopeless but noble crusade on behalf of a powerless neighborhood group. The *Chicago Tribune* obituary said that "she came to embody the struggle of regular people trying to preserve their communities." Legendary Chicago broadcaster and author Studs Terkel, who had interviewed Scala frequently during and after the

Near West Side battle, called her "my heroine." Terkel, the oracle of the city's common man, said, "She tried with intelligence and courage to save the soul of our city. She represented to me all that Chicago could have been."[18]

Her earnest efforts notwithstanding, Scala's neighborhood vanished swiftly. The city uprooted approximately eight thousand people and 630 businesses to make way for the campus, and several thousand more residents left along with family and friends or departed out of fear of dislodgement. "A lot of the people had lived in that neighborhood their whole lives, the old Italian people," recounted a newspaper reporter. "A lot of them died—they just couldn't make the move." The Near West Side's housing stock fell from an estimated 6,850 units in 1960 to 3,400 units in 1970. "All that housing they were going to put up for us?" grumbled Scala. "I think they put up forty-four units in one place and about fifty units in another. And most of it was too high-priced for the people who lived there." The new university uneasily coexisted with survivors from the old neighborhood—the relatively few Italian Americans, many of them elderly, living on the western fringe of the campus—who competed daily with commuting students for parking spots on streets, alleyways, and driveways. The university administration attempted to pacify critics by renovating the two structures in the historic Hull House complex left standing. (Scala observed sardonically that one of the refurbished Hull House buildings looked like a Howard Johnson's restaurant.) Daley pointed proudly to the striking university buildings visible from the expressways that converged west of downtown, claiming to have made higher education more accessible and affordable for his constituents. Most important for the mayor and other growth-oriented businesspeople obsessed with preservation of the Loop, the campus became an island of high land values close to downtown that slowed the entry of black and Latino populations into the area.[19]

## Who Paid the Price for Near West Side Development?

The downtown-first strategy seemed to work for the mayor and his allies. Yet the cost of protecting the Loop arguably amounted to the dismemberment of three separate communities—East Garfield Park, West Garfield Park, and the Near West Side. (The park itself, the proposed site of the campus, separated East Garfield Park and West Garfield Park.) Unlike the residents of the Valley, the Garfield Park Improvement Association, elected officials, merchants, and several homeowner organizations eagerly welcomed the University of Illinois campus. A blue-collar enclave populated largely by factory workers, the entire Garfield Park area was declining economically in the 1950s as white people began moving out and poor black people from the South and Chicago's South Side replaced them. The community newspaper, the *Garfieldian*, regularly warned that the area would turn into an African American ghetto. The arrival of the university campus, community leaders predicted, would stabilize property values and provide anxious residents with a reason to remain on the West Side. No such salutary developments ensued, however, and the pace of racial turnover accelerated. The area's population skyrocketed from 16 percent African American in 1960 to 85 percent in 1965. By the late 1960s, intense overcrowding, business abandonment, high unemployment, and exploding crime rates turned East Garfield Park and West Garfield Park into two Chicago neighborhoods where ordinary citizens, black and white, would not purchase a home or raise a family.[20] The price of a downtown-first redevelopment plan—the abandonment of three working-class neighborhoods—may well have been regrettable to Chicago's mayor and his business allies. Nevertheless, the power brokers considered the expense, borne exclusively by those residents, acceptable in a high-stakes game.

In a less fortunate metropolis such as Detroit, industry's downfall was more pronounced and the stakes were even higher. The plight of abandoned neighborhoods became arguably more precarious as the city's growth coalition assigned greater value to salvation of the central business district. In the Motor City, the protection of working-class residential areas became—if anything—more challenging than in Chicago. The role of primary spokesperson for neglected neighborhood interests there fell to Mel Ravitz, a leading community activist and politician for more than four decades. Unlike Scala, whose endeavors revolved essentially around the defense of her home turf, Ravitz rallied the troops throughout the city to oppose downtown redevelopment schemes. First as a community organizer, then as an administrator in social welfare agencies, and finally during a protracted tenure on the Detroit Common Council, Ravitz became the undisputed champion of Detroit's forgotten neighborhoods—and the bête noir of the commercial-civic elite.

## Mel Ravitz—the Professor and Detroit's Neighborhoods

Melvin Jerome (Mel) Ravitz was born in New York City in 1924 and moved with his parents to Detroit five years later. After graduating from Central High School in 1942, he earned a bachelor of arts degree in history from Wayne University in 1948, a master of arts degree in sociology from the New School for Social Research in 1949, and a doctor of philosophy degree in sociology from the University of Michigan in 1955. He began teaching as an adjunct instructor in 1949 at Wayne University, which became Wayne State University in 1956, and subsequently rose up the ranks to become a tenured full professor. Teaching intermittently, he remained a member of the university's faculty during his many years of community involvement. A prolific scholar of urban sociology and planning, he presented countless papers at professional meetings and published dozens of articles in refereed journals. As a public intellectual, he filled Detroit newspapers and popular magazines with op-ed pieces, dissents, commentaries, letters to the editor, and book reviews. From 1953 to 1960, he served as the director of community organization for the Detroit Planning Commission, overseeing neighborhood conservation projects as mandated for cities receiving urban renewal funding.[21]

Ravitz's dedication to neighborhood agency became evident during his seven years as the city's director of community organization. In that capacity, he worked tirelessly to form block clubs in which residents assumed responsibility for improving their own environments. In the process, he labored to forge interracial bonds wherein neighborhood residents of different racial and nationality backgrounds worked together to achieve common goals. By 1959, the level of citizen participation in Detroit achieved national recognition as a result of the establishment of approximately six hundred neighborhood organizations with twelve thousand members. Yet despite Ravitz's success at galvanizing disparate groups, actual improvements in declining neighborhoods came grudgingly if at all. The scant progress, city planners agreed, were primarily due to white flight. Ravitz concurred, saying, "Many white families living now in neighborhoods that are beginning to be occupied by Negroes will not invest any sizable sum of money in home improvement." Assessing the disappointing results years later, he concluded, "We couldn't stop the racial and social-economic tides." Frustrated and impatient, Ravitz turned to electoral politics as a better way of building strong communities. The associations he formed during his seven years as director of community organization provided the political base necessary to enter the world of Detroit politics and government.[22]

## An Intellectual in City Politics

In 1961, Ravitz successfully ran for Detroit Common Council, the city's legislative body, composed of nine members chosen in at-large elections; he was reelected in 1965 and 1969 (in the latter year as council president) before relinquishing his seat in 1973 to run in the Democratic mayoral primary won by Coleman Young. From 1974 to 1982, he served as staff director of the Detroit-Wayne County Community Mental Health Services Board before leaving to begin the first of another four terms on the common council.

**Figure 7.2** Mel Ravitz meeting with Detroit's Black Panthers (Credit: Walter P. Reuther Library, Archives of Labor and Urban Affairs, Wayne State University)

He retired from elective office in 1997. A staunch advocate of regional solutions to urban problems, Ravitz also chaired the Wayne County Board of Supervisors from 1966 to 1968 and the Southeast Michigan Council of Governments, which he helped to create, in 1970–1971. Detroit's best-known white liberal city official from the 1960s through the 1990s, he championed racial equality, urban planning, grassroots democracy, and community empowerment. (See figure 7.2.)[23]

As a member of the Detroit Common Council for twenty-eight years, Ravitz earned a reputation for fairness, integrity, hard work—and eccentricity. In many ways the embodiment of an ivory-tower intellectual, he wore horn-rimmed glasses, smoked a pipe, and gave long-winded speeches couched in pretentious language. Opponents in the council and elsewhere in local government often mocked the erudite professor as impractical, naïve, and hopelessly idealistic. They ridiculed "Councilman Egghead" for such visionary proposals as cross-district busing to achieve racial desegregation of public schools, taxing suburbanites to ease Detroit's fiscal distress, and consolidating the dozens of municipal governments in southeastern Michigan into a single regional authority. His supporters tolerated his peculiarities and seemingly outlandish ideas, appreciating that he ceaselessly advanced creative new solutions to the city's many problems. The voters repeatedly returned him to the common council because he never waffled on controversial issues and always defended the powerless against the powerful. In a city with a growing and eventually hegemonic black electorate, the white Ravitz won election after election because of his unwavering condemnation of racial inequality and defense of all declining neighborhoods. He chastised Ford, General Motors, and Chrysler for their meager investment in the city's welfare. In his view, the automobile conglomerates freely used city services and facilities but remained isolated in their suburban refuges when urban crises called for huge doses of corporate investment. In particular, he chided the Big Three for failing to maintain blue-collar jobs inside the city accessible to his black constituents. Most important to the survivors in Detroit's beleaguered neighborhoods, Ravitz never hesitated during his seven terms in elective office to call attention to their main concerns. Ravitz always defended community requests for better schools and safer streets against the rapacious interests of downtown-oriented businesspeople and the politicians in league with them.[24]

Ravitz earned his reputation as the common council's perennial contrarian by questioning one downtown redevelopment proposal after another. His obstinacy, he explained to the city's director of community and economic development in 1982, was owing to historical, geographical, and practical concerns, as well as his determination to oppose an unequal distribution of resources that operated to the detriment of neighborhoods. Ravitz believed that, for such a big city, Detroit had always been distinguished by a compact central business district concentrated on a handful of thoroughfares—Woodward Avenue, Washington Boulevard, and Broadway Street, principally— which made a downtown-first strategy even more questionable. The city was traditionally composed of a plentitude of single-family houses with factories scattered throughout residential neighborhoods, and the population's preference for home ownership rather than renting minimized the demand for apartments and condominiums in the urban core. The automobile giants had historically located their corporate headquarters—as well as a plethora of production facilities—in Dearborn, Highland Park, and other suburbs, minimizing their influence in the heart of Detroit. For decades, wrote Ravitz, the city acquiesced in the demise of downtown by spurning mass transit, building a massive freeway system that facilitated business and family decentralization, ignoring the economic impact of suburban shopping malls, and unquestioningly doing the bidding of the automobile magnates. The chickens were coming home to roost.[25]

To save a city in freefall, said Ravitz, members of the ruling class such as automobile mogul Henry Ford II and real-estate tycoon Max Fisher were banking on the enhancement of a downtown that had never played much of a role in Detroit's economic well-being. Worse, without sharing their plans with the common council or the public, the business elite was forsaking the commercial district encompassing Woodward, Washington, and Broadway while attempting to relocate the downtown southward and eastward along the river. In doing so, Ravitz charged, the city would be abandoning "those businesses and buildings that have tried to stay and serve in the older parts of downtown. They will continue to experience the loss of tenants as the downtown shift occurs." The decision to fashion an entirely new epicenter for the metropolitan region, a daunting prospect in any event, seemed particularly unfeasible in a city lacking experience with a large and magnetic central business district—especially when the people living in Detroit's residential expanses desperately needed help.[26]

Most important, said Ravitz, there remained the overriding concerns of equity and fairness. City hall's favoritism for downtown in the allocation of funding left neighborhoods with poorly maintained streets, alleys, and parks; reduced budgets for public safety made it impossible for a shrinking police force to curb crime or an understaffed and underequipped fire department to keep pace with an arson epidemic. (Vandals torched thousands of abandoned houses a year during the 1970s and 1980s after pilfering the plumbing, copper wiring, and anything else of value they could find in the vacant structures.) City hall's neglect resulted in high rates of teenage pregnancy, infant mortality, school delinquency, illiteracy, drug abuse, unemployment, and homelessness—all factors that drove taxpayers out of moldering neighborhoods. Ravitz congratulated Joe Stroud, editor of the *Detroit Free Press*, for publishing a scathing editorial that condemned city government for shoring up downtown while ignoring the rest of the city. "For years," wrote the councilman, "I have been urging, pleading, and battling to assure a fairer balance of City resources to support our residential neighborhoods." Furious that the city's leadership had disregarded his warnings, Ravitz lamented to Stroud that "we will awake one day and find that everyone who could leave the neighborhoods has done so and that, while we have a shiny new core area, all the rest of Detroit has become a throw-away town."[27]

## Fights with Mayor Young

Ravitz clashed repeatedly with Mayor Coleman Young, who devoted his five mayoral terms to the revitalization of the central business district. The very public disagreements between the iconoclastic councilman and the autocratic mayor became increasingly vitriolic in the 1980s and 1990s as economic conditions in Detroit rapidly deteriorated and the local administration persisted in looking downtown for solutions. Young used funds earmarked for neighborhoods in downtown renewal schemes, repeatedly diverting grants from federal programs in a manner that somehow escaped notice in Washington, DC. Ravitz singled out the mayor's brazen misuse of Community Development Block Grant (CDBG) funding as particularly egregious. Although the mayor had blamed steep cuts in CDBG funding imposed by the Reagan administration as the cause of reduced support for neighborhood investment in 1985, Ravitz identified $18 million hijacked by city hall for downtown projects as an unjustifiable action that made an untenable situation worse. The CDBG initiative, intended to benefit low- and moderate-income people, had become essentially a slush fund for riverfront and Woodward Avenue redevelopment.[28]

To Young's claim that Detroit was indeed disbursing substantial CDBG funds to neighborhoods, Ravitz insisted that the mayor was dissembling to avoid providing financial support of low- and moderate-income residents. The councilman revealed that the million dollars allocated to six neighborhoods in the 1986–1987 CDBG budget underwrote public improvements only to streets and sidewalks in areas adjoining major economic redevelopment projects launched by the city. In the Corktown neighborhood, for example, infrastructure upgrades complemented the municipality's renovation of Tiger Stadium. Ravitz objected that the money designated ostensibly for community improvement that year allocated less than 12 percent of the sum to housing rehabilitation, earmarked only 1 percent for public services to residents, and spurned the development of small commercial strips altogether.[29]

Nor did Ravitz approve of the local incentives devised by the mayor and other members of the common council in their recurring effort to retain and recruit businesses. He disputed the claim that tax-increment financing (TIF) benignly created capital for redevelopment by simply requiring the city to forego tax collections for greater rewards at a later time. He warned that the city lost the revenue traditionally placed in its general fund—money used on a regular basis for schools, roads, public safety, and other service provision—to the cost of downtown and industrial redevelopment. For Ravitz, TIFs became a pernicious form of "trickle-down economics" whereby the commercial-civic elite made immediate use of newly created capital and then expected neighborhoods to wait and hope for the benefits to reach them.[30]

Ravitz likewise condemned tax abatements, the use of which Young touted as a crucial means of attracting business, for their consistent failure to create jobs for Detroiters. Speaking to his common council colleagues in 1989, he disclosed that corporations that had recently received tax abatements from the city had actually reduced the number of workers they employed by more than forty-five thousand. Moreover, Detroit, under the mayor's direction, had accrued hundreds of millions of dollars in debt underwriting the construction or rehabilitation of manufacturing facilities—and, he warned, the municipality would be stuck with those financial obligations whether the investments paid off handsomely for businesses or factories closed. The fundamental problem was lack of accountability. Why, he asked rhetorically, should the city instead of the corporation incur the risk?[31]

## Ravitz and the Politics of Corporate Markets

Detroit's love affair with tax abatements, suggested Ravitz, stemmed from a widely accepted view of marketplace economics encouraged by corporations that compelled government jurisdictions to compete for business in Darwinian fashion against other communities, states, and even foreign countries. To the great benefit of business executives, cities engaged in fierce bidding wars that drove tax incentives ever higher. According to the conventional wisdom, which the skeptical Detroit councilman viewed as myth, the failure to provide businesses with lower taxes would inevitably lead to dire consequences for the city. If nothing else, the failure to offer incentives would appear to the voters as though elected officials were not doing everything possible to preserve and attract jobs. Moreover, the refusal to offer generous incentives might saddle the city with the reputation of having an unfavorable business climate. Ravitz reported that a number of published studies had dismissed the allure of low taxes as the most compelling factor in luring business to an area, citing as more important such factors as sound local governance, high-quality education, good transportation, satisfactory wages, and public safety. Nevertheless, Detroiters accepted as an article of faith that municipalities utilized tax abatements effectively to recruit business.[32]

Because Ravitz felt that corporations had every incentive to make pie-in-the-sky promises to municipalities in exchange for lucrative inducements—and had no disincentive against doing so—the time had come for local governments to establish rules to hold business firms accountable. In 1989, he introduced a resolution to the common council requiring the city to negotiate contracts with all recipients of financial incentives. The contracts would stipulate that companies accepting economic development packages honor three conditions: First, the firm must provide the number of jobs promised at the facility or reimburse the city proportionately. Second, employment must continue throughout the duration of the city's debt-service obligations. Third, if the facility closed, the corporation must compensate Detroit for any portion of the outstanding debt for which the city remained liable. The mayor rejected the resolution as an unrealistic set of conditions that no astute chief executive officer of a major corporation would even consider.[33]

Ravitz also opposed industrial redevelopment efforts launched by the mayor as yet additional ill-conceived schemes that would likely fail and transfer resources away from neighborhoods in the process. He roundly criticized Young's support for the Central Industrial Park (Poletown) automobile assembly plant built by General Motors, which Detroit had approved during Ravitz's eight-year hiatus from the common council, because of the destruction of a healthy working-class neighborhood to make way for the factory. He pointed to the massive cost overruns that accumulated during completion of the project but especially emphasized the indefensible disruptions imposed on the people uprooted by the plant's construction. Once again, he suggested, a corporate leviathan abetted by city hall had trampled on the interests of workers and residents. Always distrustful of the promises made by corporate shills and complicit government spokesmen, he correctly predicted that the number of workers hired by the plant would fall far short of the optimistic projections offered in advance. Whereas the automobile maker had promised 6,000 new jobs, Ravitz wrote, the company hired barely 3,700. Even if 6,000 new jobs had materialized, each new position would have cost the city between $40,000 and $50,000 from the outlay of incentives. Ravitz warned that the city would never achieve much of a financial return from its investment in the industrial renewal project. Poletown "will be a very advantageous thing for GM," he said in 1984, "but I am doubtful whether the city will find it equally bright and smiley down the road."[34]

The mayor followed the Poletown investment with a strategy similar to the one at Chrysler's aged Jefferson Avenue plant, eliciting the same rebuke from Ravitz. Chrysler threatened to shutter its antiquated factory and, in order to salvage thousands of jobs that would be lost when the plant closed, the city granted the corporation six tax abatements between 1974 and 1988. When the company proposed to build a new facility nearby on Jefferson Avenue, the city provided a host of inducements in exchange for the corporation's promise to retain 15,000 jobs. Only 2,500 workers found employment when the new plant opened in 1992, however. The disappointing dealings with Chrysler, no less than in the General Motors debacle, confirmed for Ravitz the pitfalls inherent in the city's bargaining with corporations in pursuit of industrial redevelopment.[35]

Ravitz became convinced that subservience to corporations and an obsession with downtown redevelopment would only further bifurcate Detroit, completing the division of the metropolis into two glaringly unequal communities. Along the riverfront and in the central business district, the prescient Ravitz foresaw, a select group of suburbanites, downtown residents, visitors, and conventioneers would enjoy jazz concerts, ball games, ethnic festivals, yacht regattas, and Fourth of July fireworks in a new playground for the well-to-do paid for by tax dollars. "Detroit's future seems to be that of recreation and entertainment center for the region," said the councilman in 1985, "but only for those who can afford the events and the facilities." Meanwhile, the people who lived in residential neighborhoods sadly watched the areas around their homes decline. Even if it meant taking a loss on the sale of their houses, many despairing Detroiters—an estimated 75–80 people a day that year—fled the city. Despite the frenetic activity downtown, municipal budget shortages kept city agencies from providing the basic services necessary for them to stay and raise their families. "I've become increasingly disturbed and even angry," said Ravitz; "I think Detroit has become a worse place to live for the vast majority of Detroiters."[36]

By the time that Ravitz retired from public life in 1997, he had become even more despondent about Detroit's future. He believed that investment in a downtown-first redevelopment strategy, which had been entrenched in the city for decades despite his efforts, had borne little fruit. Meanwhile, population and jobs had continued to disappear from the Motor City. After Coleman Young decided in 1994 not to seek a seventh mayoral term, Ravitz hoped that a regime change would initiate a new approach that took full account of the importance of neighborhoods. The councilman supported Dennis Archer, a respected attorney and justice of the Michigan Supreme Court whose progressive campaign rhetoric seemed like a breath of fresh air after twenty years of Young's bellicose oratory. Archer served two terms as Detroit mayor and, much to Ravitz's disappointment, helped to finalize his predecessor's work to build new stadiums and casinos in the central business district. Ignoring his earlier allusions to neighborhood restoration, Young's successor found governance easier when working cooperatively with Detroit's commercial-civic elite. A disappointed Ravitz detected a substantial discrepancy between candidate Archer's words and Mayor Archer's deeds. "I think that he is somewhat the captive of the corporate world," Ravitz observed sadly in 1997, "and is not focusing on what he ought to build the kind of city I want to see."[37]

## The Road Not Taken

Ravitz's exertions as an elected official on behalf of Detroit's many ailing neighborhoods cut across racial lines, defending the imperiled interests of black and white residents alike. Few at the time commented on the apparent anomaly of Ravitz, a well-educated white male, defending black neighborhoods against a high school–educated African American man defending white, downtown interests. Scala's leadership contained the equally unlikely fact (at that time) of a high school–educated female taking on the powerful Daley. Selected for a leadership position by her neighbors, Scala fought for Chicago's Near West Side to protect homes, businesses, and cherished institutions. Altogether, however, the efforts of these two community leaders repeatedly foundered against powerful alliances that melded political power and financial influence. Scala, Ravitz, and their mostly unorganized constituents were no match for Mayor Daley, Mayor Young, and top executives such as Hughston McBain and Holman Pettibone and automobile magnates like Henry Ford. Corporate and political leaders and their enormous legal staffs worked full-time on resolving disputes in their favor; Scala's and Ravitz's overwhelmed followers mounted protests after long days at work. It should be no surprise that the allure of private-public partnerships to restore decaying downtowns among Chicago's and Detroit's corporate and political leaders would carry the day. And, in turn, Ravitz's and Scala's warnings about the destruction of lower- and working-class communities gained little traction among political and business leaders still hoping to restart growth in troubled industrial cities. The idea of a prosperous downtown that would eventually pull outlying neighborhoods into their cash-flow orbits was impervious to challenge. The majority of elected officials in Detroit, Chicago, and many other cities clung tightly to the vision of a revived central business district as the vanguard of urban renaissance. From their well-appointed offices in city hall, surrounded by like-minded bureaucrats and politicians, rubbing elbows daily with the metropolitan region's richest and most influential citizens, mayors almost always followed the path of least resistance and enlisted in the crusade for downtown redevelopment.[38]

During heated mayoral election campaigns, candidates espousing the need for a revitalized downtown invariably issued pro forma assurances that they would not forget about needy residential neighborhoods. In truth, the exigencies of local politics demanded as much. Once the mayors were ensconced in city hall, however, those promises receded in importance to the allure of building new stadiums, convention centers, casinos, and other downtown attractions. The very few mayors who put neighborhoods first during the campaign and refused to deviate once in city hall encountered great resistance to their progressive platforms. The story of Cleveland mayor Dennis Kucinich served as a cautionary tale for any mavericks intent on defying urban elites. Kucinich seemed to go out of his way to antagonize Cleveland's wealthiest businesspeople, warred openly with the city council, narrowly survived a recall vote, and saw his reputation as a populist erode as he lost a series of ill-conceived confrontations with his wealthy and powerful adversaries. His single term in office, agreed opponents and supporters alike, achieved little to improve the quality of the city's neighborhoods. Kucinich's unceremonious departure from city hall paved the way for his successor, George Voinovich, the quintessential businessperson's mayor, who promptly cultivated an era of good feelings downtown.[39]

Another severe critic of unrestricted downtown redevelopment, Chicago Mayor Harold Washington, seemed at first blush to have replicated Kucinich's failure. In fact, different circumstances in Chicago and Cleveland produced decidedly different outcomes. A deft and experienced politician who never considered waging open warfare against the Windy City's elite, Washington worked hard to forge alliances with State Street merchants and LaSalle Street bankers. Rather than terminate all local government support for economic growth in the Loop, he wanted to redress historical inequities by granting neighborhoods an expanded (if not equal) share of resources. Signaling a shift in priorities, he emphasized jobs and not real estate. In a series of documents and pronouncements, Washington made clear his desire to seek a balance between downtown and neighborhood redevelopment. Along the way, he met opposition of a sort different from what Kucinich encountered. Having become the city's first African American mayor by winning a racially charged election in 1983, Washington spent most of his time in office battling a hostile white city council majority that openly espoused racism and opposed his programs at every turn. Stymied throughout most of his time in office, Washington was able to redirect resources from the Loop to the neighborhoods only to a very limited extent. Just months after winning reelection in 1987, he died tragically of a massive heart attack with no chosen successor in the wings to implement his agenda. A toxic mix of race and politics conspired against his ambitious plans for redistribution. Absent Washington's cajoling to ensure neighborhoods a larger slice of the fiscal pie, Chicago's political economy quickly reverted to normal. Mayors Richard M. Daley and Rahm I. Emanuel embraced downtown redevelopment with a vengeance in the decades after Washington's death, determined to secure Chicago's recognition as a global city. The neighborhoods again became an afterthought.[40]

Mayors Kucinich and Washington came up short in their advocacy of neighborhood uplift, the inefficacy of their contrasting approaches in very different cities underscoring the resiliency of the dominant preference for downtown redevelopment. Because of the disinclination of mayors to redirect the spotlight from the central business district and tony neighborhoods to decaying areas of their cities, skeptics fully expected the defeats suffered by Scala, Ravitz, and other activists at the hands of the investment class. Neither the few reform-minded politicians who managed to win mayoral races nor the greater number of community activists who fought city halls on behalf of their constituents successfully challenged the drive for downtown redevelopment. The determination to turn downtown into a lucrative magnet for tourists, sports fans, and other pleasure-seekers, a hardheaded business decision made by the municipality's most influential citizens, left the poor and working-class inhabitants of residential neighborhoods expendable. The people left behind in Pittsburgh, Chicago, and other cities fared no better at the start of the twenty-first century.[41]

# III

# Downtown's Continuing Allure, 2000–2020

I n the late 1940s, Richard King Mellon and David L. Lawrence launched a pathbreaking public-private partnership aimed at reviving downtown Pittsburgh. More than a half-century later, a new generation of the city's politicians and boosters described the makeover as extraordinary in scope. Academics and journalists from around the nation and the world pointed to Pittsburgh as a prime example of how fruitful collaboration between city halls and local business elites could rescue cities from postindustrial squalor. The gritty steel center, corporate executives asserted, had become a model for downtown redevelopment, its beautiful skyscrapers, lively culture center, and enthusiastic sports fans bringing vibrancy to a previously somnolent area. Health care, higher education, high-technology enterprises, and finance had replaced environmentally perilous mills and factories in and around the central business district. Once the unsightly and noisome component of an industrial system that relentlessly polluted air, land, and water, the three rivers converging at downtown had become a scenic and usable asset for the municipality. Pittsburgh enthusiasts also pointed to several inhospitable neighborhoods that had morphed into well-appointed middle-class sanctuaries with affordable housing and accessible leisure options. The expansion of universities and hospitals, while displacing many longtime residents, had infused tired neighborhoods with a new energy and purpose. Indeed, according to metrics applied by the Rand McNally map company in 1985, Pittsburgh had become "America's most livable city"—a designation echoed by several business associations and magazines in the following years. From the exquisitely furnished boardrooms of corporate headquarters, banks, and financial institutions in the Golden Triangle, the investments in downtown revitalization undertaken by Lawrence's successors in the mayor's office, including Richard S. Caliguiri (1977–1988) and Thomas J. "Tom" Murphy Jr. (1994–2006), appeared to have paid off handsomely. Such in short form were the celebratory statements of downtown Pittsburgh's corporate boosters.[1]

In the first two decades of the twenty-first century, Pittsburgh's leadership continued along the same path of prioritizing downtown redevelopment. With the opening of the Rivers Casino next to the Carnegie Science Center in 2009, the city enhanced its pursuit of the tourist dollar by embracing legalized gambling. When telltale signs of aging began to show in Three Rivers Stadium, Mayor Tom Murphy's administration doubled down on the commitment to professional sports by building two new venues to replace the deteriorating one. After the demolition of Three Rivers Stadium in 2001, PNC Park for baseball and Heinz Field for football opened that same year on the north bank of the Allegheny River. Two years later, the city completed a $354 million renovation of the David L. Lawrence Convention Center that more than doubled the size of the facility. The State of Downtown Pittsburgh Report, issued in 2018, found that $8.5 billion had been invested within the targeted area during the previous ten years. As well, construction had begun that year on twenty-eight new projects worth approximately $1 billion, including hotels, parking garages, and retail outlets, with more designs for future ventures on the drawing board.[2]

But, despite the impressive transformation of the Pittsburgh economy—celebrated by boosters as "Brawn Forged into Brain"—the extent of the redevelopment achievement remained dubious. While the most prosperous members of the city clearly benefited from the heralded private-public partnership, questions persisted about the efficacy and fairness of the Pittsburgh Renaissance for most community residents. According to the 2010 U.S. Census, a quarter-million residents of the Pittsburgh metropolitan area's 2.3 million persons lived in poverty. The lot of the city's African American population, historically lamentable, remained hazardous. In 2010, Pittsburgh's African Americans suffered a much higher unemployment rate than white workers, as well as the highest incidence of African American poverty of any major U.S. city. The unabashed boosterism notwithstanding, overhauled Pittsburgh had done nothing to address the problems of poverty and racial inequality.[3]

Moreover, skeptics of the much-ballyhooed renaissance pointed at the incongruity of a supposedly resurgent city, hamstrung by declining revenue and crippling deficits, surrendering its financial operation to the Commonwealth of Pennsylvania. In 2003, Pittsburgh entered the distressed city program under Act 47, passed in 1987 as a temporary measure to allow cash-strapped communities to regain their financial equilibrium. In the program, elected officials in distressed cities answered to unelected, state-appointed overseers authorized to approve all municipal expenditures. In 2014, Mayor William M. Peduto rejected a recommendation that Pittsburgh withdraw from the program, conceding that the city still remained incapable of paying for daily operations, funding employee pensions, and maintaining infrastructure. How could a city enjoying such a glorious rebirth remain "temporarily" distressed for more than a decade? Many of Mayor Tom Murphy's critics blamed the chronic financial problems on his unwise annual diversion of tax dollars from the regular operating budget to the speculative development fund. Others seeking more enduring causes for the city's mounting indebtedness singled out the proliferation of nonprofit corporations, especially universities and hospitals, which left fully 40 percent of the municipality's land tax-exempt. In both explanations, Pittsburgh's willing embrace of the "distressed" designation underscored serious flaws in its reputed success story.[4]

Pittsburgh's executives and political leaders had indeed countered deindustrialization with a sweeping plan to alter the fundamentals of the city's economy, remaking great swaths of the cityscape in the process. Yet fervid talk about Pittsburgh's rebound emanated mostly from persons connected to downtown's renovated areas or comfortable residence in higher-income districts. Chamber of Commerce members who issued grandiose claims of success ignored glaring shortcomings in the city's less-valued precincts. Vulnerable workers and members of racial minorities in slumping residential neighborhoods registered dissatisfaction with the narrow scope of the redevelopment effort. Despite all the praise for the emerging service-oriented economy, distraught workers with insufficient skills for the new high-technology emphasis found themselves unable to maintain the good wages and benefits they had enjoyed before mills and foundries closed. Enrollment in Pittsburgh's underfunded public schools fell steadily throughout the 1990s, and those pupils who remained performed poorly on standardized tests. In 2000, for example, the city's schoolchildren scored 84 points below the state mean on the SAT test. As historian Tracy Neumann concluded in her study of Pittsburgh and Hamilton, Ontario, "Local officials abandoned social democratic goals in favor of corporate welfare programs, fostering an increasing economic inequality among their residents in the process."[5]

Leaders in St. Louis and our other cities followed a similar course of action. In the search for new economic lifelines after the collapse of their manufacturing base, politicians and top-level executives chose to rehabilitate downtowns while ignoring the plight of impoverished minority neighborhoods nearby. While local media hyped business success stories, conditions in troubled neighborhoods remained dire. In Chicago, widely praised for its vitality under business-friendly mayors Richard M. Daley and Rahm Emanuel, lingering poverty and astronomical homicide rates left large sections of the metropolis and its inhabitants on the outside looking in at the uplifting changes downtown. Inhabitants of the Windy City's feral neighborhoods constantly lived in fear of mass shootings and innocent children killed by stray bullets. Detroit lost residents by the hundreds of thousands and teetered on the edge of fiscal collapse for decades, finally tumbling into insolvency when the State of Michigan put it in bankruptcy and assumed total control of local government in 2013. St. Louis lost nearly two-thirds of its population from its level in the 1950 census while the Gateway Arch and new stadiums downtown failed to lure the members of the middle-class from the county back into the city. Local governments in Cleveland and Philadelphia, in close cooperation with economic elites, likewise spent liberally to make their downtowns more accessible and attractive to suburbanites, tourists, and other visitors in the vain hope that the ailing cities would thrive in the new leisure economy. At the same time, as the flight of the middle class reduced revenue, quality in the public schools suffered—which, in turn, drove more families to the suburbs in search of better schools. In each city, the disillusioned inhabitants of the aging blue-collar neighborhoods staged grassroots demonstrations. Those irate protestors hoped to stave off their ongoing economic and cultural losses.[6]

In the twenty-first century, no metropolis fared as well as Chicago in the search among embattled Rustbelt cities for inspiring comeback stories. Of course, praise for the Windy City owed overwhelmingly to the impression created by the bustling financial district, Rubloff's North Michigan Avenue, and exquisite lakeside neighborhoods. Charged with explaining Chicago's resilience in the midst of the kind of wrenching economic change that devastated other communities, experts have mentioned several factors that accounted for Chicago's stunning turnaround—a favorable location at the center of the nation's trade and transportation networks, economic diversification, a mature infrastructure, an abundance of powerful financial institutions, innovative commodities and securities exchanges that readily attracted capital, a cluster of first-rate research universities, and a stable and supportive local government. Blessed with such advantages, Chicago achieved the coveted status of global city.[7]

In a stark contrast that political scientist Edward Goetz termed the "Detroit Scenario," other Rustbelt cities succumbed to a vicious downward spiral of manufacturing loss and population contraction that left mighty industrial cities hollowed out. Detroit's fall, reflected in the lurid imagery of postindustrial squalor known as "ruin porn," was certainly not unique. Great swaths of the cityscape in St. Louis, Philadelphia, and Cleveland—and indeed Chicago—all bore the look of deserted wastelands. In comparison with other Rust Belt metropolises, Chicago proved most successful at establishing a highly desirable brand—a good place to do business. But, as in the other cities, the brand came at considerable cost, a price borne, once again, mostly by lower-income families and disadvantaged minorities.[8]

# 8

# Richard M. Daley and Chicago's Thriving Downtown

Richard M. Daley, who served as Chicago mayor from 1989 to 2011, was one of the most influential urban leaders of his time. Daley's remarkable successes led Philadelphia Mayor Edward G. Rendell to say "He's the best mayor in the history of the country, I think." No one could dispute the magnificence Daley engineered in and around Chicago's Loop—Millennium Park, Grant Park's beautification, the South Museum Campus, a refurbished Navy Pier, and the further aggrandizement of North Michigan Avenue that developer Arthur Rubloff had started decades earlier. Under Daley's leadership, Chicago affirmed its place as one of the world's most strikingly beautiful cities. Visitors to Daley's Chicago never failed to comment on how the attractive central business district crackled with energy. State Street businesses rebounded from an earlier period of stagnation; LaSalle Street bankers, lawyers, and commodities traders presided over multimillion-dollar deals; and North Michigan Avenue emporiums sold high-end merchandise to wealthy shoppers. Moreover, new investment invigorated doleful areas adjacent to the revitalized downtown.

But Daley's many successes remained confined to Chicago's downtown and several prosperous neighborhoods. As gentrification proceeded in sedate North Side enclaves, overlooked portions of the South and West Sides continued to endure astronomical rates of unemployment, poverty, and crime; the city's epidemic of homicides became a national scandal and a source of horror and despair for families and neighborhood residents. By the time that Daley stepped down as mayor in 2011, his unwavering commitment to downtown redevelopment had paid off handsomely for Chicago's prosperous business core, which included attorneys, developers, financial executives, and its comfortable middle-class neighborhoods. The impact of his actions on the rest of the city seemed decidedly less beneficent. For the unfortunate Chicagoans who occupied substandard housing, sent their children to underperforming public schools, and survived day-to-day in violent neighborhoods, the city offered little hope for a brighter future.[1]

## Taking Control of Chicago Politics

Richard M. Daley's election as mayor represented to many Chicagoans a regal restoration, a return to the policies and practices of his father, Richard J. Daley, who had served in that office from 1955 to 1976. Daley *père* had wholeheartedly thrown the weight of Chicago's powerful Democratic machine behind the task of downtown redevelopment during his twenty-one years in office. The unprecedented construction boom in the Loop, a breakthrough triggered by the mayor's growth-friendly policies, transformed a tired, fraying central business district into an architectural jewel and affirmed the city's reputation as a great place to do business. After his death in 1976, disruptions in the long-standing entente between corporate boardrooms and city hall led to years of uncertainty. Political tumult ensued under Daley's immediate successors, who enjoyed decidedly little success in meeting the city's manifold challenges. Mayors Michael J. Bilandic and Jane M. Byrne, machine loyalists who remained faithful to Daley's downtown-first vision, lacked his political skills and quickly succumbed to mounting voter disquietude. The city's first African American mayor, Harold Washington, assembled a rainbow coalition of black people, Latinos, and white liberals and promised reform that would dismantle downtown's monopoly on city investment and respond to neighborhood interests. The embattled mayor met implacable resistance for most of his time in city hall and then, finally blessed with a governing majority in the city council, died shortly after reelection in 1987. After the brief interim administration of a nondescript caretaker, Eugene Sawyer, the younger Daley easily won the 1989 mayoral election. The new mayor promised to be a healer in a city roiled by racial turmoil in recent years and disavowed the kind of machine politics for which his father had become infamous. At the same time, he pledged to pursue economic growth through the redevelopment of the Loop and adjacent areas—primarily via skyscraper construction and the recruitment of corporate headquarters to Chicago—an announcement widely celebrated by a corporate elite yearning for the reinstatement of political stability and the return of friendly benefactors to city hall.[2]

Subsequent to his resounding triumph in 1989, Daley won reelection five times—in 1991, 1995, 1999, 2003, and 2007—before declining to run again in 2011. His record twenty-two years in the mayor's office surpassed the previous standard for longevity established by his father. His margins of victory improved after winning an impressive 56 percent of the vote in 1989, rising to 68 percent in 1991, 60 percent in 1995, 72 percent in 1999, 78 percent in 2003, and 71 percent in 2007. A political colossus whose skillful coalition building undercut electoral challenges from minority candidates in an increasingly diverse metropolis, Daley dismembered the last remnants of the black-Latino-white liberal alliance that twice carried Harold Washington to victory in the mid-1980s. Despite his parochial background—he grew up in the tribal Irish-Catholic neighborhood of Bridgeport and received undergraduate and law degrees from DePaul University—he cultivated voter support beyond the city's insular white bungalow belts. Daley built a solid voter base within the growing Latino population and successfully cultivated support within the politically active gay community, especially in the trendy Boystown and Andersonville neighborhoods on the North Side where luxury high-rises and boutique grocery stores became commonplace. He managed to survive several embarrassing scandals implicating family members and close friends, including the revelation that the mayor's nephew and his partner had bilked the city's pension fund for $68 million, and remained extremely popular with a broad spectrum of Chicago voters. When Daley chose not to seek reelection in 2011, he did so absent a groundswell of opposition to his serving a seventh term.[3]

While stringing together an impressive series of electoral victories, Daley also dominated the local polity in a manner reminiscent of his father's suzerainty in the 1950s and 1960s. He subdued the bellicose city council, a constant source of division during the preceding years, in no small part thanks to a law that allowed the mayor to fill vacancies by appointment instead of by special elections. (At times during Daley's lengthy administration, fully one-third of the city council membership consisted of his appointees.) He solidified his mastery of local government through control of the Chicago Housing Authority, Chicago Public Schools, the Chicago Park District, and the Chicago Transit Authority, agencies that by law operated independently of the municipality. Traditional opponents of Chicago's unsavory politics feared the return of Richard J. Daley's autocratic political machine, but a modernized, streamlined political organization emerged instead in the 1990s. A "pin-striped machine" fueled by real-estate investors, attorneys, and financiers in the Loop replaced blue-collar precinct captains who had safeguarded the interests of far-flung ethnic neighborhoods. Reporters no longer spotted pinky rings and AFL-CIO windbreakers in city hall corridors but instead saw tasseled loafers and alligator briefcases. The omnipotent Daley marshaled the forces of disparate city agencies and commanded a compliant city council in the single-minded pursuit of one goal—to ensure Chicago's inclusion among the exclusive list of global cities.[4]

## Daley and the Global City Idea

In 1989, soon after his first election, Daley announced his determination to elevate Chicago's reputation as an exemplary place in which to live and transact business. Daley's key idea was to bring about a wholesale transformation of a fading manufacturing hub that was confronting an ominous postindustrial future. "You're not going to see factories back," he told an audience during his first campaign. "I think you have to look at the financial markets—banking, service industry, the development of O'Hare Field, tourism, trade. This is going to be an international city." In order to complete that conversion from smoke and noise to glass and steel as rapidly as possible, Daley warmly embraced the city's progrowth coalition that consisted of real-estate, banking, insurance, and law firms. Throughout his years in office, construction cranes and the discordant sound of rivet guns dominated downtown. Builders completed nineteen of the city's thirty tallest skyscrapers during his administration.[5]

Building on the 1958 Development Plan for the Central Area of Chicago, Daley recommended demolition of the unsightly warehouses, working-class housing, and light manufacturing in districts surrounding the Loop. In their place, Daley sought to expand the central business district's commercial, leisure, and cultural activities. Corporate headquarters, a multipurpose sports arena, high-rise condominiums, and Michelin-starred restaurants were to replace block after block of modest single-family dwellings, single-room-occupancy hotels, and outdated multistory factories just outside the downtown's perimeter. The construction of upscale housing and the renovation of old residential buildings attracted grocery stores, pharmacies, coffee shops, and other businesses to serve middle-class newcomers. The new uses for real estate promised an improvement in the tax base in economically stagnant neighborhoods. The transformation usually entailed the replacement of lower-income African American households with younger, well-off European Americans. The accommodating mayor, working hand-in-hand with eager capitalists, sought to give Chicago a completely new identity as the vital center of a modern service-based economy. Equally important, Daley strove to cultivate the city's image as a sophisticated center for fashion, music, gastronomy, and the arts equal to the great cities of Europe—the Milan of the Midwest, as the *Washington Post* put it.[6]

As an essential part of his vision for Chicago, Daley sought to effect a cultural renaissance that would attract national and international audiences. Determined to bring theater patrons downtown, he oversaw the renovation of the Harris, Selwyn, Cadillac Palace, and Ford Oriental Theaters in the North Loop, as well as the opening of the Chicago Shakespeare Theater at Navy Pier and the Lookingglass Theatre on North Michigan Avenue. Working closely with Lois Weisberg, the dynamic commissioner of cultural affairs, Daley filled the city's entertainment calendar with an eclectic array of events and activities that appealed to a broad cross section of the population. The city sponsored free concerts that attracted music lovers from around the world. More than half a million people annually flocked to the Chicago Blues Festival to hear B. B. King, Etta James, Buddy Guy, and other legendary performers. Procrastinating would-be visitors to the city likewise found no hotel vacancies downtown during the Grant Park Music Festival, the Chicago Jazz Festival, the Chicago Gospel Music Festival, or Viva Chicago. Chicago also welcomed Lollapalooza, an annual four-day music festival at which more than four hundred thousand people listened to alternative rock, heavy metal, punk rock, hip-hop, and electronic music on multiple stages in Grant Park. In 1991, Daley and Weisberg converted the old public library building, nearly vacant since the opening of the new Harold Washington Public Library a few blocks away, into the Chicago Cultural Center Gallery, which served as a venue for artistic exhibitions and performances. Gallery 37, created in 1991 at the initiative of Weisberg and Daley's wife, Maggie, offered a summer job program at which professional artists taught teenagers in an outdoor setting downtown. The Cows on Parade exhibit in 1999, a collection of life-size fiberglass sculptures painted in a variety of colors, became enormously popular and sparked an outpouring of public art throughout the nation. Daley and Weisberg converted the Chicago Sister Cities International Program from an obscure and underfunded afterthought into the largest sister-cities organization in the world, which raised the city's profile as an inviting place to visit and launch business ventures.[7]

## Having Fun Downtown

Elevating Chicago's reputation for cosmopolitanism dovetailed with a new emphasis on leisure that would appeal to middle- and upper-class residents and tourists. Daley realized that offsetting the devastating loss of the city's well-heeled inhabitants to upscale suburbs, an exodus that had been ongoing for decades, required not only improving streets, garbage collection, and police protection but also offering citizens the varied opportunities for relaxation and recreation they expected as an advantage of urban living. Blessed with a surplus of disposable income, corporate executives sought to spend their entertainment dollars on festivals, concerts, lavish meals, and spectator sports. Chicago financially aided its professional sports franchises, which had built loyal followings over the previous decades, to lure an even larger number of free-spending fans to their venues. The city provided $81 million to build a new baseball stadium for the White Sox next to the Dan Ryan Expressway south of downtown, for example, and $35 million in infrastructural costs for a new Chicago Bulls and Black Hawks arena located west of the Loop. In both cases, bulldozers leveled modest homes and small businesses owned mostly by African Americans to clear space for the sports facilities. Decades earlier, city officials in St. Louis and elsewhere also had targeted African American neighborhoods to construct sports arenas and convention centers. Reclaiming and retaining affluent populations in those cities likewise had reinforced a growing commitment to tourism, an attempt to attract affluent visitors as a staple of the new service economy.[8]

The centerpiece of Chicago tourism had for decades been the convention and trade-show industry, of which the city had been a leader since the opening of McCormick Place on the lakefront just south of the Loop in 1960. By the 1980s, New York City, Las Vegas, Atlanta, Washington, DC, and other competitors were building or expanding their own exposition centers in a fierce competition for business. Accordingly, Mayor Washington authorized the construction of a McCormick Place annex in 1986. Crafting agreements with the Metropolitan Pier and Exposition Authority, a bipartisan body composed of mayoral and gubernatorial appointees, Daley followed with a $675 million addition in 1996 and an $850 million expansion in 2007. By the time that Daley left office, McCormick Place's four interconnected buildings contained 2.7 million square feet of exhibition space, allowing the sprawling complex to maintain its position as the largest convention center in North America.[9]

Just north of McCormick Place, the mayor initiated an unprecedented public-works program that devoted hundreds of millions of dollars to the reconfiguration of the area at the southeast corner of Grant Park. In 1998, the city spent $110 million to reroute a section of Lake Shore Drive to fashion a "Museum Campus," a 57-acre showplace consisting of such venerable tourist destinations as the Field Museum, the Shedd Aquarium, the Adler Planetarium, and Soldier Field (home of the city's professional football franchise, the Chicago Bears). In 2003, the Chicago Park District followed with a $680 million renovation of timeworn Soldier Field. In its final form, the Museum Campus contained a boat basin, beaches, elevated terraces, walkways, a pedestrian tunnel, and a web of bicycle paths interspersed with its monumental buildings.[10]

Daley also played the crucial role in creating Chicago's foremost tourist attraction of the twenty-first century, Navy Pier. Opened in 1916 as Municipal Pier, the 3,300-foot-long concrete-and-wood rectangle jutting into Lake Michigan north of downtown originated as a freight terminal for maritime commerce. Renamed Navy Pier in 1927 to honor World War I veterans, the space served several functions in ensuing years, including a terminus for excursion boats, a naval training center during World War II, and, starting in 1946, the original campus of the University of Illinois at Chicago. Plans to convert the pier into a commercial emporium containing retail and entertainment venues floundered in the 1970s and 1980s until Daley moved decisively soon after taking office. In 1989, he concluded a deal with Illinois Governor James R. Thompson that created the Pier and Exposition Authority, to which the state contributed $150 million to rehabilitate the structure, thereafter sharing ownership with the city. The restyled Navy Pier opened in 1995 as a multipurpose site replete with a half-mile-long promenade, a 15-story Ferris Wheel, carnival rides, restaurants, shops, performance stages, a large ballroom, an IMAX theater, exhibition spaces, docking for water taxis and tour boats, and the Chicago Children's Museum. An immediate financial success and a popular gathering spot for Chicagoans and out-of-towners alike, the facility soon claimed to be the "#1 leisure destination in the Midwest."[11]

The same year that Daley presented his plans for a rejuvenated Navy Pier, he also introduced an $800 million gaming proposal for a flotilla of boats moored on the Chicago River. (State law prohibited land-based casinos, and so the mayor hoped to employ riverboats as a source of gambling revenue.) His lobbying for repeal of the ban on land-based casinos, which would have allowed him to build a $2 billion casino-entertainment complex south of the Loop, failed in the state capital. He contended that Chicago was losing millions of dollars annually to sites in Indiana, but his recurrent arguments failed to persuade a majority in the state legislature. The General Assembly approved casinos on other downstate rivers, but the long-standing political rivalry between the Chicago metropolitan region and the state's other ninety-six counties doomed the mayor's request. Undeterred by the rejections of his gambling proposals in Springfield, Daley continued his lakefront beautification efforts with renewed vigor.[12]

## Making Downtown a Thing of Beauty

In his drive to improve the attractiveness of the areas abutting the central business district, Daley gazed disapprovingly at the tiny waterfront airport (Meigs Field) on Northerly Island that gave business executives, politicians, and other VIPs quick access to the Loop. The few daily flights on and off the 120-acre peninsula, which connected to the mainland at the heart of the Museum Campus, spoiled the mayor's plan to create a 91-acre nature park near downtown. He met implacable opposition to his idea from state and federal authorities, who refused the city permission to disrupt air traffic that utilized Meigs Field. Daley simply took matters into his own hands, offering no warning of his intentions, to decommission the landing strip. In the middle of the night on March 30–31, 2003, he dispatched a fleet of earth-movers and steam shovels under police escort to disable the airfield's lone runway. The demolition crew ripped deep gashes into the concrete, render-ing the airport unusable, and Daley informed the Federal Aviation Admin-istration (FAA) of the midnight foray the next day. The mayor initially de-fended his actions by referring vaguely to the threat of terrorism and only later confessed his desire to replace Meigs Field with a public park. Local op-ed writers lambasted Daley's arrogance and wanton disrespect for the law, and the FAA levied fines against the city. Impervious to the criticism, Daley calmly ignored the critics and ordered city crews to begin landscaping the new park. Northerly Island quickly became a popular site for bicycling, walking, and attending outdoor music concerts at a seventy-five-hundred-seat pavilion.[13]

The transfiguration of Northerly Island fit neatly into Daley's heralded beautification efforts in Chicago. The mayor's intense interest in improving his city's aesthetic appeal supposedly stemmed from the many tours of Eu-ropean cities that he and his wife, Maggie, undertook during his administra-tion. (Insiders credited Maggie Daley with widening her husband's world-view and enhancing his appreciation of cultural affairs.) Having been inspired by the grandeur of Paris, Vienna, and other celebrated continental cities, he returned to Chicago with countless ideas for local refinements. The mayor demonstrated his interest in improving the entire city landscape by planting flowers, trees, and shrubs in barren median strips and by creating or restor-ing fifty-five school parks in various neighborhoods.

Daley's unstinting devotion to beautification showed most clearly in the adornment of the highly visible central business district. In 1991, he pushed through the city council an ordinance, strengthened eight years later, that mandated the planting of trees and flowerbeds along sidewalks and in me-dian strips, placing planters on commercial streets, and requiring builders to include landscaping designs in their architectural blueprints. His decision to plant a garden on the roof of city hall brought international acclaim, and soon airplane passengers flying over the Loop were looking down at a can-opy of vegetation on downtown buildings. Daley cheerfully accepted the sobriquet "the nation's green mayor."[14]

## Millennium Park

The mayor's most ambitious project to beautify downtown with another splash of green emerged with his commitment to convert the northwest por-tion of Grant Park into a lush public garden. In so doing, he sought to elim-

inate an unsightly jumble of railroad tracks and parking lots. The Chicago
Central Area Committee, a tireless booster of downtown improvement since
its creation in the 1950s, enthusiastically approved the endeavor. Parking
fees charged to commuters would pay off the municipal bonds for building
a garage underneath Millennium Park, as it came to be called, and corporations would assume the lion's share of the cost for construction on the surface level. In 1998, the Chicago Plan Commission approved the Lakefront
Millennium Project with its projected cost of $120 million. Because of con-
struction delays and cost overruns, the park did not open until 2004, four
years behind schedule and $330 million over budget. Taxpayers ended up
paying $230 million, with contributions from the corporate sector totaling
approximately $220 million, allowing city officials to laud the project as a
model public-private partnership. Cynical about corruption in local government, Chicagoans grumbled about graft, inefficiency, the ongoing addition
of expensive enhancements, and other hidden costs that elevated the project's final cost to somewhere between $450 million and $500 million.[15]

The muttering about the project's hefty price tag notwithstanding, Millennium Park became an instant and spectacular success. A *Financial Times*
writer called it "a genuinely 21st-century interactive park [that] could trigger
a new way of thinking about public outdoor spaces." The augmentations
added during the lengthy construction period provided many of the park's
most distinctive features and largely accounted for its enduring popularity.
Enthusiastic hordes crowded around Jaume Plensa's fifty-foot-high interactive Crown Fountain, Anish Kapoor's stainless-steel bean-shaped Cloud
Gate sculpture (popularly known as The Bean), and art exhibits scattered
throughout the park. Patrons watched performances at a 1,500-seat theater,
and concertgoers enjoyed musical presentations at an outdoor pavilion with
a bandshell designed by internationally famed architect Frank Gehry. In the
winter, ice skaters glided across a large outdoor rink. A 2.5-acre flower garden and several isolated greenswards, including Maggie Daley Park, provided the opportunity for quiet repose in the heart of the city. Along with
Navy Pier, Millennium Park provided a second immensely successful tourist magnet downtown and additional proof for the mayor's boast that Chicago had completed an economic transition away from manufacturing that
skeptics had warned would take generations. *Time* magazine credited Daley,
whom it crowned the nation's best mayor, with having "presided over the
city's transition from a graying hub to a vibrant boomtown."[16]

## The Crucial Role of Tax Increment Financing

Even as accolades multiplied for Chicago's exquisite downtown makeover,
grave problems festered away from the sight of headline writers and week-

end visitors. The realization of such grandiose aims depended on locating funds for investment, a considerable challenge for any big-city mayor chasing fiscal solvency during a time of recurring austerity budgets. Beginning in the Reagan years, presidential administrations of both political parties joined state governments in severely reducing aid to cities and leaving municipal governments to their own financial devices. Deprived of the operating funds and investment dollars to which they had become accustomed, city halls borrowed money, issued bonds, and crafted intricate public-private partnerships to underwrite the capital projects they hoped to complete in revitalizing central business districts. Municipalities offered tax abatements and offered generous incentive packages to lure businesses downtown from suburban sites and other cities. Daley's Chicago utilized all these tools in the drive for downtown enhancement, but increasingly the mayor established tax-increment financing (TIF) as the cornerstone of his quest to make Chicago a global city.[17]

State legislatures authorized cities to create TIFs as a means of underwriting public investments (usually infrastructure improvements or business subsidies) in specific geographical areas overtaken by blight. TIFs freeze property-tax distributions to local jurisdictions for a specific time span (twenty-three years in Illinois). Revenue derived from increases in property value—the tax increment—must be used for development exclusively in the TIF district. Seeking a way to generate matching funds for federal grants, California passed the first law creating TIFs in 1952, but only six other states followed suit by 1970. Declining urban conditions thereafter spurred other state governments to action, and only three states had no such laws on the books by 2000; the Illinois General Assembly passed the Illinois Tax Increment Allocation Act in 1977. Harold Washington became the first Chicago mayor to employ TIFs as he attempted to revitalize a decrepit portion of the North Loop. He made use of the new legislation on a limited exploratory basis, paving the way for Daley's wholehearted embrace of the strategy in the 1990s. Indeed, Daley relied on TIFs so heavily that critics accused him of turning downtown into a "TIF district slush pool."[18]

Negative allusions to TIFs as a "slush pool" notwithstanding, no one could deny the device's success at generating investment in Chicago. Proponents argued that the self-financing mechanism relieved city government of having to increase tax burdens or levy special assessments. (On the other hand, noted critics, municipal agencies such as the Board of Education continued to increase taxes to compensate for the funds swallowed by TIFs.) Advocates of downtown enhancement welcomed the opportunities suddenly available to developers. At the same time, they praised the exploding sums of capital flowing into the flourishing areas immediately north, west, and south of the Loop and lauded the mayor's ingenuity in funding large-scale projects and providing financial incentives for builders and developers. The example of the LaSalle/Central TIF district shows how the accumulation of tax increments could generate huge sums for investment. The designated blocks on the western edge of downtown, a flourishing area that contained the Lyric Opera as well as the headquarters of United Airlines and MillerCoors, accumulated $19 million in revenue in 2007 alone. Unregulated by any independent agency, city hall exercised autonomy in the creation of TIF districts and in the use of the tax increments.[19]

## Subsidizing Capitalist Development

Displaying considerable creativity, Daley subsidized a wide variety of projects, such as the construction of pricy downtown condominiums, the move of United Airlines headquarters onto seven floors of the Willis Tower (at a cost of $35 million), and the renovation of tax-exempt buildings on Loyola University's lakefront campus. Using TIF funds as part of generous incentive packages, Daley persuaded MillerCoors, Quaker Oats, Sara Lee Desserts, Boeing Aircraft, and other successful companies to build more lavish headquarters downtown or to move their corporate offices to Chicago from the suburbs or other cities. (The recruitment of Boeing alone cost the city and the state of Illinois $56 million in public subsidies.) The mayor used this labyrinthine funding source to create a shadow budget exceeding $500 million, approximately one-sixth of the city's official budget, that served the 158 TIF districts extant in Chicago when he left office. In 2011, TIF districts covered a full 30 percent of the city. Without doubt, TIFs became an indispensable tool in the mayor's avid pursuit of downtown growth.[20]

Yet Daley's dependence on TIFs came at a considerable cost that the people of Chicago found themselves obligated to pay. The infusion of capital into designated areas of the city diverted spending from other potential targets for investment, and the preponderance of TIF districts downtown produced an unhealthy imbalance. During the final eight years of Daley's tenure, for instance, $891 million of TIF investment (48 percent of Chicago's accumulation) went to districts in and around downtown. These districts, stretching from the Gold Coast on the north to McCormick Place on the south and from the United Center on the west to the lake, encompassed just 5 percent of the city's geographical area and included only 11 percent of its population. Districts on the North and Northwest Sides, areas where household incomes far exceeded the city median, received yet another $305 million (17 percent of TIF spending). Meanwhile, city hall directed only 23 percent of the $1.84 billion in municipal TIF outlays during those years to the city's poorest neighborhoods—the centers of blight originally targeted by the Illinois Tax Increment Allotment Act. As well, TIFs proved to be an inherently flawed tool for reversing decades of economic decline and decay in the most disadvantaged areas of the city. On blocks full of empty lots, vacant buildings, and dilapidated structures, modest increases in property values produced tax increments inadequate to the task of spurring growth. The massive push needed to effect change required an enormous infusion of capital. Endeavoring to invest in an area purportedly showing some signs of community life and avoiding ZIP codes that offered no hope of economic turnaround, private interests sought the "blight that's right."[21]

Even more insidious, as a growing number of critics maintained, TIFs quietly leeched desperately needed tax revenue from municipal agencies. Increases in property-tax collections attributable to new undertakings or appreciation in value—in excess of the "fixed" distributions to local governments—automatically accrued to development efforts within the districts. Whereas TIF investments promised a significant payoff for the districts in the future, financially strapped municipal agencies shouldered the financial burden in the short term. TIFs effectively placed a cap on the number of dollars ordinarily bound for schools, parks, libraries, and other city agencies. County Board Commissioner Jesus "Chuy" Garcia unsuccessfully proposed that the city close TIF districts in and around the Loop and divert property-tax dollars to pension payments and citywide expenses such as public education. The negative impact on the schools became an especially nettlesome issue for the mayor. A series of austerity education budgets forced several school closings as part of Daley's Renaissance 2010 reform plan, which called for shuttering underperforming schools and opening a flock of charter schools. By the time that Daley left office, approximately one hundred charter schools had replaced eighty neighborhood schools. A public outcry ensued. The leadership of the Chicago Teachers Union (CTU) drew a straight line connecting TIF encroachment and the rampant school closings, lamenting the sacrifice of public education on the altar of downtown development.[22]

## Selling the City's Infrastructure

Daley ignored the controversy swirling around his recurrent use of TIFs and avidly searched for other ways to forestall budget deficits and create capital. Chicago led the way in trimming municipal operating costs through the adoption of privatization schemes. As the mayor acknowledged, the idea met considerable opposition at the outset. Chicago had a long history as a union stronghold, and labor leaders resisted any reduction of the municipal workforce. So did Democratic council members and party leaders, who feared the loss of patronage jobs. Daley justified the outsourcing of services to private firms with references to the reputed advantages enjoyed by profit-seeking businesses. "We [the city] can't compete with the private sector," he complained. "The private sector has a complete idea of who your customers are. Government doesn't have customers. They only have citizens." Consumer advocacy groups caustically noted that privatization fitted nicely with the Daley administration's lack of accountability and transparency. Turning aspects of municipal governance over to private entities removed much decision making from public scrutiny. In short, democracy seemed to be taking a back seat to the unchecked financial plans of an entrepreneurial mayor.[23]

Undeterred by the dissent, Daley imposed privatization in both small and large doses. Some of his more modest initiatives, such as hiring independent contractors to tow abandoned automobiles, trim trees, uproot tree stumps, repair traffic lights, and polish city hall floors, met with popular approval even though the city saved little money after the changeover. Other privatization efforts brought harsh criticism when profit-seeking companies provided inferior service. In the lethal heat wave that claimed the lives of 485 Chicagoans in July 1995, for example, investigators found that tardy response times by private ambulance services and poor performance by their paramedics accounted for some of the mortality.[24]

At a time when Philadelphia Mayor Edward G. Rendell and Los Angeles Mayor Richard J. Riordan were attracting attention with their privatization experiments, Daley was taking greater financial risks by entering into significantly longer agreements with private vendors involving much more money. By entering into public asset-leasing agreements with cash-rich corporations and international consortiums, he acquired huge amounts of cash for the city at a time when urgent budget shortfalls necessitated immediate infusions of funds. Such a strategy eliminated the need for service reductions or tax hikes in the present, postponing the day of fiscal reckoning well into the future. The mayor committed Chicago to three major privatization agreements—a fourth proposal, a $2.5 billion lease of Midway Airport for ninety-nine years, fell through in 2009—at a time when other big cities were tentatively entering into modest privatization arrangements but nothing on the scale of Daley's brash ventures. In 2005, he completed a deal netting the city $1.8 billion that leased the Chicago Skyway, a 7.8-mile elevated toll road linking the city to northwestern Indiana, in a partnership including Spanish and Australian conglomerates for ninety-nine years. The following year, against strong local opposition, he forced through the city council a ninety-nine-year deal brokered by the Morgan Stanley investment firm that surrendered parking fees in four underground garages beneath Grant Park and Millennium Park for $563 million. His most controversial measure involved what seemed at first to be a relatively inconsequential matter, the privatization of the city's parking meters.[25]

In 2008, Chicago received a lump-sum payment of $1.16 billion for yielding the operation of parking meters during the next seventy-five years to

Deeside Investments, a Morgan Stanley subsidiary. Harsh criticism surfaced from the start. Although the measure sailed through the city council by the lopsided margin of forty to five, many council members expressed serious reservations; some of them frankly admitted that they had not understood all of the transaction's details at the time of the vote, while others approved the idea in principle but suspected that Daley should have demanded better terms. The city clashed repeatedly with Chicago Parking Meters LLC, the holding company created to oversee the operation, and motorists complained incessantly about a host of issues with the city's thirty-six thousand parking meters. The quadrupling of downtown parking rates, a rash of broken meters, and a flood of parking tickets—many of which were undeserved, according to furious commuters—left Chicagoans vexed with a daily parking problem. Frustrated drivers often avoided the untrustworthy parking meters altogether, creating greater congestion on unmetered side streets. The level of disquiet escalated the following year when Chicago inspector general David Hoffman released a detailed and highly critical report on the parking-meter situation. Hoffman excoriated Daley for several missteps, including the conduct of negotiations without adequate city council oversight and needlessly tying Chicago to a long-term arrangement that limited flexibility in the event of buyer remorse. Perhaps most damaging, the inspector general's accounting indicated that a good bargain for the city should have included at least a $2 billion payoff. In his rush to acquire funds quickly, Hoffman and other financial experts were charging, the mayor sold Chicago short.[26]

## The Steep Costs of Downtown Redevelopment

Financial experts saw in the mayor's innovative financial manipulations a desperation to spur downtown redevelopment at all costs, even at the risk of putting Chicago's long-term fiscal health in jeopardy. *Crain's Chicago Business*, the journalistic voice of the city's entrepreneurial class, chided Daley for the "fiscal morass created in large part by his drive to make Chicago a mecca for wealthy professionals and international corporations." His excessive reliance on TIFs and path-breaking experimentation with privatization projects shared an unhealthy eagerness to gamble on immediate remuneration while saddling future mayors and government officials with the unenviable task of making restitution. Daley's defenders opined that such financial derring-do had become necessary during hazardous economic times for urban America and pointed to the undeniable flourishing of Chicago's downtown, a stark contrast to the halting progress made in the central business districts of other Rustbelt cities such as St. Louis. Yet encouraging financial indicators early in the Daley mayoralty gradually gave way to reports of mounting budgetary imbalances. The administration's penchant for cutting financial corners, first ignored and then excused as an acceptable tactic in the 1990s, looked especially worrisome as the nation plunged into the Great Recession of 2008–2009. By the time that Daley's successor took office in 2011, the city appeared to be mired in a "fiscal mess."[27]

The Daley administration's renown for fiscal responsibility gradually evaporated, replaced by the aura of a spendthrift that put severe pressure on the city treasury. Between 2005 and 2009, while Chicago's tax revenues rose 6.5 percent, municipal spending increased by 17.3 percent. By the end of that period, tax and fee collections totaled only about $3.1 billion out of a $5.3 billion budget. The biggest culprit in the developing crisis, the unfunded pension allocation, accounted for a liability in excess of $19 billion by 2013. Diverting money designated for the city's four employee pension funds (police, fire, municipal, and labor) allowed the city to maintain a satisfactory level of services but at the expense of the dwindling pension funds. At the same time, the city turned a blind eye to an inadequate emergency reserve fund, which had been serving as yet another source of largess to disguise increasing deficits. The Civic Federation, a widely respected watchdog organization of long standing, roundly condemned the city's budgetary sleight of hand and predicted fiscal calamity if city officials continued to raid pension and emergency funds to patch over shortfalls elsewhere.[28]

Along with the city's worsening financial health, Chicagoans expressed concern about other chronic problems that seemed immune to solution by city government. In boldly assuming total control of education, low-cost housing, parks, and public transportation, Daley consolidated power in impressive fashion but also assumed responsibility for making headway against intractable forces that had stymied his predecessors for decades. No mayoral priority offered greater challenges than the improvement of the city's infamously moribund public-education system, which U.S. Secretary of Education William Bennett called the worst in the nation. "If it's not the last, I don't know who is," he bluntly stated in 1987. "There can't be very many more cities that are worse. Chicago is pretty much it." The wretched reputation of the Chicago Public Schools (CPS) besmirched the city's image, hampered the ability to recruit "knowledge-based" firms, discouraged the kind of middle-class people Daley was wooing from remaining in or moving into the municipality, and, for all these reasons, damaged the mayor's pursuit of the global city designation. In 1995, the Illinois legislature granted complete control of the CPS to the mayor, who eagerly accepted the call to battle.[29]

Daley declared education his first priority and moved swiftly to impose comprehensive reform, altering policies and practices in areas from the Board of Education to the classroom. He transformed a traditional educational bureaucracy into a corporate structure, a distinction underscored by changing the title of school board president to chief executive officer. He centralized authority, reducing the autonomy of elected local school councils established during the Harold Washington years, and demanded stringent economies to reduce waste and inefficiency. Most important, the mayor demanded a rigid accountability wherein standardized tests measured student performance with a commensurate set of rewards and punishments for schools and teachers. In the event of substandard performance, schools faced a variety of corrective actions ranging from administrative reorganization and curricular reform to closure. (The program he installed served as a template for the No Child Left Behind Act passed by Congress in 2001 and implemented thereafter by President George W. Bush.) Daley initially received positive notices for his sweeping reform effort, which President Bill Clinton called "a model for the nation" in 1998. Graduation rates in city high schools rose from 42 percent to 51 percent in the first ten years of the new accountability era, and praise increased among leading educators nationwide for Daley's hardheaded approach. He received the Education Excellence Award from the National Conference for Community and Justice in 1999, and the National Association of State Boards of Education named him Policy Leader of the Year in 2000.[30]

In 2004, the mayor and CPS chief executive officer Arne Duncan, who later became President Barack Obama's secretary of education, sought to build on the early positive results with additional reforms. They created the Renaissance 2010 program, which established more demanding standards and created private academies as alternatives to neighborhood schools. By 2011, Daley replaced eighty underachieving schools with approximately one hundred charter schools. Chicago's leading citizens applauded the decisive action taken by the no-nonsense mayor, who strongly urged members of the business elite to donate to and become closely involved with individual schools. Private-education providers benefited from the expanding opportunities to obtain contracts with the Board of Education, and boosters proudly pointed to the steps being taken by the administration to make Chicago a more livable city. Growth in the number of charter schools represented another victory for privatization. Best of all in the view of economy-minded reformers, private schools were able to save money in a labor-intensive enterprise by offering lower salaries for teachers and dispensing with the practice of tenure.[31]

## Teachers Challenge Daley

The Daley-Duncan initiatives generated determined opposition from many quarters. Opponents decried the city's draconian measures as an unwarranted assault on beleaguered teachers, who lacked the resources to offer quality instruction in overcrowded classrooms. Teachers complained about the price being paid for exclusively "teaching to the test" in order to obtain better results on highly questionable examinations. For years, a quiescent body that passively enacted directives from central administration, leaders of the CTU developed a new independence and sharply questioned the fundamental motivations of the mayor's reforms. After Karen Lewis won the CTU presidency in 2010 on a militant platform that excoriated the corporate-friendly roots of the mayor's educational-reform package, she defiantly said, "The election shows the unity of thirty thousand educators standing strong to put business in its place: out of our schools."[32]

The rift between Daley and the CTU widened with time, resulting in an acrimonious strike the year after he left office. The rising hostility amounted to a struggle for empowerment by thousands of teachers (and public workers) convinced that they had long been treated unfairly by city hall but also revolved around substantive policy issues. The CTU leadership and other critics censured Daley's commitment to corporate-style reform. They also pointed out that wrenching changes in public education, including the severe budget cuts and school closings, not coincidentally occurred most often in the city's low-income neighborhoods. African American and Latino students bore the brunt of the drastic shifts in resources. In a 2010 article headlined "Daley School Plan Fails to Make the Grade," the *Chicago Tribune* charged that the reconfiguration of district maps necessitated by school closings frequently bunched students from the most disadvantaged families together in faltering schools. Such policies set these embattled schools up for failure by concentrating violence and gang activity on the premises and on adjacent blocks while inoculating charter schools from such environmental distractions. No longer able to walk short distances to nearby schools, many students faced the prospect of having to hike much longer distances across unfamiliar terrain—a hazardous and sometimes lethal prospect in gang-infested areas of the city.[33]

The school reform initiative not only singled out disadvantaged minority students for the greatest sacrifices but also did so at a time when existing data failed to confirm that the growing number of charter schools was proving to be a panacea for the entire school system. For all the encomiums showered on Renaissance 2010, test results and other metrics of academic achievement in the public schools improved but remained well below state and national scores. Graduation rates in the public schools overall stood at only 55.8 percent in 2011, and the CPS still struggled under the burden of a $720 million deficit. Of the one hundred worst public schools in the nation, based on standardized test scores in 2009, the CPS administered seventeen of them. Disparities between a selective group of students enrolled in innovative college-preparatory programs in charter schools and students left behind to slog through antiquated curricula became more pronounced with time. Moreover, students displaced by school closings usually found themselves shuttled off to other unsatisfactory schools. The underpinnings of Daley's education reform reinforced the city's drive to serve the middle class, bolstering his agenda for remaking Chicago, but largely avoided the much more imposing task of improving schools for everyone regardless of race and economic circumstance.[34]

## Daley and Public Housing's Remaining Residents

No less daunting than the public-education conundrum, the toxic public-housing situation presented Daley with a challenge that had flummoxed Chicago mayors for decades. As with public education, the mayor's assumption of absolute control over a troubled municipal bureaucracy presented him with a unique opportunity to address a myriad of problems in the Chicago Housing Authority (CHA). The third-largest public housing entity in the nation, the CHA administered all government-subsidized housing for low-income residents in the city. The defective agency had consistently produced alarming fiscal deficits, making routine maintenance impossible; demoralized residents complained about inadequate upkeep, soaring crime rates, rising levels of gang infestation, and unresponsive lower- and mid-level management in the projects. Nine of the ten poorest census tracts in the nation were Chicago public-housing projects. In 1995, citing the city's inability to manage its own affairs competently, the U.S. Department of Housing and Urban Development (HUD) assumed operation of the CHA and its thirty thousand units of low-income housing. In short order, under the auspices of the federal Hope VI program, bulldozers began leveling high-rise buildings at the Cabrini-Green project and at Stateway Gardens. In 1999, HUD returned control of public housing to the CHA, and Daley moved immediately to try his hand at solving the low-income housing predicament.[35]

"In the case of public housing and school reform," observed Northwestern University sociologist Mary Pattillo, "the strategies were basically the same: clear the high-rises of their residents and the poorly performing schools of their students and then start from scratch." In 1999, city hall announced the Chicago Plan for Transformation, a complete reshuffling of the public-housing deck that entailed the elimination of all high-rise and midrise structures at the Robert Taylor Homes, the Henry Horner Homes, Stateway Gardens, and Cabrini-Green. The city would rehabilitate the remaining low-rise buildings at those locations. Next, the CHA would launch an extensive construction effort to erect mixed-use projects for low- and middle-income tenants. The plan prescribed healthy doses of privatization and decentralization, turning operational decisions over to independent contractors and divesting the CHA of considerable managerial authority. Daley promised a halt to decades of flawed public policy—the end, he intoned, of "a legacy of slime"—and a rebirth of hope with mixed-income communities where tenants paying market rates would live side-by-side with lifetime public housing tenants. Daley was again launching a daring social experiment on a massive scale untried anywhere else and, yet again, assuredly with mixed motives.[36]

Closing the books on the failed experiment in high-rise public housing not only promised a rescue for embattled tenants but also the creation of vast real-estate investment opportunities. The demolition of hulking public-housing towers meant the elimination of hideous eyesores, many in the shadow of the Loop, that had despoiled neighborhoods and depressed land values for several decades. Clearing public-housing sites paved the way for gentrification and signaled a bonanza for rapacious real-estate interests, opening prime land to market-rate developers. Public-housing residents uprooted by the demolition faced an uncertain future, despite the city's assurances of sufficient relocation arrangements to accommodate the displaced population. The testimony of the unhoused tenants suggested that some found shelter rather quickly, but others languished for months and even years. A study analyzing the first ten years of the CHA's Plan for Transformation found that "relocation did not help most residents improve their employment situation or incomes. . . . Those that moved into Chicago neighborhoods using housing vouchers most often relocated to neighborhoods with high poverty and deep racial segregation." Homelessness increased along with the shortage of affordable housing. Several studies found that the eradication of so much public housing made matters worse, not better, for much of the disadvantaged population.[37]

## Public Safety and Race

Many public-policy experts had predicted that the elimination of the ghastly public-housing towers, which had provided such fertile ground for homicide, juvenile delinquency, drug usage, and many other antisocial behaviors, would benefit the effort to reduce Chicago's historically high rates of violent crime. Daley saw the removal of the vertical ghettos as an important element of the city's campaign to lower crime rates, but he moved on several other fronts to curtail violence as well. He crusaded against unrestricted gun proliferation, lobbied state and federal legislators to pass more laws limiting handgun ownership, joined several other mayors in class-action lawsuits against firearm manufacturers, and hired more police officers. Daley could point to lower homicide and overall crime rates in the city when he left office than when he assumed the mayoralty twenty-two years earlier. Crime crested nationally in the early 1990s and then fell significantly, a trend reflected in Chicago, and the mayor could legitimately claim to have contributed to the improvement.[38]

Yet encouraging changes in crime statistics belied the fact that public safety continued to be a major concern of many Chicagoans, especially the residents of the city's declining neighborhoods. Despite having a significantly smaller population, Chicago continued to vie with New York City and Los Angeles as the national homicide leader. Inhabitants of high-crime areas, most of which were concentrated in minority neighborhoods, noted that they had seen no increase in police presence on their blocks. Some Chicagoans trapped in crime-ridden neighborhoods such as Englewood on the city's South Side called for the assignment of more uniformed officers to their neighborhoods—a politically untenable request in city hall when it meant the reduction of law enforcement personnel in the Loop and middle-class tracts. On the other hand, many residents of crime-infested areas hesitated to call for a heightened police presence because of their mistrust of the authorities. Police-community relations continued to suffer, especially after the sensational disclosure that police under the direction of Commander Jon Burge had tortured 137 African American suspects on the South Side to coerce confessions between 1972 and 1991—notably overlapping eight of Daley's years as state's attorney and two of his years as mayor. During that time, Daley ignored pleas for an official inquiry. Also, Daley dismissed repeated calls for the establishment of a civilian review board to investigate charges of police misconduct and, despite occasional promises to address the police force's habitual use of excessive force against racial minorities, he never took substantive action. The belief persisted in minority neighborhoods that members of the disproportionately white police force acted with impunity in administering their own form of justice in impoverished minority neighborhoods.[39]

Ongoing tensions between the residents of disadvantaged neighborhoods and police officers, who were usually the most visible representatives of city government on the streets, underscored the feeling that the Daley administration's preoccupation with downtown aggrandizement left little room for the needs and wants of the city's marginalized populations. Chicago remained one of the nation's most segregated cities, a classic example of what sociologists Douglas S. Massey and Nancy A. Denton termed hypersegregation in their influential book *American Apartheid*. According to Massey and Denton, hypersegregation concentrates poverty to create a self-perpetuating spiral of decay in African American enclaves with deleterious consequences for hapless residents. In Chicago, this phenomenon showed in the striking disparities based on race in a number of categories—school graduation rates, employment, income, pensions, wealth, access to branch banks, housing quality, life expectancy, excessive reliance on unlicensed caregivers, teenage pregnancy, drug arrests, incarceration rates, and victimization by crime. According to a study conducted by Loyola University of Chicago in 2006, the median income for African American households stood at 66 percent of the average for white households, and ten of the city's poorest neighborhoods were situated in census tracts at least 94 percent black. No one could blame Daley alone for such deplorable situations, which resulted from decades of flawed public policy and institutional racism. Nevertheless, his willingness to overlook the grim conditions and mounting hopelessness in desperate neighborhoods while zealously pursuing global-city status left a growing legion of lower-income Chicagoans frustrated and angry at the denial of their right to earn a middle-class income and reside with their families in safety.[40]

While critics warned that the widening chasm that separated the opulent downtown from decaying neighborhoods—perhaps even undermining Daley's downtown-focused accomplishments—he continued to "make no little plans" in pursuit of international prominence. In 2006, the mayor launched a full-scale campaign to have Chicago host the 2016 summer Olympics, an event that would have put the city squarely in the spotlight and serve as his crowning achievement on the world stage. Chicago's elite quickly and enthusiastically fell into line behind the mayor, but not everyone in the Windy City applauded the idea. Dissidents asked how a city with limited resources in perilous fiscal times could justify spending so much money on an elaborate spectacle that guaranteed no long-term reward for the downtrodden. Daley's promises of trickle-down economic benefits for all residents proved unconvincing on the embattled South and West Sides. Despite the generous backing of the city's business community and the endorsement of President Barack Obama and First Lady Michelle Obama, both of whom traveled to Copenhagen, Denmark, to sing their home city's praises in person to the International Olympic Committee, Chicago's bid failed. When the committee awarded the games to Rio de Janeiro, Brazil, and the crestfallen mayor expressed profound disappointment, many residents of Chicago nonchalantly shrugged off the defeat—and indeed many breathed a sigh of relief that the city avoided making a monumental investment with no foreseeable payoff for the city's ordinary residents of long-neglected neighborhoods.[41]

## A City of Contrasts

Daley left office in 2011 with signs of a divided Chicago all around him. In January of that year, a federal judge in U.S. District Court sentenced Jon Burge to 4.5 years in prison for supervising the grisly torture used by police to wring confessions from African American men. The judge denounced the state's attorney's and mayor's offices for failing to investigate charges of police impropriety, underlining Daley's role in the scandal. As the conclusion of the Burge trial fed complaints about city hall's treatment of the disadvantaged, the mayor's unvarying determination to redevelop downtown remained a winning strategy to the business elite. No one could deny that people were returning to Chicago, the city's population having increased from 1990 to 2000 for the first time since the 1940–1950 decade. (The city's black population was decreasing, many African Americans voting with their feet by decamping for the inner suburbs.) University of Chicago sociologist Terry Nichols Clark exulted that Chicago's lakefront had surpassed the Grand Canyon and Yellowstone as the nation's most visited park. The sprouting of condominiums and Starbucks coffee shops in improving neighborhoods signaled the relentless onslaught of gentrification in areas favored by city hall, a clear sign of urban renewal—but a dispiriting setback for ousted residents. The invasion of mostly white high-earners claimed a variety of victims, raising rents and driving out lower-income and elderly residents of all races—acceptable collateral damage, it seemed, in the triumphalist saga of the global city.[42]

Rahm Emanuel, who succeeded Daley in 2011 and won reelection four years later, pursued the same goal of gilding the urban core, arguably with even more verve. Fully dedicated to the goal of affirming Chicago's status as a global city, Emanuel made no apologies for appeasing corporate titans in the quest to create a business-friendly environment. He also presided over the largest mass closing of public schools in the nation's history, shuttered half the city's mental-health clinics, and failed to stem the rising number of firearm murders that was making Chicago the homicide capital of the United States—in each instance, exhibiting a callous indifference to worsening conditions in poor minority neighborhoods. As murder rates remained mordantly high, protesters charged that the administration was paying inadequate attention to the violent outbursts punctuating the inexorable economic decline on the South and West Sides. Daley's policies clearly were continuing with Emanuel, whom critics began calling "Mayor 1%" for his slavish attention to the desires of the city's wealthiest residents. The Loop and its environs continued to bloom, but at what cost? Increasingly, the forlorn residents of the forgotten neighborhoods balked at having to shoulder the burden. Defying the overwhelming political and economic power arrayed against them, the people left behind gamely fought city hall to challenge the unwavering focus on downtown.[43] Hospital construction posed yet another set of challenges and opportunities to central city residents. Like stadiums and convention centers, hospital building remained solidly in the hands of downtown-oriented executives.

Starting in the 1960s and extending to 2021, proponents of hospital construction assumed key posts in urban leadership. Hospital growth, few doubted, would soon deliver better health care to every resident and valuable connections to biotechnology firms employing medical doctors and researchers with Ph.D.s. Hospitals, by this reasoning, would create thousands of jobs, helping to replace the many positions that disappeared each month at factories and warehouses. A portion of the extravagant hopes came to pass. Hospital administrators in Chicago, St. Louis, and Philadelphia created several of the nation's best-known hospitals, for instance, Chicago's Rush University Medical Center. By the early 2000s, however, hospital administrators also began to discover that their city's earlier failures to invest in primary education, public transit, clean air, and health care for low-income workers discouraged biotechnology investors. Nor did even the best-intentioned politicians and hospital officials possess the resources needed to eradicate the deeply racialized crime and untreated illnesses that lingered next door to the nation's most distinguished medical centers. Ultimately, big-city hospitals were expensive urban renewal projects that were supposed to turn into high-technology growth centers but were only partly successful in doing so. No one, it seems, escaped their city's racial and industrial history. During the 1960s and early 1970s, Bill Rafsky, still active in Philadelphia politics, helped launch his city's hospital administrators on the path toward rapid growth, as the next chapter explores.[44]

# 9

# Big-City Hospitals

*From Urban Renewal to the Next Growth Machine*

n April 1971, Philadelphia's Metropolitan Hospital was at last ready to serve patients in its new quarters. During the early 1960s, city officials led by William L. Rafsky and Society Hill's hostile residents had brought considerable economic and legal pressure on the hospital's leaders to abandon expansion plans at their former site. In July 1964, Rafsky and the hospital's attorneys reached an accommodation that included financial support to construct a sparkling $11 million, state-of-the-art hospital. And now, nearly seven years later, journalists offered enthusiastic reports about Metropolitan's 8-story building, colored in an attractive beige and copper. The hospital's modernistic design was only one of its many exciting features. The new Metropolitan featured six operating rooms and specialized areas for pediatric and cardiovascular services. Still more, the hospital's designers had arranged patients' rooms in circles around each nursing station, guaranteeing quick access for emergencies and daily care. Metropolitan will "continue its role as a community hospital to center city," hospital president Dr. David Silverman proudly told a local reporter.[1]

Bill Rafsky and a multitude of city officials had not demanded that Silverman move his hospital only to improve patient care. Starting in the mid-1950s, Society Hill's proponents, including Rafsky and developer Albert Greenfield and Mayor Richardson K. Dilworth, sought to create an upscale community of mostly white householders who would patronize Center City retailers, work in nearby law and medical offices, and staff corporate headquarters such as those of chemical company Rohm and Haas. In 1971, Metropolitan Hospital's large and sleek exterior held out the promise of a much-sought round of rising property values. A local writer described the Independence Hall area, Metropolitan's new location, as already "buzzing with construction activity." The modernistic Metropolitan Hospital, with its rounded appearance and novel colors, would presumably add to the buzz. Two years later, leaders of the Pennsylvania College of Podiatric Medicine opened their $9 million building on the corner opposite Metropolitan Hospital. The podiatric school and Metropolitan Hospital created a small medical complex on Center City's east side. That complex also cut off the deteriorated Chinatown district from the newly glistening Independence Hall and Society Hill areas to the east. At their best, hospitals improved patients' health and added to the fortunes of neighborhoods close by.[2]

The Metropolitan and podiatric buildings were only one part of a medical construction boom taking place in the Philadelphia region. During the early 1970s, Philadelphia's hospital administrators launched still larger and more expensive projects. In 1974, executives at several local hospitals, including Thomas Jefferson University Hospital and the Hospital of the University of Pennsylvania, had plans on drawing boards to build and modernize facilities at a price tag of $125 million. And to finance those big projects, hospital executives sought Mayor Frank L. Rizzo's help. In brief, they wanted Rizzo to support an ordinance to create a new city authority. That authority would sell low-interest, tax-exempt revenue bonds and make the funds available to the hospitals. As the bonds came due, hospital officials would utilize patient and other revenues to repay the bonds, much in the way that a toll-road authority collects coins at tollbooths to repay bondholders for construction loans. The cost savings were substantial, as much as 3.5 to 4.0 percent compared to interest rates each hospital acting on its own had to pay, according to the city council's president. Interest paid on the bonds was exempt from federal income taxation, creating an added incentive for the bond buyers. With hospital officials unable to resist such an attractive program, more than twenty Pennsylvania cities had already taken advantage of state legislation authorizing creation of hospital authorities.[3]

In Philadelphia's always contentious politics, however, not even a straightforward proposal to expand the city's health-care facilities was certain of city hall's support. The hospitals' proposal "got caught in . . . a crossfire" between the mayor and the city council president, a *Philadelphia Inquirer* editorial writer observed in January 1974. Rizzo wanted to create a Philadelphia Development Authority capable of awarding tax advantaged construction to a larger number of borrowers who would, he contended, advance projects for recreation facilities, highways, sewage improvements, and the like. But with council members already making known their opposition to a wide-ranging Development Authority, Rizzo sought to win their support by naming likely board members in advance, including Bill Rafsky. By the 1970s, Rafsky's can-do attitude, his widespread connections, and his recognized willingness to work long hours to achieve a mayor's goals had followed him into the Rizzo administration. Perhaps Rafsky's faithful service and multiple accomplishments worked against him, at least in this instance. The council president was prepared to create an authority that served the hospitals' financial needs, but no others. Rafsky's presence and his reputation for creatively changing city bureaucracies represented a risk that the council president refused to take. Rizzo and the council president also disagreed about who would appoint the authority's members. The squabbling ended with an agreement that the new authority would only work with hospitals. Rizzo, however, secured the right to appoint members to the newly named Hospital Authority, subject to council's approval. During the next ten years, Rizzo's Hospital Authority issued $1.25 billion in bonds.[4] New hospital buildings, exactly as Rafsky determined in his long-running battle to relocate Metropolitan, were useful in the daunting job of obliterating aging structures and removing low-income African Americans from Center City and other valued areas.

In February 1976, Rizzo initiated another hospital redevelopment program. The city would shutter Philadelphia General Hospital (PGH), which had treated low-income and indigent patients since 1832. Like any Rizzo project in or around Center City, racial hostility ran through PGH's closing from start to finish. PGH's patients consisted mostly of lower-income African Americans who had stayed behind as wealthier neighbors fled to the suburbs and commuted on Philadelphia's expressways and trains. Each day, as many as 150 patients made their way to the PGH's emergency room, seeking treatment for lacerated necks, broken bones, and far deadlier afflictions that they lacked the ability to pay for. No one planned to construct a hospital to replace Philadelphia General, and in fact no one had a plan for what would take place when bulldozers reduced it to a field of rubble. At that point, however, the city's budget crunch made it difficult for Rizzo and other politicians to launch costly hospital projects.[5]

Rizzo turned to the Philadelphia Industrial Development Corporation (PIDC) to redevelop the PGH site. The PIDC's history extended back to the 1950s and efforts by Bill Rafsky and Mayor Richardson K. Dilworth to stem the city's job losses. In 1958, Dilworth had joined with leaders of the Chamber of Commerce of Greater Philadelphia to create the PIDC. As with the Hospital Authority, the PIDC's activist leaders sold bonds and used the proceeds to make low-interest loans to local firms to help them expand or just remain in the city. During the 1960s, PIDC officials helped develop the University City Science Center, where officials sought to attract medical, scientific, and engineering companies into the area near the University of Pennsylvania. The idea in working with those firms was to convert their devices and ideas into products, services, and profits. Just between 1971 and 1976, PIDC leaders completed 494 deals. The PIDC's seasoned managers, in other words, possessed experience both in the older field of making loans to entice corporate executives to remain in Philadelphia and in the new and complex field of organizing and financing businesses that would prosper in the expanding fields of science and medicine. Partnership with the PIDC offered alert hospital administrators the opportunity to expand clinics, research capabilities, and earnings. During the next decades, PIDC leaders regularly noted their city's promising future as a site for medical developments. "Someday Philadelphia will be known as the medical capital of the world," a PIDC vice president announced in 1985.[6]

The abundance of rhetoric surrounding hospital construction in and around the former PGH site carried a political rather than a medical promise. During the 1970s and 1980s, no one could have doubted that the Hospital of the University of Pennsylvania and the nearby Children's Hospital of Philadelphia had long featured top-tier researchers and excellent treatment centers. All that boasting, it appears, was aimed at winning approval for a new model to guide downtown hospitals, a model only dimly perceived at that time. Research hospitals and major universities, politicians and physicians had begun to judge, could do much more than cure the sick and provide higher education; they might eliminate blight, create thousands of new jobs, bring money into underdeveloped and declining areas, and in turn anchor parts of the city's economy, or at least Center City's economy.[7] The promise of the hospital as a combined downtown economic engine and urban renewal agency had a long history in Chicago. The Windy City's civic leaders called it a medical district.

## The Chicago Model

Chicago's medical district was the nation's first. In 1941, a small group of physicians persuaded the Illinois General Assembly to approve the Medical District Act, creating a medical district 1.5 miles southwest of the city's Loop. Rush Medical School, Presbyterian Hospital, and Cook County Hospital, which a Chicago journalist described as "the world's largest civilian hospital," were already located in the area. In January 1945, with World War II still ongoing, Illinois Governor Dwight H. Green asked state legislators to appropriate $250,000 to fund the district's first land purchases. The governor described the tract's growth as vital to public health and as an antidote to blight.[8]

During the next decades, growth of the district's hospitals depended on avid and energetic supporters. Dr. Walter H. Theobald made that growth his life's work. Theobald had graduated from Rush Medical School in 1911 as an ear, nose, and throat specialist. Despite having always been in private practice rather than a hospital employee, Theobald joined the seven-member commission in 1945 as its president. His work on the commission extended nearly to his death in 1974 at the age of eighty-seven. In their earlier actions, Theobald and his fellow commissioners sought to clear the dilapidated buildings that surrounded the three medical campuses on their 305-acre site, which included 50 acres dedicated to future parkland. The State of Illinois financed the commission's purchases, and government action helped in a second way. The proposed Congress Street Expressway was to run along the district's northern border, creating a hard buffer against nearby factories, warehouses, and lower-income African Americans who were moving into the area. In multiple ways, the Medical Center District served as an early demonstration project for later Chicagoans like Mayor Richard J. Daley and real-estate developer Arthur Rubloff as they contemplated ways to utilize public and private funds to enhance the value of properties along North Michigan Avenue and in their planned Fort Dearborn Project.[9]

After World War II, Theobald and his fellow commissioners envisioned the district as a major research, treatment, and educational center. They planned not only for the growth of medical schools and hospitals, but also for a University of Illinois campus with space for twenty thousand students. In November 1947, however, a *Chicago Tribune* writer headlined Theobald's plans as "a costly dream . . . in [a] blighted area." Medical students and even physicians, the reporter noted, "repair porches, stairs . . . , and roofs, [often] 'at their own expense.'"[10]

In the years that followed, a program of substantial borrowing and massive federal, state, and county spending fostered part of the sought-after growth. Cook County officials issued tax-free bonds to finance construction of hospital buildings. In 1949, Presbyterian Hospital administrators started work on a 15-story home for nurses. During the 1950s, new buildings and additional patients appeared at a faster pace. In January 1956, ABC television utilized Cook County Hospital to broadcast "Accident Medicine" to television-viewing Americans. Producers started the show with arriving ambulances and busy medical staff and then transported audience members to discussions about specialized topics such as the treatment of chest fractures. The hospital's round-the-clock life-or-death dramas made for gripping television, which was certainly useful publicity as hospital officials like Theobald planned for additional bond issues and met with legislators to plead for more funds to finance additional growth. "Development will never end," Theobald announced in December 1957, as if on cue from an ABC producer.[11]

At that juncture, uneven growth was a more accurate description of Theobald's medical district. A local journalist pointed to the area's "islands of slums." Urban renewal, even in a bountifully financed program like that underway in the district, was a lengthy undertaking, riven by politics and congressional delays in approving funds and further stymied by local property owners' refusal to sell homes and renters equally unwilling to move. As in other renewal programs, city officials including Mayor Daley promised public housing to displaced families. Only a small number secured those desired places. In April 1961, however, district officials hosted an open house for all visitors, suggesting a high level of confidence in their new facilities' appearance and the prospects for growth those buildings suggested. That confidence, it turned out, was partly justified. In 1965, University of Illinois leaders approved a plan for a Chicago campus capable of serving more than twenty-five thousand students. And yet, on weekends, the medical district, according to a member of Theobald's commission, was "deserted." A journalist described the district and surrounding blocks as "one of the toughest police districts."[12] The medical district's physical development would remain incomplete for decades into the future.

By the early 1970s, Theobald and his top hospital administrators had settled on a new approach to medical education and patient treatment. That approach revolved around the idea that hospitals and medical schools could function together as part of a regional medical system. In 1969, Rush Medical College had merged with Presbyterian Hospital and the nearby St. Luke's Medical Center. In 1971, top officials launched a $76 million expansion program that included additional patient beds and academic buildings. The investment represented more than another round of construction to add to patient capacity and laboratory space. Rather, the combined Rush-Presbyterian-St. Luke's was supposed to gather in one place all the services needed by patients from across the Chicago region. Those patients might enter treatment at a community hospital or a doctor's office in the suburbs or in another part of Chicago and conclude treatment at the recently combined hospital complex. Like so many plans generated during Theobald's entrepreneurial reign as president at the Illinois Medical District, the creation of a thoroughgoing medical system remained incomplete. In the short run, Theobald helped put the hospitals and the health-related schools in his district on a competitive footing to snag patients and medical talent away from Chicago's other fast-growing hospitals, such as the prestigious Northwestern Memorial Hospital and the University of Chicago Medical Center. By the 1970s, the city's hospitals were not simply a place to reduce a child's temperature, place a cast around a broken bone, or recover from a heart attack. Hospitals like the massive Rush-Presbyterian-St. Luke's were increasingly vital local resources both to improve health outcomes and to create jobs and businesses in cities undergoing wrenching change.[13]

Dr. William H. Danforth identified an equal number of financial and demographic challenges surrounding his hospital in St. Louis, a city shaped in the previous decades by urban-renewal projects, racial strife, and an un-relenting economic downturn.

## Another Round of Renewal in St. Louis

In December 1970, Washington University's trustees appointed the forty-four-year-old Danforth as their next chancellor. He started his new post the following July. Danforth, a Harvard University–trained physician, had completed a cardiac residency at the prestigious Barnes Hospital in St. Louis. Barnes was part of the Washington University School of Medicine, and its staff included nurses and physicians with years of experience treating the city's low-income population.[14] No physician or educator, however, possessed the skills and resources that were prerequisite to reducing St. Louis's multiple problems to one or several clear-cut fixes.

Early in 1972, a *Wall Street Journal* writer reported on his visit to St. Louis. In the article, "St. Louis: Can the Decay Be Stopped?" any regular newspaper reader since World War II would have recognized almost by instinct the publication of another gloomy account of urban deterioration. But this reporter, with a background in the city's urban-renewal history, brought still grimmer news to a national audience. During the 1950s and 1960s, the city's political leaders such as Mayor Raymond R. Tucker and members of Civic Progress, a group of top business executives that included beer baron August A. Busch Jr. had supported the Mill Creek Valley project. The Mill Creek Valley demolition took in a vast swath of buildings starting at the edge of downtown and extending as far west as Grand Avenue. That destruction, judged the reporter, had helped "recapture . . . the downtown core and part of the riverfront from blight." By any standard, the reporter overstated the degree of downtown's revival. And with Mill Creek Valley buildings eliminated and its population scattered, city and business leaders led another renewal project to clear space for a new baseball stadium to house Busch's St. Louis Cardinals. In subsequent years, the poverty, racism, joblessness, drug use, and prostitution that earlier characterized sections of downtown and parts of Mill Creek Valley relocated westward to the neighborhoods near Washington University and Barnes Hospital.[15]

Now it was Danforth's responsibility to deal with the multiple problems that an earlier generation of city leaders had failed to resolve. By 1975, Danforth and his fellow hospital executives had determined that their medical school, hospital, and more than 5,800 employees would remain in the city. The decision to stay put, by one estimate, also guaranteed "a $166 million shot in the arm for the local economy." If Barnes remained in St. Louis, however, Danforth insisted that the hospital play a decisive role in restoring the surrounding area.[16] Like hospital administrators in Philadelphia and Chicago,

Danforth relied on cooperative politicians to provide a portion of the finances and most of the governmental foundation for that redevelopment.
Barnes administrators and St. Louis lawmakers created an area much like
the Illinois Medical District in Chicago and its decades-long effort to redevelop real estate near the Loop.

In February 1975, St. Louis's Board of Alderman approved a contract
with the Washington University Medical Center Redevelopment Corporation. Starting immediately, the corporation's officers received authority to
guide development of a thirty-six-block tract surrounding Barnes Hospital.
Barnes physicians often worked closely with their counterparts at the nearby Jewish Hospital, and cooperative aldermen added it to the district. Aldermen and medical officers highlighted their reliance on private investments
rather than city funds, but their calculations failed to include the tax abatement that would help fund a $48 million development over nine years. In
the 1960s, August Busch had constructed his stadium with a similar tax abatement, bulldozing homes and businesses along the way. By the mid-1970s,
however, wholesale demolition and removal of African American households violated accepted political practice. "There will be no rampaging bulldozers," a university publicist promised in June 1975. Race remained a central theme in the organization of any big-city hospital. Yet Danforth stood
in a stronger position to redevelop his neighborhood, called the Central
West End, than members of that earlier generation of downtown-oriented
renewal enthusiasts like August Busch and Mayor Tucker. Danforth's resources included federal financing (Medicare and Medicaid), insurance payments, a burgeoning patient population in the suburbs, and his hospital's
reputation for delivering medical miracles nearly every day. During the next
two decades, Danforth presided over a program including both rehabilitation and new construction.[17]

The neighborhood rebranding started with favorable publicity placed in
national newspapers. The Central West End, a *Chicago Tribune* writer announced in May 1981, "is one of the liveliest neighborhoods in the country"
for watching people. In 1987, a *Philadelphia Inquirer* reporter described St.
Louis as "a gem sparkling in the heartland" and recommended "concentrations of worthwhile restaurants" in the Central West End. In January 1988,
Danforth and others scored an even bigger coup when Barbara P. Bush, wife
of presidential candidate George H. W. Bush, attended a fund-raising event
at the home of supporters in the Central West End. In March 1992, however, a civil-rights leader described the Central West End as an area with
"prostitutes and dope dealers," and urged "people . . . to reclaim the neighborhood." Up to the late 1980s, the area's redevelopment varied between
drug-ridden and upscale from block to block. The improvements continued
during the next decade. Because police patrolled the area with "persistence

and tenacity," the vice president and security chair of the Central West End Association reported in June 1999, "crime has dropped as much as 60 to 90 percent over the past three years."[18] As the decade concluded, a combination of intense policing, heavy spending on rehabilitation, and a barrage of mostly upbeat publicity distributed around the United States had substantially remade the Central West End's reputation—from shabby and dangerous to a smart place to visit, shop, work, and seek medical attention.

To be sure, William Danforth was not a home builder, architect, property developer, or real-estate speculator. He headed a nationally respected university and hospital. From the start, Danforth's goal in leading the Central West End's redevelopment was to make the area more attractive to patients and staff, which, he trusted, would maintain or perhaps enlarge Barnes Hospital's dominance in the St. Louis region. Improving the hospital's image in areas such as women's health was another exercise aimed at gaining additional patients. But Danforth did not seek only to add patients. Most fundamentally, he set about the business of expanding his patient base among suburban women.

Outside observers had always placed Barnes on any list of the nation's best hospitals. "Most physicians in this part of the country believe Barnes . . . is the premier teaching and research hospital in the Midwest," the authors of a glowing report on the nation's major hospitals observed in 1987. Barnes, however, failed to score high among those who rated women's medical services. "To a great extent," a writer for *Ladies' Home Journal* informed his readers in January 1976, "hospital care in the U.S. means women's care," as, for instance, hysterectomies and partial or full mastectomies. That reputation stuck. "Most of our 'best doctors' are on the teaching staffs of medical schools," a nurse writing for *Harper's Bazaar* told her largely female readership. But in specialized areas for women such as infertility and breast and gynecological cancer, however, only Dr. Falls B. Hershey, a breast cancer specialist affiliated with Barnes, appeared on her list of "best medical specialists."[19] The process of bringing about an improved rank for the treatment of women rested on construction of a strong record treating diseases such as breast cancer.

Danforth created specialized facilities in which many female patients could begin and complete breast cancer treatments. Medical doctors like Diane Radford, a surgical oncologist, assembled, translated, and presented diagnostic test results to patients facing wrenching choices between radical surgeries and degrees of disfigurement. "The center gives them every surgical option," Radford reported. Still more, Radford's patients no longer had to travel into the Central West End for treatment. Early in 1992, Barnes opened a one-stop center for breast cancer treatment at their West County satellite hospital. Danforth and his colleagues had extended the medical system idea to attract women with breast cancer and other diseases as patients, even if they were located miles away from the Central West End. The area St. Louisans identified as West County consisted mostly of wealthy (and white) residents in cities such as Creve Coeur and Ladue as well as nearby Clayton. The medical system idea was deeply racialized from the start. Yet the undeniable financial fact of the matter was that Danforth needed cash-rich or insured patients to help offset part of the hospital's expenses for large staffs, complex research, daily patient treatment (including indigent patients), and costly equipment. A medical historian describes that equipment, in Barnes and in other hospitals, as a "biomedical showcase." In turn, Danforth, by extending his hospital system into places like West County, sought to locate well-off patients who would make Barnes their first choice for every type of medical care.[20] Merger with a nearby hospital constituted another strategy to reduce Barnes's expenses and simultaneously locate a larger number of suburban patients who brought cash or insurance cards to the hospital's check-in desk.

In 1995, Danforth presided over the merger of Barnes and the nearby Jewish Hospital, creating St. Louis's largest medical center. The combined hospitals held a "commanding 12.4 percent market share in the St. Louis area," a local writer calculated. Reports about market share no doubt instructed readers in the businesslike language increasingly invoked to describe hospitals. Less noticed was the fact that Danforth had also refashioned Barnes-Jewish into a medical system, like Chicago's Rush-Presbyterian-St. Luke's twenty years earlier. The idea, as before, was to connect medical services to wealthier patients in a vast catchment area, starting in West County but also extending in every direction across the region. Once underway, suburban patients continued to visit local doctors for health checkups, including laboratory tests. Physicians in those suburban centers directed patients in need of specialized services for kidney disease or difficult pregnancies to operating rooms, beds, and clinics located at Barnes-Jewish's main buildings in the Central West End. Danforth led an effort to make relentless suburbanization work for his hospital's growth and national reputation as a center of high-technology medicine.[21] Danforth also launched Barnes-Jewish into the complex business of converting medical research into profitable businesses and an extension of his Central West End renewal. During the next twenty years, only the renewal portion succeeded.

## Hospitals and the Business of Biotechnology

Danforth's interest in turning his researchers' ideas into lucrative businesses started in the late 1990s, after a surprising loss. A faculty member in engineering had developed a device to speed the movement of data across the internet. For two years, a *New York Times* writer reported, the engineer sought funding to start a business that would make his device into a salable product. No one in St. Louis stepped forward. The engineer then relocated to San Francisco, where financing appeared quickly, or so ran this account. A year later, he sold his company to Cisco Systems, a leading manufacturer of internet equipment, for $350 million. "Tech had flash, ambition, and billions to spend," reports Silicon Valley historian Margaret Pugh O'Mara, but that sparkle and excitement had not reached dull St. Louis. "We have great research here," Danforth asserted at one point, "but we have not done so well with the commercialization of that science." Innovative thinkers like that engineer, ran Danforth's reasoning, required start-up capital and modern facilities. And that same engineer, no doubt real, also served as a stand-in for the perception among St. Louis's political and businesses leaders like Danforth that St. Louis firms lacked risk-takers and failed to innovate—especially in comparison with cutting-edge firms in and near San Francisco like Cisco Systems that held a dominant position in supplying devices to build the internet. Hospitals, however, did not build high-technology machines. Scientists and physicians at Barnes-Jewish worked with organs and cells. In earlier decades, researchers at major corporations such as Genentech had taken a lead in the field, converting esoteric cell research into profitable, life-enhancing discoveries. Genentech's researchers, for example, had developed drugs derived from Chinese hamster ovaries that were used to treat cancers and asthma. "Boosters of an economy organized around health care, education, and high technology," historian Gabriel Winant observes, "often seemed to imagine that everyone involved would be a professional."[22]

In the early 2000s, Danforth sought to put Barnes-Jewish into the prestigious and potentially lucrative hunt for useful drug therapies. In the future, his talented researchers would promptly convert laboratory experiments and scientific articles lacking cash value into marketable products. "Venture capitalists have seen the future—and it's biotech," a writer for *Investment Dealers' Digest* reported in October 2001. By this fervid reasoning, if St. Louis captured one or more of these biotechnology firms, the adjoining neighborhoods would prosper again, fueled by the ready availability of deep research funds and the presence of well-paid scientists. Danforth's Washington University (and nearby St. Louis University) stood to benefit as well. Those biotechnology firms would in the future pay royalties to university officials for the patents developed in their laboratories. *Incubated* was a favorite term to describe the way startup firms would reshape esoteric scientific investigations into blockbuster drugs that earned massive royalties for university laboratories. Public-private partnership was another often-expressed term to describe a close working relationship among university officials, public agencies, and the firms that converted laboratory discoveries into useful products. Of course, federal agencies such as the National Institutes of Health had regularly financed that expensive research; and, starting in 1980, the Bayh-Dole Patent and Trademark Act permitted private universities to own and commercialize their research results.[23] Here again, government set the terms and smoothed the way for Danforth's engagement with biotechnology. But still, like any new or old enterprise, Danforth needed one person to steer it in a useful and profitable direction.

John P. Dubinsky took charge of the development. Dubinsky, a former bank president and chair of Jewish Hospital's board at the time of the 1995 merger, brought decades of experience to the business and politics of banking and hospital management. Starting in the mid-1960s, his first tasks at the bank included sizing up credit histories, assessing property values, and approving mortgage loans to homeowners. Prior to making business loans, Dubinsky and his senior officers evaluated each firm's viability in competitive markets. Dubinsky was also alert to state politics. Up to the 1990s, bankers like Dubinsky, who operated under a Missouri charter, looked to state politicians and regulators to determine rules about lending or expansion plans. Dubinsky was in regular contact with State of Missouri officials—often, the very persons and agencies to whom any biotechnology executive would turn for startup funds. Dubinsky had served fewer years as a hospital board official, but he developed connections with Danforth that extended far into the future. Danforth and Dubinsky worked as a team on several hospital projects, and, in fact, it was Danforth who recruited Dubinsky to the new post. Dubinsky's predecessor as chair of the Jewish Hospital's board described him as "hands on."[24]

In December 2001, Dubinsky took up his new responsibilities as president of Cortex—the acronym for his Center of Research, Technology and Entrepreneurial Expertise. "Biology is the next revolution," he announced in May 2002 after he and Danforth visited successful biotechnology firms near the MIT campus in Cambridge. Dubinsky and Danforth probably did not realize that they followed the very same path as earlier St. Louis leaders who had trekked to cities such as Pittsburgh to learn political growth formulas. Dubinsky and Danforth's trip failed to reassure jittery businesspeople, however. During the next months, heads of several small biotechnology companies spoke openly about relocating to East and West Coast cities that already featured readily available business services and laboratory space. After half a century of business and population loss, St. Louis's research infrastructure suffered in comparison with the facilities already established in cities like Boston, San Francisco, Seattle, and Los Angeles.[25]

Cortex never emerged as a center of biotechnology investment and employment. Missouri politicians permanently crimped Dubinsky and Danforth's growth plans. Biotechnology firms were in the business of converting cells, including human cells, into useful products and, in March 2007, state legislators refused to fund research that made use of cells taken from human embryos. Suddenly, $5.5 million earmarked for Cortex's wet laboratory was zeroed out of the state budget. "We are sacrificing . . . the growth of biotechnology," Dubinsky lamented, adding that biotechnology was "the greatest opportunity in our lifetime in terms of jobs and economic development." The next day, a newspaper writer headlined that "Biotech leaders are back to square one."[26]

Dubinsky turned Cortex in a new direction. The state's rough-and-tumble politics and the arrival of few new companies forced him to redefine the district as a business park with a new name, the Cortex Innovation Community. In subsequent years, many of the companies that leased space at Cortex bore no relationship to the much-touted biotechnology revolution. In 2014, Ikea, which sells Swedish furniture, rented space in Cortex. Ikea brought retail customers to its locations. In 2018, Microsoft opened a regional office and technology center where customers and employees would create new software designs. By 2019, Cortex rented space in attractive buildings to 390 firms, including corporate giants such as Boeing. More than 5,500 persons worked in the Cortex district, most of whom were not engaged in biotechnology. Under Dubinsky's supervision, in sum, Cortex emerged as a successful urban renewal project.[27] Proximity to Barnes-Jewish Hospital was no doubt an asset as Dubinsky pitched likely tenants on the area's advantages, which included restaurants, ethnically diverse neighborhoods, first-class health care, and the presence of a large pool of well-educated future employees.

The Cortex district extended the middle-class themes Danforth had established in his renewed Central West End. From 1975, he had directed a program to remake the area surrounding Barnes Hospital into a comfortable place for mostly white, higher-income St. Louisans to reside, work, and seek medical treatment. Suburban patients could drive into the Central West End, consult their physicians, schedule procedures, and remain for lunch. Dubinsky's Cortex added taxpaying firms and a workforce—mostly young and, again, mostly white—earning salaries sufficient to rent nearby apartments. In sharp contrast, earlier downtown renewal programs had failed to maintain jobs in the city. Yet Dubinsky and Cortex proved equally uninterested in dealing with the city's often hateful racial history. Setting Cortex on a sound financial footing was their highest priority. As well, Cortex employees at firms like Boeing and Microsoft were by training and habit accustomed to following managers' directions in detail. As a result, Dubinsky and his successor were never able to begin the arduous process of transferring the entrepreneurial, startup mentality that animated small biotechnology firms in other cities to St. Louis's large and traditional corporations.[28] Chicago's biotechnology promoters achieved similarly limited results.

Leaders of the Illinois Medical District opened their Chicago Technology Park in 1987. Ten years later, the park hosted only sixteen companies. Still, the medical district's executive director promised rapid growth, at some point to include ten thousand employees. What "silicon did this century," he predicted, "biotech will do in the next." As that new century started, Chicago's hospital leaders increasingly sounded like Dubinsky and Danforth in their rapt descriptions of biotechnology's medical and financial promise. Words such as *incubator* were standard fare in the district. Just as standard, federal and Illinois officials had already awarded grants totaling $20 million to aid startup firms. And, without doubt, Dubinsky and Danforth would have recognized the difficulty the medical district encountered in recruiting firms to the park, securing additional funds for their research, and then translating that research into marketable products. In mid-2001, only twenty-seven firms had set up operations and research to convert laboratory investigations into commercial products.[29]

During the next decade, the Chicago Technology Park fizzled as a center of biotechnology investment and innovation. Between 2004 and 2012, as one sign that plans had gone unfulfilled, the district lost $18.7 million; and, as another, in 2012, a $40 million bond issue edged toward default. Much like Dubinsky in St. Louis, the park's managers hunted for new tenants such as a Costco store and a helicopter landing pad for executives. In 2014, only thirty firms operated in the park, an increase of three since 2001. Nor did those firms' executives fulfill the ambitions of the park's founders that laboratory discoveries would soon improve health and achieve commercial successes. Most basically, managers of the park's biotechnology firms never established an intimate and near-daily flow among their employees and the basic science researchers in the Illinois Medical District's distinguished hospitals. Much as Danforth and Dubinsky discovered in building Cortex, the presence of a hospital, even a distinguished hospital, did not necessarily bring technology entrepreneurs to their doorstep. During the decade's remaining years, district leaders sought new commercial developments such as medical offices and two Hyatt-branded hotels to be constructed in the shuttered Cook County Hospital's former location. Hyatt Hotel and Hyatt House opened in 2020. Like their counterparts in St. Louis, leaders of the Illinois Medical District had succeeded in making their technology park into an attractive area for middle-class Chicagoans to attend college, rent an apartment, and devote an afternoon to shopping. Government remained a vital part in enabling Illinois Hospital District managers to amass the cash and political power that were prerequisite to successfully renewing areas near their hospitals and universities. Yet that government support proved useless as Illinois Medical District administrators failed to assemble competitive biotechnology districts.[30] But without doubt, hospitals in Chicago and other cities served as vital actors in shaping their regions' health-care employment.

## Race, Class, and Gender on Hospital Floors

Every day and night, ambulance sirens screeched warnings to pedestrians and motorists to clear the way for their cargos of sick and injured patients. And whether at Barnes-Jewish or another hospital, dedicated nurses and physicians met patients at emergency room doors to begin lifesaving therapies and administer pain-reducing medicines. In 2014, Barnes-Jewish counted more than ninety-five thousand emergency room visits. In each decade, moreover, nurses and physicians attended to patients stricken with new ailments such as HIV-AIDS and crack cocaine addiction, as well as the scourge of gunshot wounds. In 2020 brave medical staffs began treating patients struck low by COVID-19, a profoundly contagious virus for which neither therapies nor vaccines existed at that time. And whether it was crack cocaine or COVID-19, persons of color made up a disproportionate number of patients. They resided near downtown, often within sight of luxury apartments and gated communities that housed their fellow, mostly white, citizens in guard-protected comfort. Residents of the left-behind neighborhoods inhaled the polluted air discharged each day by their cities' remaining industrial plants and waste disposal sites (as did, in a few cases, upscale residents of recently gentrified districts). But health and wealth remained starkly imprinted on city maps. In 2012, as one example, Philadelphia researchers found that all the Society Hill–area women forty years old and above had had mammograms. But a few miles away, in predominantly low-income, African American North Philadelphia, only 52 percent of the women had had a mammogram. No wonder then, as a *New York Times* writer observed in May 2020, "a baby born in one neighborhood in Chicago is now expected to die 30 years sooner than a baby born in a wealthier neighborhood just eight miles to the north."[31]

Nothing about the economic and racial geographies or the astonishingly higher death rates near downtown Cleveland, Detroit, and Philadelphia was natural or inevitable. But those geographies created a paradox in U.S. political understanding. Every adult urban resident has known (or should have known) their city's changing racial boundaries, at least in rough outline.[32] Yet, curiously, even well-educated Americans were profoundly unaware of the decisions made by political and business leaders such as Cleveland's Mayor Voinovich, both of Chicago's Daleys, and Philadelphia's Rafsky that since the 1950s had framed residents' chances to achieve a middling class lifestyle. But, each day, Voinovich's and his mayoral counterparts' cumulated decisions (and multiple federal policies) favoring downtown had ushered their cities and their overworked hospital staffs to these uneven (and often deadly) outcomes.[33]

Medical personnel were no more knowledgeable about urban history than other city residents. Nurses and doctors remained uninformed about the vital role city leaders had played since the 1960s in fostering the growth of major medical centers as urban renewal projects. Medical personnel, mostly shift workers, attended to patients as they arrived. And, as those patients' friends and family members lulled around crowded waiting rooms, they perhaps observed portions of the hospital's hurried work life. Hospital staff were ubiquitous. Those staff members included mostly white and male surgeons dressed in scrubs. They performed specialized interventions and complex surgical procedures that sometimes required standing over anesthetized patients for up to eight or ten hours. In 2019, however, women constituted 74.9 percent of hospital workers. That predominantly female (and often heavily minority) staff prepared patients for surgery, implemented postoperative procedures, and monitored hoped-for recoveries. An identically female staff maintained patient flow in and out of busy clinics for patients seeking treatments as diverse as chemotherapy and hearing disorders. African Americans, usually women, often took up of the harder tasks such as room cleanup. In May 2019, the mean hourly average wage for all workers in the United States stood at $25.72. Cleveland's health-care support workers earned $14.91 an hour. Hospital employment replicated the racialized economy of minorities filling less-skilled positions.[34] At hospitals like Barnes-Jewish and the University of Pennsylvania, moreover, the workday started at 5:30 in the morning in surgical preparation units and concluded around 10:30 in the evening, when second shift personnel headed home in automobiles and more often on public transportation. Starting in the early 1990s, the Metrolink platform across the street from the Barnes-Jewish entrance served hundreds of modest-wage employees at a time. And beginning in 2008, Cleveland's less-well-paid hospital employees rode the HealthLine from downtown to the Cleveland Clinic. In both cities, health-care employees, often attired in multicolored garb, boarded and returned to predominantly African American neighborhoods located miles from their hospitals' massive buildings. They, too, stood on their feet up to ten hours each day, moving from one assignment to the next such as relocating equipment, cleaning bathrooms, and bathing feverish patients.

In the 1960s, hospital administrators like Metropolitan's Dr. Silverman and Barnes's Dr. Danforth began to make precedent setting judgments about hospital organization and size. They emphasized growth as a device to improve patient outcomes, boost revenues, and deal with relentless suburbanization. The expansion of hospitals obliterated old neighborhoods and created phenomenal medical complexes that dominated entire sections of cities.

The growth extended across subsequent decades. In 2018, the University of Pennsylvania Health System employed more than twenty-three thousand physicians, nurses, and staff members to treat patients and also to carry forward complex research programs in areas as varied as breast cancer, male infertility, and Parkinson's disease. Throughout the day, well-paid physicians traveled between laboratory and clinic to check on cell research at one moment and speak with anxious patients and their families at another. In similar fashion, Barnes-Jewish employed more than twenty-eight thousand persons at the start of 2020. Like hospitals in many cities, Barnes-Jewish and the University of Pennsylvania hospitals were their city's largest employers. In 2017, some 17 percent of St. Louis County's workforce held jobs associated with health care and social assistance, often in hospitals. Those same large hospitals and universities were also their city's biggest spenders. By 2011, according to former Cleveland city planner Norman Krumholz, university and medical purchasing and payrolls accounted for approximately two-thirds of the growth in the city's economy. Urban publicists and collegiate researchers described these massive operations with sobriquets such as "eds and meds," and "anchor institutions."[35]

But the growing number of jobs at university hospitals was always relative to employment in earlier years. During the postwar decades, the largest employers of earlier decades such as meat packers and steel manufacturers in Chicago or Philadelphia's once-mighty Pennsylvania Railroad had closed, shrunk, or moved away. In 1967, Philadelphia still possessed 264,000 manufacturing jobs, but that number had declined to 23,000 in 2012. In 2018, only 7,300 manufacturing jobs remained in Pittsburgh while 90,000 persons worked in education and health care. In these cities, it appears, only universities and hospitals remained to recruit employees in large numbers. Whether in St. Louis or Chicago, medical personnel restored Americans' health.[36] After 2000, physicians and medical assistants routinely managed diseases such as HIV-AIDS, a death sentence a few years earlier. But neither Frank Rizzo, Bill Rafsky, John Dubinsky, nor William Danforth possessed the wisdom combined with the political and cash resources to cure the afflictions of racism, poverty, and inadequate health care that surrounded every city's downtown and nearby hospitals.[37] Detroit's poorest and mostly African American residents experienced no greater luck when a pair of billionaire visionaries, Mike Ilitch and Dan Gilbert, invested vast sums of money and relegated local government to a supporting role in a decades-long quest to revitalize their city's downtown, whose history is told in the next chapter.

# 10

## "Gilbertville," "Ilitchville," and
## the Redevelopment of Detroit

D etroit was at one time among the nation's wealthiest cities. Publicists and residents decorously referred to it as "the Paris of the Midwest." The city had risen to prominence along with other Midwestern Rust Belt communities tied to the triumph of Fordism, and for decades residents of the boomtown enjoyed steady employment and high wages. During World War II, Detroit's remarkable transformation from the nexus of the automobile industry to the nation's leading producer of arms and munitions led President Franklin D. Roosevelt to dub the Motor City the Arsenal of Democracy. In daily headlines and in lawmakers' pronouncements, winning the war took precedence over growing problems of race relations, access to steady jobs, a decaying infrastructure, and falling retail sales.[1]

The descent from manufacturing leviathan to postindustrial wreckage came inexorably after the war. By 1945, "downtown decay was a major problem," the distinguished planning historian June Manning Thomas observed, "but so was industrial decline." The automobile business, for decades the city's economic bellwether, suffered repeated setbacks at the hands of Japanese and European competitors. Disaster mounted in the last decades of the twentieth century as corporations built plants and opened new headquarters outside city limits. Workers, skilled and unskilled alike, suffered the jarring loss of employment. Detroit's overreliance on production of a single commodity backfired when the automobile industry floundered.[2]

Along with industrial contraction and the attendant job loss came a dramatic population exodus. A horrific race riot in 1967, continuous racial tension, and a series of embarrassing political scandals contributed to a growing consensus among white residents (and a smaller number of middle-income African Americans) that the city of Detroit was no longer a fit place to buy a house, raise a family, or even look for a job. From 1.8 million residents in 1950, which ranked Detroit the fifth-largest city in the nation, the population fell to 673,000 in 2017. Images of barren lots, deserted storefronts, and burned-out homes made Detroit's denuded landscape an international symbol of urban decay.[3]

The City of Detroit's fiscal collapse added yet another layer of despair. A drastically reduced tax base, falling real-estate valuations, taxpayer delinquency, and fiscal mismanagement in city hall created huge shortfalls in the municipal budget. The city's credit rating sank to junk-bond status, negating the possibility of borrowing money to meet recurring financial obligations. A paucity of resources led to a steep reduction in services. Residents complained about darkened streetlights, erratic bus service, sporadic garbage pickup, escalating crime rates, and delayed response times by police cars, fire trucks, and ambulances. In 2013, Michigan governor Richard D. Snyder suspended Detroit's home rule, appointing an emergency manager with virtually limitless authority to govern as he saw fit. Unable to pay off its estimated $20 billion debt, Detroit filed for bankruptcy later that year. The city yielded managerial control of Cobo Hall, Eastern Market, Belle Isle, and other community assets to several nonprofit, professionally managed, quasi-public boards. Detroit's elected leaders had surrendered their city's autonomy. The overwhelming sense of doom among left-behind residents and remaining business owners allowed little hope for the future.[4]

In the first decades of the twenty-first century, however, two wealthy entrepreneurs bought numerous tracts of land and launched sweeping rebuilding initiatives in Detroit as part of arguably the largest private urban revival effort in the nation's history. Native Detroiters who grew up in modest circumstances and founded successful corporations, billionaires Michael Ilitch and Daniel B. Gilbert separately commenced reclamation activities designed to rehabilitate the fortunes of the ailing Motor City. Working at different tempos and operating in contiguous areas of the city, the self-made men subscribed to the prevailing wisdom that the rebirth of residential neighborhoods would necessarily follow the resuscitation of the downtown. Ilitch frequently secured generous taxpayer subsidies for his projects, and Gilbert more often utilized his own capital exclusively. Both men, however, operated independently of public direction while developing strategies and devising projects wholly on their own. Their ardent advocacy and massive investment elevated Ilitch and Gilbert from local success stories to potential saviors of the city.[5]

## Mike Ilitch's Dream of an Entertainment District

The most recent crusade to salvage Detroit began with the rags-to-riches story of Mike Ilitch, the son of poor Macedonian immigrants who grew up in a working-class neighborhood on the city's West Side. His father repaired machinery at a Chrysler factory. After graduating from high school and completing a four-year hitch in the U.S. Marine Corps, Ilitch signed a minor-league baseball contract with the hometown Tigers. Failing to advance to the big leagues, he sold awnings and kitchen equipment door-to-door. By 1959, Ilitch had saved $10,000 and founded Little Caesars pizza in Garden City, a Detroit suburb. Ilitch by one account wanted to name the firm Pizza Treat. Ilitch's wife Marian, however, recommended Little Caesars, from her favored nickname for him. In the early days, Mike made pizzas and Marian kept the books. Mike and Marian quickly opened additional stores and sold franchises throughout the metropolitan region, state, and nation. By the early 1990s, Little Caesars claimed to be the world's largest carry-out pizza chain with more than 4,300 outlets. While the earnings of the pizza conglomerate rose and fell during subsequent decades, the family added other enterprises that consistently earned substantial profits. In 2015, Ilitch Holdings, the parent company overseeing dozens of other business concerns, reported total revenue of $3.3 billion. At the time of his death in 2017, according to *Forbes* magazine, the family's net wealth exceeded $6 billion.[6]

Mike Ilitch's story involved much more than simply making enormous sums of money. Ilitch invested much of his firm's capital in the construction and rehabilitation of entertainment venues, speculating that leisure activities would be the cornerstone of Detroit's downtown revival—a cornerstone that he meticulously laid over a period of thirty years. He began with the purchase in 1988 of the iconic Fox Theatre on Woodward Avenue at the northern edge of the central business district. The magnificent 10-story art deco building opened in 1928 as one of the five flagship movie palaces in the Fox Theatre national chain; the ornate 5,041-seat emporium remained Detroit's premier film destination for decades. In the 1950s and 1960s, the venue hosted live performances by Elvis Presley, various Motown recording groups, and other musical headliners in addition to its regular film offerings. As much of the middle-class moviegoing public fled to the suburbs and other downtown movie theaters closed in the 1970s, the Fox struggled along offering poor-quality blaxploitation and martial-arts films. Despite its election to the National Register of Historic Places in 1985 and its designation as a National Historic Landmark in 1989, decades of neglect and postponed maintenance became evident in its crumbling facades, peeling plaster, and threadbare seat cushions in the antiquated theater. Mike and Marian Ilitch purchased the Fabulous Fox in 1988 for $12 million and promised to restore its earlier luster. After the completion of the eighteen-month refurbishing project, the National Trust for Historic Preservation awarded Ilitch the National Preservation Award in 1990 for his renovation. Local preservationists hailed the restoration project as a wonderful contribution to the city's cultural scene.[7]

Ilitch had much larger plans. He proclaimed the Fox Theatre restoration merely the first step in his design to revive downtown Detroit by creating an entertainment district north of Grand Circus Park. He immediately moved the headquarters of several Ilitch Holdings subsidiaries (principally Little Caesars Pizza, Olympia Entertainment, and Olympia Development) from suburban Farmington Hills into offices in the Fox Theatre—a dramatic first step, he explained, in reversing the exodus of businesses from the city core to outlying suburbs. He also opened the Hockeytown Café, City Theatre, and Second City Detroit on the same block to spark additional nightlife in the area. The next move in creating an entertainment quarter along the Woodward corridor would be to build a new stadium for the Detroit Tigers baseball team, which Ilitch had purchased after the Fox reopening, in the surrounding area.[8]

## A New Baseball Stadium

Having acquired the Detroit Red Wings professional hockey team in 1982 and the Detroit Drive of the Arena Football League in 1988, Ilitch fulfilled a lifelong dream when he purchased the Tigers in 1992. The previous owner had talked about the need to build a new baseball stadium, and Ilitch immediately confronted questions about his intentions for the existing facility, Tiger Stadium. The Tigers had played at the intersection of Michigan and Trumbull Avenues in the Corktown neighborhood west of downtown since 1901. Local fans loved Tiger Stadium, which they viewed as an irreplaceable symbol of the city's athletic tradition. Not Ilitch. Where baseball aficionados saw a charming old ballpark rich with history, the Tiger owner saw a weatherworn structure desperately in need of expensive overhauls; and any repairs, he contended, only postponed the eventual destruction of an unattractive and outdated building. Where local fans saw an accessible venue comfortably removed from downtown traffic congestion, Ilitch complained about the dearth of lighted parking lots near the stadium that forced fans to leave their cars during games in nearby front yards, alleys, and vacant lots. Most important, Tiger Stadium languished in a deteriorated residential area more than a mile from Ilitch's proposed entertainment zone. Prospects for redeveloping the area around the ballpark were meager. When Ilitch purchased the team, he publicly praised Tiger Stadium's many charms. Shortly thereafter, however, he began to hint about the need to construct a new stadium.[9]

The location of a new home for the Tigers became a topic of widespread discussion in the 1990s with fans, local politicians, state legislators, and members of the Detroit financial community eagerly weighing in. Mayor Coleman A. Young quickly affirmed the need to vacate Tiger Stadium, saying, "It's obvious the damned thing is falling down." Young, the enthusiastic champion of the Renaissance Center, Joe Louis Arena, and other gigantic bricks-and-mortar projects downtown, jumped aboard the new stadium bandwagon as an integral addition to the central business district's rebirth. He also argued that the city must find a new site for the baseball club within city limits to head off the team's possible departure for greener pastures elsewhere. (The Detroit Lions professional football team had moved to suburban Pontiac in 1975, and the Detroit Pistons professional basketball team followed three years later.) A Michigan legislator advanced a proposal for a 200-acre site at the state-owned Michigan Fairgrounds eight miles north of downtown where cheap land and abundant freeway access existed, but his bill stalled in committee. Speculation centered on the construction of a new stadium with a retractable dome on the riverfront adjacent to Joe Louis Arena, home of the Red Wings, that would conveniently place the homes of Ilitch's hockey and baseball teams next to each other. The Tiger owner demurred, however, continuing to favor a site at the northern edge of downtown.[10]

## Bulldozing Part of Downtown

Ilitch moved slowly to ensure that the new baseball stadium would be constructed near the Fox Theatre, intimating that eventually venues for the Lions and the Red Wings would be added nearby to create an "ultra-sports entertainment district." While continuing to acquire properties along Woodward Avenue, he assembled a team of architects and urban design firms to develop a plan for situating all of his sports facilities in a compact area of the city. The stockpiling of land parcels occurred at a glacial pace, and critics complained when Olympia Development proceeded slowly in razing dilapidated buildings. Vacant lots remained empty for years. Historic preservationists, who had lauded Ilitch for the beautiful restoration of the Fox Theatre, turned against him as it became clear that his new stadium plan called for the purchase and demolition of several historic buildings north of downtown. Members of Preservation Detroit, the Michigan Historic Preservation Network, and other groups balked at the demolition of three historically significant and structurally sound buildings, the Adams Theatre/Fine Arts Building on Grand Circus Park, the United Artists Theatre, and the Park Avenue Hotel. The greatest uproar occurred over the fate of the Madison-Lenox Hotel, one of downtown Detroit's last remaining turn-of-the-century residential buildings, which Olympia Development had designated for destruction to build a parking lot near the new ballpark.[11]

The fate of the Madison-Lenox Hotel, which became a cause célèbre among preservationists nationally, involved the fate of a once-stately hotel that had declined and by the 1980s was occupied only by low- and fixed-income elderly residents. Ilitch bought the building in 1997. Olympia Development allowed the vacant hotel to deteriorate for several years, culminating in a "demolition by neglect watch" decree issued by the Detroit Historic District Commission. Mayor Kwame M. Kilpatrick agreed to provide Ilitch with a $700,000 interest-free loan to flatten the building. When the commission withstood pressure from Kilpatrick and denied the owner permission to raze the hotel, ordering Olympia Development to repair the structure or sell it, the two sides settled into a prolonged stalemate. In violation of state law and city ordinances, wrecking crews appeared unannounced on May 18, 2005, and began bulldozing the structure. City officials claimed that the hotel was "in imminent danger of collapse and its removal was justified as an emergency." Ilitch's Olympia Development denied having been consulted beforehand about the city's decision to level the building. Authorities never brought charges for the illegal demolition, and preservationists could only rail against the fait accompli. Ilitch preserved historic buildings or razed them, whatever best suited his needs.[12]

The careful assembly of properties, sometimes met by fierce criticism and at other times quietly without opposition, finally paid off on October 29, 1997, when the Detroit Tigers held groundbreaking ceremonies for the new ballpark. (In 1998, Comerica Bank paid $66 million over the next thirty years for naming rights to the stadium.) Originally planned to occupy a site behind the Fox Theatre, the ballpark ended up a block east of Woodward Avenue because of difficulties in acquiring land farther west. The team agreed to spend $145 million, the state promised $55 million, and the city committed a portion of special commercial property taxes to pay off bonds worth $40 million. The amounts required increased prior to Comerica Park's opening in 2000, and state and local contributions eventually totaled 37 percent of the final $360 million cost. Disgruntled taxpayers sued to forestall construction, contending that the state legislature had failed to approve funding, but the Michigan Court of Appeals ruled that Governor John M. Engler possessed the necessary authority to authorize expenditures and ruled in favor of the team. "Comerica Park will help restore the excitement of urban living that has been missing far too long from downtown Detroit," Mayor Dennis W. Archer predicted. Ilitch's search for allies in his downtown redevelopment plans even extended to Pontiac, a suburb twelve miles north of Detroit.[13]

Starting in 1996, Ilitch played a large role in coaxing the Detroit Lions owner William Clay Ford to vacate the Pontiac Silverdome and construct a new stadium next to Comerica Park. Ilitch trumpeted the many financial and logistical advantages of creating a sports center for the city's professional teams. He also made the case for the return to the central city as a public-spirited gesture that would enhance the downtown redevelopment campaign. Mayor Archer again wholeheartedly endorsed the idea of the city contributing substantial subsidies for the construction of a privately owned stadium, and the electorate approved the proposal in a referendum on November 5, 1996. Ford Field, the $430 million professional football stadium, opened next to Comerica Park in 2002.[14]

## Hockey, New Neighborhoods, and a Sports District

Ilitch next began laying the groundwork for the construction of an arena for his Red Wings hockey team in the shadow of the Tiger-Lion complex, the area he called Wildcat Corner. (He likewise attempted to buy the Detroit Pistons basketball team, with plans to move the team back downtown, but lost to another bidder.) The Red Wings had played at Joe Louis Arena on the riverfront since 1979, after Mayor Coleman Young had persuaded President Jimmy Carter to authorize a federal loan of $38 million for construction costs. "Revitalize the riverfront," Young had proclaimed at the time, "and I guarantee you'll revitalize the whole city." But Ilitch's blueprint for revitalizing the whole city concentrated on the blighted area north of the central business district. Olympia Development bought parcels of land in a forty-five-block area north of the Fisher Freeway (Interstate 75) for the hockey arena and, as Ilitch made clear from the outset, for a host of other uses as well. The sports venue would serve as the centerpiece of a vast urban renewal effort, replacing hollowed-out buildings, seedy bars, and weed-strewn vacant lots with a mixed-use project that included market-rate housing, retailing, entertainment, and office space. The new district would connect the riverfront with the medical center, Wayne State University campus, and museums in the lively Midtown neighborhood to the north, a link that had been severed by the completion of the Fisher Freeway barrier. "If the development that they're proposing happens at that capacity they're proposing," said the city manager of suburban Oak Park, "it's an absolute game changer for the city of Detroit, no doubt about it."[15]

Christopher Ilitch, the son of Mike and Marian Ilitch and chief executive officer and president of Ilitch Holdings after his father's death in 2017, echoed his family's intention to lead Detroit's rebirth with their investments. Surrounding the 650,000-square-foot hockey and events center, Ilitch prom-

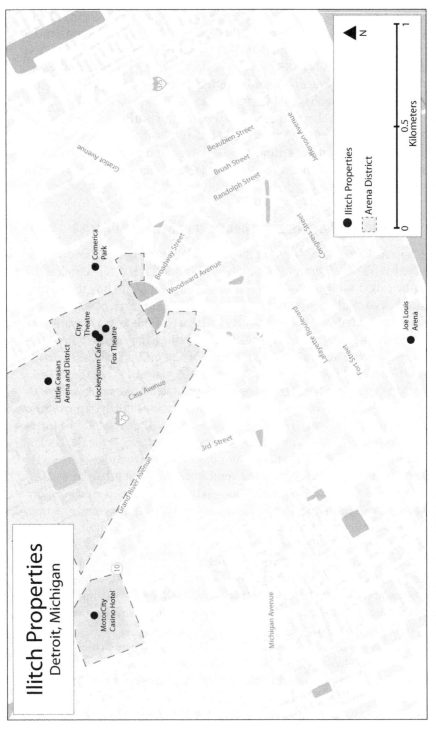

**Figure 10.1** Map of Ilitch Properties (Credit: Megan Maher, GeoMaps, Department of Geography and Geology, Illinois State University, Bloomington)

ised, Olympia Development would create five separate neighborhoods within the entire renewal district—one each for a sports arena, residential housing, entertainment, dining, and green space. The redeveloped area would extend from Wildcat Corner on the east to a northwest boundary abutting the MotorCity Casino Hotel, owned by Marian Ilitch. Within that space, the Ilitches vowed to spend "tens of millions" of additional dollars on ancillary improvements such as road repairs, new streetlights, and landscaping that "frees the city up to spend its resources on other priorities." No wonder that members of Detroit's Downtown Development Authority endorsed the expenditure of $200 million in public funds, after which the city council approved the deal. The Ilitches in turn agreed to contribute the balance of the estimated $650 million to complete the project. The comprehensiveness of the daring development plan, Chris Ilitch asserted in 2014, could only be described as revolutionary. In short, he boasted, "there is nothing like this going on in our country." Moreover, the Ilitch plan, with its proposal to privately underwrite infrastructure improvements traditionally provided by municipalities, offered an innovative approach to service delivery—an unprecedented blurring of public and private roles in the city.[16]

Mike and Chris Ilitch soon claimed that their initiative had also resulted in the creation of the nation's foremost sports district. On November 22, 2016, Olympia Development and Detroit Pistons owner Tom Gores jointly announced that the Pistons would join the Red Wings in the new arena being constructed north of Interstate 75. The Pistons had fled Detroit in 1978 for two Oakland County locations, playing the first ten years in Pontiac and thereafter in Auburn Hills, but Gores indicated a desire to return the team to its proper home in the central city and join the Ilitches in the downtown redevelopment effort. When Little Caesars Arena opened in the fall of 2017 with the Red Wings and Pistons as tenants, a mere six blocks away from Comerica Park and Ford Field, Detroit's sports district indeed became the most compact in urban America.[17] (See figure 10.1.)

## The Ilitch Family and District Detroit

In addition to the sports venues, Olympia Development continued to add new construction projects along Woodward Avenue in what the media began referring to as District Detroit. In 2014, the Ilitches unveiled architectural plans for a new 8-story office complex next door to the Fox Theatre, which would more than double the size of the cramped Ilitch Holdings headquarters. The following year, the Ilitch family donated the land immediately north of Little Caesars Arena and $40 million for the construction of a new Wayne State University building, the future home of the Mike Ilitch School of Business. The location of the business school next to the arena some distance south of the main Wayne State University campus, university administrators contended, would move students and faculty closer to the central business district, foster engagement with the city, and provide more opportunities for internships and mentorships. University officials expected that students, faculty, administrators, and staff would reside near the business school, in the new housing under construction and planned for District Detroit.[18]

Transportation improvements came next. Ilitch and other entrepreneurs called for the construction of a light rail system along Woodward Avenue. They sought to spark redevelopment north of downtown, eradicate the blight separating District Detroit from the Wayne State campus, and link the riverfront with the bustling Midtown neighborhood to the north. The M-1 Rail Consortium, which included representatives from Ilitch Holdings, General Motors, the Ford Foundation, Chrysler Group, the Kresge Foundation, Quicken Loans, and other local corporations and foundations, submitted a 1,200-page proposal to U.S. Department of Transportation Secretary Ray H. La-Hood pledging generous private financial support in return for federal funding. The inability to secure substantial financing from the bankrupt city of Detroit, argued the consortium members, must not be allowed to derail the completion of an essential catalyst to the city's recovery. After many years of struggle to raise the necessary funding, the 3.4-mile system commenced operation in 2017 as a public-private partnership underwritten by corporations and foundations along with the local, state, and federal governments. The streetcar line, originally given the working title of M-1, became known as the QLine when Quicken Loans purchased naming rights. At the direction of Dan Gilbert, the founder and chief executive officer of Quicken Loans, the prosperous mortgage company had contributed $10 million of the project's total cost of $140 million.[19]

The investment in the area north of the central business district of an estimated $2 billion over thirty years by the Ilitch family occurred during disastrous decades, when Detroit's dire financial situation kept most other risk takers at bay. Their investments in the downtown area had launched an era of redevelopment in the city. "Without Mr. Ilitch taking a shot when nobody else would, none of this would be where it is today," commented an appreciative observer of the city's putative turnaround. "He said yes when others were saying no." In February 2017, at the time of Ilitch's death, a prominent local resident described him as "a visionary leader whose lifelong investments in Detroit helped us become the comeback city we are today."[20]

## Dan Gilbert and Downtown Revival

Dan Gilbert, another Detroit success story, cooperated with Ilitch in the city's redevelopment effort. Gilbert, however, turned his attention to an adjoining section of downtown and acted at a much more rapid pace than Ilitch. Like Ilitch, Gilbert spent lavishly on behalf of his hometown. Again like Ilitch, Gilbert identified downtown renovation as the key to the city's revival. As impressive as Ilitch's gradual reworking of the area north of downtown proved to be, Gilbert's headlong rush to remake the central business district left Detroiters in awe.[21]

Born in Detroit and raised in suburban Southfield, Gilbert spent little time in the Motor City during his formative years. His father, who owned and operated a bar and grill in Detroit, described to his son how the urban core had declined over decades. The young Gilbert received a bachelor's degree at Michigan State University and a law degree at Wayne State University. He earned a real-estate agent's license during his undergraduate years and worked part-time for a real estate company while in law school. Theorizing that he could earn more money providing mortgages than listing and selling houses, Gilbert founded a mortgage lending company (Rock Financial) in 1985 with $5,000 he earned delivering pizzas while in college. The firm became one of the nation's most successful mortgage providers, pioneering in online lending. In 1999, he sold Rock Financial to a software company, which renamed the web operation Quicken Loans. Gilbert reacquired the company three years later. Quicken Loans soon emerged as the nation's largest online lender and in 2018 surpassed Wells Fargo as the second leading retail mortgage lender. Under the umbrella of Rock Ventures, the corporation that managed his investments and real-estate holdings, Gilbert owned the Greektown Casino-Hotel in Detroit as well as a number of entertainment enterprises in Cleveland, including the National Basketball Association's Cavaliers, Quicken Loans Arena, the Arena Football League's Gladiators, the American Hockey League's Monsters, and the Horseshoe Casino.[22]

Having achieved phenomenal success in business and having amassed a huge personal fortune, the billionaire Gilbert followed the path of urban restoration pioneered by Ilitch. Allowing that he intended to spend wisely and hoped to earn handsome returns on his investments, Gilbert maintained that his actions would also benefit Detroit. "There's no conflict in doing good and doing well," he insisted. He identified as one of his primary goals the restoration of his birthplace to greatness. "People my age," he related, "we would hear from our parents and grandparents who were raised in Detroit about how great this city was, from 1900 to the 1960s. But none of us had any memory of that." Gilbert's plan, which he sometimes referred to as Detroit 2.0, called for the wholesale conversion of the downtown as the linchpin of urban reclamation. He strove to transform the central business district from an after-hours ghost town bereft of retail and entertainment, where only government buildings and financial institutions survived, into a high-technology mecca where entrepreneurs worked, lived, and played.

His vision entailed a vibrant urban core where young business owners and workers resided, shopped, and spent much of their leisure time rather than fleeing to their suburban homes daily at 5:00 P.M.[23]

## The Urban Core as a Zone for the Young and the Well-Paid

In 2007, Gilbert announced that he would transfer the headquarters of Quicken Loans from locations in suburban Troy, Livonia, and Farmington Hills to downtown Detroit, but the recession of 2008–2009 delayed the move. The relocation began in 2010, bringing 1,700 employees to offices in the Compuware Building, one of the buildings near Campus Martius he had selected to provide office space for the mortgage giant. In the following two years, 2,500 more Quicken Loans workers completed the shift from outlying municipalities to Chase Tower (nicknamed the Qube) and other buildings Gilbert purchased. In 2011, Quicken Loans hired two hundred interns from universities around the country, the first of thousands he brought to the city in subsequent years, as the next step in populating the downtown with new workers. The influx of young people visibly increased foot traffic downtown and provided an infusion of energy. Office workers spilled out of skyscrapers into restyled Campus Martius at noontime to buy lunch from one of the many food trucks parked on the streets, sip wine around a newly installed artificial beach, listen to live music, or patronize the bicycle rentals on a sunny day. A short distance away, other young people played basketball and volleyball at the Quicken Loans Sports Zone in Cadillac Square. His goals, Gilbert reiterated repeatedly, included not only the concentration of his financial empire in Detroit's central business district but also convincing the company's employees that they could enjoy living as well as working in the central city. At the time of the initial move in 2010, Gilbert reported, only seventy-five of the firm's workers resided within Detroit's borders; six years later, the total had increased to approximately 3,500.[24]

A handful of Quicken Loans employees settled into the few comfortable districts remaining in Detroit's barren landscape on the Northwest and Far East Sides. Still, Gilbert believed, most of the newcomers desired the walking lifestyles available downtown or the convenience of a short daily commute from neighboring Midtown. Accordingly, the makeover of the central business district should include all the amenities that young professionals sought. Such a list included, in addition to suitable housing, establishments that made urban life attractive to a well-educated middle-class population with ample disposable income and leisure time—trendy restaurants, coffee shops, clothing stores, and entertainment venues. The desiccated Detroit downtown, littered with empty skyscrapers, shuttered storefronts, vacant lots, and crumbling sidewalks, offered forbidding prospects to potential urban homesteaders when the influx of Quicken Loans employees began. The absence of grocery stores, pharmacies, hardware stores, and national chain retailers further clouded the picture. Gilbert's plan required a total reconfiguration of the dormant downtown, for which he became a tireless cheerleader. His assistants affixed "Opportunity Detroit" posters to billboards, lampposts, storefronts, buses, and taxicabs.[25]

In 2011, Gilbert's Bedrock Detroit, the real-estate arm of his business empire, began buying land, buildings, surface parking lots, and parking garages in downtown Detroit. Most noticeably, he snapped up half-empty, undervalued skyscrapers. The flurry of acquisitions in the following years reflected Gilbert's belief in a "big bang" of development, by which frenetic financial activity would create an irresistible momentum. The buildings received thorough renovations; most of the properties acquired initially, such as the Chase Tower, Madison Theatre Building, the Albert Kahn–designed First National Building, and the Daniel Burnham–designed Dime Building, housed the offices of Quicken Loans and other Gilbert-owned enterprises under the control of Rock Ventures. Having satisfied the spatial needs of his own firms, Gilbert continued to buy downtown buildings and restore them for lease as first-floor retail, office space, apartments, condominiums, lofts, and, especially, high-technology firms. There was no reason Detroit could not become the Silicon Valley of the Midwest, Gilbert often proclaimed. (He renamed the Madison Theatre Building, whose new tenants included a local Twitter office and a designer of iPhone apps, the M@dison Building.) In 2012, he bought the Federal Reserve Bank of Chicago's Detroit Branch Building, the Kresge Building, the Minoru Yamasaki–designed One Woodward Avenue, and five smaller buildings on Woodward Avenue, adding a total of 630,000 square feet of commercial space in the central business district. He added the 1001 Woodward office tower and several smaller buildings nearby in 2013, One Campus Martius (formerly the Compuware Building) in 2014, and the historic Book Tower in 2015.[26] (See figure 10.2.)

The purchase of so much prime real estate in the heart of Detroit, at bargain-basement prices because of the decades-long decline of the city's downtown, left Gilbert in possession of some of the city's most architecturally striking buildings and potentially valuable land. Between 2011 and 2016, as a result of what he blithely described as a "skyscraper sale," Gilbert spent $451 million to buy sixty-two properties and an estimated 17,000 parking spaces in downtown Detroit. (Bedrock Detroit reported that its investments in property acquisition and renovation during those years totaled $2.2 billion, which included the purchase and restoration of buildings in the central business district, the 8.4-acre Brush Park housing development north of the

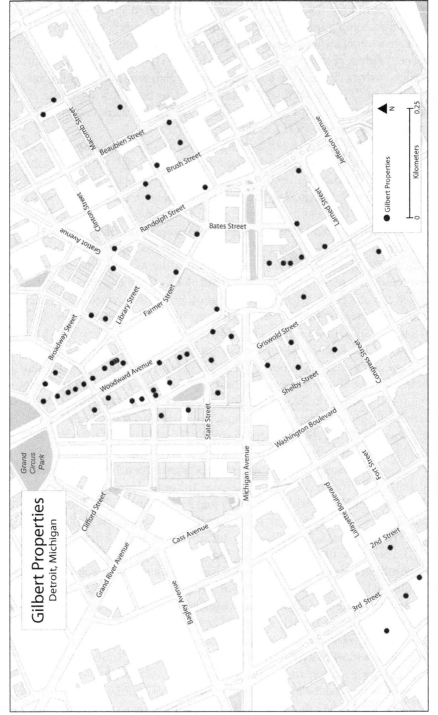

**Figure 10.2** Map of Gilbert Properties (Credit: Megan Maher, GeoMaps, Department of Geography and Geology, Illinois State University, Bloomington)

Fisher Freeway, the Greektown Casino-Hotel, a data analysis center in Cork-town, and other projects outside the central business district.) Most of the properties were located on Woodward Avenue, the spine of the central business district, although other holdings were scattered throughout the greater downtown area. The regenerating central business district came to be so closely identified with Quicken Loans and Bedrock Detroit that admirers and skeptics alike referred to the city hub as Gilbertville.[27]

## A New Skyscraper to Replace
## Hudson's Department Store

In 2017, Gilbert proposed constructing the greatest adornment yet to Wood-ward Avenue, a new skyscraper on the site of the old J. L. Hudson's Depart-ment Store that would become the tallest structure in Michigan. The resi-dential tower would rise nearly 800 feet in the air—slightly higher than the riverfront's Renaissance Center—with a public sky deck perched atop its 58 stories. (Dedicated principally to high-technology businesses, according to local wags, the tower would transform Woodward Avenue into Webward Avenue.) The building's 1.2 million square feet would also include apart-ments, offices, retail, a movie theater, event and conference space, a street-level market, and an underground parking garage. Even though Gilbert's downtown holdings had previously been assembled essentially with his own capital, the $900 million estimated cost of the building forced him to try a different tack. Gilbert lobbied aggressively in the state legislature to help underwrite his most ambitious project, and the avid support of Detroit may-or Michael E. Duggan and several local corporations carried the day. The new incentive package for large-scale developments in Michigan included tax-increment financing, state sales-tax exemptions, state income-tax abate-ment, and reductions in city income taxes. A jubilant Mayor Duggan ex-ulted, "Detroit is finally going vertical. . . . Today this site is a sign of our recovery."[28]

Gilbert said that the completion of the new building, scheduled for 2022, would be especially significant for Detroit in several respects. Long the pre-mier department store in the city and a bellwether of the central business district, Hudson's had been viewed as an irreplaceable institution. "For me, Hudson's *was* Detroit," commented a long-time patron at the time of its de-mise, "and when it's gone, there will be nothing left." The victim of metro-politan decentralization, the store had steadily lost business to suburban competitors prior to closing in 1983. The stately 25-story building sat vacant until its demolition in 1998, after which the gaping hole in the city core served as a constant reminder of downtown's lost glory and an ominous symbol of current lethargy. Replacing the 2.3-acre eyesore with a breathtaking architectural masterpiece, Gilbert asserted, would "bridge the past to the future."[29]

Moreover, the decision to erect a new skyscraper underscored the financial need to move beyond the refurbishment of antiquated structures and to expand the downtown's footprint. The project's launch represented proof, asserted Gilbert, that his plan to revive the central business district was working. "If a few years ago somebody told you that we'd be out of office space, we'd be out of residential, and retail is almost filled up in downtown and Midtown, I think you'd probably put them in some sort of institution," he said. Gilbert touted the edifice arising from the old Hudson's site—no name had yet been chosen for the new building—as the economic engine of future growth and development in downtown Detroit.[30]

Along with the new skyscraper, Gilbert announced the start of three other massive construction projects to be completed as part of a further $2.1 billion investment in downtown's ongoing facelift. His new agenda included an addition to One Campus Martius, another skyscraper, and an extensive restoration of the Book Tower. The new buildings would continue to transform the city skyline and create an estimated twenty-four thousand permanent and temporary jobs. "For us," Gilbert explained, "it's jobs, jobs, jobs." At the time of the announcement, he boasted, Quicken Loans and its affiliated enterprises had surpassed the Detroit Medical Center as the city's largest employer with an estimated seventeen thousand workers. He also hinted that Detroit would compete to secure the second headquarters of e-commerce colossus Amazon, a prize that represented a $5 billion investment by the Seattle-based corporation and that would potentially bring fifty thousand jobs to the Motor City.[31]

## What Did Amazon Think of Detroit's Rebirth?

When Amazon announced that it was seeking a home for its second headquarters, dozens of cities from across the country submitted bids to the corporation's judges. Mayor Duggan immediately enlisted Gilbert to chair the local committee charged with preparing the city's submission. Gilbert and his committee members worked in conjunction with Windsor, Ontario, the Canadian city situated immediately across the Detroit River. The committee prepared an impressive 242-page spiral-bound book that hailed the metropolitan area's economic resurgence since the 2008–2009 recession, lavishly praised the impressive reconstruction of Detroit's downtown, and listed a stunning series of plans for future economic growth. The proposal responded to Amazon's expressed need for 8 million square feet of office space in the next 15–17 years with a detailed outline for satisfying the demand, weaving together the rehabilitation of existing structures and the construction of new skyscrapers and midrise buildings. Capitalizing on the inclusion of Windsor, Gilbert and the fifty-nine people who worked with him in preparing the document emphasized the international dimension in a bid that included a U.S. and a Canadian city. Gilbert confidently asserted that the persuasive, attractively packaged Detroit-Windsor offer would prove highly competitive in the development sweepstakes.[32]

He was wrong. On January 18, 2018, Amazon announced the identities of the twenty finalists with Detroit-Windsor conspicuously absent from the list. The Amazon selection committee praised several elements of the Detroit submission, acknowledging that the Motor City no longer could be dismissed simply as a forlorn Rust Belt casualty, but it identified two fundamental weaknesses in the city's bid: talent and transit. First, unable to compete with Boston, Austin, Denver, and other cities as a magnet for high-technology workers, Detroit suffered from an unacceptably low number of residents with college degrees—an outcome largely explained by the dreadful test scores and low graduation rates in the city's public schools. The existence of excellent universities in the region notwithstanding, Amazon officials contended, the talent base simply could not measure up to the highly efficient work forces in other big cities. Second, the lack of an extensive mass-transit system and the near-total reliance on the automobile placed extraordinary stress on the commuting population, a shortcoming exacerbated by the inclusion of Windsor across the Detroit River.[33]

Unaccustomed to losing, the combative Gilbert vehemently rejected Amazon's reasoning. Amazon's leaders had failed to select Detroit, he contended, because of the "elephant in the room," a reference to the city's notoriety as a financial disaster that recently had required emergency measures applied by the state to remain solvent. The city continued to suffer under the burden of, as Gilbert put it, a "unique radioactive-like reputational fallout of 50–60 years of economic decline, disinvestment, municipal bankruptcy, and all of the other associated negative consequences of that extraordinarily long period of time." Detroit had as much to offer as any other large city, but evaluators could not see beyond the mismanagement and disastrous decision making in the city's past. Gilbert admitted that Detroit needed to improve its metropolitan transportation system, an invaluable asset in attracting a millennial workforce, but stopped short of recognizing the deficiency as an insurmountable hurdle. When outsiders viewed the remarkable turnaround being achieved in the downtown, they were soon won over, he regularly contended. "Once we get them here," he added, "we've got them." The rejection by Amazon would not impede the progress, the unabashed optimist believed, that he, Ilitch, and others were making in fashioning a Detroit renaissance.[34]

Yet some disinterested observers saw good reason to temper Gilbert's boundless confidence about the city's turnaround and found valuable insights in Amazon's rationale for rejecting the Detroit proposal. Although the central business district was undergoing a remarkable change as a result of Gilbert's investments, much of the area still appeared rundown and uninviting. The streets around Campus Martius thrummed with energy, but crumbling buildings and empty lots dominated the landscape just a few blocks east and west of Woodward Avenue. Additional parcels of land had been identified for development, but the enormity of the undertaking meant that complete redevelopment of the downtown would require decades. "In short," concluded *Detroit Free Press* columnist John Gallagher, "downtown Detroit could improve for another decade at the same rate as the past ten years and still not 'finish' the work of bringing downtown back."[35]

The Amazon selection committee's criticism of the local transportation network also exposed crucial inadequacies in citywide service delivery. The continuation of rampant population loss and the wholesale abandonment of homes, along with the poverty afflicting many of the hardy survivors who remained in Detroit, pointed to systemic urban failures. For all the laudable work done from the riverfront along the Woodward corridor to Midtown, much of the city remained untouched by the reclamation effort. The rehabilitation of the entire area targeted by Gilbert and Ilitch would have salvaged a modest portion—at best, a few square miles—of Detroit's sprawling 139 square miles. In pondering what the future held for residents of the neighborhoods, community leaders feared they were settling for two Detroits—a resurgent downtown in the midst of a desperately impoverished city. Race figured in the criticism as well. In a city where the African American population exceeded 80 percent, some people of color saw evidence of "cultural gentrification" because the influx of young college educated, technology-savvy workers was turning the downtown whiter while the demographic makeup and sorry financial condition of outlying precincts remained unchanged.[36]

Both Ilitch and Gilbert insisted that their quest for profits firmly aligned with a desire to save the city and that a downtown-first strategy remained the best means of achieving both goals. Benefits would accrue in the neighborhoods as a result of a prosperous downtown creating jobs, increasing the tax base, and stimulating economic growth. Spokespersons for both the Ilitch and Gilbert conglomerates acknowledged the criticism leveled against them—that their downtown-first focus was shortchanging the much larger remainder of a suffering city but defended their decisions. "It still doesn't solve all of Detroit's very important issues," said Chris Ilitch of his family's transactions, but "I'm not apologetic about it at all. In our community, there was nothing happening on any vacant land. Our vision was to go big. To get the footprint, that's what you need to do." Gilbert denied having turned a blind eye to squalid conditions in the neighborhoods, pointing out that he had served as part of the Motor City Mapping endeavor and cochaired the Detroit Blight Removal Task Force, which had assessed 382,000 parcels of property and razed nearly 11,000 deserted homes, respectively. He explained his obsession with resuscitating the downtown as simply a necessary prelude to transforming the entire city. "This is not the only solution," he said. "The education system needs to be addressed. But what we're doing is a big part of the solution. I can't think of a great American city that doesn't have a great downtown."[37]

## Ilitch, Gilbert, and the Fate of Urban Planning

Gilbert and Ilitch had consistently received rave reviews from Detroit's political and civic leadership for their labors on behalf of the city. A series of mayors dutifully acceded to the development projects undertaken downtown and lobbied aggressively in state capital Lansing for financial aid. As Detroit plummeted in a downward economic spiral, the beleaguered mayors welcomed any economic lifeline tossed their way. The city's chief executives readily relinquished their say in planning future development. "My job," allowed Mayor Dave Bing in 2013, "is to knock down as many barriers as possible and get out of the way." Mayor Duggan commented two years later, "I walk down Woodward today and I see these storefronts filled with businesses, and I couldn't be more pleased with what Dan [Gilbert] has done and his contributions to the community."[38]

Whether commending or condemning the exertions of Ilitch and Gilbert, observers marveled at the profound influence the two entrepreneurs wielded in Detroit—often at the expense of municipal government. The Ilitch family's commitment to pay for infrastructure improvements in District Detroit not only demonstrated Olympia Development's single-minded drive to improve the neighborhood around the new arenas but also signaled city hall's willing cession of municipal government's traditional responsibilities to private entities. Gilbert's Bedrock Detroit evinced the same willingness to usurp municipal housekeeping tasks. Convinced that the I-375 exit to Lafayette Street failed to accommodate incoming traffic at an important access point to downtown, Gilbert volunteered to pay the $1.25 million cost to widen the ramp from one lane to three and eliminate the bottleneck. To aid an underfunded and understaffed Detroit Police Department, which was hard-pressed to ensure pedestrian safety downtown, Gilbert installed a state-of-the-art surveillance system by which security guards in the Qube

monitored live feeds from more than five hundred cameras perched downtown. Some Detroiters rued the usurpation of civic duties by the private
sector, and civil libertarians inveighed against covert invasions of people's
privacy; members of Gilbert's safety team muted dissent with a report that
they had initiated more than five hundred calls to 911 for emergency medical assistance and assisted almost 750 motorists with car trouble. His company actively recruited new businesses to the central business district, squir-
ing corporate executives and other out-of-towners on walking tours to point
out the positive changes underway. His boosterism "fill[ed] some of the
void" created by years of government malfeasance, Gilbert explained. "If it
serves as some form of a bridge until the city gets financially healthier, that's
OK. If we have to do that, we'll do it. We can afford it." By the second decade
of the twenty-first century, it had become so commonplace for Gilbert to
assume such a role that a national affairs magazine referred to him as "Detroit's de facto CEO."[39]

Gilbert's prominence proved to be the perfect complement to the influence wielded by the Ilitch family. Both parties subscribed to the salience of
downtown refurbishment to urban reclamation. Ilitch focused his investments on the north-central segment of the downtown, and Gilbert concentrated on the adjacent south-central portion. By all accounts, their business
dealings in side-by-side tracts of land never came into conflict. Their approaches differed in some fundamental ways. With the exception of the Fox
Theatre, Ilitch relied primarily on clearance and new construction, while
Gilbert typically preserved the architectural integrity of old buildings utilizing cosmetic external flourishes and extensive interior renovation. In their
public statements, each praised the work done by the other and acknowledged a common mission. Gilbert lavishly extolled the District Detroit plan,
saying, "The thoughtful and impressive design will be transformative for
downtown. . . . This tops a lifetime of Detroit accomplishments for Mike and
Marian which Chris is carrying out with passion and diligence." Chris Ilitch
returned the compliment, observing that "We love what Dan Gilbert is doing, and we try to collaborate wherever we can. It's really important what
everybody's doing—not just Dan, but all the stakeholders." Their herculean
attempts to rebuild Detroit's core demonstrated an unmistakable synergy,
as if part of a grand design.[40]

And yet perhaps most striking, the momentous handiwork of the two
tycoons proceeded without a master plan. Other than seeking to achieve the
broad goal of downtown reclamation, these entrepreneurs proceeded extem-
poraneously. Neither Mike nor Chris Ilitch spoke of eliminating the decrepitude between Grand Circus Park and Midtown along the Woodward
corridor as a specific goal; downtown improvement remained a vague objec-

tive. Gilbert described his skyscraper-buying spree as "opportunistic," not premeditated. "I just didn't have any kind of clue about it," he confessed. "These buildings were available and obviously inexpensive, and it happened very quickly." Indeed, their successes bespoke a heavy dose of serendipity. Their expanded influence was owing to several factors that rearranged the dynamic of public-private partnerships, consigning a discredited municipal government that had repeatedly failed to provide leadership to the back seat. No one could deny the impact of an estimated $4 billion investment on Detroit's downtown by Ilitch and Gilbert. Still, the eventual significance of that vast infusion of funds for the entire city's tax base and for the ability of its officials to provide police and fire services, well-educated employees, and a public transportation system sufficient to meet the prerequisites of first-class corporate executives like Amazon's remained very much unclear. To what extent, in other words, had the city's residents ultimately benefited from the private largess disbursed in what some Detroiters feared was becoming a real-estate plutocracy?[41]

The undeniable influence on the shape of downtown exerted by Ilitch and Gilbert, along with their commensurate ability to plan Detroit's future growth, call to mind the immense power wielded by ambitious boosters in earlier years. Examples of such entrepreneurship abound, which proved fundamental in the city's growth and evolving spatial arrangements. Between the 1880s and 1920s, a new generation of Detroit investors struck their fortunes in timber, shipbuilding, and copper and iron mining. Corporate executives assembled factories that produced high-value products such as automobiles and railroad parts. To focus only on three among the best-known factory executives, Henry Ford and James J. Couzens (also at Ford) and General Motors' William C. Durant presided over manufacturing complexes that employed thousands of workers and whose labors also fouled rivers and spewed noise and smoke throughout Detroit. As important, Ford, Couzens, Durant, and their successors made decisions about plant location (such as in nearby Dearborn) that have influenced the city's form up to the present day.[42]

Mike Ilitch and Dan Gilbert, in contrast, presided over modest-sized office staffs that guided employees in the business of writing loans, preparing food, dealing cards, operating slot machines, and providing attractive venues for sports teams that employed dozens of the nation's most admired and well-paid athletes. Ilitch and Gilbert's businesses fit right into a nation where the balance of wealth and employment had shifted decades earlier from production to consumption. Around 1990, family fun often began to consist of weekends in downtown hotels for visits to museums, plays, sports contests, and casinos. Ilitch and Gilbert both created entertainment markets and catered to them.[43]

Despite many differences, Ilitch and Gilbert on the one hand and indus-trial leaders like Ford, Couzens, and Durant on the other shared important elements. Contemporaries and historians described them with similar and highly adulatory terms. No word appeared more often in these tributes than *entrepreneurial*. Scholars, of course, have long debated the exact behaviors and attitudes covered by the term. Among plainspoken Americans, how-ever, *entrepreneur* has served as a concept cluster of valued qualities. Inno-vativeness is certainly among those qualities, as are brashness and farsight-edness. Altogether, businesspersons described as entrepreneurs seemingly possessed a nearly innate ability to foster material abundance that existed alongside a fast-growing leisure economy. By this reasoning, Ford in an ear-lier period had built factories that led to steady, if grimy, factory jobs for thousands and paid the workers a wage that allowed them to engage in more leisure activities. And in the recent period, no one doubted the importance to their city and region of entrepreneurs like Ilitch and Gilbert, who made dinner preparations as convenient as a telephone call, allowed ordinary res-idents to secure home mortgages on line, and fielded sports teams of such high caliber that loyal fans bragged about snagging a pair of tickets to Tigers, Red Wings, and Lions games.[44]

As well, Gilbert and Ilitch set themselves apart from contemporary busi-ness executives in a significant way. They exercised a direct and often deci-sive hand in planning for downtown Detroit's development. At this point, it is useful to remind ourselves of the way in which Detroit and other cities had been planned and governed before Gilbert and Ilitch's arrival in politics and planning. Starting in the 1940s and extending to the 1980s, business leaders in Detroit (and elsewhere) had mostly stayed away from deeply po-liticized efforts to determine the location of people, roads, and buildings. Members of that generation of executives allowed planners and road engi-neers to frame their city's geography. During this period, in turn, city-plan-ning departments, led and staffed by persons with advanced degrees in ar-chitecture, engineering, urban planning, and urban affairs, laid out street and highway coordinates. Those vast and expensive projects allowed power-ful and politically savvy planners such as Edmund Bacon in Philadelphia, Edward Logue in Boston, and Robert Moses in New York to initiate a vast remodeling of their city's landscape. At the hands of Bacon, Logue, and their counterparts around the nation, fleets of bulldozers leveled buildings judged to lack undeniable commercial prospects or aesthetic up-to-dateness.[45]

Downtown renewal at the hands of planners had not yet run its course. In the 1990s, city leaders and their planning department's officers began to coalesce with downtown business executives to force construction and ex-pansion of massive convention centers, including Detroit's Cobo Hall. Like earlier projects aimed at boosting downtown property values, advocates promised that new and expanded convention centers would, at last, return affluent visitors to downtown hotels and restaurants. And, as in earlier renewal efforts, convention center projects cost far more than they returned to cities in the form of jobs, sales reports, rental income, property values, and tax receipts.[46]

In retrospect, advocates of those vast construction projects, including Mayor Albert Cobo and members of his planning team in Detroit, had presided over one of the gravest domestic policy miscalculations in the postwar decades. By the early 1970s, construction of the major airport and the interstate highway system permitted countless Detroit householders and businesses to move up to one hundred miles from downtown. Factory owners, including the major Detroit manufacturers, followed highways and trucks out of town, as far as cities like Flint, where they constructed sprawling plants that, in turn, attracted employees and small-business owners to locate nearby. Those new suburbanites then built a network of suburban governments to stand vigil against the next set of newcomers, especially African Americans. By the 1990s, metropolitan area commuters were more likely to travel between Detroit suburbs (like Warren and Pontiac) than from suburb to core city for work and recreation. By 2000, retailing and tourism had practically ceased to exist in downtown Detroit. Construction of the interstate highway system in metropolitan Detroit and other urban areas had not single-handedly caused all the city's problems, but those freeways, admitted a senior official in the Federal Highway Administration in 2013, played an outsize role. In 2017, Gilbert declared that his twin towers at the Hudson's site would serve as the starting point for a new downtown. No one at that groundbreaking ceremony for Gilbert's twin towers could have doubted that, in Detroit at least, Gilbert and Ilitch were firmly in charge of city planning. Gilbert and Ilitch's many businesses thrived in part because they had mastered the urban political economy of their era.[47]

Surely, Ilitch and Gilbert took large risks with their limited resources. But their impressive achievements must also be seen as a product of the environment in which they operated. Ilitch and Gilbert found success within a political economy reshaped by historical forces ascendant in Detroit by the early twenty-first century. Sweeping demographic change, prolonged economic calamity, the inefficacy of local government, and the terrible reputation planners had left behind with their flawed projects had combined to create a unique situation in which a pair of brash entrepreneurs invested billions of dollars to determine the city's future economic growth, including the intense focus on downtown. If the massive intervention by Ilitch and Gilbert gains traction in coming decades, will the Detroit experiment become a model for other struggling postindustrial cities? If elected officials and influential corporate executives judge the efforts of these entrepreneurs successful, will municipal planning departments still have an important role to play in urban development? Similarly, will the influence of Gilbertville and Ilitchville be seen as a decisive victory for private over public action in the battle to save postindustrial cities?

# Notes

### PREFACE

1. Harold James, "Neoliberalism and its Interlocutors," *Capitalism: A Journal of History and Economics* 1, no. 2 (Spring 2020): 484–518, including quotation on 485.

### PART I

1. Tracy Neumann, *Remaking the Rust Belt: The Postindustrial Transformation of North America* (Philadelphia: University of Pennsylvania Press, 2016), 26–27; John F. Bauman and Edward K. Muller, *Before Renaissance: Planning in Pittsburgh, 1889–1943* (Pittsburgh, PA: University of Pittsburgh Press, 2006), 1; "Mellon Will Leave Half to His Widow," *Chicago Tribune*, July 2, 1970; "First Boston Tops List of Syndicate Managers," *New York Times*, March 23, 1971; "Richard K. Mellon, Financier, Is Dead," *New York Times*, June 4, 1970; "Death of a King," *Time*, June 15, 1970. In 1983, historian John N. Ingham, in *Biographical Dictionary of American Business Leaders* (Westport, CT: Greenwood, 1983), 2: 928, estimated the family's wealth at $5 billion. Other members of Mellon's immediate family of eleven owned portions of the estate.

2. "Richard K. Mellon, Financier, Is Dead"; Michael C. Jensen, "Four Generations of Mellons," *New York Times*, May 2, 1971.

3. Mark H. Rose, *Market Rules: Bankers, Presidents, and the Coming of the Great Recession* (Philadelphia: University of Pennsylvania Press, 2018). Historian Albert J. Churella kindly shared portions of his manuscripts-in-progress focused on the Pennsylvania Railroad after 1917.

4. In this period, reports historian John Ingham in "The American Urban Upper Class: Cosmopolitans or Locals?" *Journal of Urban History* 2, no. 1 (November 1975): 67–87, Pittsburgh's upper-class families "felt they had important roles as social arbiters in their own local community" (73).

5. Ingham, *Biographical Dictionary of American Business Leaders*, 926; Jensen, "Four Generations of Mellons"; Michael P. Weber, *Don't Call Me Boss: David L. Lawrence, Pittsburgh's Renaissance Mayor* (Pittsburgh, PA: University of Pittsburgh Press, 1988), 236.

6. Edward K. Muller, "Downtown Pittsburgh: Renaissance and Renewal," in *Pittsburgh and the Appalachians: Cultural and Natural Resources in a Postindustrial Age*, ed. Joseph L. Scarpaci and Kevin J. Patrick (Pittsburgh, PA: University of Pittsburgh Press, 2006), 8; Roy Lubove, *Twentieth-Century Pittsburgh*, vol. 1, *Government, Business, and Environmental Change*, (Pittsburgh, PA: University of Pittsburgh Press, 1995), 108–9; "Hotchkiss to Speak," *Pittsburgh Press*, December 1, 1943; Gabriel Winant, *The Next Shift: The Fall of Industry and the Rise of Health Care in Rust Belt America* (Cambridge, MA: Harvard University Press, 2021), 106. In 1944, Allegheny Conference founders incorporated as the Allegheny Conference on Postwar Community Planning. In 1945, they changed the legal name to the Allegheny Conference on Community Development (Sherie R. Mershon, "Corporate Social Responsibility and Urban Revitalization: The Allegheny Conference on Community Development, 1943–1968," (unpublished Ph.D. diss., Carnegie Mellon University, 2000), 153n1.

7. Mark H. Rose and Raymond A. Mohl, *Interstate: Highway Politics and Policy since 1939*, 3rd ed., rev. (Knoxville: University of Tennessee Press, 2012), 20–23, 55–67; Dale McFeatters, "Communities Urged to Begin Mapping Post-war Jobs Now," *Pittsburgh Press*, May 18, 1944; Weber, *Don't Call Me Boss*, 235. Brent Cebul and Mason B. Williams, in "'Really and Truly a Partnership': The New Deal's Associational State and the Making of Postwar American Politics," in *Shaped by the State: Toward a New Political History of the Twentieth Century*, ed. Brent Cebul, Lily Geismer, and Mason B. Williams (Chicago: University of Chicago Press, 2019), 115, identify "a localist brand of politics, which disparaged the state not as an expression of ideological preference but as a means of expressing boosters' sense of greater entitlement to state support." Finally, historians Destin Jenkins and Justin Leroy, in their introduction to *Histories of Racial Capitalism*, ed. Destin Jenkins and Justin Leroy (New York: Columbia University Press, 2021), 1, include race among capitalism's constitutive elements.

8. McFeatters, "Communities Urged to Begin Mapping Post-war Jobs Now." Also see Roger S. Ahlbrandt and Morton Coleman, *The Role of the Corporation in Community Economic Development as Viewed by Twenty-One Corporate Executives* (Pittsburgh, PA: University of Pittsburgh Press, 1987); Brian D. Robick, "Blight: The Development of a Contested Concept," (unpublished Ph.D. diss., Carnegie Mellon University, 2011), 109–66; Edward K. Muller, "Post–World War II, Renaissance Pittsburgh," unpublished manuscript, last revised 2018, which Professor Muller kindly shared with us.

9. William Allan, "'Mr. Renaissance' Glad He Gets Lost in Crowd," *Pittsburgh Press*, September 28, 1958; "Redevelopment was not possible," contends historian Michael Weber, "without the cooperation of Lawrence and Mellon." See Weber, *Don't Call Me Boss*, 235.

10. Jeanne R. Lowe, *Cities in a Race with Time: Progress and Poverty in America's Renewing Cities* (New York: Random House, 1967), 112–13; Lubove, *Twentieth-Century Pittsburgh*, 106, 114–15; Muller, "Downtown Pittsburgh, Renaissance and Renewal," 8–9; Jon C. Teaford, *The Rough Road to Renaissance: Urban Revitalization in America, 1940–1985* (Baltimore, MD: Johns Hopkins University Press, 1990), 46–47.

11. Barbara Ferman, *Challenging the Growth Machine: Neighborhood Politics in Chicago and Pittsburgh* (Lawrence: University Press of Kansas, 1996), 53; Allan, "Mr. Renaissance"; James Neal Primm, *Lion of the Valley: St. Louis, Missouri* (Boulder, CO: Pruett, 1981), 474–77; Thomas R. Bullard, "Raymond R. Tucker," in *Biographical Dictionary of American Mayors, 1820–1980: Big City Mayors*, ed. Melvin G. Holli and Peter d'A. Jones

(Westport, CT: Greenwood, 1981), 368; Allen Dieterich-Ward, *Beyond Rust: Metropolitan Pittsburgh and the Fate of Industrial America* (Philadelphia: University of Pennsylvania Press, 2016), 75–80; Weber, *Don't Call Me Boss,* 171.

12. Mershon, "Corporate Social Responsibility," 796–806; Neumann, *Remaking the Rust Belt,* 26–27.

13. Allan, "Mr. Renaissance"; Weber, *Don't Call Me Boss,* 233–34; Lubove, *Twentieth-Century Pittsburgh,* 110–11.

14. "Wabash Terminal Future in Doubt following Million Dollar Fire," *Pittsburgh Press,* March 24, 1946; Lubove, *Twentieth-Century Pittsburgh,* 119–20.

15. "Smoke Control Called Key to Pittsburgh Renaissance," *Pittsburgh Press,* December 10, 1953; Lubove, *Twentieth-Century Pittsburgh,* 122–24, including 123n42, where Lubove directs our attention to the December 10, 1953, article in the *Pittsburgh Press.*

16. Dieterich-Ward, *Beyond Rust,* 82–83; Lubove, *Twentieth-Century Pittsburgh,* 122–24.

17. "Four Gateway Center Building Formally Dedicated," *Pittsburgh Press,* June 24, 1960; "Equitable Executive 'Man on the Spot,'" *Pittsburgh Press,* June 24, 1960, including quotation.

18. Rose and Mohl, *Interstate,* 58–59; "Grand Ball Caps Opening of Hilton," *Pittsburgh Press,* December 4, 1959; Edward K. Muller, "Downtown Pittsburgh: Relentless Change," in *Making Industrial Pittsburgh Modern: Environment, Landscape, Transportation, Energy, and Planning,* ed. Edward K. Muller and Joel A. Tarr (Pittsburgh, PA: University of Pittsburgh Press, 2019), 392–443.

19. Arthur R. Friedman, "Latest Steel Equipment on View," *Pittsburgh Post-Gazette,* September 24, 1964.

20. See for example, Frank P. I. Somerville, "'Pittsburgh's Renaissance' Rolls Along,'" *The Baltimore Sun,* February 13, 1966.

21. Jim Schottelkotte, "Pittsburgh Levels Its Hovels, and Now Beauty Rakes the Sky," *Cincinnati Inquirer,* November 2, 1956; Gregory J. Crowley, *The Politics of Place: Contentious Urban Redevelopment in Pittsburgh* (Pittsburgh, PA: University of Pittsburgh Press, 2005), 59.

22. Francesca Russello Ammon, *Bulldozer: Demolition and Clearance of the Postwar Landscape* (New Haven, CT: Yale University Press, 2016), masterfully describes the "culture of clearance" that fostered rural, suburban, and urban renewal in Pittsburgh and other cities.

23. Schottelkotte, "Pittsburgh Levels Its Hovels"; Tracy Neumann, "Reforging the Steel City: Symbolism and Space in Postindustrial Pittsburgh," *Journal of Urban History* 44, no. 4 (July 2018): 583.

24. Neumann, *Remaking the Rust Belt,* 1–2. Neumann describes the visitors as "policy tourists," an apt concept.

25. Neumann, *Remaking the Rustbelt,* 1; Muller, "Downtown Pittsburgh," 421–22.

26. Neumann, *Remaking the Rust Belt,* 27.

27. Winant, *Next Shift,* 20; Teaford, *Rough Road,* 46–54. Allegheny Conference executives also sponsored studies of important local topics such as truck congestion, mass transit services, and changing employment among wage and salary workers. From start to finish, the ACCD's many studies were inherently political documents.

28. Stefan Link and Noam Maggor, "The United States as a Developing Nation: Revisiting the Peculiarities of American History," *Past and Present* 246, no. 1 (February 2020): 294 (quotation); Douglas J. Flowe, *Uncontrollable Blackness: African American Men and Criminality in Jim Crow New York* (Chapel Hill: University of North Carolina Press,

2020); David Farber, *Crack: Rock Cocaine, Street Capitalism, and the Decade of Greed* (New York: Cambridge University Press, 2019).

29. Russell F. Weigley, ed., *Philadelphia: A 300-Year History* (New York: W. W. Norton, 1982), 1–154; Walter Licht, *Getting Work: Philadelphia, 1840–1950* (Philadelphia: University of Pennsylvania Press, 1999), 4.

30. Licht, *Getting Work*, 10–11. Also see Philip Scranton, *Proprietary Capitalism: The Textile Manufacture at Philadelphia, 1800–1885* (Cambridge: Cambridge University Press, 2003); and Scranton, *Figured Tapestry: Production, Markets, and Power in Philadelphia Textiles, 1885–1941* (Cambridge: Cambridge University Press, 1989). The two volumes by Scranton provide a detailed history of the rise and fall of the textile industry in Philadelphia. Jerome J. Hodos, *Second Cities: Globalization and Local Politics in Manchester and Philadelphia* (Philadelphia: Temple University Press 2011), discusses Philadelphia's prominence in the colonial era and decline to second city status in the nineteenth century.

31. Lincoln Steffens, *The Shame of the Cities* (New York: Hill and Wang, 1957), 134 (quotations); Weigley, ed., *Philadelphia, 1840–1950*, 496–98. Also see Peter McCaffery, *When Bosses Ruled Philadelphia: The Emergence of the Republican Machine, 1867–1933* (University Park: Pennsylvania State University Press, 1993); and Daniel Amsterdam, *Roaring Metropolis: Businessmen's Campaign for a Civic Welfare State* (Philadelphia: University of Pennsylvania Press, 2016), especially chapter 3.

32. Melvin G. Holli, ed., *Detroit* (New York: New Viewpoints, 1976), 1–60; Olivier Zunz, *The Changing Face of Inequality: Urbanization, Industrial Development, and Immigrants in Detroit, 1880–1920* (Chicago: University of Chicago Press, 1982), 2–3; Robert Conot, *American Odyssey* (New York: William Morrow, 1974), 65–67; Willis F. Dunbar, "The Speeding Tempo of Urbanization," *Michigan History* 35, no. 3 (September 1951), 292–93.

33. Conot, *American Odyssey*, 130–31.

34. Allan Nevins, *Ford: The Times, the Man, the Company* (New York: Charles Scribner's Sons, 1954), 1: 156–57; Jon C. Teaford, *Cities of the Heartland: The Rise and Fall of the Industrial Midwest* (Bloomington: Indiana University Press, 1993), 106–7; Holli, ed., *Detroit*, 117–21.

35. Sidney Fine, *Sit-Down: The General Motors Strike of 1936–1937* (Ann Arbor: University of Michigan Press, 1969), 4–5, 327–41; Teaford, *Cities of the Heartland*, 184–85; J. David Greenstone, *Labor in American Politics* (New York: Alfred A. Knopf, 1969), 110–40.

36. Carol Poh Miller and Robert A. Wheeler, "Cleveland: The Making and Remaking of an American City, 1796–1993," in *Cleveland: A Metropolitan Reader*, ed. W. Dennis Keating, Norman Krumholz, and David C. Perry (Kent, OH: Kent State University Press, 1995), 31–33.

37. Barney Warf and Brian Holly, "The Rise and Fall and Rise of Cleveland," *Annals of the American Academy of Political and Social Science* 551 (May 1997): 209–10; Miller and Wheeler, "Cleveland," 35–37; Edward W. Hill, "The Cleveland Economy: A Case Study of Economic Restructuring," in Keating, Krumholz, and Perry, eds., *Cleveland*, 56–57.

38. Lincoln Steffens, *The Struggle for Self-Government* (New York: McLure, Phillips, 1906), 161 (quotation); Diane Tittle, *Rebuilding Cleveland: The Cleveland Foundation and Its Evolving Urban Strategy* (Columbus: Ohio State University Press, 1992), 14–30.

39. William Cronon, *Nature's Metropolis: Chicago and the Great West* (New York: W. W. Norton, 1991); Dominic A. Pacyga, *Chicago: A Biography* (Chicago: University of Chicago Press, 2009), chapters 1–2.

40. Cronon, *Nature's Metropolis*, chapters 3–5; Roger Biles, *Illinois: A History of the Land and Its People* (DeKalb: Northern Illinois University Press, 2005), 128–29.

41. Pacyga, *Chicago*, 70–76; Biles, *Illinois*, 130–32. Also see Melvin G. Holli and Peter d'A. Jones, eds., *The Ethnic Frontier: Group Survival in Chicago and the Midwest* (Grand Rapids, MI: William B. Eerdmans, 1977); Melvin G. Holli and Peter d'A. Jones, eds., *Ethnic Chicago* (Grand Rapids, MI: William B. Eerdmans, 1981); Perry Duis, *Chicago: Creating New Traditions* (Chicago: University of Chicago Press, 1977); and Dominic A. Pacyga and Ellen Skerrett, *Chicago: City of Neighborhoods* (Chicago: Loyola University Press, 1986).

42. John M. Allswang, *A House for All Peoples: Ethnic Politics in Chicago, 1890–1936* (Lexington: University Press of Kentucky, 1971); Alex Gottfried, *Boss Cermak of Chicago: A Study of Political Leadership* (Seattle: University of Washington Press, 1962); and Roger Biles, *Big City Boss in Depression and War: Mayor Edward J. Kelly of Chicago* (DeKalb: Northern Illinois University Press, 1984).

43. Primm, *Lion of the Valley*, chapters 1–4; Richard C. Wade, *The Urban Frontier: The Rise of Western Cities, 1790–1830* (Urbana: University of Illinois Press, 1996), 200–202.

44. Primm, *Lion of the Valley*, 201–9; Biles, *Illinois*, 129–30.

45. Selwyn K. Troen and Glen E. Holt, eds., *St. Louis* (New York: New Viewpoints, 1977), xxi–xxii; Colin Gordon, *Mapping Decline: St. Louis and the Fate of the American City* (Philadelphia: University of Pennsylvania Press, 2008), 69–71.

46. Primm, *Lion of the Valley*, 314–20, 472–73, 508–9; Gordon, *Mapping Decline*, 10.

47. David R. Goldfield and Blaine A. Brownell, *Urban America: A History*, 2nd ed. (Boston: Houghton Mifflin, 1990), 324 (quotation); Sidney Fine, *Frank Murphy: The Detroit Years* (Ann Arbor: University of Michigan Press, 1975), 246–47.

48. Alison Isenberg, *Downtown America: A History of the Place and the People Who Made It* (Chicago: University of Chicago Press, 2004), 135 (first quotation); Robert M. Fogelson, *Downtown: Its Rise and Fall, 1880–1950* (New Haven, CT: Yale University Press, 2001), 227, 234 (second quotation).

49. Teaford, *Cities of the Heartland*, 185–86; Isenberg, *Downtown America*, 160–65.

50. Dennis McClendon, "Expressways," in *The Encyclopedia of Chicago*, ed. James R. Grossman, Ann Durkin Keating, and Janice L. Reiff (Chicago: University of Chicago Press, 2004), 286–87; Joseph Heathcott and Máire Agnes Murphy, "Corridors of Flight, Zones of Renewal: Industry, Planning, and Policy in the Making of Metropolitan St. Louis, 1940–1980," *Journal of Urban History* 31, no. 2 (January 2005): 151–52, 157; Primm, *Lion of the Valley*, 479–84; Gordon, *Mapping Decline*, 12.

51. Clarence N. Stone, *Regime Politics: Governing Atlanta, 1946–1988* (Lawrence: University Press of Kansas, 1989), xi; Martin Horak et al., "Change Afoot," in *Urban Neighborhoods in a New Era*, ed. Clarence N. Stone and Robert P. Stoker (Chicago: University of Chicago Press, 2015), 1. See as well Dennis R. Judd and Todd Swanstrom, *City Politics: The Political Economy of Urban America*, 8th ed. (New York: Taylor and Francis, 2014), 180, for the valuable contention that "groups opposing renewal were small and often divided, [and] residents . . . put a priority on protecting their own turf but rarely saw any reason to expend scarce resources to help someone else."

52. Jenkins and Leroy, Introduction.

## CHAPTER 1

1. "Anheuser-Busch Sales High," *New York Times*, January 5, 1954; "Ralston Co. Sales Dip but Net Rises," *New York Times*, December 19, 1953; "St. Louis Theatre Ends Segre-

gation," *New York Times*, January 6, 1953; "Sees Protestant Flight from City," *Christian Century* 70, no. 22 (June 3, 1953); and also see Mark Wild, *Renewal: Liberal Protestants and the American City after World War II* (Chicago: University of Chicago Press, 2019), which contextualizes white churchgoers' outmigration from the 1930s to the 1960s. For urban social and economic change in St. Louis, including the presence of intense racial animosities that started after the Civil War and extended to the 1980s and beyond, we relied on James Neal Primm, *Lion of the Valley: St. Louis, Missouri, 1764–1980*, 3rd ed. (St. Louis: Missouri Historical Society Press, 1998); Clarence Lang, *Grassroots at the Gateway: Class Politics and Black Freedom Struggle in St. Louis, 1936–75* (Ann Arbor: University of Michigan Press, 2009); Clarence Lang, "Between Civil Rights, Black Power, and the Mason-Dixon Line: A Case Study of Black Freedom Movement Militancy in the Gateway City," in *Race Struggles*, ed. Theodore Koditschek, Sundiata Keita Cha-Jua, and Helen A. Neville (Urbana: University of Illinois Press, 2009), 231–59; Mark Benton, "'Just the Way Things Are around Here': Racial Segregation, Critical Junctures, and Path Dependence in Saint Louis," *Journal of Urban History* 44, no. 6 (November 2018): 1113–30; Clarence Lang, "Civil Rights versus 'Civic Progress': The St. Louis NAACP and the City Charter Fight, 1956–1957," *Journal of Urban History* 34, no. 4 (May 2008): 609–38. As we narrowed the number of cities to study and focused closely on St. Louis, we relied on helpful conversations with historians Colin Gordon and Joseph Heathcott. See especially Colin Gordon, *Mapping Decline: St. Louis and the Fate of the American City* (Philadelphia: University of Pennsylvania Press, 2008); Gordon, *Citizen Brown: Race, Democracy, and Inequality in the St. Louis Suburbs* (Chicago: University of Chicago Press, 2019); and Joseph Heathcott and Máire Agnes Murphy, "Corridors of Flight, Zones of Renewal: Industry, Planning, and Policy in the Making of Metropolitan St. Louis, 1940–1980," *Journal of Urban History* 32, no. 2 (January 2005): 151–89. Paige Glotzer, *How the Suburbs Were Segregated: Developers and the Business of Exclusionary Housing, 1890–1960* (New York: Columbia University Press, 2020), explains the ways in which whiteness was embedded in suburban building practices that extended back to the nineteenth century.

2. "Urges Using Blighted Areas for Industries," *St. Louis Post-Dispatch*, January 9, 1953.

3. "Large Area Rezoned for Store in County," *St. Louis Post-Dispatch*, January 5, 1954; "Heffern-Neuhoff Jewelry Firm Goes Out of Business," *St. Louis Post-Dispatch*, February 26, 1955; "New Woolworth Store to Open Tomorrow at Sixth and Locust, "*St. Louis Globe-Democrat*, September 30, 1956; "Retailers Step Up Shift to Suburbs," *New York Times*, January 3, 1955, including T. V. Hauser's remarks. Robert Bussel, *Fighting for Total Person Unionism: Harold Gibbons, Ernest Calloway, and Working-Class Citizenship* (Urbana: University of Illinois Press, 2015), 110, describes the politics that guided Famous-Barr's tearoom integration. "As stores followed their markets to the suburbs in the 1950s," observes historian Vicki Howard in *From Main Street to Mall: The Rise and Fall of the American Department Store* (Philadelphia: University of Pennsylvania Press, 2015), "many merchants, academic observers, and consumers still saw downtown as the place to be" (136). Historian Lizabeth Cohen, *Saving America's Cities: Ed Logue and the Struggle to Renew Urban America in the Suburban Age* (New York: Farrar, Straus and Giroux, 2019), 44, describes downtown Boston's two department stores, as well as shops that were "comfortably dowdy to downright dilapidated." Race was a central factor in every city's politics and social geography. Economist Leah Platt Boustan, in *Competition in the Promised Land: Black Migrants in Northern Cities and Labor Markets* (Princeton, NJ: Princeton University Press, 2017), concludes that white shoppers and ordinary white urban residents—in Detroit, Chicago, and other cities—slowly arrived at the conclusion that they did not wish to share space or responsibility for their city with African Amer-

icans. By the 1970s, in Heather Thompson's excellent phrasing in "Rethinking the Politics of White Flight in the Postwar City: Detroit, 1945–1980," *Journal of Urban History* 25, no. 2 (January 1999): 193, white householders joined the suburban migration when they determined that African Americans would assume leadership positions in their cities and that "the racial status quo was forever undone." Naturally, Arnold R. Hirsch, *Making the Second Ghetto: Race and Housing in Chicago, 1940–1960* (Chicago: University of Chicago Press, 1998), and Thomas J. Sugrue, *The Origins of the Urban Crisis: Race and Inequality in Postwar Detroit*, rev. ed. (Princeton, NJ: Princeton University Press, 2014), informed our thinking about racial geography and politics during the twentieth century.

4. Joseph Heathcott, "The City Quietly Remade: National Programs and Local Agendas in the Movement to Clear the Slums, 1942–1952," *Journal of Urban History* 34, no. 2 (January 2008): 226; Heathcott, "Black Archipelago: Politics and Civic Life in the Jim Crow City," *Journal of Social History* 38, no. 3 (Spring 2005): 708–9, and especially Heathcott's finding of intense crowding among African American householders in areas north and west of downtown that helped construct a "racist spatial and social order on the land" ("Black Archipelago," 707). As well, reports historian Taylor H. Desloge, "The Tortured Pre-history of Urban Blight: African American St. Louis and the Politics of Public Health," (unpublished Ph.D. diss., Washington University, 2019), white St. Louisans had long identified African American bodies with diseases such as tuberculosis. Similar, and equally inaccurate, fears about African Americans and disease proclivity haunted white New Yorkers, determines historian Douglas J. Flowe in *Uncontrollable Blackness: African American Men and Criminality in Jim Crow New York* (Chapel Hill: University of North Carolina Press, 2020), 37. Also see Aaron Cowan, *A Nice Place to Visit: Tourism and Urban Revitalization in the Postwar Rustbelt* (Philadelphia: Temple University Press, 2016), 13, and Mark H. Rose and Raymond A. Mohl, *Interstate: Highway Politics and Policy since 1939*, 3rd ed. (Knoxville: University of Tennessee Press, 2012), 55–67.

5. Richard G. Baumhauf, "Prospect Called Excellent for Success of New Civic Program," *St. Louis Post-Dispatch*, January 28, 1953.

6. Ibid.; "Progress, Inc.," *St. Louis Post-Dispatch*, January 20, 1953; "Mayor for Using Unissued, Unspent $50,000,000 Bonds," *St. Louis Post-Dispatch*, March 9, 1950. Daniel Amsterdam, *Roaring Metropolis: Businessmen's Campaign for a Civic Welfare State* (Philadelphia: University of Pennsylvania Press, 2016), explains the importance of businesspeople's committees to build support for street improvements, new schools, and large museums in Detroit, Philadelphia, and Atlanta from the first days of the twentieth century to the mid-1930s.

7. Harry Wilensky, "Pittsburgh's Project Scope Is Impressive," *St. Louis Post-Dispatch*, October 27, 1953 (quotation). Historian Laura Grantmyre, in "Selling Pittsburgh as America's Renaissance City," *Journal of Urban History* 41, no. 1 (January 2015): 5–13, explains the efforts of Park Martin and other ACCD leaders to represent Pittsburgh as the nation's urban renewal leader. For the regular acknowledgment among urban political and business leaders that Pittsburgh's Allegheny Conference served as their model for directing redevelopment, see Tracy Neumann, *Remaking the Rust Belt: The Postindustrial Transformation of North America* (Philadelphia: University of Pennsylvania Press, 2016), 1–2.

8. "St. Louisans Ask Tips on City Advance," *Pittsburgh Post-Gazette*, October 27, 1953; "St. Louis Studies Progress Here," *Pittsburgh Press*, October 26, 1953. St. Louis's top businesspeople, like August Busch and David Calhoun, were ready participants in a dialogue with their counterparts in Pittsburgh, Chicago, and other cities undergoing rapid social and economic change. In November 1956, for example, Holman D. Pettibone and New-

ton C. Farr, leaders of the newly formed Chicago Central Area Committee, traveled to St. Louis to meet with Civic Progress members (Minutes of the Meeting of Civic Progress, Inc., October 29, 1956, Raymond R. Tucker Records [WUA00366], 1953–1965, series 5, box 1, folder "Civic Progress, Inc.," Washington University Archives, St. Louis, Missouri [cited hereafter as Tucker Records, WUA]. Whether in St. Louis, Pittsburgh, or Chicago, downtown business leaders (mostly Republicans) worked closely with Democratic mayors.

9. Lang, "Civil Rights versus 'Civic Progress,'" 618; "Mayor Has Plan to Finish Three Expressways within Five Years," *St. Louis Post-Dispatch*, October 11, 1954; "New Highway Building Era Proposed under Detroit Plan That Would Drop Pay-as-You-Go for U.S. Credit Financing," *St. Louis Post-Dispatch*, October 24, 1954; "City Will Draw Off-Street Parking Plans," *St. Louis Post-Dispatch*, November 2, 1955.

10. Gordon, *Mapping Decline*, 49–53; Lang, "Civil Rights versus 'Civic Progress,'" 618; Heathcott, "Black Archipelago," 713.

11. Robert E. Cantwell, "St. Louis Snaps Out of It," *Fortune*, July 1956, 119 (quotation); "Sidney R. Baer, 65, St. Louis Merchant," *New York Times*, August 26, 1956; "David R. Calhoun Jr. Dead at 71; Banker Active in Civic Affairs," *St. Louis Post-Dispatch*, May 16, 1974; Lang, "Civil Rights versus 'Civic Progress,'" 618; Heywood T. Sanders, *Convention Center Follies: Politics, Power, and Public Investment in American Cities* (Philadelphia: University of Pennsylvania Press, 2014), 343–45; Gordon, *Mapping Decline*, 52, brought the Cantwell article to our attention.

12. Lang, "Civil Rights versus 'Civic Progress,'" 618; Harry Wilensky, "Pittsburgh's Project Scope Is Impressive," including Mellon quotation; "A New St. Louis Rips Up Its Past," *Business Week*, September 10, 1955, 132; Heathcott and Murphy, "Corridors of Flight," 159, alerted us to the *Business Week* article.

13. Heathcott, "City Quietly Remade," 231. We should not doubt the accuracy of historian Destin Jenkins's contention in *The Bonds of Inequality: Debt and the Making of the American City* (Chicago: University of Chicago Press, 2021), 14, that "the racial welfare state, of which infrastructure and social services were a crucial part, became acceptable only insofar as the allocation of borrowed funds helped secure white rights while keeping taxes low."

14. "Pass Bond Issue for Plaza Plan, Spokesmen for 3 Faiths Urge," *St. Louis Post-Dispatch*, September 26, 1953; "Plaza Bond Vote Spurs Plans for Big Improvement Program," *St. Louis Post-Dispatch*, September 30, 1953.

15. "Light Vote Will Mean Bond Issue Defeat: Tucker," *St. Louis Post-Dispatch*, May 18, 1955; "Civic Bond Issue Appeals to Be Made in Many Churches Today," *St Louis Post-Dispatch*, May 22, 1955.

16. Harry Wilensky, "City Program Wins by Heavy Margins; School by 5 to 1," *St. Louis Post-Dispatch*, May 27, 1955; "Quick Start Promised on Improvements as All Bond Propositions Carry," *St. Louis Post-Dispatch*, May 27, 1955, including Busch quotation. Harry Wilensky, "Civic Progress, Inc.: Twenty St. Louisans Leading the Way," *St. Louis Post-Dispatch*, June 19, 1955, describes the voluntary approach Busch, McHaney, and other Civic Progress members brought to bond issues and renewal projects.

17. Cowan, *Nice Place to Visit*; Tracy Campbell, *The Gateway Arch: A Biography* (New Haven, CT: Yale University Press, 2013).

18. Lang, "Civil Rights versus 'Civic Progress,'" 619–20, 623 (quotation). Republican and Democratic politicians joined forces to oppose the election of freeholders proposed by Civic Progress. "Politicians are afraid," a *St. Louis Post-Dispatch* journalist reported, that the freeholders "might recommend elimination of many city patronage jobs, a

reduction in the number of city elective offices or a smaller Board of Aldermen" ("G.O.P. Leaders Join Democrats in Support of Charter Slate," *St. Louis Post-Dispatch*, May 1, 1956).

19. Lang, "Civil Rights versus 'Civic Progress,'" 620, 622; Cowan, *Nice Place to Visit*, 80.

20. Herbert A. Trask, "New Charter Defeated by Margin of 35,000 in Big Setback for Tucker," *St. Louis Post-Dispatch*, August 7, 1957; "Defeated Charter Was Product of Year's Work by Freeholders," *St. Louis Post-Dispatch*, August 7, 1957; "Taxes, 7-7-1, Mayor's Power Cited as Causes in Charter Loss," *St. Louis Post-Dispatch*, August 8, 1957; "Tucker Says Charter Must Be Amended for Progress," *St. Louis Post-Dispatch*, August 11, 1957; "New Charter Beaten by 51,200," *St. Louis Post-Dispatch*, August 2, 1950; Joe Alex Morris, "How to Rescue a City," *Saturday Evening Post*, August 18, 1956, 33; Minutes of the Monthly Meeting of Civic Progress, Inc., October 24, 1957, series 5, box 1, Tucker Records, WUA. October 24, 1957. And for perceptive observations about race, class, and conflict between African American labor leaders like Calloway and Mayor Tucker, see Bussel, *Fighting for Total Person Unionism*, 104, 107.

21. Colin Gordon, "Dividing the City: Race-Restrictive Covenants and the Architecture of Segregation in St. Louis," *Journal of Urban History*, first published March 26, 2021, https://doi.org/10.1177%2F0096144221999641, locates the origins of official segregation in restrictive covenants executed among home sellers and buyers as early as 1893. Also see Edwin M. Clark, as cited in Lang, "Civil Rights versus 'Civic Progress,'" 630; Heathcott, "City Quietly Remade," 226. For Clark's intense focus on downtown redevelopment, see his remarks in Minutes of the Meeting of Civic Progress, Inc., September 27, 1956, series 5, box 1, Tucker Records, WUA. Bussel, *Fighting for Total Person Unionism*, 102, nicely characterizes the perception among Civic Progress leaders like telephone executive Clark that their loss in the battle to rewrite the city charter portended a loss of control in St. Louis politics.

22. Gordon, *Mapping Decline*, 167–68; Walter Johnson, *The Broken Heart of America: St Louis and the Violent History of the United States* (New York: Basic Books, 2020), 307–8, 9 (first quotation); "A Bold Design . . . for a Quarter of a Billion Dollars" [advertisement], *St. Louis Post-Dispatch*, January 3, 1958. Regarding people who move from one public housing project to another, see Lawrence Vale, *Purging the Poorest: Public Housing and the Design Politics of Twice-Cleared Communities* (Chicago: University of Chicago Press, 2013), for the perceptive observation that "low-income people and high municipal aspirations remain in frequent conflict" (xiii).

23. We are pleased to acknowledge Francesca Russello Ammon, *Bulldozer: Demolition and the Clearance of the Postwar Landscape* (New Haven, CT: Yale University Press, 2016), for the concept of a postwar "culture of clearance" that swept across U.S. cities. In St. Louis, reports urban historian Eric Sandweiss, in *St. Louis: The Evolution of an American Urban Landscape* (Philadelphia: Temple University Press, 2001), 183–229, the urge to level areas in and around downtown in fact extended back to the late nineteenth century. After World War II, determines historian Clarence Lang, in *Grassroots at the Gateway*, "municipal reform, and 'urban renewal' and 'downtown revitalization,' had become hegemonic in the thinking of many big-city Democratic mayors, central district businesspeople, federal officials, and urban planners" (198). "In 1947," Lang continues, "St. Louis's City Plan Commission had issued an influential report declaring the city virtually 'unlivable' due to the blight covering half of its residential area, and calling for the destruction of properties surrounding the downtown business area" (199). In subsequent years, displaced residents had only a few organizations such as trade unions, neighborhood groups, and the NAACP to secure a place in conversations about their futures. See, for examples of African American community vitality and political mobilization in

St. Louis, Joseph Heathcott, "Black Archipelago": 705–36; and Sarah Siegel, "'Dominant Decision-Making Authority': Resident Leadership in St. Louis, Missouri, Model Cities Planning," *Journal of Urban History* 45, no. 2 (March 2019): 333–53. Finally, the concept of blight had a decades-long history in St. Louis politics (Desloge, "Tortured Pre-history of Urban Blight"). In early 2021, Desloge's dissertation remained embargoed, but Rose Miyatsu, "Rediscovering St. Louis's Lung Block," Washington University, Department of African American Studies, May 9, 2019, provides a valuable introduction to a portion of Desloge's findings, https://history.wustl.edu/news/rediscovering-st-louis's-lung-block.

24. "He's Changing the Face of the City," *St. Louis Post-Dispatch*, November 13, 1960 (Farris quotation); "$2,873,915 Value Put on Property Sought by City between Plazas," *St. Louis Post-Dispatch*, August 19, 1951; Heathcott and Murphy, "Corridors of Flight"; Heathcott, "City Quietly Remade." Our great thanks to Joseph Heathcott and Maire Murphy for valuable conversations about Farris's approach to renewal and for ideas about downtown renewal as part of a metropolitan project.

25. Regarding urban renewal funding, see Roger Biles, *The Fate of Cities: Urban America and the Federal Government, 1945–2000* (Lawrence: University Press of Kansas, 2011); Jon C. Teaford, *The Rough Road to Renaissance: Urban Revitalization in America, 1940–1985* (Baltimore, MD: Johns Hopkins University Press, 1990). Gordon, *Mapping Decline*, 161–74, delineates the legal grounds that supported Farris's renewal projects.

26. "C. of C. Gets Plan for Downtown Sports Stadium," *St. Louis Post-Dispatch*, December 9, 1958; Benjamin D. Lisle, *Modern Coliseum: Stadiums and American Culture* (Philadelphia: University of Pennsylvania Press, 2017), 210; "Stadium a Part of $80,935,000 Downtown Plan Ok'd by C. of C.," *St. Louis Post-Dispatch*, September 10, 1959; "Stadium Stock, Debenture Plan Gets State Approval," *St. Louis Post-Dispatch*, January 18, 1962; "Chance to Build a Dream," *St. Louis Post-Dispatch*, December 10, 1958, including quote.

27. "11 City Bond Items Defeated; Tucker Considers Resubmission," *St. Louis Post-Dispatch*, January 24, 1962; "Comfort Denies Offer to Drop Stadium Fight," *St. Louis Post-Dispatch*, March 7, 1962; "Work to Be Done," *St. Louis Post-Dispatch*, January 25, 1962; "Aldermen Vote Unanimously to Resubmit Bond Issues March 6," *St. Louis Post-Dispatch*, February 9, 1962. Jenkins, *Bonds of Inequality*, 16, describes a bond approval process that kept members of the "white working class—and, more precisely, members of segregated building trades—employed in the construction of innumerable capital improvement projects."

28. "St. Louis Cardinals Team History and Encyclopedia," https://www.baseball-reference.com/teams/STL/index.shtml, last updated February 2, 2022; "Stan Musial," https://www.baseball-reference.com/players/m/musiast01.shtml, last updated February 2, 2022; Luke Epplin, "The Problem with Remembering Stan Musial as Baseball's 'Perfect Knight,'" *Atlantic*, January 24, 2013, https://www.theatlantic.com/entertainment/archive/2013/01/the-problem-with-remembering-stan-musial-as-baseballs-perfect-knight/272489/; George Vecsey, "The Star Who Stood Out by Not Standing Out," *New York Times*, January 20, 2013. Ann Levin, "Oral History About Overlooked Living Legend Musial," *San Diego Union-Tribune*, May 9, 2011, https://www.sandiegouniontribune.com/sdut-oral-history-about-overlooked-living-legend-musial-2011may09-story.html, including quote.

29. "School Board to Submit Bond Issue to Voters Again March 6," *St. Louis Post-Dispatch*, February 1, 1962; "Musial Gets Fellow Pros to Work for Stadium Vote," *St. Louis Post-Dispatch*, February 25, 1962; "Instead of a Dilapidated, Tax-Poor Wasteland, 11 Competing Cities Are Paying for Their Own Stadiums" [advertisement], *St. Louis Post-Dispatch*, March 4, 1962; Gordon, *Mapping Decline*, 168.; Lisle, *Modern Coliseum*,

217–28; Cowan, *Nice Place to Visit*, 66; Huping Ling, *Chinese St. Louis: From Enclave to Cultural Community* (Philadelphia: Temple University Press, 2004), 103–4, 128–31.

30. Robert A. Dunlap, "Seven of 11 Bond Issues Are Approved, including $23,180,000 for Schools," *St. Louis Post-Dispatch*, March 7, 1962; "His Honor Has Honor for Musial," *St. Louis Post-Dispatch*, September 26, 1962.

31. "St. Louis Cardinals Attendance Data," last updated 2020, http://www.baseball -almanac.com/teams/cardatte.shtml. Jenkins, *Bonds of Inequality*, 17, highlights the support among "merchants, athletes, labor unions and civic groups" for bond issues to support playgrounds and streetlighting.

32. Downtown St. Louis, Inc., "Show Me Downtown" [advertisement], *St. Louis Post-Dispatch*, September 14, 1966; J. A. Baer II, "Foresees Further Increases in Business Downtown Here," *St. Louis Post-Dispatch*, January 8, 1967 (quotation).

33. Cowan, *Nice Place to Visit*, 72; Gordon, *Mapping Decline*, including quotation on 168; "Plan Group Rejects Blighting Proposal," *St. Louis Post-Dispatch*, June 4, 1968; Charles Haddad, "Woolworth's Nightmare Turned into a Dream," *St. Louis Post-Dispatch*, August 8, 1983; Charlene Prost, untitled report in the *St. Louis Post-Dispatch*, 3C, February 28, 1994.

34. E. S. Evans, "Mill Creek Job, Nearly Complete, Is Acclaimed as Great Success," *St. Louis Post-Dispatch*, July 12, 1970; Cowan, *Nice Place to Visit*, 73–77; Sanders, *Convention Center Follies*.

35. Ammon, *Bulldozer*; Neumann, *Remaking the Rust Belt*; Roy Lubove, *Twentieth-Century Pittsburgh*, vol. 2, *The Post-steel Era* (Pittsburgh, PA: University of Pittsburgh Press, 1996); "Farris Program for Downtown," *St. Louis Post-Dispatch*, June 10, 1976; Gordon, *Mapping Decline*, 225; "Greater St. Louis was a poster child for urban renewal and its limits," observes historian Colin Gordon in *Citizen Brown*, 83.

36. Gordon, *Mapping Decline*, 51; Barbara Ferman, *Challenging the Growth Machine: Neighborhood Politics in Chicago and Pittsburgh* (Lawrence: University Press of Kansas, 1996), 29.

37. Stein, *St. Louis Politics*, 3; "Colony Hotel Is Opened on Gradual Basis," *St. Louis Post-Dispatch*, March 21, 1965; "New Office Building Begun by Clayton Inn," *St. Louis Post-Dispatch*, October 6, 1969; "Ample Services Support Clayton Growth," *St. Louis Post-Dispatch*, December 8, 1969, including quotation; Gordon, *Mapping Decline*, 53. We used Clayton, a prospering city located at St. Louis's western border, as a particularly luminescent example of one of those local growth machines. For areas west of Clayton, also see historian Johnson, *Broken Heart of America*, 334, who notes residents' mantra of "'good schools, nice neighborhoods,' and 'high property values.'"

38. Eric Avila, *Popular Culture in the Age of White Flight: Fear and Fantasy in Suburban Los Angeles* (Berkeley: University of California Press, 2004), is an excellent place to launch a study of suburban whiteness coupled to homeowner self-interest and chamber of commerce boosting. Elizabeth Tandy Shermer, *Sunbelt Capitalism: Phoenix and the Transformation of American Politics* (Philadelphia: University of Pennsylvania Press, 2013), chronicles growth politics in Phoenix. Also see Sanders, *Convention Center Follies*, for competition among city leaders throughout the United States to build the largest and most inviting convention centers, only to fall behind within a few years.

## CHAPTER 2

1. Jack Houston and Stanley Ziemba, "Arthur Rubloff, 83, Colossus of Real Estate Development," *Chicago Tribune*, May 25, 1986, including citation; "Bergdorf Goodman

Chicago Store," *Wall Street Journal*, November 10, 1965. In a letter dated December 6, 1948, Rubloff told *Chicago Tribune* publisher Robert R. McCormick that a public-relations firm had suggested "Magnificent Mile." Twenty-five years later, however, Rubloff credited McCormick with having chosen the name from a list Rubloff had presented to him. Memories are necessarily faulty, but, perhaps more likely, Rubloff was prepared to award credit as he judged wisest in order to promote a project or curry an image. Compare Arthur Rubloff to Colonel Robert R. McCormick, "December 6, 1948, box 1, folder 2; and Arthur Rubloff, "Greater North Michigan Avenue Assn.," November 15, 1973, box "Speeches," folder "Greater North Michigan Avenue Association," both in Arthur Rubloff Papers, Chicago History Museum [cited hereafter as Rubloff papers]. On the development of North Michigan Avenue prior to Rubloff's Magnificent Mile, see John W. Stamper, *Chicago's North Michigan Avenue: Planning and Development, 1900–1930* (Chicago: University of Chicago Press, 1990).

2. Susie J. Pak, *Gentlemen Bankers: The World of J.P. Morgan* (Cambridge, MA: Harvard University Press, 2013), encourages us to perceive Rubloff and his associates as members of cooperating and competing networks that revolved around business, political, and social affairs and that were necessarily both public and private in nature. Sociologist Gerald D. Suttles, *The Man-Made City: The Land-Use Confidence Game in Chicago* (Chicago: University of Chicago Press, 1990), 121, highlights the sharp splits among Chicago's business and political leaders during the 1970s and 1980s.

3. "East Side of Michigan Avenue," February 13, 1947; "Guests to Be Invited to Press Luncheon," March 20, 1947; Thomas W. Hughes to Arthur Rubloff, May 9, 1947, all in box 1, folder 1, Rubloff Papers; Michael Sterne, "William Zeckendorf, Real Estate Developer, 71, Dies," *New York Times*, October 2, 1976.

4. For case studies of real-estate professionals engaged in this block-by-block treatment of property in Chicago's neighborhoods, see Amanda I. Seligman, *Block by Block: Neighborhoods and Public Policy on Chicago's West Side* (Chicago: University of Chicago Press, 2005); and Beryl Satter, *Family Properties: Race, Real Estate, and the Exploitation of Black, Urban America* (New York: Metropolitan, 2009). Also see Destin Jenkins and Justin Leroy, "Introduction: The Old History of Capitalism," in *Histories of Racial Capitalism*, ed. Destin Jenkins and Justin Leroy (New York: Columbia University Press, 2021), 1–14.

5. Arnold R. Hirsch, *Making the Second Ghetto: Race and Housing in Chicago, 1940–1960* (Cambridge, MA: Cambridge University Press, 1983), 102–12; Ross Miller, "Chicago Title and Trust," *Encyclopedia of Chicago*, http://www.encyclopedia.chicagohistory.org/pages/272.html.

6. "Rubloff Plan Publicity" [c. February 1, 1947]; Arthur Rubloff to William Zeckendorf, March 14, 1947; untitled description of Rubloff's background, including quotation, all in box 1, folder 1, Rubloff Papers. For the centrality of race in urban renewal politics, see Lizabeth Cohen, *Saving America's Cities: Ed Logue and the Struggle to Renew Urban America in the Suburban Age* (New York: Farrar, Straus and Giroux, 2019), 126–36.

7. Joseph R. Frey to Arthur Rubloff, June 17, 1949; Arthur Rubloff to Frederick M. Bowes, April 8, 1950; Gordon Lang to Arthur Rubloff, June 29, 1949; Frederick M. Bowes to Gordon Lang, March 31, 1950; Arthur Rubloff to Col. Robert McCormick, December 20, 1948, including quotation, all in box 1, folder 2, Rubloff Papers; Stamper, *Chicago's North Michigan Avenue.*

8. "Excerpts from First Annual Meeting of the North Michigan Avenue Association," November 17, 1949, box 1, folder 2, Rubloff Papers.

9. Tracy Neumann, *Remaking the Rust Belt: The Postindustrial Transformation of North America* (Philadelphia: University of Pennsylvania Press, 2016), 19–20, 26–27, explains the factors leading to creation of these growth coalitions in general, as well as the ACCD's origins and activities. For Pittsburgh's lengthy planning tradition prior to 1944, see John F. Bauman and Edward K. Muller, *Before Renaissance: Planning in Pittsburgh, 1889–1943* (Pittsburgh, PA: University of Pittsburgh Press, 2006). Tracy Neumann, "Reforging the Steel City: Symbolism and Space in Postindustrial Pittsburgh," *Journal of Urban History* 44, no. 4 (July 2018): 582, notes that leaders in cities throughout the United States judged the ACCD's activities "a template for their own urban redevelopment activities." Throughout this book we also relied on Neumann, "Reforging the Steel City," for the concept of urban branding.

10. Ann Durkin Keating, "Fort Dearborn," *Encyclopedia of Chicago History*, http:// www.encyclopedia.chicagohistory.org/pages/477.html; Joshua A. T. Salzmann, *Liquid Capital: Making the Chicago Waterfront* (Philadelphia: University of Pennsylvania Press, 2017), 26–27. Henry Dearborn was President Thomas Jefferson's secretary of war from 1801 to 1809. Also see Ann Durkin Keating, *Rising Up from Indian Country: The Battle of Fort Dearborn and the Birth of Chicago* (Chicago: University of Chicago Press, 2012). By early 1954, Rubloff had alerted perhaps a dozen business leaders about his Project X.

11. Clayton Kirkpatrick, "Outline Vast Civic Center!" *Chicago Tribune*, March 17, 1954; and for a more detailed description, see Greater North Michigan Avenue Association, "Fort Dearborn Project," c. March 1954, both in box 5, folder 2, Rubloff Papers; "Rubloff Calls Huge Project Five Year Job," *Chicago Tribune*, April 6, 1954, in box 2, folder 10a, Fort Dearborn Project Records, Special Collections, MSFDP_67, Richard J. Daley Library, University of Illinois at Chicago [cited hereafter as Fort Dearborn Records, UIC].

12. Ross Miller, *Here's the Deal: The Buying and Selling of a Great American City* (New York: Alfred A. Knopf, 1996), 67, 78, describes the prestige and undeniable authority that business leaders traditionally brought to planning and Rubloff's already outsize role. As in any large real-estate project, developers like Rubloff sought to know the area's existing demographics. Among several studies Rubloff had access to, see Chicago Commission on Human Relations, Department of Community Services, "Population and Housing Characteristics of Community Areas 7 and 8," June 1956, in box 4, folder 27, Fort Dearborn Records, UIC. Historian D. Bradford Hunt and planner Jon B. Devries, *Planning Chicago* (Chicago: American Planning Association, 2013), 58, identify architects at Skidmore, Owings and Merrill as Chicago's unofficial planners starting in 1973 and extending to 2009, with plans for the Olympics.

13. Greater North Michigan Avenue Association, "Fort Dearborn Project"; Hirsch, *Making the Second Ghetto*, 105–7. Vicki Howard, *From Main Street to Mall: The Rise and Fall of the American Department Store* (Philadelphia: University of Pennsylvania Press, 2015), 132–65, explains the predicament of department-store operators like McBain in dealing with federal highway and housing programs that fostered the outmigration of affluent shoppers. "State Street vs. Suburbs," *Business Week*, June 26, 1954, in box 2, folder 10b, Fort Dearborn Records, UIC, places downtown retailing in a national context.

14. Hirsch, *Making the Second Ghetto*, 212–14; "Fort Dearborn Project" [meeting notes], July 7, 1954, box 5, folder 5; "Planners Offer Revised Fort Dearborn Project," *Chicago Sun-Times*, July 16, 1954, box 2, folder 10a, both in Rubloff Papers. Also see Kribben's observation at a meeting on January 18, 1955, that "the job was so complex and difficult that it would take years in accomplishment under the most favorable circum-

270 / Notes to Chapter 2

stances and with all elements of the community working together, and that progress could be impaired or prevented by political interference or selfish opposition," in Kribben meeting with Byron Dalton and Hayward Hirsch, January 18, 1955, box 4, folder 26, Fort Dearborn Records, UIC.

15. Frederick M. Bowes to fellow directors, November 28, 1955, box 1, folder 6; W. N. Sutherland, "Seek Ideas at Detroit Civic Center," *Chicago Herald American*, May 15, 1956; Roy M. Fisher, "Another Tale of Two Cities," *Chicago Daily News*, May 18, 1956, the last two in box 2, folder 11b, all in Fort Dearborn Records, UIC. Also see William McGaffin, "Daley in New York Seeks City Saving," *Chicago Daily News*, May 18, 1955, for a report of Daley's visit to New York City, where he met with a senior executive at Moody's Investor Service about securing a higher rating (and lower interest expenses) for city bonds. "We are on the threshold of a new era," Daley told a reporter, "and with a little impetus can accomplish things too long delayed," such as the Fort Dearborn project. Moody's hard-edged executive reported "a pleasant chat with Mr. Daley, but that is as far as it went." See further Roman Pucinski, "Mayor Daley Gets Brush-Off on Upgrading City Bonds," *Chicago Sun-Times*, May 19, 1955, last two in box 2, folder 10b, and all in Fort Dearborn Records, UIC.

16. Editors, *Downtown Idea Exchange*, January 1, 1957, box 6, folder 48, Fort Dearborn Records, UIC. Compare "State St. Holds World Retail Stature" and "Shop Centers Springing Up," both in *Chicago Tribune*, January 2, 1957. "Reveal 28 Men Backing Loop Building Drive," *Chicago Tribune*, January 29, 1957. Joseph M. Siry, *Carson Pirie Scott: Louis Sullivan and the Chicago Department Store* (Chicago: University of Chicago Press, 1988, 2012), is an architectural history of the store.

17. Greater North Michigan Avenue Association, Minutes of the Executive Committee Meeting, March 14, 1957; George H. Dovenmuehle to Earl Kribben, March 15, 1957, both in box 6, folder 48; Gilbert H. Scribner to Peter B. Clark, February 11, 1959, box 1, folder 9, all in Fort Dearborn Records, UIC.

18. Fort Dearborn project minutes, January 14, 1957, Fort Dearborn Records, UIC; Joel Rast, "Creating a Unified Business Elite: The Origins of the Chicago Central Area Committee," *Journal of Urban History* 37, no. 4 (July 2011): 594–95, 598, 604; "Urges Better Transport in Business Area," *Chicago Tribune*, November 21, 1956; Charles Gotthart, "Pirie Asserts Chicago 'Is Truly on the March,'" *Chicago Tribune*, August 7, 1957.

19. Edward C. Banfield, *Political Influence* (New York: Free Press, 1961), 141–46; "Downtown Chicago's Future," *Chicago Tribune*, January 18, 1956. Pettibone founded the Chicago Central Area Committee, reports Joel Rast, *Remaking Chicago: The Political Origins of Urban Industrial America* (DeKalb: Northern Illinois University Press, 1999), 27.

20. Thomas Buck, "Campaign to Improve Loop Gets under Way," *Chicago Tribune*, September 20, 1956; Fort Dearborn project minutes, January 14, 1957, October 22, 1957, Fort Dearborn Records, UIC. Rubloff at first thought he could strike an accord with Pettibone. An upcoming meeting between Pettibone and Rubloff "is a very good thing," Rubloff wrote Nelson Forrest in June 1956. See Arthur Rubloff to Holman D. Pettibone, June 18, 1956, including Rubloff's typed note to Forrest added to the copy, box 2, folder 2, Rubloff Papers. Finally, see political scientist Heywood T. Sanders, *Convention Center Follies: Politics, Power, and Public Investment in American Cities* (Philadelphia: University of Pennsylvania Press, 2014), 259, for the perceptive observation that in Chicago's fractured renewal politics, "a single project, in one location, would simply not suffice to ensure business unity." On Daley's leadership, see Roger Biles, *Richard J. Daley: Politics, Race, and the Governing of Chicago* (DeKalb: Northern Illinois University Press, 1995).

21. Sanders, *Convention Center Follies*, 211, including *Chicago Tribune* quotation.

22. Sanders, *Convention Center Follies*, is the standard and most valuable account of convention-center politics. See contemporary reports about the number of convention-goers, their spending, and Chicago as an important convention center in Victor Hillary, "Convention Trade," *Wall Street Journal*, June 8, 1946; Ray Vicker, "Confab Crescendo," *Wall Street Journal*, January 12, 1955; Jerry Flint, "Many Cities Put Up Lavish New Buildings to Woo Conventions," *Wall Street Journal*, November 8, 1960.

23. Sanders, *Convention Center Follies*, 223; "New $15 Million Convention Hall Proposed for Chicago," *Wall Street Journal*, March 31, 1953.

24. Sanders, *Convention Center Follies*, 222–24, 232; Banfield, *Political Influence*, 228–31; "Convention Bureau Value in 1960 Put at 250 Million," *Chicago Tribune*, November 13, 1960.

25. Philip Hampson, "The Road to Success: Sketch of Newton C. Farr, Long Time Chicago Real Estate Man," *Chicago Tribune*, October 2, 1954; Nelson Forrest to Newton C. Farr, November 25, 1955, box 1, folder 5, Rubloff Papers, including quotation; James Janega, "Nelson Forrest; Led Michigan Ave. Group," *Chicago Tribune*, October 13, 2000; Lilia Fernandez, *Brown in the Windy City: Mexicans and Puerto Ricans in Postwar Chicago* (Chicago: University of Chicago Press, 2012), 139. Only a few years later, reports historian Mike Amezcua in "A Machine in the Barrio: Chicago's Conservative Colonia and the Remaking of Latino Politics in the 1960s and 1970s," *The Sixties* 12, no. 1 (2019): 95–120; leaders among portions of the city's Mexican American community took an active role in the Daley organization, emerging as "Amigos for Daley." And, finally, sociologists Michael T. Maly and Heather M. Dalmage, in *Vanishing Eden: White Construction of Memory, Meaning, and Identity in a Racially Changing City* (Philadelphia: Temple University Press, 2016, describe "defended communities" in parts of Chicago's South Side during the 1960s–1980s, where householders built "nostalgia narratives . . . that validate[d] a social hierarchy of white as good and justifiably dominant" (27).

26. *The Area* [newsletter of the Greater North Michigan Avenue Association], June 13, 1956, and Nelson Forrest to Phillip Doyle, July 17, 1956 (quotation), both in box 2, folder 2, Rubloff Papers. Developers never doubted that the success of one project enhanced their chances to secure bank and insurance-company loan approvals to build a similar project down the block or around the corner.

27. Fernandez, *Brown in the Windy City*, 141; Lawrence J. Vale, *Purging the Poorest: Public Housing and the Design Politics of Twice-Cleared Communities* (Chicago: University of Chicago Press, 2013), 249. Andrew J. Diamond, *Chicago on the Make: Power and Inequality in a Modern City* (Oakland: University of California Press, 2017), 151, describes urban renewal as a "battle to hold the color line" and finds Daley "the perfect battlefield commander." In 1929, a University of Chicago sociologist characterized those white, upper-income neighborhoods and the nearby area populated by lower-income brown and black residents as the Gold Coast and the slum. See historian Howard Chudacoff's introduction to Harvey Warren Zorbaugh, *The Gold Coast and the Slum: A Sociological Study of Chicago's Near North Side* (Chicago: University of Chicago Press, 1929, 1976), vii–xv. Mike Amezcua, "Beautiful Urbanism: Gender, Landscape, and Contestation in Latino Chicago's Age of Urban Renewal," *Journal of American History* 104, no. 1 (June 2017): 98, describes a process by which "Latinos repurpose[d] the architecture of the blighted neighborhood to make it their own."

28. Houston and Ziemba, "Arthur Rubloff"; Joanne Knoch, "Detail Plan for Bergdorf Store," *Chicago Tribune*, November 9, 1965; Steven R. Strahler, "Rubloff: How a Great Name in Real Estate Lost Its Way," *Crain's Chicago Business*, October 29, 1990. In 1995, Jane Adler, "City Review: Chicago," *National Real Estate Investor* 37, no. 4 (April 1995),

characterized retail sales on North Michigan Avenue as "hot." Two years later, Jane Adler, "A Luxury Conversion," *Journal of Property Management* 62, no. 5 (September–October 1997), described North Michigan Avenue as "home to the city's highest concentration of upscale units."

29. Miller, *Here's the Deal*, 74, 99 (quotations); Strahler, "Rubloff."

30. Miller, *Here's the Deal*, 55 (quotation).

31. Larry Bennett, "Beyond Urban Renewal: Chicago's North Loop Redevelopment Project," *Urban Affairs Review* 22 (December 1986): 242–60; Miller, *Here's the Deal*, 179–79.

32. Roger Biles, *Mayor Harold Washington: Champion of Race and Reform in Chicago* (Urbana: University of Illinois Press, 2018), 135–36, 177–78, 217–18, 265, 274, 323.

33. The literature on urban renewal is vast. See these excellent examples published across four decades: Arnold R. Hirsch, *Making the Second Ghetto: Race and Housing in Chicago, 1940–1960* (Chicago: University of Chicago Press, 1983, 1998); Jon C. Teaford, *The Rough Road to Renaissance: Urban Revitalization in America, 1940–1985* (Baltimore, MD: Johns Hopkins University Press, 1990); Barbara Ferman, *Challenging the Growth Machine: Neighborhood Politics in Chicago and Pittsburgh* (Lawrence: University Press of Kansas, 1996); Eric Avila, *Popular Culture in the Age of White Flight: Fear and Fantasy in Suburban Los Angeles* (Berkeley: University of California Press, 2004); Alison Isenberg, *Downtown America: A History of the Place and the People Who Made It* (Chicago: University of Chicago Press, 2004); Isenberg, *Designing San Francisco: Art, Land, and Urban Renewal in the City by the Bay* (Princeton, NJ: Princeton University Press, 2017); Thomas J. Sugrue, *The Origins of the Urban Crisis: Race and Inequality in Postwar Detroit* (Princeton, NJ: Princeton University Press, 2005); Colin Gordon, *Mapping Decline: St. Louis and the Fate of the American City* (Philadelphia: University of Pennsylvania Press, 2008); Guian McKee, *The Problem of Jobs: Liberalism, Race, and Deindustrialization in Philadelphia* (Chicago: University of Chicago Press, 2008); Samuel Zipp, *Manhattan Projects: The Rise and Fall of Urban Renewal in Cold War New York* (New York: Oxford University Press, 2010); N.D.B. Connolly, *A World More Concrete: Real Estate and the Remaking of Jim Crow South Florida* (Chicago: University of Chicago Press, 2014); Andrew Highsmith, *Demolition Means Progress: Flint, Michigan and the Fate of the American Metropolis* (Chicago: University of Chicago Press, 2015); Aaron Cowan, *A Nice Place to Visit: Tourism and Urban Revitalization in the Postwar Rustbelt* (Philadelphia: Temple University Press, 2016); Allan Dietrich-Ward, *Beyond Rust: Metropolitan Pittsburgh and the Fate of Industrial America* (Philadelphia: University of Pennsylvania Press, 2016); Tracy Neumann, *Remaking the Rust Belt: The Postindustrial Transformation of North America* (Philadelphia: University of Pennsylvania Press, 2016); Kim Phillips-Fein, *Fear City: New York's Fiscal Crisis and the Rise of Austerity Politics* (New York: Metropolitan, 2017); Mark Souther, *Believing in Cleveland: Managing Decline in "The Best Location in the Nation"* (Philadelphia: Temple University Press, 2017); Heather Ann Thompson, *Whose Detroit? Politics, Labor, and Race in a Modern American City* (Ithaca: Cornell University Press, 2017); Edward K. Muller and Joel A. Tarr, eds., *Making Pittsburgh Modern: Environment, Transportation, Energy, and Planning* (Pittsburgh: University of Pittsburgh Press, 2019); Joel Rast, *The Origins of the Dual City: Housing, Race & Redevelopment in Twentieth-Century Chicago* (Chicago: University of Chicago Press, 2019); Keeanga-Yamahtta Taylor, *Race for Profit: How Banks and the Real Estate Industry Undermined Black Homeownership* (Chapel Hill: University of North Carolina Press, 2019); J. Rosie Tighe and Stephanie Ryberg-Webster, eds., *Legacy Cities: Continuity and Change Amid Decline and Revival* (Pittsburgh: University of Pittsburgh

Press, 2019); A. K. Sandoval-Strausz, *Barrio America: How Latino Immigrants Saved the American City* (New York: Basic Books, 2019); Walter Johnson, *The Broken Heart of America: St. Louis and the Violent History of the United States* (New York: Basic Books, 1920); Robert Lewis, *Chicago's Industrial Decline: The Failure of Redevelopment, 1920–1975* (Ithaca, NY: Cornell University Press, 2020); Destin Jenkins, *The Bonds of Inequality: Debt and the Making of the American City* (Chicago: University of Chicago Press, 2021); Mitchell Schwarzer, *Hella Town: Oakland's History of Development and Disruption* (Oakland: University of California Press, 2021); Gabriel Winant, *The Next Shift: the Fall of Industry and the Rise of Health Care in Rust Belt America* (Cambridge, MA: Harvard University Press, 2021); Howard Gillette, Jr., *Camden After the Fall: Decline and Renewal in a Post-Industrial City* (Philadelphia: University of Pennsylvania Press, 2006); Gillette, *The Paradox of Urban Revitalization: Progress and Poverty in America's Postindustrial Era* (Philadelphia: University of Pennsylvania Press, 2022); Diamond, *Chicago on the Make*; Cohen, *Saving America's Cities*, and Biles, *Mayor Harold Washington*.

34. We borrowed "grinding politics" from Michael R. Fein, *Paving the Way: New York Road Building and the American State, 1880–1956* (Lawrence: University Press of Kansas, 2008).

35. On Washington's ambivalence about downtown redevelopment, see Biles, *Mayor Harold Washington*. We have few assessments of Mayor Richard M. Daley's administration. But see Keith Koeneman, *First Son: The Biography of Richard M. Daley* (Chicago: University of Chicago Press, 2013); Larry Bennett, *The Third City: Chicago and American Urbanism* (Chicago: University of Chicago Press, 2010); and Costas Spirou and Dennis R. Judd, *Building the City of Spectacle: Mayor Richard M. Daley and the Remaking of Chicago* (Ithaca, NY: Cornell University Press, 2016).

36. Rachel Weber, *From Boom to Bubble: How Finance Built the New Chicago* (Chicago: University of Chicago Press, 2015), describes the important part played by building developers in the city's post-2000 downtown construction boom. On the future of postindustrial Chicago, see Dominic A. Pacyga, *Chicago: A Biography* (Chicago: University of Chicago Press, 2009), chapter 11. The decades-long efforts in Chicago and elsewhere to reconstruct a downtown populated mostly by wealthy, white householders and related businesses leads inevitably to historian Keeanga-Yamahtta Taylor's observation on the ways in which "perceptions of insurmountable difference steeped in the permanence of blood, race, and culture constituted the underwriting criteria that determined who was to be excluded and who should be included" (Taylor, *Race for Profit: How Banks and the Real Estate Industry Undermined Black Homeownership* [Chapel Hill: University of North Carolina Press, 2019], 11). Destin Jenkins's review of Yamahtta Taylor in *Enterprise & Society* 22, no. 1 (March 2021): 288–91, brought this sentence to our attention.

37. Hirsch, *Making the Second Ghetto*, 115–34; Ferman, *Challenging the Growth Machine*, 29; Joel Rast, *The Origins of the Dual City: Housing, Race, and Redevelopment in Twentieth-Century Chicago* (Chicago: University of Chicago Press, 2019), 192.

## CHAPTER 3

1. Andrew Feffer, "Show Down in Center City: Staging Redevelopment and Citizenship in Bicentennial Philadelphia, 1974–1977," *Journal of Urban History* 30, no. 6 (September 2004): 791–825.

2. Carolyn T. Adams, "Greater Philadelphia Movement," *The Encyclopedia of Greater Philadelphia* (New Brunswick, NJ: Rutgers University, 2016), https://philadelphiaen

cyclopedia.org/archive/greater-philadelphia-movement/. For an early example of non-partisan language in a partisan city, see Joseph H. Miller, "23 to Accelerate Phila. Movement," *Philadelphia Inquirer*, March 13, 1949. Also see R. Daniel Wadhwani and Christina Lubinski, "Reinventing Entrepreneurial History," *Business History Review* 91 (Winter 2017): 767–99. Wadhwani and Lubinski determine that entrepreneurs perceive opportunities, make decisions about resource allocation, and "legitim[ate] novelty," 769. Needless to add, Rafsky, like other policy entrepreneurs, sometimes failed to measure up to all these idealized criteria.

3. "William L. Rafsky—Civil Servant, 81," *New York Times*, June 29, 2001. Articles mentioning Rafsky's years at City College of New York include "11 Groups Named at City College," *New York Times,* December 4, 1938; and "Students Elect at City College," *New York Times,* February 12, 1939.

4. Mark R. Wilson, *Destructive Creation: American Business and the Winning of World War II* (Philadelphia: University of Pennsylvania Press, 2016); "Philadelphia Out to Regain Hosiery Leadership," *Philadelphia Inquirer,* May 30, 1948; "Live and Learn [and] Learn to Live! At the Junto" [advertisement], *Philadelphia Inquirer,* September 19, 1948; "Henry Klein Heads Adult School Group," *Philadelphia Inquirer,* January 29, 1950.

Factory closures and job losses informed every aspect of Philadelphia's politics and planning. McKee, *The Problem of Jobs,* is the standard (and excellent) account of local efforts to retain and even increase manufacturing employment. Between 1956 and 1962, reports historian Philip Scranton in "Large Firms and Industrial Restructuring: The Philadelphia Region, 1900–1980," *Pennsylvania Magazine of History and Biography* 116, no. 4 (October 1992): 454, "the area's classic job generators . . . underwent an extended sequence of liquidations." Those firms were in and around Center City. "The depression combined with decades of disinvestment and decay to crush Philadelphia's economic foundations," as historian Timothy J. Lombardo writes, "just as the migration of southern African Americans and Puerto Ricans began to outnumber white immigrants," in his review of "Envisioning Philadelphia: The Politics of Civic Identify in the City of Brotherly Love," *Journal of Urban History* 47, no. 5—first published online August 7, 2020, https://doi.org/10.1177%2F0096144220948800.

5. "Big Enough for Both Sides" (letter to the editor), *Philadelphia Inquirer,* December 8, 1947; "Meade Indorses New Charter as Aid to Business," *Philadelphia Inquirer,* April 1, 1951; James A. Reichley, *The Art of Government: Reform and Organization Politics in Philadelphia* (New York: Fund for the Republic, 1959), 5, reprinted in Brown Reprints (Dubuque, IA, 1972); "Rebuild 'Society Hill' in Colonial Style, City Adviser Urges," *Philadelphia Inquirer,* June 9, 1950; "Mayor Gets 6-Yr., Half Billion Plan to Improve Phila.," *Philadelphia Inquirer,* September 9, 1951; "Charter Backers Hail Vote as People's Victory," *Philadelphia Inquirer,* April 18, 1951; Joseph D. Crumlish, *A City Finds Itself: The Philadelphia Home Rule Charter Movement* (Detroit, MI: Wayne State University Press, 1959), 29–31, 82–91; John F. Bauman, *Public Housing, Race, and Renewal: Urban Planning in Philadelphia, 1920–1974* (Philadelphia: Temple University Press, 1987), 102–3, 149; McKee, *Problem of Jobs,* 19–20; and Kirk R. Petshek, *The Challenge of Urban Reform: Policies and Programs in Philadelphia* (Philadelphia: Temple University Press, 1973), 55–56. Finally, Lizabeth Cohen, *Saving America's Cities: Ed Logue and the Struggle to Renew Urban America in the Suburban Age* (New York: Farrar, Straus and Giroux, 2019), 33–34, captures the excitement surrounding Philadelphia's 1952 election and the arrival of "a promising new frontier for liberal experimentation." Historian and planner Domenic Vitiello helped us perceive individual restoration projects planned for downtown Philadelphia as part of larger whole.

6. Memo from the Mayor's Office to Byrne et al., January 22, 1952; Time Records (J. Clark), February 18, 21, 1952, and March 12, 1952, all in box 2, folder 53, William L. Rafsky Papers, Accession 355, Temple University Urban Archives, Philadelphia, PA [cited hereafter as Rafsky Papers]; McKee, *Problem of Jobs*, 1–17. "Racial Discrimination," historian Keeanga-Yamahtta Taylor shows, "continued to add value to racially exclusive suburbs" (Taylor, *Race for Profit: How Banks and the Real Estate Industry Undermined Black Homeownership* [Chapel Hill: University of North Carolina Press, 2019], 7). Destin Jenkins's review of Yamahtta Taylor in *Enterprise & Society* 22, no. 1 (March 2021): 288–91, brought this sentence to our attention.

7. In May 1948, the peripatetic Martin and other top ACCD officials spoke to more than one hundred Philadelphia business leaders about the importance of nonpartisanship and cooperation between labor and management ("Pittsburgh Plan Outlined Here," *Philadelphia Inquirer*, May 13, 1948; Kurtz as quoted in Miller, "23 to Accelerate Phila. Movement"; Petshek, *Challenge of Urban Reform*, 28–30; Bauman, *Public Housing, Race, and Renewal*, 148–49), including quotation.

8. Guian A. McKee, "Blue Sky Boys, Professional Citizens, and Knights-in-Shining-Money: Philadelphia's Penn Center Project and the Constraints of Private Development," *Journal of Planning History* 6, no. 1 (February 2007): 50–51, describes tearing down the wall and station as "an opportunity for economic development unparalleled in Philadelphia." "Officials Urge Penn Center Supervision," *Philadelphia Inquirer*, November 15, 1954; Gregory L. Heller, "Salesman of Ideas: The Life Experiences That Shaped Edmund Bacon," in *Imaging Philadelphia: Edmund Bacon and the Future of the City*, ed. Scott Gabriel Knowles (Philadelphia: University of Pennsylvania Press, 2009), 36–37; statement by Mayor Joseph S. Clark Jr., March 23, 1952, box 7, folder "PRR Legal Dept. Philadelphia Improvements—General Correspondence, 1952," Hagley Museum and Library, Wilmington, DE [cited hereafter as PRR Records].

9. "For the Information of the Public," February 21, 1952, box 7, folder "PRR Legal Department, Philadelphia Improvements—News Clippings and Publicity Penn Center 1952 (A)," PRR Records; McKee, "Blue Sky Boys," 53; Heller, "Salesman of Ideas," 37; "Architects' Model of the New Penn Center Plan on Display in Our Grand Court through Saturday, March 1" [advertisement], *Philadelphia Inquirer*, February 24, 1952; Time Records (J. Clark), March 14, 1952, Rafsky Papers.

10. "Mid-Philadelphia Starts Big Center," *New York Times*, November 25, 1953; "Citizen Groups Urged to Aid in Midcity Projects," *Philadelphia Inquirer*, May 30, 1955; McKee, "Blue Sky Boys," 59–61. Also see McKee, "Edmund Bacon and the Complexity of the City," in Knowles, ed., *Imagining Philadelphia*, 55, 62.

11. "Philadelphia's New Problem," *Time*, February 24, 1958. Timothy J. Lombardo, *Blue Collar Conservatism: Frank Rizzo's Philadelphia and Populist Politics* (Philadelphia: University of Pennsylvania Press, 2018), 35, brought Dilworth's "white noose" to our attention.

12. For the rhetoric of white racial hate in Philadelphia's neighborhoods, see Lombardo, *Blue Collar Conservatism*. In 1950, report city planners Chester Rapkin and William G. Grigsby in *Residential Renewal in the Urban Core: An Analysis of the Demand for Housing in Center City Philadelphia, 1957 to 1970* (Philadelphia: University of Pennsylvania Press, 1960), 34, one new housing unit was built in Philadelphia for each built in the metropolitan area; and, by 1956, that ratio was one for every five. "For all intents and purposes," historian Eric C. Schneider contends, Philadelphia's African American population "lived in a different city" (s.v. "Crime," *The Encyclopedia of Greater Philadelphia*, New Brunswick, NJ: Rutgers University, 2014, https://philadelphiaencyclopedia .org/archive/crime/).

13. Time Records (J. Clark), December 22, 1955, box 2, folder 38, Rafsky Papers; E. Digby Baltzell, *Philadelphia Gentlemen: The Making of a National Upper Class* (Glencoe, IL: Free Press, 1958), 40; "PRR Seeks City Stadium at 30th St.," *Philadelphia Inquirer,* January 11, 1956; Guian McKee, "A Utopian, a Utopianist, or Whatever the Heck It Is: Edmund Bacon and the Complexity of the City," in Knowles, ed., *Imagining Philadelphia,* 55.

14. "110,000-Seat Stadium Planned in New York," *Philadelphia Inquirer,* April 5, 1956; "Stadium Plan Raises Questions," editorial, *Philadelphia Inquirer,* August 2, 1956.

15. "Citizens' Unit Assails Plan for New Stadium in S. Phila.," *Philadelphia Inquirer,* January 30, 1958; Guian McKee, "Stadiums and Arenas," *The Encyclopedia of Greater Philadelphia* (New Brunswick, NJ: Rutgers University), https://philadelphiaencyclopedia.org/archive/stadiums-and-arenas/.

16. Accomplishments of Development Director, n.d., box 1, folder "Personal Biographical Data," Rafsky Papers.

17. Howard Whitman, "In Our Food," *Redbook,* May 1952, 37; "Food Center Set for Philadelphia," *New York Times,* October 28, 1954; Greater Philadelphia Movement, *The New Food Distribution Center* (Philadelphia: Greater Philadelphia Movement, 1954), unpaged; Greater Philadelphia Movement, "What to Do before Skid Row Is Demolished" (Philadelphia: Greater Philadelphia Movement, 1958); U.S. Senate, Committee on Banking and Currency, *Urban Renewal in Selected Cities* (testimony of William L. Rafsky), 85th Cong., 1st sess. (Washington, DC: U.S. Government Printing Office, 1957), 783; "Redevelopment Plan Is Good Investment, Rafsky Tells Realtors," *Philadelphia Inquirer,* March 15, 1959; "Rites Mark Closing of Dock St. Market," *Philadelphia Inquirer,* June 18, 1959. Guian A. McKee, "Urban Deindustrialization and Local Public Policy: Industrial Renewal in Philadelphia, 1953–1976," *Journal of Policy History* 16, no. 1 (January 2004): 75–76, highlights the centrality of racial conflicts in each of the city's renewal projects. Philadelphia's "wholesale district," reports sociologist Andrew Deener, "became tied to the narrative of urban deterioration" in *The Problem with Feeding Cities: The Social Transformation of Infrastructure, Abundance, and Inequality in America* (Chicago: University of Chicago Press, 2020), 45.

18. Charlene Mires, *Independence Hall in American Memory* (Philadelphia: University of Pennsylvania Press, 2002), 213–26; "Historic Shrine Park Bill Signed," *Philadelphia Inquirer,* June 29, 1948; "Dilworth Pushes Program in Talk at White House," *Philadelphia Inquirer,* March 6, 1957; "Council Delays Final Action on FEPC Bill," *Philadelphia Inquirer,* February 27, 1948.

19. "City Leaders Plan to Rebuild Blighted Midtown Area," *Philadelphia Inquirer,* June 5, 1956; Peter Binzen with Jonathan Binzen, *Richardson Dilworth: Last of the Bare-Knuckled Aristocrats* (Philadelphia: Camino, 2014), 158–19; Roul Tunley, "Comeback of a Shabby City," *Saturday Evening Post,* December 5, 1959, 76.

20. Dan Rottenberg, *The Outsider: Albert M. Greenfield and the Fall of the Protestant Establishment* (Philadelphia; Temple University Press, 2014); Time Records (Rafsky), January 21, 1952, February 21, 28, 1955, Rafsky Papers.

21. Rottenberg, *Outsider,* 118, 236–45; "Charter Sought to Aid Midcity Development," *Philadelphia Inquirer,* November 9, 1956.

22. Rottenberg, *Outsider,* 245, 332n56; "Greenfield Gets OK to Form Midcity Rebuilding Group," *Philadelphia Inquirer,* July 3, 1956; "Charter Sought"; "U.S. Earmarks 11 Million for Society Hill Slum Area," *Philadelphia Inquirer,* October 20, 1957; "Accomplishments of Development Coordinator," box 1, folder "Personal Biographical Data," Rafsky Papers.

23. Rapkin and Grigsby, *Residential Renewal*, 128. Society Hill's redevelopment had been on the city planning commission's official list since 1948, reports historian Gregory L. Heller in *Ed Bacon: Planning, Politics, and the Building of Modern Philadelphia* (Philadelphia: University of Pennsylvania Press, 2013), 120.

24. "Developers Set in Philadelphia," *New York Times*, November 22, 1958; "Big Man with Big Ideas: William Zeckendorf," *New York Times*, March 19, 1956; "Allegheny Buys Denver Project," *New York Times*, July 28, 1959; Rottenberg, *Outsider*, 243–45; William G. Weart, "Philadelphia Set to Begin Project," *New York Times*, December 4, 1960; William G. Weart, "Old Site Revived by Philadelphia," *New York Times*, June 4, 1961. In 1963, reports historian Heller in *Ed Bacon*, 133, Zeckendorf encountered financial difficulties and sold his development projects.

25. George Kiseda, "Tate Cites Wrong Jack at Luncheon," *Philadelphia Inquirer*, April 16, 1963; "Ground Broken for Rohm, Haas Headquarters," *Philadelphia Inquirer*, April 16, 1963; "Rafsky to Be 'Deployed' to Another City Job," *Philadelphia Inquirer*, December 12, 1962, including quotation; Charlie Bannister, "Camden Bank Shows Its Dog-Eared Bill," *Philadelphia Inquirer*, January 2, 1962; Gustave G. Amsterdam, "Demolition Perils" (letter to the editor), *Philadelphia Inquirer*, March 14, 1962; Rafsky, "Report for Week Ending Wednesday, April 10, 1963," Rafsky Papers.

26. Heller, *Ed Bacon*, 125; "Just like the Old Days," *Time*, June 23, 1961; "Saks Fifth Avenue Expands in Philadelphia," *Women's Wear Daily*, January 16, 1961; "Dresses: Beatrice Katz at Gimbels Phila.," *Women's Wear Daily*, April 5, 1961; "The Maternity Shop: Retail Ads Are Saying," *Women's Wear Daily*, March 3, 1964, 42. "Society Hill Towers," reports historian Francesca Russello Ammon in "Reversing the Tide of Suburban Families? The Design, Marketing, and Occupancy of Urban Renewal's High-Rise Housing," *Journal of Planning History* 19, no. 4 (November 2020): 246, attracted "twice as many children and dramatically fewer seniors" than similar high-rise, higher-income redevelopment projects in New Haven, Connecticut, or Washington, DC.

27. "Ground Broken"; "Philadelphia's Society Hill: A Salvage Job in History," *New York Times*, November 27, 1965.

28. "Society Hill Folks Divided over Hospital," *Philadelphia Inquirer*, May 10, 1963; "Change in Hospital's Zoning Opposed," *Philadelphia Inquirer*, May 10, 1963; "Hospital Wing at 3d and Spruce Stirs a Furor," *Philadelphia Inquirer*, May 14, 1963; "Metropolitan Hospital Is Refused U.S. Grant," *Philadelphia Inquirer*, June 29, 1963; also see Lombardo, *Blue-Collar Conservatism*, 130, on Philadelphians' increasing substitution of "class-based arguments" for older, racial appeals.

29. "Zoning Board Approves Hospital Wing Permits," *Philadelphia Inquirer*, September 7, 1963; "Scranton, Tate Fight Hospital Expansion Aid," *Philadelphia Inquirer*, October 24, 1963; "Phila. Hospital Grant Is Rejected by U.S.," *Philadelphia Inquirer*, November 2, 1963; "Hospital Will Relocate at Independence Mall," *Philadelphia Inquirer*, July 15, 1964.

30. Heller, *Ed Bacon*, 153; "Plan to Shift Express Route Wins Approval," *Philadelphia Inquirer*, October 11, 1956; William F. Feist and C. Allen Keith, "State Eliminates 'Chinese Wall' from Expressway in Society Hill," *Philadelphia Inquirer*, December 19, 1964; Mark H. Rose and Raymond A. Mohl, *Interstate: Highway Politics and Policy since 1939*, 3rd ed. (Knoxville: University of Tennessee Press, 2012), 135–57.

31. Jerome Cahill, "Covered Expressway Test Tuesday," *Philadelphia Inquirer*, February 27, 1966; Rem Rieder, "Highway Section Is Opened," *Philadelphia Inquirer*, July 1, 1967; Gerald McKelvey, "More U.S. Aid on Road Cover Sought," *Philadelphia Inquirer*, July 5, 1970; William F. Feist and C. Allen Keith, "City Seeks Fund for Cover on Expressway," *Philadelphia Inquirer*, February 9, 1966, including quotation.

32. Desmond Ryan, "U.S. Won't Give Extra Funds Sought for Expressway Cover," *Philadelphia Inquirer*, August 19, 1970, including quotation. Marcus Anthony Hunter, *Black Citymakers: How the Philadelphia Negro Changed Urban America* (New York: Oxford University Press, 2013), 115–65, explains the successful efforts of African Americans residing south of Society Hill to block an expressway that would have destroyed part of their neighborhood. Equally, Christopher Klemek, *The Transatlantic Collapse of Urban Renewal: Postwar Urbanism from New York to Berlin* (Chicago: University of Chicago Press, 2011), places Society Hill's redevelopment squarely in the middle of Philadelphia's long-term plans for downtown renewal.

33. Lombardo, *Blue-Collar Conservatism*, 131 (quotation). Anthropologist Ana Y. Ramos-Zayas, in "Ordinary Whiteness: Affect, Kinship, and the Moral Economy of Privilege," *Journal of Urban History* 47, no. 2 (March 2021): 459–60, explains "the inextricable ways in which white supremacy becomes grounded in affective, emotive, and psychological dynamics that intersect with structural and institutional inequalities."

34. Sandy Padwe, "Involved Lady Does Homework," *Philadelphia Inquirer*, October 2, 1970; Lombardo, *Blue Collar Conservatism*, 1–17, 32, 116–32, 197, quotation on 130. Cohen, *Saving America's Cities*, 128–29, documents African American support for expanded public housing in cities like New Haven, Connecticut. Historians Destin Jenkins and Justin Leroy, in "Introduction: The Old History of Capitalism," in *Histories of Racial Capitalism*, ed. Jenkins and Leroy (New York: Columbia University Press, 2020), 1–15, demonstrate the importance of treating both white and black Americans as part of a focus on racial capitalism.

35. Lombardo, *Blue-Collar Conservatism*, 32; Padwe, "Involved Lady"; Marcus Anthony Hunter, Kevin Loughran, and Gary Alan Fine, "Memory Politics: Growth Coalitions, Urban Pasts, and the Creation of 'Historic' Philadelphia," *City and Community* 17, no. 2 (June 2018): 342; Bauman, *Public Housing, Race, and Renewal*, 148–49. For Rafsky's extensive role in directing renewal projects beyond Center City, see Bauman, *Public Housing, Race, and Renewal*. Barbara Ferman, *Challenging the Growth Machine: Neighborhood Politics in Chicago and Pittsburgh* (Lawrence: University Press of Kansas, 1996), 29, determines that neighborhood groups usually failed to stop downtown-oriented projects. "Race was contested at nearly every turn," reports historian Eric C. Schneider in *The Ecology of Homicide: Race, Place, and Space in Postwar Philadelphia* (Philadelphia: University of Pennsylvania Press, 2020), 17.

36. McKee, *Problem of Jobs*, is a penetrating account of Philadelphia's postwar industrial redevelopment programs. Also see 361*n*15, for a list of closed firms and the many jobs that evaporated. Eric Avila, "Popular Culture in the Age of White Flight: Film Noir, Disneyland, and the Cold War (Sub) Urban Imaginary," *Journal of Urban History* 31, no. 1 (November 2004): 3–22. Also see Sean McComas, "Gallery at Market Street," *Encyclopedia of Greater Philadelphia* (New Brunswick, NJ: Rutgers University), https://philadelphiaencyclopedia.org/archive/gallery-at-market-east; "William L. Rafsky—Civil Servant, 81." Cohen, in *Saving America's Cities*, 397, makes the valuable observation that "urban renewal was driven as much by improvisation as by orthodoxy."

## CHAPTER 4

1. Dan Austin, "Meet the Five Worst Mayors in Detroit History," *Detroit Free Press*, July 23, 2014; Brie Zetner, "Ernest Bohn Was Director of First U.S. Housing Authority," *Cleveland Plain Dealer*, November 19, 2017.

2. Roger Biles, *The Fate of Cities: Urban America and the Federal Government, 1945–2000* (Lawrence: University Press of Kansas, 2011), 47–51; Jon C. Teaford, *The Rough Road to Renaissance: Urban Revitalization in America, 1940–1985* (Baltimore, MD: Johns Hopkins University Press, 1990), 46–54; Arnold R. Hirsch, *Making the Second Ghetto: Race and Housing in Chicago, 1940–1960* (Cambridge: Cambridge University Press, 1983), chapter 4. Also see Thomas J. Sugrue, *The Origins of the Urban Crisis: Race and Inequality in Postwar Detroit* (Princeton, NJ: Princeton University Press, 1996); John H. Mollenkopf, *The Contested City* (Princeton, NJ: Princeton University Press, 1983); Mark I. Gelfand, *A Nation of Cities: The Federal Government and Urban America, 1933–1965* (New York: Oxford University Press, 1975); Robert M. Fogelson, *Downtown: Its Rise and Fall, 1880–1950* (New Haven, CT: Yale University Press, 2001); and Peter Dreier, John Mollenkopf, and Todd Swanstrom, *Place Matters: Metropolitics for the Twenty-First Century* (Lawrence: University Press of Kansas, 2004).

3. Raymond A. Mohl, "Planned Destruction: The Interstates and Central City Housing," in *From Tenements to the Taylor Homes: In Search of an Urban Housing Policy in Twentieth-Century America*, ed. John F. Bauman, Roger Biles, and Kristin M. Szylvian (University Park: Pennsylvania State University Press, 2000), 226–45. The standard history of the interstates remains Mark H. Rose and Raymond A. Mohl, *Interstate: Express Highway Politics since 1939*, 3rd ed. (Knoxville: University of Tennessee Press, 2012).

4. Roger Biles, "Expressways before the Interstates: The Case of Detroit, 1945–1956," *Journal of Urban History* 40, no. 5 (September 2014): 843–54; Bruce E. Seely, *Building the American Highway System: Engineers as Policy Makers* (Philadelphia: Temple University Press, 1987), 193–202; Owen D. Gutfreund, *20th-Century Sprawl: Highways and the Reshaping of the American Landscape* (New York: Oxford University Press, 2004), 53–59. Also see Mark H. Rose, Bruce E. Seely, and Paul F. Barrett, *The Best Transportation System in the World: Railroads, Trucks, Airlines, and American Public Policy in the Twentieth Century* (Philadelphia: University of Pennsylvania Press, 2010); Richard O. Davies, *The Age of Asphalt: The Automobile, the Freeway, and the Condition of Metropolitan America* (Philadelphia: J. B. Lippincott, 1975); and Tom Lewis, *Divided Highways: Building the Interstate Highways, Transforming American Life* (New York: Viking, 1977).

5. Carl S. Wells, "Proposals for Downtown Detroit," Washington, DC: Urban Land Institute, 1942, 9–30. On postwar deindustrialization in Detroit, see June Manning Thomas, "Detroit: The Centrifugal City," in *Unequal Partnerships: The Political Economy of Urban Redevelopment in Postwar America*, ed. Gregory D. Squires (New Brunswick, NJ: Rutgers University Press, 1989), 142–60; Joe T. Darden, Richard Child Hill, June Thomas, and Richard Thomas, *Detroit: Race and Uneven Development* (Philadelphia: Temple University Press, 1987); and B. J. Widick, *Detroit: City of Race and Class Violence* (Chicago: Quadrangle, 1972).

6. Wells "Proposals for Downtown Detroit," 19, 23, 29. The lack of parking remained a nettlesome problem in downtown Detroit for decades. See "Parking: Scourge of Downtown," *Detroit News* clipping, December 6, 1970, in Roman S. Gribbs Papers, box 7A, folder 2, Burton Historical Collection, Detroit Public Library, Detroit, Michigan.

7. Albert E. Cobo to Detroit Common Council, memorandum, April 16, 1945, box 3, folder "Expressway," Detroit Mayors Papers [hereafter cited as Detroit Mayors Papers], 1953, Burton Historical Collection, Detroit Public Library, Detroit, Michigan; City of Detroit, "Detroit Plan," 2; Alan Clive, *State of War: Michigan in World War II* (Ann Arbor: University of Michigan Press, 1979), 112; June Manning Thomas, *Redevelopment and Race: Planning a Finer City in Postwar Detroit* (Baltimore, MD: Johns Hopkins Uni-

versity Press, 1997), 48–52; Darden et al., *Detroit*, 156–57; Glenn Richards to Albert E. Cobo, December 16, 1949, box 4, folder "Expressway Reports," 2, Detroit Mayors Papers, 1950.

8. Glenn C. Richards to deLesseps S. Morrison, July 20, 1950, box 4, folder "Expressway Reports," 1, Detroit Mayors Papers, 1950; Glenn C. Richards, "How Detroit Is Financing Its Expressways," in box 3, folder "John Lodge and Edsel Ford," Detroit Mayors Papers, 1952.

9. *Detroit Free Press*, September 13, 1957 [Obituary]; Robert Bolt, "Albert Eugene Cobo," in *Biographical Dictionary of American Mayors, 1820–1980: Big City Mayors*, ed. Melvin G. Holli and Peter d'A. Jones (Westport, CT: Greenwood, 1981), 69–70; Sugrue, *Origins of the Urban Crisis*, 82–84; Teaford, *Rough Road*, 55.

10. Bolt, "Albert Eugene Cobo," 69–70; Robert Conot, *American Odyssey* (Detroit, MI: Wayne State University Press, 1986), 403–5; Thomas, *Redevelopment and Race*, 58–59; Sugrue, *Origins of the Urban Crisis*, 73–75, 82–84.

11. Albert E. Cobo to Homer Ferguson, May 17, 1950, box 4, folder "Expressway Reports," 2, Detroit Mayors Papers, 1950; Laurence G. Lenhardt to G. Mennen Williams, June 30, 1950, box 2, folder "Detroit 1949," G. Mennen Williams Papers, Michigan Historical Collection, Bentley Historical Library, University of Michigan, Ann Arbor, Michigan [hereafter cited as Williams Papers]; Albert E. Cobo to G. Mennen Williams, March 31, 1950, box 4, folder "Expressway Reports," 2, Detroit Mayors Papers, 1950; Albert E. Cobo to G. Mennen Williams, April 24, 1950, box 27, folder "Detroit 1950," Williams Papers; "$180-Million Expressway Program Passes the One-Third Mark," box 4, folder "Expressways," Detroit Mayors Papers, 1951; Conot, *American Odyssey*, 445.

12. Glenn C. Richards to John W. Warner, March 10, 1958, box 3, folder "Expressways," Detroit Mayors Papers, 1958, DPW; David Greenstone, *A Report on the Politics of Detroit* (Cambridge, MA: Joint Center for Urban Studies, 1961), VI-19 (quotation).

13. Teaford, *Rough Road*, 95 (quotation); Detroit City Plan Commission, "Detroit Master Plan, 1951"; Rupert Spade, *Eero Saarinen* (New York: Simon and Schuster, 1971), 10–11; Thomas, *Redevelopment and Race*, 66–72. An Urban Land Institute study of Detroit in 1955 found the expressway system "remarkably well thought out" (Leo Adde, *Nine Cities: The Anatomy of Downtown Renewal* [Washington, DC: Urban Land Institute, 1969], 221).

14. Albert E. Cobo to Homer Ferguson, May 17, 1950, box 4, folder "Expressway Reports," 2, Detroit Mayors Papers, 1950; American Municipal Association, "Washington Summary," n.d., box 4, folder "Expressway Reports," 1, Detroit Mayors Papers, 1950; "An Address to Be Given Thursday, November 20, Engineering Society of Detroit, by Glenn C. Richards, Expressway Coordinator, City of Detroit," 5, box 3, folder "Expressways—Survey for New," Detroit Mayors Papers, 1952; Rose and Mohl, *Interstate*, 37–40.

15. Cobo to Detroit Common Council (first quotation); City of Detroit, Proposed System of Trafficways, Master Plan Report no. 4 (Detroit, MI: Detroit City Planning Commission, December 1946), 10 (second quotation); Sugrue, *Origins of the Urban Crisis*, 47.

16. Adde, *Nine Cities*, 221.

17. Charles M. Ziegler to G. Mennen Williams, March 10, 1954, box 4, folder "Expressways," Detroit Mayors Papers, 1954, all quotations; Sugrue, *Origins of the Urban Crisis*, 48. Also see Paul Barrett and Mark H. Rose, "Street Smarts: The Politics of Transportation Statistics in the American City," *Journal of Urban History* 25, no. 3 (March 1999), 412–18, for the authority that origin-destination studies conferred on highway engineers in selecting routes.

18. Sugrue, *Origins of the Urban Crisis*, 47.

19. Ibid., 47–48; Harvey Royal to G. Mennen Williams, May 4, 1950, box 27, folder "Detroit 1950," Williams Papers; "Profile of Critical Problems Facing Negro People in the Detroit Community," April 18, 1959, box 39, folder A3-14, Detroit Urban League Papers, Michigan Historical Collection, Bentley Historical Library, University of Michigan, Ann Arbor, Michigan.

20. "Minutes, Relocation Advisory Council," February 26, 1958, box 42, folder A6-6, Detroit Urban League Papers; "Report on Expressway Displacement," June 7, 1950, box 41, folder A4-18, Detroit Urban League Papers; Thomas, *Redevelopment and Race*, 59–65; Sugrue, *Origins of the Urban Crisis*, 48.

21. Bolt, "Albert Eugene Cobo," 69–70; James Ransom, "Cobo Seeks Clean City," *Detroit Free Press*, November 15, 1949; Sugrue, *Origins of the Urban Crisis*, 48 (quotation). For comparable situations in other large U.S. cities, see Raymond A. Mohl, "Race and Space in the Modern City: Interstate-95 and the Black Community in Miami," in *Urban Policy in Twentieth-Century America*, ed. Arnold R. Hirsch and Raymond A. Mohl (New Brunswick, NJ: Rutgers University Press, 1993), 100–58; Christopher Silver, *Twentieth-Century Richmond: Planning, Politics, and Race* (Knoxville, TN: University of Tennessee Press, 1984); and Ronald H. Bayor, "Roads to Racial Segregation: Atlanta in the Twentieth Century," *Journal of Urban History* 15, no. 1 (November 1988): 3–21.

22. Carl H. Chatters to Albert E. Cobo, July 1, 1952, box 3, folder "Expressways 1952," Detroit Mayors Papers, 1952; "Address to Be Given Thursday," 6; Albert E. Cobo, "American Municipal Association Testimony—October 8, 1954, General Lucius Clay's Highway Committee," box 4, folder "Expressways—President's Highway Committee," Detroit Mayors Papers, 1954; Rose and Mohl, *Interstate*, 103 (first quotation); Biles, *Fate of Cities*, 70–71; Glenn C. Richards to Louis C. Miriani, February 3, 1958, box 3, folder "Expressways," DPW, Detroit Mayors Papers, 1958; Conot, *American Odyssey*, 445 (second quotation).

23. City of Cleveland, *Cleveland Today . . . Tomorrow: The General Plan of Cleveland* (Cleveland, OH: City Planning Commission, 1950), 30; "Planning in Cleveland: 1903–1963," box 4, folder 26, Ernest J. Bohn Papers, Special Collections Research Center, Kelvin Smith Library, Case Western Reserve University, Cleveland, Ohio [hereafter cited as Bohn Papers]; Teaford, *Rough Road*, 95 (quotation). On the 1949 general plan, see Andrew Chakalis, Dennis Keating, Norman Krumholz, and Ann Marie Wieland, "A Century of Planning in Cleveland," *Journal of Planning History* 1, no. 1 (February 2002): 85.

24. "Ernest J. Bohn," in *The Encyclopedia of Cleveland History*, ed. David D. Van Tassel and John J. Grabowski (Bloomington: Indiana University Press, 1987), 110–11; William D. Jenkins, "Ernest J. Bohn and the Configuration of Public Housing and Urban Planning, 1932–1945," *Proceedings of the Fifth National Conference on American Planning History* (Hilliard, OH: Society for American City and Regional Planning History, 1994), 109–23; William D. Jenkins, "Before Downtown: Cleveland, Ohio, and Urban Renewal, 1949–1958," *Journal of Urban History* 27, no. 4 (May 2001): 475. Useful biographical information can be found using the finding aid for the Ernest J. Bohn Papers, Special Collections Research Center, Kelvin Smith Library, Case Western Reserve University, Cleveland, Ohio.

25. "Business Now Backs Cleveland," *Business Week*, September 21, 1968, 118–19; Ernest J. Bohn to Mayor Thomas A. Burke, October 3, 1947, box 11, folder 33, Bohn Papers (quotation).

26. David Stradling and Richard Stradling, *Where the River Burned: Carl Stokes and the Struggle to Save Cleveland* (Ithaca, NY: Cornell University Press, 2015), 32; J. Mark

Souther, *Believing in Cleveland: Managing Decline in "The Best Location in the Nation"* (Philadelphia: Temple University Press, 2017), 18; "Business Now Backs Cleveland," 122 (quotation). Philip W. Porter, *Cleveland: Confused City on a Seesaw* (Columbus: Ohio State University Press), agrees with this characterization of Cleveland's political leadership in the 1940s and 1950s.

27. Cleveland City Planning Commission, *Downtown Cleveland 1975: The Downtown General Plan* (Cleveland, OH: Cleveland City Planning Commission, 1959), 1–6; Chakalis et al., "Century of Planning," 86; Stradling and Stradling, *Where the River Burned*, 96–98.

28. City of Cleveland, *Cleveland Today . . . Tomorrow*, 22–23; Cleveland City Planning Commission, *Downtown Cleveland 1975*, 3–6; "Introduction," n.d., box 69, folder 1326, Carl B. Stokes Papers, Western Reserve Historical Society, Cleveland, Ohio; Stradling and Stradling, *Where the River Burned*, 97–99.

29. "Planning in Cleveland: 1903–1963"; *Cleveland Press*, November 27, 1959; Souther, *Believing in Cleveland*, 18, 20, 23; Porter, *Cleveland*, 137–38. Mayor Carl B. Stokes said, "It was virtually impossible to obtain any sizable chunk of investment capital in Cleveland that didn't involve [George] Gund and his Cleveland Trust Company" (Carl B. Stokes, *Promises of Power: A Political Autobiography* [New York: Simon and Schuster, 1973], 122).

30. *Cleveland Press*, November 27, 1959; Souther, *Believing in Cleveland*, 19–26. A full discussion of the subway question can be found in J. Mark Souther, "A $35 Million 'Hole in the Ground': Metropolitan Fragmentation and Cleveland's Unbuilt Downtown Subway," *Journal of Planning History* 14, no. 3 (August 2015): 179–203.

31. "Status of the Express Highway Program," May 1, 1949, box 11, folder 29, Bohn Papers; "Capital Improvement Program/Cleveland, 1962–167," box 13, folder 20, Bohn Papers; Carol Poh Miller and Robert A. Wheeler, *Cleveland: A Concise History, 1796–1996*, 2nd ed. (Bloomington: Indiana University Press, 1997), 152–54; Thomas F. Campbell, "Cleveland: The Struggle for Stability," in *Snowbelt Cities: Metropolitan Politics in the Northeast and Midwest since World War II*, ed. Richard M. Bernard (Bloomington: Indiana University Press, 1990), 110; Thomas E. Bier, "Housing Dynamics of the Cleveland Area, 1950–2000," in *Cleveland: A Metropolitan Reader*, ed. W. Dennis Keating, Norman Krumholz, and David C. Perry (Kent, OH: Kent State University Press, 1995), 252–53. Bohn carefully described the key role played by the inner beltway in a 1947 letter to Mayor Thomas A. Burke (Ernest J. Bohn to Mayor Thomas A. Burke, October 3, 1947, box 11, folder 33, Bohn Papers).

32. Souther, *Believing in Cleveland*, 86.

33. Stradling and Stradling, *Where the River Burned*, 182 (quotation). The origins of the antifreeway revolt are discussed in A. Q. Mowbray, *Road to Ruin* (Philadelphia: J. B. Lippincott, 1969). For a more thorough examination of freeway revolts, see Raymond A. Mohl, "Stop the Road: Freeway Revolts in American Cities," *Journal of Urban History* 30, no. 5 (July 2004): 674–706; and Mohl, "The Interstates and the Cities: The U.S. Department of Transportation and the Freeway Revolt, 1966–1973," *Journal of Policy History* 20, no. 2 (2008): 193–226.

34. Bier, "Housing Dynamics," 252; Campbell, "Cleveland," 110; Eric Johannsen, *Cleveland Architecture: 1876–1976* (Cleveland, OH: Western Reserve Historical Society, 1979), 216.

35. Ira J. Bach, "Chicago Expands Its Burnham Plan," *American City* 76 (September 1961): 103; Dennis McClendon, "Expressways," in *The Encyclopedia of Chicago*, ed. James R. Grossman, Ann Durkin Keating, and Janice L. Reiff (Chicago: University of Chicago

Press, 2004), 286–87; Roger Biles, *Richard J. Daley: Politics, Race, and the Governing of Chicago* (DeKalb: Northern Illinois University Press, 1995), 49; Harold M. Mayer and Richard C. Wade, *Chicago: Growth of a Metropolis* (Chicago: University of Chicago Press, 1969), 440–42; Carl W. Condit, *Chicago, 1930–1970: Building, Planning, and Urban Technology* (Chicago: University of Chicago Press, 1974), 235–48; Teaford, *Rough Road*, 96, 103. For more background, see Paul Barrett, *The Automobile and Urban Transit: The Formation of Public Policy in Chicago, 1900–1930* (Philadelphia: Temple University Press, 1983).

36. Robert A. Beauregard, "The Spatial Transformation of Postwar Philadelphia," in *Atop the Urban Hierarchy*, ed. Robert A. Beauregard (New York: Rowman and Littlefield, 1989), 215 (quotation); Teaford, *Rough Road*, 95–96.

37. "St. Louis Waited Twenty-Five Years," *Business Week*, November 14, 1953, 194–96; Mark Abbott, "The 1947 Comprehensive City Plan and Harland Bartholomew's St. Louis," in *St. Louis Plans: The Ideal and Real St. Louis*, ed. Mark Tranel (Columbia: University of Missouri Press, 2007), 109–49; Colin Gordon, *Mapping Decline: St. Louis and the Fate of the American City* (Philadelphia: University of Pennsylvania Press, 2008), 158–61, 258n12; Teaford, *Rough Road*, 27–28, 97, 165; James Neal Primm, *Lion of the Valley: St. Louis, 1764–1980* (Boulder, CO: Pruett, 1981), 495–96.

38. Biles, "Expressways before the Interstates," 843–54.

## PART II

1. Robert A. Beauregard, *Voices of Decline: The Postwar Fate of U.S. Cities* (Cambridge, MA: Blackwell, 1993), 195 (quotation); Peter Dreier, John Mollenkopf, and Todd Swanstrom, *Place Matters: Metropolitics for the Twenty-First Century* (Lawrence: University Press of Kansas, 2004), 164; "An Erosion of Aid to the Cities," *Business Week*, August 15, 1977, 36. On the federal government's retreat from urban America, see Roger Biles, *The Fate of Cities: Urban America and the Federal Government, 1945–2000* (Lawrence: University Press of Kansas, 2011). Also see Alice O'Connor, "Swimming against the Tide: A Brief History of Federal Policy in Poor Communities," in *Urban Problems and Community Development*, ed. Ronald F. Ferguson and William T. Dickens (Washington, DC: Brookings Institution Press, 1999), 77–137. Essential background on federal-local relations is provided in Mark I. Gelfand, *A Nation of Cities: The Federal Government and Urban America, 1933–1965* (New York: Oxford University Press, 1975).

2. The literature on tourism and leisure activities in cities has grown rapidly in recent years. A good introduction can be found in J. Mark Souther, "Landscapes of Leisure: Building an Urban History of Tourism," *Journal of Urban History* 30 (January 2004): 257–65; Dennis R. Judd and Susan S. Fainstein, eds., *The Tourist City* (New Haven, CT: Yale University Press, 1999); Dennis R. Judd, ed., *The Infrastructure of Play: Building the Tourist City* (Armonk, NY: M. E. Sharpe, 2003); Sharon Zukin, *Landscapes of Power: From Detroit to Disney World* (Berkeley: University of California Press, 1991); and Aaron Cowan, *A Nice Place to Visit: Tourism and Urban Revitalization in the Postwar City* (Philadelphia: Temple University Press, 2016). On deindustrialization, especially in Pittsburgh, see John McCarthy's review essay, "Rust Belt Requiem: Understanding Postindustrial Regions, Cities, and Spaces," *Journal of Urban History* 45, no. 6 (November 2019): 1299–1306.

3. Edward K. Muller, "Downtown Pittsburgh: Renaissance and Renewal," in *Pittsburgh and the Appalachians: Cultural and Natural Resources in a Postindustrial Age*, ed. Joseph L. Scarpaci and Kevin J. Patrick (Pittsburgh, PA: University of Pittsburgh Press,

2006), 12–13; Jon C. Teaford, *The Rough Road to Renaissance: Urban Revitalization in America, 1940–1985* (Baltimore, MD: Johns Hopkins University Press, 1990), 221–22; "Copious Coping: How Other Mayors Fare," *Time*, June 15, 1981, 31 (quotations); Roy Lubove, *Twentieth-Century Pittsburgh*, vol. 2, *The Post-steel Era* (Pittsburgh, PA: University of Pittsburgh Press, 1996), 58–61. A thorough discussion of Flaherty's administration can be found in Shelby Stewman and Joel A. Tarr, "Four Decades of Public-Private Partnerships in Pittsburgh," in *Public-Private Partnerships in American Cities: Seven Case Studies*, ed. R. Scott Fosler and Renee A. Berger (Lexington, MA: D. C. Heath, 1982), 59–127. Also see Tracy Neumann, "Reforging the Steel City: Symbolism and Space in Postindustrial Pittsburgh," *Journal of Urban History* 44, no. 4 (July 2018): 582–602.

4. Lubove, *Twentieth-Century Pittsburgh*, 2: vii–x, 60–63; Jonathan Barnett, "Designing Downtown Pittsburgh," *Architectural Record* 170, no. 1 (January 1982): 92; Stefan Lorant, *Pittsburgh: The Story of an American City*, 3rd ed. (Lenox, MA: Authors Edition, 1980), 553; Gregory J. Crowley, *The Politics of Place: Contentious Urban Redevelopment in Pittsburgh* (Pittsburgh, PA: University of Pittsburgh Press, 2005), 100–105; Brian J. L. Berry, Susan W. Sanderson, Shelby Stewman, and Joel A. Tarr, "The Nation's Most Livable City: Pittsburgh's Transformation," in *The Future of Winter Cities*, ed. Gary Gappert (Newbury Park, CA: Sage, 1987), 180–82; Teaford, *Rough Road*, 270; Tracy Neumann, *Remaking the Rust Belt: The Postindustrial Transformation of North America* (Philadelphia: University of Pennsylvania Press, 2016), 110–14.

5. Neumann, *Remaking the Rust Belt*, 117–20; Muller, "Downtown Pittsburgh," 15–16. Also see Lubove, *Twentieth-Century Pittsburgh*, vol. 2, chapter 9, for a fuller discussion of cultural development.

6. Cowan, *A Nice Place to Visit*, 109–12, 113 (quotation). On professional sports and cities, see Michael N. Danielson, *Home Team: Professional Sports and the American Metropolis* (Princeton, NJ: Princeton University Press, 1997); Robert Trumpbour, *The New Cathedrals: Politics and Media in the History of Stadium Construction* (Syracuse, NY: Syracuse University Press, 2007); and Timothy Jon Curry, Kent Schwirian, and Rachael A. Woldoff, *High Stakes: Big Time Sports and Downtown Redevelopment* (Columbus: Ohio State University Press, 2004).

7. Muller, "Downtown Pittsburgh," 18–19. On new uses of the rivers surrounding Pittsburgh, see Edward K. Muller, "River City," in *Devastation and Renewal: An Environmental History of Pittsburgh and Its Region*, ed. Joel A. Tarr (Pittsburgh, PA: University of Pittsburgh Press, 2003), 41–63; and Timothy M. Collins, Edward K. Muller, and Joel A. Tarr, "Pittsburgh's Three Rivers: From Industrial Infrastructure to Environmental Asset," in *Rivers in History: Perspectives on Waterways in Europe and North America*, ed. Christof Mauch and Thomas Zeller (Pittsburgh, PA: University of Pittsburgh Press, 2008), 41–62.

8. Teaford, *Rough Road*, 282 (quotation); Roger S. Ahlbrandt Jr., "Public-Private Partnerships for Neighborhood Renewal," *Annals of the American Academy of Political and Social Science* 488 (November 1986): 127–30; Robert H. Lurcott and Jane A. Downing, "A Public-Private Support System for Community-Based Organizations in Pittsburgh," *Journal of the American Planning Association* 53 (Autumn 1987): 459–68. Also see Alberta Sbragia, "The Pittsburgh Model of Economic Development: Partnership, Responsiveness, and Indifference," in *Unequal Partnerships: Urban Economic Development in Postwar America*, ed. Gregory Squires (New Brunswick, NJ: Rutgers University Press, 1989), 103–20.

9. Neumann, *Remaking the Rust Belt*, 208 (first quotation), 209; Muller, "Downtown Pittsburgh," 17; Scarpaci, "Pittsburgh's Suburbs: Hollowing Out the Core," in Scarpaci

and Patrick, eds., *Pittsburgh and the Appalachians,* 136; Allen Dietrich-Ward, *Beyond Rust: Metropolitan Pittsburgh and the Fate of Industrial America* (Philadelphia: University of Pennsylvania Press, 2016), 288 (second quotation). Richard L. Florida described the "creative class" in *The Rise of the Creative Class* (New York: Basic Books, 2002). Also see Donald Carter, Tom Murphy, Richard Stafford, Stanley Lowe, and Morton Coleman (moderator), "The Pittsburgh Story" (video), Remaking Cities Congress, Pittsburgh, Pennsylvania, October 15–18, 2013, https://www.youtube.com/channel/UC6hrVs96jVk vZF8BUzM_xsg; and Anthony Pennao, "Changing Images of Twentieth Century Pittsburgh," *Pennsylvania History* 43 (January 1976): 49–63.

10. McCarthy, "Rust Belt Requiem," 1302; Dietrich-Ward, *Beyond Rust,* 260.

11. Joe W. Trotter and Jared N. Day, *Race and Renaissance: African Americans in Pittsburgh since World War II* (Pittsburgh, PA: University of Pittsburgh Press, 2010), 90–105; Roy Lubove, *Twentieth-Century Pittsburgh,* vol. 1, *Government, Business, and Environmental Change* (Pittsburgh, PA: University of Pittsburgh Press, 1969), 144–55; Dietrich-Ward, *Beyond Rust,* 175–78.

12. Neumann, *Remaking the Rust Belt,* 123; Robert McLean, *Countdown to Renaissance II: The New Way Corporate America Builds* (Pittsburgh, PA: Urban Marketing Associates, 1984), 94–95.

## CHAPTER 5

1. *Cleveland Plain Dealer,* December 6, 1967. For information on the campaign to improve Cleveland's image, we relied on J. Mark Souther, *Believing in Cleveland: Managing Decline in "The Best Location in the Nation"* (Philadelphia: Temple University Press, 2017). The history of the Cleveland Development Foundation is outlined in Diana Tittle, *Rebuilding Cleveland: The Cleveland Foundation and Its Evolving Urban Strategy* (Columbus: Ohio State University Press, 1992); and Richard Pogue, *The Cleveland Foundation at Seventy-Five: An Evolving Community Resource* (New York: Newcomen Society, 1989). On the Cuyahoga River fire, see David Stradling and Richard Stradling, *Where the River Burned: Carl Stokes and the Struggle to Save Cleveland* (Ithaca, NY: Cornell University Press, 2015); and David Stradling and Richard Stradling, "Perceptions of the Burning River: Deindustrialization and Cleveland's Cuyahoga River," *Environmental History* 13, no. 3 (July 2008): 515–35.

2. Roldo Bartimole, "Keeping the Lid On: Corporate Responsibility in Cleveland," *Business and Society Review* 5 (Spring 1973): 97, no. 7 (quotations).

3. Eric Johannesen, *Cleveland Architecture, 1876–1976* (Cleveland, OH: Western Reserve Historical Society, 1979), 223–28; George E. Condon, *Cleveland: The Best Kept Secret* (New York: Doubleday, 1967), 354–55; Philip W. Porter, *Cleveland: Confused City on a Seesaw* (Columbus: Ohio State University Press, 1976), 180–86; Souther, *Believing in Cleveland,* 32–44.

4. Ada Louise Huxtable, "Revitalization of Cleveland at a Turning Point," *New York Times,* November 23, 1973; Carol Poh Miller and Robert A. Wheeler, *Cleveland: A Concise History, 1796–1996,* 2nd ed. (Bloomington: Indiana University Press, 1997), 184; Alex Kotlowitz, "All Boarded Up," *New York Times Magazine,* March 8, 2009, 28; Thomas F. Campbell, "Cleveland: The Struggle for Stability," in *Snowbelt Cities: Metropolitan Politics in the Northeast and Midwest since World War II,* ed. Richard M. Bernard (Bloomington: Indiana University Press, 1990), 129; Souther, *Believing in Cleveland,* 197–204.

5. James C. Davis to Ralph J. Perk, May 1, 1972, box 50, folder 753, Ralph J. Perk Papers, Western Reserve Historical Society, Cleveland, Ohio; "The Mayoral Administra-

tion of Ralph J. Perk," in Van Tassel and Grabowski, eds., *Encyclopedia of Cleveland History*, 670; Thomas J. Campbell, "Ralph J. Perk," in *Biographical Dictionary of American Mayors, 1820–1980: Big City Mayors*, ed. Melvin G. Holli and Peter d'A. Jones (Westport, CT: Greenwood, 1981), 283; Roldo Bartimole, "Who Governs: The Corporate Hand," in *Cleveland: A Metropolitan Reader*, ed. W. Dennis Keating, Norman Krumholz, and David C. Perry (Kent, OH: Kent State University Press, 1995), 167 (first quotation); Dr. Joseph P. Furber to Richard A. Clark, November 22, 1976, box 73, file 1129, Perk Papers, Cleveland, Ohio (second quotation); Jon C. Teaford, *The Rough Road to Renaissance: Urban Revitalization in America, 1940–1985* (Baltimore, MD: Johns Hopkins University Press, 1990), 222, 224; Miller and Wheeler, eds., *Cleveland*, 178–79.

6. Todd Swanstrom, *The Crisis of Growth Politics: Cleveland, Kucinich, and the Challenge of Urban Populism* (Philadelphia: Temple University Press, 1985), 111–12; Alison Bick Hirsch, *City Choreographer: Lawrence Halprin in Urban Renewal America* (Minneapolis: University of Minnesota Press, 2014), 260–62; Daniel R. Kerr, *Derelict Paradise: Homelessness and Urban Development in Cleveland, Ohio* (Amherst: University of Massachusetts Press, 2011), 197; Souther, *Believing in Cleveland*, 132–38. Also see Lawrence Halprin and Associates, *Concept for Cleveland: A Strategy for Downtown* (Cleveland, OH: Greater Cleveland Growth Association, 1975). For more information on social equity planning, see Norman Krumholz and John Forester, *Making Equity Planning Work: Leadership in the Public Sector* (Philadelphia: Temple University Press, 1990); Norman Krumholz, "A Retrospective View of Equity Planning: Cleveland, 1969–1979," *Journal of the American Planning Association* 48, no. 2 (1982): 163–83; Norman Krumholz, Janice M. Cogger, and John H. Linner, "The Cleveland Policy Planning Report," *Journal of the American Institute of Planners* 41, no. 5 (September 1975): 298–304; and Norman Krumholz, "Government, Equity, Redistribution, and the Practice of Urban Planning," in Keating et al., *Cleveland*, 311–20.

7. Swanstrom, *Crisis of Growth Politics*, 119–35; Campbell, "Cleveland," 124–25.

8. Myron Magnet, "How Business Bosses Saved a Sick City," *Fortune*, March 27, 1989, 106 (quotations); Jason Hackworth, *The Neoliberal City: Governance, Ideology, and Development in American Urbanism* (Ithaca, NY: Cornell University Press, 2007), 1–2; Pierre Clavel, *The Progressive City: Planning and Participation, 1969–1984* (New Brunswick, NJ: Rutgers University Press, 1986), 86–87. For background on the public power question in Cleveland, see W. Dennis Keating, Norman Krumholz, and David C. Perry, "The Ninety-Year War over Public Power in Cleveland," *Journal of Urban Affairs* 13, no. 4 (December 1991): 397–418.

9. Swanstrom, *Crisis of Growth Politics*, 138–39; Campbell, "Cleveland," 125 (quotation); Souther, *Believing in Cleveland*, 185–87, 189; Stephen A. Blossom, "Republic Plans $200 Million Dollar Fixup," *Cleveland Plain Dealer*, December 20, 1978.

10. Souther, *Believing in Cleveland*, 185 (quotation).

11. "Cleveland Is on the Brink," *Business Week*, November 20, 1978, 129–30 (quotations); Teaford, *Rough Road*, 229–30. Standard and Poor's late-1970s downgrade of Cleveland's borrowing ability, reports historian Destin Jenkins in *The Bonds of Inequality: Debt and the Making of the American City* (Chicago: University of Chicago Press, 2021), 200, "was a partial reflection of a very real urban fiscal crisis" that affected a large number of cities.

12. John H. Beck, "Is Cleveland Another New York?" *Urban Affairs Quarterly* 18 (December 1982): 207; Teaford, *Rough Road*, 230 (quotation). For a detailed description and analysis of events, see U.S. Congress, House of Representatives, Ninety-sixty Congress, First Session, *Role of Commercial Banks in Financing the Debt of the City of Cleve-*

*land, Hearing before the Subcommittee on Financial Institutions, Supervision, Regulation, and Insurance of the Committee on Banking, Finance, and Urban Affairs* (Washington, DC: U.S. Government Printing Office, 1980).

13. Thomas R. Bullard, "George Vutor Voinovich," in *Biographical Dictionary of American Mayors*, 376; Campbell, "Cleveland," 127.

14. Magnet, "How Business Bosses Saved a Sick City," 107 (first quotation); Campbell, "Cleveland," 127 (second and third quotations).

15. Iver Peterson, "Boom and Bust Overlap in Cleveland," *New York Times*, February 5, 1982; Magnet, "How Business Bosses Saved a Sick City," 106–10; Souther, *Believing in Cleveland*, 200 (quotation).

16. Carole F. Hoover to George V. Voinovich, November 13, 1979, box 2, folder 10, George V. Voinovich Papers, Western Reserve Historical Society, Cleveland, Ohio [hereafter cited as Voinovich Papers]; "Running a City like a Business," *Business Week*, June 2, 1980, 100 (quotation); Mark Weinberg, "The Urban Fiscal Crisis: Impact on Budgeting and Financial Planning Practices of Urban America," *Journal of Urban Affairs* 6 (Winter 1984): 41–43; Swanstrom, *Crisis of Growth Politics*, 247–50; Campbell, "Cleveland," 128–29; "The Mayoral Administration of George V. Voinovich," in Van Tassel and Grabowski, eds., *Encyclopedia of Cleveland History*, 670–71. The length of the mayoral term changed from two years to four years in 1981.

17. "Mayoral Administration of George V. Voinovich," 670; Peterson, "Boom and Bust Overlap in Cleveland;" *Cleveland Plain Dealer*, January 27, April 8, 1982; Campbell, "Cleveland," 129.

18. *Cleveland Plain Dealer*, April 7, 1987; Magnet, "How Business Bosses Saved a Sick City," 108; Richard A. Shatten, "Cleveland Tomorrow: A Practicing Model of New Roles and Processes for Corporate Leadership in Cities," in Keating et al., *Cleveland*, 321–24.

19. George V. Voinovich to Bradley Jones, December 21, 1983, box 4, folder 27, Voinovich Papers (quotation); Carol Poh Miller and Robert A. Wheeler, "Cleveland: The Making and Remaking of an American City, 1796–1993," in Keating et al., *Cleveland*, 46–47; Bartimole, "Who Governs," 172; *Cleveland Plain Dealer*, November 12, 1981. Also see John J. Grabowski and Walter C. Leedy, *The Terminal Tower, Tower City Center: A Historical Perspective* (Cleveland, OH: Western Reserve Historical Society, 1990).

20. Dennis Keating, Norman Krumholz, and John Metzger, "Cleveland: Post-Populist Public-Private Partnerships," in *Unequal Partnerships: The Political Economy of Urban Redevelopment in Postwar America*, ed. Gregory D. Squires (New Brunswick, NJ: Rutgers University Press, 1989), 129–33; George V. Voinovich to Richard S. Williamson, May 17, 1982, box 36, folder "Urban Policy," Voinovich Papers; George V. Voinovich to President Ronald Reagan, March 14, 1985, box 36, folder "Urban Policy" (quotation). On UDAG, see Roger Biles, *The Fate of Cities: Urban America and the Federal Government, 1945–2000* (Lawrence: University Press of Kansas, 2011), especially chapters 7 and 8.

21. George V. Voinovich to Gary Conley, Hunter Morrison, Ed Richard, and Vince Lombardi, May 19, 1983, box 13, folder 29, Voinovich Papers; Kerr, *Derelict Paradise*, 197. A complete list of projects can be found in Downtown Development Department, Greater Cleveland Growth Association, "Downtown Development Projects and Proposals, 1980 to Present," n.d., box 13, folder 6, Voinovich Papers.

22. W. Dennis Keating, "Cleveland: The Comeback City," in *Reconstructing Urban Regime Theory: Regulating Urban Politics in a Global Economy*, ed. Mickey Lauria (Thousand Oaks, CA: Sage, 1997), 194–205; "Cleveland Arena," in Van Tassel and Grabowski, eds., *Encyclopedia of Cleveland History*, 202. In 2021, the Cleveland Indians became the Cleveland Guardians.

23. Edward M. Richard to Dr. Walter B. Waetgen, May 2, 1983, box 32, folder 7, Voinovich Papers (quotation); Kevin J. Delaney and Rick Eckstein, *Public Dollars, Private Stadiums: The Battle over Building Sports Stadiums* (New Brunswick, NJ: Rutgers University Press, 2003), 66; James A. Toman and Gregory G. Deegan, *Cleveland Stadium: The Last Chapter, 1931–1996* (Cleveland, OH: Cleveland Landmarks Press, 1997), 40–42.

24. George V. Voinovich, "Voinovich, Growth Association to Help Tribe," news release, February 6, 1986, box 30, folder 26, Voinovich Papers (quotation); Ziona Austrian and Mark S. Rosentraub, "Cleveland's Gateway to the Future," in *Sports, Jobs, and Taxes: The Economic Impact of Sports Teams and Stadiums*, ed. Roger G. Noll and Andrew Zimbalist (Washington, DC: Brookings Institution Press, 1997), 359; *Cleveland Plain Dealer*, September 4, 1991; Delaney and Eckstein, *Public Dollars, Private Stadiums*, 71, 73, 79; Toman and Deegan, *Cleveland Stadium*, 42.

25. "Playhouse Square," in Van Tassel and Grabowski, eds., *Encyclopedia of Cleveland History*, 771–72; Gary N. Conley, Vincent Lombardi, and Hunter Morrison to Mayor George V. Voinovich, May 9, 1983, box 13, folder 29, Voinovich Papers; Johannesen, *Cleveland Architecture*, 251; Souther, *Believing in Cleveland*, 125–30.

26. Heywood T. Sanders, *Convention Center Follies: Politics, Power, and Public Investment in American Cities* (Philadelphia: University of Pennsylvania Press, 2014), 42–43; *Cleveland Plain Dealer*, December 10, 1981, February 27, 2005, October 9, 2011; George V. Voinovich to Thomas Vail, October 8, 1984, box 14, folder 16, Voinovich Papers (quotation); Ed Richard to George V. Voinovich, November 23, 1983, box 14, folder 16, Voinovich Papers.

27. Souther *Believing in Cleveland*, 102–4; *Wall Street Journal* clipping, September 24, 1987, in box 4, folder 11, Voinovich Papers. See the promotional materials on the RiverFest in box 121, folder 11, Voinovich Papers.

28. Herb Strawbridge, *Remembering Higbee's* (Cleveland, OH: Western Reserve Historical Society, 2004), 223–35; Souther, *Believing in Cleveland*, 133–36.

29. George V. Voinovich to Gary Conley et al., May 19, 1983; Gary N. Conley et al. to Mayor George V. Voinovich, May 9, 1983; Souther, *Believing in Cleveland*, 38–39; George V. Voinovich to Bradley Jones, December 21, 1983, box 4, folder 27, Voinovich Papers.

30. George V. Voinovich to Gary Conley et al., May 19, 1983; George V. Voinovich to Cleveland City Council, November 24, 1986, box 28, folder 2, Voinovich Papers; Campbell, "Cleveland," 130; Gary N. Conley et al. to Mayor George V. Voinovich, May 9, 1983 (quotations).

31. "Cleveland's Hotel Development Strategy," n.d., box 25, folder 15, Voinovich Papers; Souther, *Believing in Cleveland*, 28–31; Teaford, *Rough Road*, 298–99; *Cleveland Plain Dealer*, December 10, 1981; Aaron S. Gurwitz and G. Thomas Kingsley, *The Cleveland Metropolitan Economy* (Santa Monica, CA: RAND Corporation, 1982), 177.

32. George V. Voinovich to unspecified persons, February 23, 1983, box 13, folder "Dev.-Priorities," Voinovich Papers (quotation); George V. Voinovich to Gary Conley et al., May 19, 1983; *Cleveland Plain Dealer*, February 6, 1994; Philip W. Porter, *Cleveland*, 259. On the past glory of Euclid Avenue, see Jan Cigliano, *Showplace of America: Cleveland's Euclid Avenue, 1850–1910* (Kent, OH: Kent State University Press, 1991). The best discussion of University Circle's historical development is J. Mark Souther, "Acropolis of the Middle-West: Decay, Renewal, and Boosterism in Cleveland's University Circle," *Journal of Planning History* 10, no. 1 (February 2011): 30–58.

33. National Association of City Transportation Officials, "Euclid Avenue BRT, Cleveland, OH," https://nacto.org/case-study/euclid-avenue-brt-cleveland-oh; George V. Voinovich to unspecified persons, February 23, 1983; Souther, "Acropolis," 52; Gary Conley

to Mayor George Voinovich, September 9, 1986, box 10, folder 22, Voinovich Papers; Souther, *Believing in Cleveland*, 199. On the impact of ISTEA, see Mark H. Rose, Bruce E. Seely, and Paul F. Barrett, *The Best Transportation System in the World: Railroads, Trucks, Airlines, and American Public Policy in the Twentieth Century* (Columbus: Ohio State University Press, 2006), 213, 238; and Biles, *Fate of Cities*, 302–3, 347, 353.

34. Campbell, "Cleveland," 131; Barney Warf and Brian Holly, "The Rise and Fall and Rise of Cleveland," *Annals of the American Academy of Political and Social Science* 551, no. 1 (May 1997): 217; "Mayor of Cleveland to Run for Governor and Not Re-election," *New York Times*, April 28, 1989 (quotation). On Civic Vision 2000, see Cleveland City Planning Commission, *Cleveland Civic Vision 2000* (Cleveland, OH: Cleveland City Planning Commission, 1988). Also see City of Cleveland, "Greater Cleveland's Public-Private Partnerships: A Review of Local Programs That Have Changed Cleveland," n.d., box 24, folder 17, Voinovich Papers.

35. William E. Nelson Jr., "Cleveland: The Evolution of Black Political Power," in Keating et al., *Cleveland*, 294 (quotations); *Cleveland Plain Dealer*, January 5, 1992.

36. "Memorandum of Understanding" [for the Rock and Roll Hall of Fame], n.d., box 25, folder 10, Voinovich Papers; Keating et al., "Post-Populist Public-Private Partnerships," 347–48; Kerr, *Derelict Paradise*, 219–21; Toman and Deegan, *Cleveland Stadium*, 43–46; Delaney and Eckstein, *Public Dollars, Private Stadiums*, 79–83; Nelson, "Cleveland," 294–98. In 2019, Gilbert changed the name of the basketball facility from Quicken Loans Arena to Rocket Mortgage FieldHouse.

37. Warf and Holly, "Rise and Fall," 218 (quotation); *Cleveland Plain Dealer*, November 4, 2009, October 2, 2010, February 4, 2011, May 1, 2011, January 26, 2012.

38. *Cleveland Plain Dealer*, September 10, 2000; Iver Peterson, "'Mistake by the Lake' Wakes Up Roaring," *New York Times*, September 10, 1995 (quotation).

39. *Cleveland Plain Dealer*, September 10, 2000 (quotation); Warf and Holly, "Rise and Fall," 219–21; Keating et al., "Post-Populist Public-Private Partnerships," 337–39.

## CHAPTER 6

1. Mark Binelli, *Detroit City Is the Place to Be: The Afterlife of an American Metropolis* (New York: Metropolitan, 2012), 129 (quotations).

2. Binelli, *Detroit City Is the Place to Be*, 129; Melvin G. Holli, ed., *Detroit* (New York: New Viewpoints, 1976), 222; Heather Ann Thompson, *Whose Detroit? Politics, Labor, and Race in a Modern American City* (Ithaca, NY: Cornell University Press, 2001), 206; Roger Biles, "Public Policy Made by Private Enterprise: Bond Rating Agencies and Urban America," *Journal of Urban History* 44, no. 6 (November 2018): 1106. A consensus has developed that, because of the destructive forces of economic decay in Detroit long before Coleman Young became mayor, it is unfair to blame him for the city's decline. On this point, see Thomas J. Sugrue, *The Origins of the Urban Crisis: Race and Inequality in Postwar Detroit* (Princeton, NJ: Princeton University Press, 1996); Dan Georgakas and Marvin Surkin, *Detroit: I Do Mind Dying* (New York: St. Martin's, 1975); B. J. Widick, *Detroit: City of Race and Class Violence* (Chicago: Quadrangle, 1972); Robert E. Conot, *American Odyssey: A Unique History of America Told through the Life of a Great City* (New York: William Morrow, 1974); David Maraniss, *Once in a Great City: A Detroit Story* (New York: Simon and Schuster, 2015); and Suzanne Smith, *Dancing in the Streets: Motown and the Cultural Politics of Detroit* (Cambridge, MA: Harvard University Press, 2000).

3. Sharon Zukin, *Landscapes of Power: From Detroit to Disney World* (Berkeley: University of California Press 1991), 106; Ron Stodghill II, "Coleman's Greatest Hits," *Detroit*

*Free Press Magazine*, November 17, 1991, in box 3, folder 9, Detroit Renaissance Papers, Walter P. Reuther Library, Wayne State University, Detroit, Michigan [cited hereafter as Detroit Renaissance Papers]; Coleman A. Young and Lonnie Wheeler, *Hard Stuff: The Autobiography of Coleman Young* (New York: Viking, 1994), 228 (first quotation); Remer Tyson, "Mayor Young a Year Later," *The Nation*, March 1, 1975, 238 (second quotation).

4. Stodghill, "Coleman's Greatest Hits"; Thomas J. Anton, *Federal Aid to Detroit* (Washington, DC: Brookings Institution, 1983), 48. Also see June Manning Thomas, *Redevelopment and Race: Planning a Finer City in Postwar Detroit* (Baltimore, MD: Johns Hopkins University Press, 1997), especially chapter 7.

5. Binelli, *Detroit City*, 128–29; Melvin G. Holli, "Coleman Alexander Young," in *Biographical Dictionary of American Mayors, 1820–1980: Big City Mayors*, ed. Melvin G. Holli and Peter d'A. Jones (Westport, CT: Greenwood, 1981), 402; Edward L. Lach Jr., "Coleman Young," in *African American Lives*, ed. Henry Louis Gates Jr. and Evelyn Brooks Higginbotham (New York: Oxford University Press, 2004), 924–25. On Young's life and political career, see Wilbur C. Rich, *Coleman Young and Detroit Politics: From Social Activist to Power Broker* (Detroit, MI: Wayne State University Press, 1989); Thompson, *Whose Detroit?*; Heather Thompson, "Rethinking the Collapse of Postwar Liberalism: The Rise of Mayor Coleman Young and the Politics of Race in Detroit," in *African-American Mayors: Race, Politics, and the American City*, ed. David R. Colburn and Jeffrey S. Adler (Urbana: University of Illinois Press, 2001), 227–48; and Heather Thompson, "Coleman A. Young: Race and the Reshaping of Postwar Urban Politics," in *The Human Tradition in Urban America*, ed. Roger Biles (Wilmington, DE: Scholarly Resources, 2002), 187–203. Also see Young's provocative autobiography, *Hard Stuff*, written with Lonnie Wheeler. For a discussion of Detroit's post–World War II politics, see Colleen Doody, *Detroit's Cold War: The Origins of Postwar Conservatism* (Urbana: University of Illinois Press, 2013).

6. *Crain's Detroit Business*, November 17, 1997 (first quotation); Rich, *Coleman Young*, 112; Heather Thompson, "Coleman A. Young," 197–98; Sidney Fine, *Violence in the Motor City: The Cavanagh Administration, Race Relations, and the Detroit Riot of 1967* (Ann Arbor: University of Michigan Press, 1989), 457 (second quotation). Heather Ann Thompson discusses conservative white people's hatred of Young in *Whose Detroit?*, 205–7. On the hollow prize identified by Hudson, see H. Paul Friesema, "Black Control of Central Cities: The Hollow Prize," *Journal of the American Institute of Planners* 35, no. 2 (March 1969): 75–79; Roger Biles, "Black Mayors: A Historical Assessment," *Journal of Negro History* 77, no 3 (Summer 1992): 115–17; John H. Mollenkopf, "The Post-war Politics of Urban Development," *Politics and Society* 5, no. 3 (September 1975): 292; and Adolph Reed Jr., "The Black Urban Regime: Structural Origins and Constraints," in *Power, Community, and the City*, ed. Michael Peter Smith (New Brunswick, NJ: Transaction, 1988), 161. Many white people saw the 1967 racial disturbance as the beginning of Detroit's decline. See, for instance, Ze'ev Chafets, *Devil's Night and Other True Tales of Detroit* (New York: Random House, 1990).

7. Thomas, *Redevelopment and Race*, 157 (quotation); Rich, *Coleman Young*, 280; Stodghill, "Coleman's Greatest Hits."

8. "Moving Detroit Forward: A Plan for Urban Economic Revitalization," April 1975, box 103, folder 5, Coleman A. Young Papers II, Walter P. Reuther Library, Wayne State University, Detroit, Michigan [cited hereafter as Young Papers II]; Rich, *Coleman Young*, 139; City of Detroit, "The Detroit Plan, February 1947." Roger Biles, *The Fate of Cities: Urban America and the Federal Government, 1945–2000* (Lawrence: University Press of

Kansas, 2011), 212–14; Kathy Warbelow, "Young Feels U.S. Owes Detroit Help," *Detroit Free Press*, May 5, 1975.

9. "Moving Detroit Forward: A Plan for Urban Economic Revitalization," June 1977, box 106, folder 17, Coleman Young Papers, Detroit Public Library, Burton Historical Collection, Detroit, Michigan [cited hereafter as Coleman Young Papers]; Coleman Young to Jimmy Carter, April 29, 1977, box 107, folder 6, Coleman Young Papers (quotation).

10. William Clay Ford to James H. Wineman, February 5, 1971, box 4, folder 11, Detroit Economic Development Corporation Papers, Walter P. Reuther Library, Wayne State University, Detroit, Michigan; Young and Wheeler, *Hard Stuff*, 231 (quotation); *Detroit News* clipping, May 27, 1979, in box 4, folder 42, Detroit Renaissance Papers; Coleman Young to Bruce Norris, February 18, 1977, box 80, folder 25, Maryann Mahaffey Papers, Detroit Public Library, Burton Historical Collection, Detroit, Michigan; Tyson, "Mayor Young a Year Later," 237–38; Biles, *Fate of Cities*, 225–26; Thomas, *Redevelopment and Race*, 157–58; Rich, *Coleman Young*, 171–80.

11. Young and Wheeler, *Hard Stuff*, 256 (first quotation); Biles, *Fate of Cities*, 251; Binelli, *Detroit City*, 132; Bryan D. Jones and Lynn W. Bachelor, *The Sustaining Hand: Community Leadership and Corporate Power*, 2nd ed., rev. (Lawrence: University Press of Kansas, 1993), 36–37; Biles, "Public Policy Made by Private Enterprise," 1108 (second quotation). "Pinched by local and statewide cuts on one side," historian Destin Jenkins reports in *Bonds of Inequality: Debt and the Making of the American City* (Chicago: University of Chicago Press, 2021), 208, "cities were squeezed further by the cutting of the federal financial lifeline."

12. Stodghill, "Coleman's Greatest Hits"; *Detroit News* clipping, July 20, 1986, in box 4, folder 4.3, Detroit Renaissance Papers. David Maraniss, *Once in a Great City: A Detroit Story* (New York: Simon and Schuster, 2015), chapter 3, describes the Detroit Auto Show festivities.

13. John E. Fetzer, Inc., to Coleman A. Young, July 13, 1977, box 84, folder 23, Mahaffey Papers; Dwight Havens and Bob Sweany to Mayor Roman S. Gribbs, Max Fisher, Tom Adams, and Tom Reid, February 8, 1971, box 4, folder 15, Detroit Economic Development Corporation Papers, Walter P. Reuther Library, Wayne State University, Detroit, Michigan; Michael Betzold and Ethan Casey, *Queen of Diamonds: The Tiger Stadium Story* (West Bloomfield, MI: Altwerger and Mandel, 1992), 108.

14. Betzold and Casey, *Queen of Diamonds*, 133 (quotation).

15. "General Statement of Recommendations from the Downtown Stadium Working Group," n.d., box 32, folder 30, Developing Urban Detroit Area Research Project Papers, Walter P. Reuther Library, Wayne State University, Detroit, Michigan; Gregory Huskisson, "City, County Team Up for Stadium," *Detroit Free Press*, July 27, 1991; Betzold and Casey, *Queen of Diamonds*, 295.

16. Detroit Alliance for a Rational Economy, "No Tax Break for Riverfront West," n.d., box 11, folder 3, Ken and Sheila Cockrell Papers, Walter P. Reuther Library, Wayne State University, Detroit, Michigan; Rick Ratliff, "What's Ahead for Detroit Riverfront"? *Detroit Free Press*, September 1, 1985; Tyson, "Mayor Young a Year Later," 238; Thomas, *Redevelopment and Race*, 158–59.

17. Joe T. Darden, Richard Child Hill, June Thomas, and Richard Thomas, *Detroit: Race and Uneven Development* (Philadelphia: Temple University Press, 1987), 46–54; Lynda Ann Ewen, *Corporate Power and Urban Crisis in Detroit* (Princeton, NJ: Princeton University Press, 2015), 210–15; June Manning Thomas, "Detroit: The Centrifugal City,"

in *Unequal Partnerships: The Political Economy of Urban Redevelopment in Postwar America*, ed. Gregory D. Squires (New Brunswick, NJ: Rutgers University Press, 1989), 149; Stephen A. Horn, "Detroit's Renaissance Center," *Urban Land* 46 (July 1987): 6–7. A partial list of the leading businesspeople who joined Ford in Detroit Renaissance is provided in a *Detroit News* clipping, June 24, 1973, box 4, folder 14, Coleman Young Papers.

18. Horn, "Detroit's Renaissance Center," 7–8.

19. Rachel B. Mullen, "Renaissance Center," in *The Critical Edge: Controversy in Recent American Architecture*, ed. Tod A. Marder (Cambridge, MA: MIT Press, 1985), 175–87; Horn, "Detroit's Renaissance Center," 8 (quotation), 9–10; Binelli, *Detroit City*, 24.

20. "Detroit's Downtown Gets a Tonic," *Business Week*, August 9, 1976, 52; Thomas, *Redevelopment and Race*, 154–57.

21. Horn, "Detroit's Renaissance Center," 9–11; Bruce N. Wright, "Megaform Comes to Motown," *Progressive Architecture* 59 (February 1978): 51 (quotation).

22. *Detroit Free Press* clipping, October 31, 1979, in box 4, folder 4.3, Detroit Renaissance Papers; *Detroit Free Press* clipping, January 18, 1990, in box 2, folder 7, Detroit Renaissance Papers; *Wall Street Journal*, April 30, 1985 (quotation); Rich, *Coleman Young*, 192, 195, 203–4; Thomas, "Detroit," 150.

23. Detroit Historical Society, "Detroit Grand Prix," *Encyclopedia of Detroit*, https://detroithistorical.org/learn/encyclopedia-of-detroit/detroit-grand-prix; *Detroit Free Press*, September 21, 1991.

24. John Holusha, "Detroit Has Hard Times and One Man in Charge," *New York Times*, October 16, 1988, Isabel Wilkerson, "Fresh Trouble for Familiar Face in Detroit Politics," *New York Times,* May 1, 1989; Jon C. Teaford, *The Rough Road to Renaissance: Urban Revitalization in America, 1940–1985* (Baltimore, MD: Johns Hopkins University Press, 1990), 280 (quotation); Young and Wheeler, *Hard Stuff,* 313–14; Rich, *Coleman Young*, 121.

25. *Michigan Senate Public Hearing* (statement of Councilman Mel Ravitz, July 17, 1987), box 52, folder 10, Mel Ravitz Papers, Walter P. Reuther Library, Wayne State University, Detroit, Michigan [cited hereafter as Ravitz Papers]. On Atlantic City, see Bryant Simon, *Boardwalk of Dreams: Atlantic City and the Fate of Urban America* (New York: Oxford University Press, 2004). The history of Las Vegas is told by Hal K. Rothman in a series of books: *Neon Metropolis: How Las Vegas Started the Twenty-First Century* (New York: Routledge: 2003); *Playing the Odds: Las Vegas and the Modern West* (Albuquerque: University of New Mexico Press, 2007); and *Devil's Bargains: Tourism in the Twentieth-Century American West* (Lawrence: University Press of Kansas, 2000).

26. *Michigan Senate Public Hearing* (statement of Councilman Mel Ravitz).

27. Coleman A. Young to the Honorable City Council, October 27, 1987, box 52, folder 10, Ravitz Papers; Mayor's Press Release, February 12, 1988, box 52, folder 10, Ravitz Papers (quotation); *Detroit News* clipping, May 13, 1988, in box 4, folder 23, Detroit Renaissance Papers.

28. "Detroit Balloting to Weigh Casinos," *New York Times*, August 2, 1988; Wilkerson, "Fresh Trouble for Familiar Face in Detroit Politics," *Crain's Detroit Business*, November 17, 1997.

29. City of Detroit, "Detroit Casino Development Projects," October 1999, box 2, folder 9; Mayor Dennis W. Archer, "Will Detroit Be Dealt a Winning Hand? Criteria for Casino Gambling" (speech, n.d.), box 45, folder 12 (quotation), both in Dennis W. Archer Papers, Detroit Public Library, Burton Historical Collection, Detroit, Michigan; *Detroit Free Press*, June 20, 2016, July 17, 2017.

30. "The High Rollers Hit Motown," *Business Week*, September 8, 1997, 62–63; *Crain's Detroit Business*, November 11, 1996, April 19, 1999, April 25, 2005.

31. Katherine Warner, John Ehrmann, Luther Jackson, and Jerry Lax, "Detroit's Renaissance Includes Factories," *Urban Land* 41 (June 1982): 3–4; Anton, *Federal Aid to Detroit*, 7–8; Thomas, "Detroit," 151–52; Young and Wheeler, *Hard Stuff*, 240–41.

32. Rich, *Coleman Young*, 181–83; Stodghill, "Coleman's Greatest Hits"; Warner et al., "Detroit's Renaissance," 4–5.

33. Warner et al., "Detroit's Renaissance," 4–6; Young and Wheeler, *Hard Stuff*, 244–45; Jeanie Wylie, *Poletown: Community Betrayal* (Urbana: University of Illinois Press, 1989), 54; Jones and Bachelor, *Sustaining Hand*, 83–86, 95; Rich, *Coleman Young*, 183–88, 203 (first quotation); Luther Jackson, "Court Rules Against Poletown Council," *Detroit Free Press*, March 14, 1981 (second quotation).

34. Thomas, *Redevelopment and Race*, 162–66; Darden et al., *Detroit*, 176–81; Jones and Bachelor, *Sustaining Hand*, 211.

35. June Manning Thomas, "Detroit," 152; Darden et al., *Detroit*, 177; Jones and Bachelor, *Sustaining Hand*, 215–16; Wylie, *Poletown*, 202 (quotation). On the unreliability of work in the automobile factories, see Daniel J. Clark, *Disruption in Detroit: Autoworkers and the Elusive Postwar Boom* (Urbana: University of Illinois Press, 2018).

36. City of Detroit, "Economic Diversification and Revitalization Plan," n.d., box 101, folder 101.13, Young Papers II; Walter Guzzardi Jr., "A Determined Detroit Struggles to Find a New Economic Life," *Fortune* April 21, 1980, 76, 78, 85; Richard Child Hill, "Transnational Capitalism and Urban Crisis: The Case of the Auto Industry and Detroit," in *Cities in Recession: Critical Responses to the Urban Policies of the New Right*, ed. Ivan Szelenyi (Beverly Hills, CA: Sage, 1984), 156; Jones and Bachelor, *Sustaining Hand*, 210; June Manning Thomas, "Planning and Industrial Decline: Lessons from Postwar Detroit," *Journal of the American Planning Association* 56, no. 3 (Winter 1990): 304; Young and Wheeler, *Hard Stuff*, 233–34, 235 (quotation), 250–51; Thomas, *Redevelopment and Race*, 165–66.

37. *Detroit News*, September 16, 1988; Jones and Bachelor, *Sustaining Hand*, 221–25; Thomas, *Redevelopment and Race*, 165–66; Young and Wheeler, *Hard Stuff*, 252 (quotation).

38. John Gallagher, "Michigan Tried to Lure Amazon with $4 Billion," *Detroit Free Press*, May 26, 2018. The most graphic description of the fire and police departments' sorry condition can be found in Charlie LeDuff, *Detroit: An American Autopsy* (New York: Penguin, 2013). The arson story is covered in Chafets, *Devil's Night*.

39. Young and Wheeler, *Hard Stuff*, 317.

40. Gallagher, "Michigan Tried to Lure Amazon with $4 Billion;" Young and Wheeler, *Hard Stuff*, chapter 10.

41. Gallagher, "Michigan Tried to Lure Amazon with $4 Billion;" Young and Wheeler, *Hard Stuff*, 315 (including quotation).

## CHAPTER 7

1. The literature on neighborhoods and community activism is modest. See, for example, Robert Fisher, *Let the People Decide: Neighborhood Organizing in America* (Boston: Twayne, 1984); Robert Halpern, *Rebuilding the Inner City: A History of Neighborhood Initiatives to Address Poverty in the United States* (New York: Columbia University Press, 1995); Larry Bennett, *Fragments of Cities: The New American Downtowns and*

*Neighborhoods* (Columbus: Ohio State University Press, 1990); Alexander von Hoffman, *House by House, Block by Block: The Rebirth of America's Urban Neighborhoods* (New York: Oxford University Press, 2004); Amanda I. Seligman, *Chicago's Block Clubs: How Neighbors Shape the City* (Chicago: University of Chicago Press, 2016); Maria Kefalas, *Working-Class Heroes: Protecting Home, Community, and Nation in a Chicago Neighborhood* (Berkeley, CA: University of California Press, 2003); Benjamin Looker, *A Nation of Neighborhoods: Imagining Cities, Communities, and Democracy in Postwar America* (Chicago: University of Chicago Press, 2015); and Peg Knoepfle, *After Alinsky: Community Organizing in Illinois* (Springfield, IL: Sangamon State University, 1990). Clarence Stone and Robert P. Stoker, *Urban Neighborhoods in a New Era: Revitalization Politics in the Postindustrial City* (Chicago: University of Chicago Press, 2015), examines the interplay between neighborhood organizations and city halls, suggesting on page 5 that the former has been "bargaining for benefits" with the latter. On activism in African American communities, see Jeffrey Helgeson, *Crucibles of Black Empowerment: Chicago's Neighborhood Politics from the New Deal to Harold Washington* (Chicago: University of Chicago Press, 2014). The review essay by Susanne Cowan, "Back to the Neighborhood: Ideas and Practices of Local Governance," *Journal of Urban History* 45 (September 2019): 1070–75, provides useful historiographical background. A description of the area can be found in Jane Addams, *Twenty Years at Hull House* (New York: Penguin, 1981), and Ira Berkow, *Maxwell Street: Survival in a Bazaar* (New York: Doubleday, 1977).

2. Studs Terkel, "Ya Gotta Fight City Hall," *Chicago Guide*, September 1973, 145, clipping, in box 1, folder 24, Florence Scala Papers, Richard J. Daley Library, Special Collections, University of Illinois at Chicago, Chicago, Illinois [cited hereafter as Scala Papers]; George Rosen, *Decision-Making Chicago-Style: The Genesis of a University of Illinois Campus* (Urbana: University of Illinois Press, 1980), 94–97, 128–32; Gerald D. Suttles, *Social Order of the Slum: Ethnicity and Territory in the Inner City* (Chicago: University of Chicago Press, 1968), 15–20.

3. On Daley's mayoralty, see Roger Biles, *Richard J. Daley: Politics, Race, and the Governing of Chicago* (DeKalb: Northern Illinois University Press, 1995).

4. "Miss Scala," interview by Robert H. Young, n.d., 2 (quotation), box 1, folder 4, Scala Papers; Adam Cohen and Elizabeth Taylor, *American Pharaoh: Mayor Richard J. Daley, His Battle for Chicago and the Nation* (Boston: Little, Brown, 2000), 228–29; Mike Royko, *Boss: Richard J. Daley of Chicago* (New York: Signet, 1971), 126–27; Dominic A. Pacyga, *Chicago: A Biography* (Chicago: University of Chicago Press, 2009), 327.

5. Rosen, *Decision-Making Chicago-Style*, 20–59, 65–85, 112–18; Biles, *Richard J. Daley*, 74–75.

6. Carolyn Eastwood, *Near West Side Stories: Struggles for Community in Chicago's Maxwell Street Neighborhood* (Chicago: Lake Claremont, 2002); 165; "Miss Scala" interview, 3–4, 8; Biles, *Richard J. Daley*, 75; Rosen, *Decision-Making Chicago-Style*, 82.

7. "Miss Scala" interview, 4, 14; Royko, *Boss*, 127; Biles, *Richard J. Daley*, 75–76.

8. "Plan to Raze Hull House is Hit by Board," *Chicago Tribune*, February 11, 1961; "Campus Site Residents to Protest Today," February 14, 1961; Rosen, *Decision-Making Chicago-Style*, 114–16; Eastwood, *Near West Side Stories*, 166. Several authors describe in detail the difficulties of organizing low-income residents, many of whom were immigrants who spoke little English, to challenge city policies. See, for example, Amanda I. Seligman, *Block by Block: Neighborhoods and Public Policy on Chicago's West Side* (Chicago: University of Chicago Press, 2005); Beryl Satter, *Family Properties: Race, Real Estate, and the Exploitation of Black Urban America* (New York: Metropolitan, 2009);

and Lilia Fernandez, *Brown in the Windy City: Mexicans and Puerto Ricans in Postwar Chicago* (Chicago: University of Chicago Press, 2012). In *Challenging the Growth Machine: Neighborhood Politics in Chicago and Pittsburgh* (Lawrence: University Press of Kansas, 1996), Barbara Ferman notes the stark differences that often divided community groups seeking to compete with downtown interests.

9. Eastwood, *Near West Side Stories*, 135–59.

10. Royko, *Boss*, 127–28.

11. Rosen, *Decision-Making Chicago-Style*, 116; Cohen and Taylor, *American Pharaoh*, 230; Eastwood, *Near West Side Stories*, 172, 176–77.

12. John Bartlow Martin, "A New Attack on Delinquency: How the Chicago Area Project Works," *Harper's Magazine*, May 1944, 502–3; Pacyga, *Chicago*, 268–70. On the Back of the Yards Neighborhood Council, see Robert A. Slayton, *Back of the Yards: The Making of a Local Democracy* (Chicago: University of Chicago Press, 1986); and Thomas J. Jablonsky, *Pride in the Jungle: Community and Everyday Life in Back of the Yards Chicago* (Baltimore, MD: Johns Hopkins University Press, 1993). On Alinsky, see Sanford D. Horwitt, *Let Them Call Me Rebel: Saul Alinsky, His Life and Legacy* (New York: Alfred A. Knopf, 1989); Nicholas von Hoffman, *Radical: A Portrait of Saul Alinsky* (New York: Nation Books, 2010); and Satter, *Family Properties*. On the Woodlawn Organization, see John Hall Fish, *Black Power/White Control: The Struggle of the Woodlawn Organization in Chicago* (Princeton, NJ: Princeton University Press, 1973); and Arthur Brazier, *Black Self-Determination: The Story of the Woodlawn Organization* (Grand Rapids, MI: William B. Eerdmans, 1969). Following in the Alinsky tradition, Barack Obama tried his hand at community organizing in Chicago during the 1980s. Obama relates his experiences as a community organizer in *Dreams from My Father: A Story of Race and Inheritance*, 2nd ed. (New York: Three Rivers, 2004).

13. "Angry Women Sit in Daley's Office 3 Hours," *Chicago Tribune*, April 19, 1961.

14. "Council Gets U. of I. Site Laws," *Chicago Tribune*, March 31, 1961 (first and second quotations); "Angry Women Sit in Daley's Office 3 Hours;" Cohen and Taylor, *American Pharaoh*, 231 (third quotation).

15. Ashby G. Smith, "Statement to Planning and Housing Committee of Chicago City Council," April 13, 1961, box 5, folder 80, Scala Papers; Carmen Mendoza to Planning and Housing Committee of City Council, April 13, 1961, box 5, folder 81, Scala Papers; Rosen, *Decision-Making Chicago-Style*, 116–17.

16. "Highest Court Upholds U.I. Campus Site," *Chicago Tribune*, May 14, 1963 (quotation); Rosen, *Decision-Making Chicago-Style*, 117–18; Eastwood, *Near West Side Stories*, 177–79.

17. Eastwood, *Near West Side Stories*, 181, 197 (quotation).

18. Emma Graves Fitzsimmons, "'Heroine' Led Fight Against City Hall in '60s," *Chicago Tribune*, August 29, 2007.

19. Biles, *Richard J. Daley*, 76–77; Cohen and Taylor, *American Pharaoh*, 232 (first quotation); Royko, *Boss*, 129 (second quotation); Terkel, "Ya Gotta Fight City Hall," 145.

20. Ferman, *Challenging the Growth Machine*, 68; Rosen, *Decision-Making Chicago-Style*, 66–67. Also see Seligman, *Block by Block*, chapter 4.

21. Relatively little has been written about Ravitz's public career, although he is mentioned in some of the secondary literature on post–World War II Detroit. See, for example, June Manning Thomas, *Redevelopment and Race: Planning a Finer City in Postwar Detroit* (Baltimore, MD: Johns Hopkins University Press, 1997); and Heather Ann Thompson, *Whose Detroit? Politics, Labor, and Race in a Modern American City* (Ithaca,

NY: Cornell University Press, 2001). The best source for background information is the finding aid for the Mel Ravitz Papers, Walter P. Reuther Library, Wayne State University, Detroit, Michigan.

22. Mel Ravitz, "Urban Renewal Faces Critical Roadblocks," *Journal of the American Institute of Planners* 21, no. 1 (1955): 17–21; Mel Ravitz and Adelaide Dinwoodie, "Detroit Social Workers Mobilize Citizen Aid for Urban Renewal," *Journal of Housing* 13 (1956): 232–34; Thomas, *Redevelopment and Race*, 96–97 (quotations).

23. Bill McGraw, "Remembering Ravitz," *Metrotimes*, April 21, 2010, https://www.metrotimes.com/detroit/remembering-ravitz/Content?oid=2197294.

24. McGraw, "Remembering Ravitz."

25. Mel Ravitz to Emmett S. Moten Jr., November 5, 1982, box 78, folder 11, Ravitz Papers.

26. Ibid.

27. *Detroit Free Press*, December 30, 1986; Mel Ravitz to Joe Stroud, January 6, 1987, box 78, folder 1, Ravitz Papers (quotations). On the epidemic of arson in Detroit, see Charlie LeDuff, *Detroit: An American Autopsy* (New York: Penguin, 2013), 46–57. Also see Ze'ev Chafets, *Devil's Night: And Other True Tales of Detroit* (New York: Random House, 1990).

28. Mel Ravitz to Madame Chairperson, Members of the Planning Department, April 3, 1985, box 52, folder 13, Ravitz Papers; Ann Mullen, "A Gadfly Reflects," *Metrotimes*, September 24–30, 1997, clipping, box 67, folder 37, Mel Ravitz Papers.

29. Mel Ravitz to My [common council] Colleagues, memorandum, April 18, 1986, box 52, folder 13, Ravitz Papers.

30. Mel Ravitz, "Community Development: Salvation or Suicide," n.d., box 79, folder 7, 9–10, Ravitz Papers.

31. Mel Ravitz to [common council] Colleagues, memorandum, July 24, 1989, box 270, folder 23, Ravitz Papers; Thomas, *Redevelopment and Race*, 166.

32. Mel Ravitz and Richard Robinson, "False Promises: Tax Abatements as Business Incentives," *City Views*, August–September 1987, 19–21, clipping, box 66, folder 29, Ravitz Papers; Mel Ravitz, "The Many Facets of Community Development," n.d., box 82, folder 72, Ravitz Papers.

33. Mel Ravitz to [common council] Colleagues, memorandum, July 24, 1989, box 270, folder 23, Ravitz Papers. Also see Mel Ravitz, "Statement of Mel Ravitz to the United Automobile Workers Executive Board," November 16, 1983, box 54, folder 32, Ravitz Papers.

34. Mel Ravitz, "Economic Development: Salvation or Suicide," *Social Policy* 19, no. 2 (Fall 1988): 19; McGraw, "Remembering Ravitz" (quotation). Also see Carter Wilson, "A Study of Organized Neighborhood Opposition to the General Motors Plant Redevelopment Project in Poletown," (unpublished Ph.D. diss., Wayne State University, 1982); and Jeanie Wylie, *Poletown: Community Betrayed* (Urbana: University of Illinois Press, 1989).

35. Ravitz, "Community Development," 10–11; Thomas, *Redevelopment and Race*, 165–66.

36. "Another Tale of Two Cities," Detroit city councilman Mel Ravitz reports, March 1985, box 83, folder 2, Ravitz Papers; Mel Ravitz, "Perils of Planning as an Executive Function," *Journal of the American Planning Association* 54 (Spring 1988): 165.

37. Mullen, "Gadfly Reflects" (quotation).

38. On public-private partnerships and downtown revitalization, see Jon C. Teaford, *The Rough Road to Renaissance: Urban Revitalization in America, 1940–1985* (Baltimore,

MD: Johns Hopkins University Press, 1990), especially chapters 7 and 8. Dennis Keating, Norman Krumholz, and Philip Star, eds., *Revitalizing Urban Neighborhoods* (Lawrence: University Press of Kansas, 1996), detailed the role of local activists in reversing urban job losses and rebuilding communities.

39. The best account of Kucinich's mayoralty can be found in Todd Swanstrom, *The Crisis of Growth Politics: Cleveland, Kucinich, and the Challenge of Urban Populism* (Philadelphia: Temple University Press, 1985). Also see the biographical sketch of Kucinich in David D. Van Tassel and John J. Grabowski, eds., *The Encyclopedia of Cleveland History* (Bloomington: Indiana University Press, 1987), 669.

40. For a comprehensive assessment of Washington's mayoralty, see Roger Biles, *Mayor Harold Washington: Champion of Race and Reform in Chicago* (Urbana: University of Illinois Press, 2018). On Mayor Washington and the neighborhoods, see Pierre Clavel and Wim Wiewel, eds., *Harold Washington and the Neighborhoods: Progressive City Government in Chicago, 1983–1987* (New Brunswick, NJ: Rutgers University Press, 1991). On Richard M. Daley and the resumption of a downtown-first redevelopment policy, see Costas Spirou and Dennis R. Judd, *Building the City of Spectacle: Mayor Richard M. Daley and the Remaking of Chicago* (Ithaca, NY: Cornell University Press, 2016); and Larry Bennett, *The Third City: Chicago and American Urbanism* (Chicago: University of Chicago Press, 2010). On Richard M. Daley as a person, see Keith Koeneman, *First Son: The Biography of Richard M. Daley* (Chicago: University of Chicago Press, 2013).

41. A broader discussion of downtown as the focus of urban redevelopment can be found in such books as Robert A. Beauregard, *Voices of Decline: The Postwar Fate of U.S. Cities* (New York: Routledge, 2003); Larry Ford, *America's New Downtowns: Revitalization or Reinvention?* (Baltimore, MD: Johns Hopkins University Press, 2003); Bernard Frieden and Lynne Sagalyn, *Downtown, Inc.: How America Rebuilds Cities* (Cambridge, MA: MIT Press, 1989); and Dennis R. Judd, ed., *The Infrastructure of Play: Building the Tourist City* (Armonk, NY: M. E. Sharpe, 2003).

## PART III

1. Aaron Cowan, *A Nice Place to Visit: Tourism and Urban Revitalization in the Postwar Sunbelt* (Philadelphia: Temple University Press, 2016), 104 (quotation); Francesca Levy, "America's Most Livable Cities," *Forbes*, April 29, 2010, http://www.forbes.com /2010/04/29/cities-livable-pittsburgh-lifestyle-real-estate-top-ten-jobs-crime-income .html#1a7b927d6346. Also see Franklin Toker, *Pittsburgh: An Urban Portrait* (University Park: Pennsylvania State University Press, 1986). Edward K. Muller and Joel A. Tarr, *Making Industrial Pittsburgh Modern: Environment, Landscape, Transportation, and Planning* (Pittsburgh, PA: University of Pittsburgh Press, 2019), brings the redevelopment story into the twenty-first century.

2. Cowan, *Nice Place to Visit*, 123–24; Allen Dietrich-Ward, *Beyond Rust: Metropolitan Pittsburgh and the Fate of Industrial America* (Philadelphia: University of Pennsylvania Press, 20160, 281; Mark Belco, "28 Projects Worth $1 Billion under Construction and More on the Way: Downtown in Midst of Building Boom," *Pittsburgh Post-Gazette*, May 1, 2018, https://www.post-gazette.com/business/development/2018/05/01/Report -finds-significant-investment-in-Greater-Downtown-Pittsburgh/stories/201805010129 (accessed January 2020).

3. Dietrich-Ward, *Beyond Rust*, 225 (quotation); Cowan, *Nice Place to Visit*, 157; Edward K. Muller, "Downtown Pittsburgh: Renaissance and Renewal," in *Pittsburgh and the Appalachians: Cultural and Natural Resources in a Postindustrial Age*, ed. Joseph L.

Scarpaci and Kevin J. Patrick (Pittsburgh, PA: University of Pittsburgh Press, 2006), 18; Tracy Neumann, *Remaking the Rust Belt: The Postindustrial Transformation of North America* (Philadelphia: University of Pennsylvania Press, 2016), 215–16.

4. Dietrich-Ward, *Beyond Rust*, 264, 288–89.

5. Joseph L. Scarpaci, "Pittsburgh's Suburbs: Hollowing Out the Core," in Scarpaci and Patrick, eds., *Pittsburgh and the Appalachians*, 138; Neumann, *Remaking the Rustbelt*, 3 (quotation).

6. *Wall Street Journal*, July 28, 2008, February 28, 2010. In *Cities in the Urban Age: A Dissent* (Chicago: University of Chicago Press, 2018), urban planner Robert A. Beauregard argues that the concentration of great wealth and the deepening of poverty naturally occur in cities; in particular, see chapter 2. Rachel Weber, *From Boom to Bubble: How Finance Built the New Chicago* (Chicago: University of Chicago Press, 2015), says that developers built downtown not because of greater demand but because financial markets made more capital available. Joel Rast, *The Origins of the Dual City: Housing, Race, and Redevelopment in Twentieth-Century Chicago* (Chicago: University of Chicago Press, 2019), contends that, after long trying to eliminate slums and blight, Chicago's leaders accepted the "dual city" by the late twentieth century. Robert J. Sampson, *Great American City: Chicago and the Enduring Neighborhood* (Chicago: University of Chicago Press, 2012), emphasizes the importance of making policy at the neighborhood level. Kimberly Kinder, *DIY Detroit: Making Do in a City without Services* (Minneapolis, MN: University of Minnesota Press, 2016), relates how residents provisioned themselves to compensate for the city's failure to provide services.

7. Larry Bennett, *The Third City: Chicago and American Urbanism* (Chicago: University of Chicago Press, 2010), 191–98. On Chicago's economic transformation, see Gregory D. Squires, Larry Bennett, Kathleen McCourt, and Philip Nyden, *Chicago: Race, Class, and the Response to Urban Decline* (Philadelphia: Temple University Press, 1989); and John P. Koval, Larry Bennett, Michael I. Bennett, Fassil Demissie, Roberta Garner, and Kiljoong Kim, *The New Chicago: A Social and Cultural Analysis* (Philadelphia: Temple University Press, 2006). The identification of global cities began with Saskia Sassen, *The Global City: New York, London, Tokyo* (Princeton, NJ: Princeton University Press, 1991). Also see Saskia Sassen, "A Global City," in *Global Chicago*, ed. Charles Madigan (Urbana: University of Illinois Press, 2004).

8. Edward Goetz, *Clearing the Way: Deconcentrating the Poor in Urban America* (Washington, DC: Urban Institute Press, 2003), 105 (quotation).

## CHAPTER 8

1. Evan Osnos, "The Daley Show," *New Yorker* 86, March 8, 2010, 41 (quotation); Adele Simmons, "Chicago's Amazing 10-Year Turnaround," *Chicago Tribune*, January 4, 2000; Dominic A. Pacyga, *Chicago: A Biography* (Chicago: University of Chicago Press, 2009), 384–89. In the brief time since Daley left office, two comprehensive treatments of his mayoralty have been published—Keith Koeneman, *First Son: The Biography of Richard M. Daley* (Chicago: University of Chicago Press, 2013); and Costas Spirou and Dennis R. Judd, *Building the City of Spectacle: Mayor Richard M. Daley and the Remaking of Chicago* (Ithaca, NY: Cornell University Press, 2016). Two other books that deal substantially with the younger Daley's impact on Chicago are Larry Bennett, *The Third City: Chicago and American Urbanism* (Chicago: University of Chicago Press, 2010); and Andrew J. Diamond, *Chicago on the Make: Power and Inequality in a Modern City* (Oakland: University of California Press, 2017), especially chapter 7. Also see Larry Bennett,

"The Mayor among His Peers: Interpreting Richard M. Daley," in *The City, Revisited: Urban Theory from Chicago, Los Angeles, and New York*, ed. Dennis R. Judd and Dick Simpson (Minneapolis, MN: University of Minnesota Press, 2011), 242–72. As well, Costas Spirou, "Both Center and Periphery: Chicago's Metropolitan Expansion and the New Downtowns," in Judd and Simpson, *City Revisited*, 273–301, notes that satellite cities such as Aurora, Elgin, Joliet, and Waukegan followed Chicago in focusing on downtown redevelopment.

2. Roger Biles, *Richard J. Daley: Politics, Race, and the Governing of Chicago* (DeKalb: Northern Illinois University Press, 1995), 223–41. On the Bilandic, Byrne, and Sawyer mayoralties, see Paul M. Green and Melvin G. Holli, eds., *The Mayors: The Chicago Political Tradition*, 3rd ed. (Carbondale: Southern Illinois University Press, 2005). On the 1989 election, see Paul M. Green and Melvin G. Holli, eds., *Restoration 1989: Chicago Elects a New Daley* (Chicago: Lyceum, 1991). On the Washington mayoralty, see Roger Biles, *Mayor Harold Washington: Champion of Race and Reform in Chicago* (Urbana: University of Illinois Press, 2018). Also see Joel Rast, *The Origins of the Dual City: Housing, Race, and Redevelopment in Twentieth-Century Chicago* (Chicago: University of Chicago Press, 2019).

3. Biles, *Mayor Harold Washington*, 315–16; Melvin G. Holli, "The Daley Era: Richard J. to Richard M.," in Green and Holli, eds., *The Mayors*, 229–34; Pacyga, *Chicago*, 398–400; Bennett, *Third City*, 91; John Kass, "Daley Is Ill, But Not Over Nephew's Deal," *Chicago Tribune*, June 10, 2009. On Daley's political support in the gay community, see Timothy Stewart-Winter, *Queer Clout: Chicago and the Rise of Gay Politics* (Philadelphia: University of Pennsylvania Press, 2016).

4. David Moberg, "The Fuel of a New Machine," *Chicago Reader*, March 30, 1989, http://www.chicagoreader.com/chicago/the-fuel-of-a-new-machine/Content?oid= 873612; Mary Pattillo, *Black on the Block: The Politics of Race and Class in the City* (Chicago: University of Chicago Press, 2007), 152–53; Dick Simpson, *Rogues, Rebels, and Rubber Stamps: The Politics of the Chicago City Council from 1863 to the Present* (Boulder, CO: Westview, 2011), 287–90; Bennett, *Third City*, 91–92; Biles, *Mayor Harold Washington*, 315–16. For a clear statement of Daley's vision of Chicago as a global city, see Economic Club of Chicago speech, February 15, 2011, youtube.com/watch?y=oWs84eJd8oY. On global cities, see Saskia Sassen, *The Global City: New York, London, Tokyo*, 2nd ed. (Princeton, NJ: Princeton University Press, 2001).

5. Fassil Demissie, "Globalization and the Remaking of Chicago," in *The New Chicago: A Social and Cultural Analysis*, ed. John P. Koval, Larry Bennett, Michael I. J. Bennett, Fassil Demissie, Roberta Garner, and Kiljoong Kim (Philadelphia: Temple University Press, 2006), 22 (quotation), 27, 29.

6. City of Chicago, *Development Plan for the Central Area of Chicago* (Chicago: City of Chicago, Department of City Planning, 1958); Osnos, "Daley Show," 40; Timothy J. Gilfoyle, *Millennium Park: Creating a Chicago Landmark* (Chicago: University of Chicago Press, 2006), 84. For a critique of the 1985 plan, see Joel Rast, *Remaking Chicago: The Political Origins of Urban Industrial Change* (DeKalb: Northern Illinois University Press, 1999). Also see the essays in Charles Madigan, ed., *Global Chicago* (Urbana: University of Illinois Press, 2004).

7. Gilfoyle, *Millennium Park*, 84, 351–52; Koeneman, *First Son*, 128, 173–76.

8. Richard C. Longworth, "The Political City," in *Global Chicago*, ed. Charles Madigan (Urbana: University of Illinois Press, 2004), 76–77; Diamond, *Chicago on the Make*, 285. The literature on urban tourism has increased exponentially in recent decades. Begin with Dennis R. Judd and Susan S. Fainstein, eds., *The Tourist City* (New Haven,

CT: Yale University Press, 1999); Aaron Cowan, *A Nice Place to Visit: Tourism and Urban Revitalization in the Postwar Rustbelt* (Philadelphia: Temple University Press, 2016); and J. Mark Souther, "Landscapes of Leisure: Building an Urban History of Tourism," *Journal of Urban History* 30, no. 2 (January 2004): 257–65. In *Bulls Markets: Chicago's Basketball Business and the New Inequality* (Chicago: University of Chicago Press, 2018), Sean Dinces examines the case of professional basketball.

9. McCormick Place home page, http://www.mccormickplace.com; Costas Spirou, "Urban Beautification: The Construction of a New Identity in Chicago," in Koval et al., eds, *The New Chicago*, 295–97. The best discussion of McCormick Place's history can be found in Heywood T. Sanders, *Convention Center Follies: Politics, Power, and Public Investment in American Cities* (Philadelphia: University of Pennsylvania Press, 2014), especially chapter 6.

10. Spirou, "Urban Beautification," 297–98; Alison True, "TIFs: Where It All Began and How Joravsky Sussed It from the Start," *Chicago Reader*, October 26, 2009, https://www.chicagoreader.com/Bleader/archives/2009/10/26/tifs-where-it-all-began-and-how-joravsky-sussed-it-from-the-start; Spirou and Judd, *Building the City of Spectacle*, 1–3; Diamond, *Chicago on the Make*, 285–86.

11. Douglas Bukowski, *Navy Pier: A Chicago Landmark* (Chicago: Metropolitan Pier and Exposition Authority, 1996); Douglas Bukowski, "Navy Pier," in *The Encyclopedia of Chicago*, ed. James R. Grossman, Ann Durkin Keating, and Janice L. Reiff (Chicago: University of Chicago Press, 2004), 561; Navy Pier home page, http://navypier.com; Koeneman, *First Son*, 131; Biles, *Mayor Harold Washington*, 219 (quotation).

12. *Chicago Tribune*, April 30, 2011; James Atlas, "The Daleys of Chicago," *New York Times Magazine*, August 25, 1996, 58.

13. "Gambling Loses," *Chicago Tribune*, April 1; "Pension: Bond Plan 1 Vote Short in Senate," *Chicago Tribune*, April 3, 2003; Koeneman, *First Son*, 224–27; Diamond, *Chicago on the Make*, 370n75; Spirou and Judd, *Building the City of Spectacle*, 99–103.

14. Sadhu Johnston, "The Green Development in Chicago," *Economic Development Journal* 4 (Spring 2005): 12–19; Gilfoyle, *Millennium Park*, 83–84; Bennett, *Third City*, 100; J. Diamond, *Chicago on the Make*, 285.

15. Gilfoyle, *Millennium Park*, 95–96, 167–70.

16. *Financial Times*, July 20, 2004 (first quotation); Diamond, *Chicago on the Make*, 285; Nancy Gibbs, "The Five Best Big-City Mayors," *Time*, April 25, 2005, 17 (second quotation).

17. The federal government's declining financial support of cities is discussed in Roger Biles, *The Fate of Cities: Urban America and the Federal Government, 1945–2000* (Lawrence: University Press of Kansas, 2011), especially chapters 8–11; and Peter Dreier, John Mollenkopf, and Todd Swanstrom, eds., *Place Matters: Metropolitics for the Twenty-First Century*, 2nd ed. (Lawrence: University Press of Kansas, 2004). On urban financial solutions to this problem, see the following: Rachel Weber, "Selling City Futures: The Financialization of Urban Redevelopment Policy," *Economic Geography* 86, no. 3 (July 2010): 251–74; Joel Rast, "The Politics of Alternative Economic Development: Revisiting the Stone-Imbroscio Debate," *Journal of Urban Affairs* 27, no. 1 (March 2005): 53–69; Roger Biles, "Public Policy Made by Private Enterprise: Bond Rating Agencies and Urban America," *Journal of Urban History* 44, no. 6 (November 2018): 1098–112.

18. Craig L. Johnson and Joyce Y. Man, *Tax Increment Financing and Economic Development: Uses, Structures, and Impact* (Albany, NY: State University of New York Press, 2001), 1–3; Colin Gordon, "Blighting the Way: Urban Renewal, Economic Development,

and the Elusive Definition of Blight," *Fordham Urban Law Journal* 31, no. 2 (January 2004): 313–14; Biles, *Mayor Harold Washington*, 317 (quotation).

19. Charles S. Suchor, "Chicago's Central Area," in Koval et al., eds., *The New Chicago*, 56–76; Ben Joravsky, "Million-Dollar Lies," *Chicago Reader*, August 10, 2006, https://www.chicagoreader.com/chicago/million-dollar-lies/; Diamond, *Chicago on the Make*, 281.

20. Joravsky, "Million-Dollar Lies"; David Moberg, "Economic Restructuring," in Koval et al., eds., *The New Chicago*, 32; Diamond, *Chicago on the Make*, 281 (quotation), 283; David Orr, "Renewed Call for a TIF Moratorium," *HuffPost*, April 8, 2011; Kari Lydersen, *Mayor 1%: Rahm Emanuel and the Rise of Chicago's 99%* (Chicago: Haymarket, 2013), 193–96.

21. Thomas L. Friedman, "A Progressive in the Age of Austerity," *New York Times*, October 16, 2011; Johnson and Man, *Tax Increment Financing*, 224; Ben Joravsky and Mick Dumke, "Who Wins and Loses in Rahm's TIF Game?" *Chicago Reader*, March 26, 2015, https://chicagoreader.com/news-politics/who-wins-and-loses-in-rahms-tif-game/; Gordon, "Blighting the Way," 322 (quotation). In *Slaughterhouse: Chicago's Union Stockyard and the World It Made* (Chicago: University of Chicago Press, 2015), 183, historian Dominic A. Pacyga points out that the Stock Yard District TIF was a rare "example of how the TIFs were intended to be used."

22. Joravsky, "Million-Dollar Lies"; True, "TIFs"; Micah Uetricht, *Strike for America: Chicago Teachers against Austerity* (New York: Verso, 2014), 86–87; Joravsky and Dumke, "Who Wins and Loses?"; Spirou and Judd, *Building the City of Spectacle*, 167–68.

23. Richard M. Daley, "No Pain, No Gain," *New York Times*, June 16, 1991; Tony Dutzik, Brian Imus, and Phineas Baxandall, *Privatization and the Public Interest: The Need for Transparency and Accountability in Chicago's Public Asset Lease Deals* (Chicago: Illinois PIRG Education Fund, 2009), 8; Diamond, *Chicago on the Make*, 13.

24. On the 1995 heat wave, see Eric Klinenburg, *Heat Wave: A Social Autopsy of Disaster in Chicago* (Chicago: University of Chicago Press, 2002).

25. Dutzik et al., *Privatization*, 10–26; Spirou and Judd, *Building the City of Spectacle*, 139, 151–52, 171–73. Rendell's efforts are described in detail in Buzz Bissinger, *A Prayer for the City* (New York: Vintage, 1997).

26. Matt Taibbi, *Griftopia: A Story of Bankers, Politicians, and the Most Audacious Power Grab in American History* (New York: Spiegel and Grau, 2011, 166–69; Dan P. Blake, "Daley Takes Blame for Meters," *Chicago Tribune*, May 20, 2009; Jeff Long, "Illinois' Gambling Problem," *Chicago Tribune*, December 4, 2008; Spirou and Judd, *Building the City of Spectacle*, 171–73; Koeneman, *First Son*, 279–81, 286–87.

27. David Moberg, "How Does Richie Rate? Opening Up the Mayor's Report Card," *Chicago Reader*, February 18, 1999, https://www.chicagoreader.com/chicago/how-does-richie-rate/Content?oid=898456; *Crain's Chicago Business*, June 12, 2010 (first quotation); Spirou and Judd, *Building the City of Spectacle*, 171 (second quotation).

28. Craig Malin, "It Takes a Pro to Run a City," *Chicago Tribune*, November 1, 2013; Spirou and Judd, *Building the City of Spectacle*, 171; Koeneman, *First Son*, 280–81.

29. Biles, *Mayor Harold Washington*, 289 (quotation); John Kass, "Daley Quickly Flexes School Muscle," *Chicago Tribune*, May 25, 1995.

30. Moberg, "How Does Richie Rate?"; Diamond, *Chicago on the Make*, 269 (quotation); Spirou and Judd, *Building the City of Spectacle*, 167.

31. Dorothy Shipps, *School Reform, Corporate Style: Chicago, 1880–2000* (Lawrence: University Press of Kansas, 2006), 135–69; Uetricht, *Strike for America*, 8, 87. Also see

Anthony S. Bryk, David Kerbow, and Sharon Rollow, "Chicago School Reform," in *New Schools for a New Century*, ed. Diane Ravitch and Joseph Viteritti (New Haven, CT: Yale University Press, 1997), 164–200.

32. Uetricht, *Strike for America*, 37 (quotation).

33. Stephanie Banchero, "Daley School Plan Fails to Make Grade," *Chicago Tribune*, January 17, 2010. The 2012 CTU strike is covered thoroughly in Uetricht, *Strike for America*, 53–79.

34. *Chicago Tribune*, January 17, 2010; Pauline Lipman, "Chicago School Reform: Advancing the Global City Agenda," in Koval et al., eds., *The New Chicago*, 248–55;" Monica Davey, "From Daley, No Endorsements or Regrets," *New York Times*, September 12, 2010. Koeneman, *First Son*, 155–64, offers a more upbeat analysis of the education reform movement.

35. D. Bradford Hunt, *Blueprint for Disaster: The Unraveling of Chicago Public Housing* (Chicago: University of Chicago Press, 2009), 259–95. Also see Larry Bennett, Janet S. Smith, and Patricia A. Wright, eds., *Where Are Poor People to Live? Transforming Public Housing* (Armonk, NY: M. E. Sharpe, 2006); and Lawrence J. Vale, *Purging the Poorest: Public Housing and the Design Politics of Twice-Cleared Communities* (Chicago: University of Chicago Press, 2013). Additional background on Chicago public housing can be found in Devereux Bowly Jr., *The Poorhouse: Subsidized Housing in Chicago* (Carbondale: Southern Illinois University Press, 1978); and J. S. Fuerst, *When Public Housing Was Paradise: Building Community in Chicago* (Urbana: University of Illinois Press, 2003).

36. Pattillo, *Black on the Block*, 153 (first quotation); Spirou and Judd, *Building the City of Spectacle*, 164 (second quotation); Hunt, *Blueprint for Disaster*, 278–79. Catherine Fennell, *Last Project Standing: Civics and Sympathy in Post-welfare Chicago* (Minneapolis, MN: University of Minnesota Press, 2015), examines Henry Horner Homes.

37. Erin M. Graves and Lawrence J. Vale, "Planning Note: The Chicago Housing Authority's Plan for Transformation: Assessing the First Ten Years," *Journal of the American Planning Association* 78 (Autumn 2012): 464 (quotation); Paul L. Street, *Racial Oppression in the Global Metropolis: A Living Black Chicago History* (Lanham, MD: Rowman and Littlefield, 2007), 261; R. C. Longworth, "Chicago Has Entered the Global Era," *Chicago Tribune*, August 25, 2002.

38. Moberg, "How Does Richie Rate?"

39. Moberg, How Does Richie Rate?" Also see Jeffrey S. Adler, *First in Violence, Deepest in Dirt: Homicide in Chicago, 1875–1920* (Cambridge, MA: Harvard University Press, 2006); Richard C. Lindberg, *To Serve and Collect: Chicago Politics and Police Corruption from the Lager Beer Riot to the Summerdale Scandal* (Westport, CT: Praeger, 1991); Wesley G. Skogan, *Police and Community in Chicago: A Tale of Three Cities* (New York: Oxford University Press, 2006); Simon Balto, *Occupied Territory: Policing Black Chicago from Red Summer to Black Power* (Chapel Hill, NC: University of North Carolina Press, 2019); and Andrew S. Baer, *Beyond the Usual Beating: The Jon Burge Police Torture Scandal and Social Movements for Police Accountability in Chicago* (Chicago: University of Chicago Press, 2020).

40. Douglas S. Massey and Nancy A. Denton, *American Apartheid: Segregation and the Making of the Underclass* (Cambridge, MA: Harvard University Press, 1993), 74–78, 148; James Warren, "City's Inequities Belie World-Class Imagery," *New York Times*, February 5, 2011.

41. Monica Davey, "Chicago Absorbs its Latest Defeat," *New York Times*, October 4, 2009; "Bumpy Road Awaits USOC Chief," *Chicago Tribune*, December 10, 2008; "Daley's Dream Dashed," October 4, 2009; Koeneman, *First Son*, 289–91.

42. Jason Meisner, "26 Years for Teen in Fatal Beating," *Chicago Tribune*, January 22, 2011; Bennett, *Third City*, 105; Warren, "City's Inequities"; Longworth, "Political City," 76.

43. Megan Stielstra, "What Should Chicago Celebrate?" *New York Times*, December 31, 2015; Lydersen, *Mayor 1%*, 111–26; Biles, *Mayor Harold Washington*, 318; Street, *Racial Oppression*, 261; Diamond, *Chicago on the Make*, 299–300.

44. Colin Gordon, *Mapping Decline: St. Louis and the Fate of the American City* (Philadelphia: University of Pennsylvania Press, 2008); David Farber, *Crack: Rock Cocaine, Street Capitalism, and the Decade of Greed* (New York: Cambridge University Press, 2019).

## CHAPTER 9

1. "Hospital Will Relocate at Independence Mall," *Philadelphia Inquirer*, July 15, 1964; "Patients Move into New Metropolitan Hospital," *Philadelphia Inquirer*, April 4, 1971; Alan L. Phillips, "Hospitals Here Keep Patients Too Long, U.S. Official Says," *Philadelphia Inquirer*, March 15, 1971; Charlie Bannister, "Hospital to Dedicate Its Roundhouse 'Twin,'" *Philadelphia Inquirer*, March 12, 1971. Important books by historians of medicine have informed our understanding of hospital growth, physician training and specialization, and medical care in teaching hospitals. We relied on Colin Gordon, *Dead on Arrival: The Politics of Health Care in Twentieth-Century America* (Princeton, NJ: Princeton University Press, 2003); Kenneth M. Ludmerer, *Learning to Heal: the Development of American Medical Education* (New York: Basic Books, 1985); Charles E. Rosenberg, *The Care of Strangers: The Rise of the America's Hospital System* (Baltimore, MD: Johns Hopkins University, 1987); Andrew T. Simpson, *The Medical Metropolis: Health Care and Economic Transformation in Pittsburgh and Houston* (Philadelphia: University of Pennsylvania Press, 2019); Rosemary Stevens, *In Sickness and in Wealth: American Hospitals in the Twentieth Century* (New York: Basic Books, 1989); Morris J. Vogel, *The Invention of the Modern Hospital, Boston, 1870–1930* (Chicago: University of Chicago Press, 1980); and Keith Wailoo, *Dying in the City of the Blues: Sickle Cell Anemia and the Politics of Race and Health* (Chapel Hill: University of North Carolina Press, 2001).

2. "Independence Hall Section Holds Construction Spotlight," *Philadelphia Inquirer*, March 21, 1971; Frank Dougherty, "Things Are Looking Up as Midcity Construction Booms," *Philadelphia Daily News*, February 29, 1972. Our thanks to Domenic Vitiello for calling the podiatric school's location to our attention and for identifying that part of Center City as a small medical center. And also see Kathryn E. Wilson, *Ethnic Renewal in Philadelphia's Chinatown: Space, Place, and Struggle* (Philadelphia: Temple University Press, 2015), 64, for connections between urban renewal plans aimed at Chinatown and Rafsky as an "urban entrepreneur."

3. Aaron Epstein, "Schwartz Scuttles Rizzo Bond Plan," *Philadelphia Inquirer*, January 11, 1974; Epstein, "Bill to Establish Hospitals Authority Passed by Council," *Philadelphia Inquirer*, January 25, 1974; "A Hospital Authority—Now!" *Philadelphia Inquirer*, January 15, 1974. By the late 1970s, reports historian Guian A. McKee ("The Hospital City in an Ethnic Enclave: Tufts-New England Medical Center, Boston's Chinatown, and the Urban Political Economy of Health Care," *Journal of Urban History* 42, no. 2 [March 2016]: 281n65), only a few hospitals had made use of tax-exempt bonds to finance construction projects.

4. Aaron Epstein, "Who in City Has Authority to Appoint an Authority?" *Philadelphia Inquirer*, August 17, 1973; "Hospital Authority—Now"; Zachary Stalberg, "Council to Push Hospital Plan," *Philadelphia Daily News*, December 28, 1973; Guian A. McKee, "Hospitals (Economic Development)," *Encyclopedia of Greater Philadelphia* (New Bruns-

wick, NJ: Rutgers University), https://philadelphiaencyclopedia.org/archive/hospitals
-economic-development/.

5. "Elton Barclay, Ex-Head of Philadelphia General," *Philadelphia Inquirer*, April 9,
1945; Paul Carpenter, "Hospitals Reflect Life in City," *Philadelphia Inquirer*, January 18,
1974; McKee, "Hospitals (Economic Development)."

6. Guian A. McKee, "Urban Deindustrialization and Local Public Policy: Industrial
Renewal in Philadelphia, 1953–1976," *Journal of Policy History* 16, no. 1 (January 2004):
66–98; PIDC vice president as quoted in Gregory R. Byrnes, "At PHG Site, Health Center
Is Planned," *Philadelphia Inquirer*, November 10, 1985. Historian Destin Jenkins, in *The
Bonds of Inequality: Debt and the Making of the American City* (Chicago: University of
Chicago Press, 2021), 11, highlights the important role played by "municipal technocrats
and creditors" in managing bond issues that lay outside voters' purview.

7. Kenneth M. Ludmerer, *Time to Heal: American Medical Education from the Turn
of the Century to the Era of Managed Care* (New York: Oxford University Press, 1999),
267; Margaret Pugh O'Mara, *Cities of Knowledge: Cold War Science and the Search for
the Next Silicon Valley* (Princeton, NJ: Princeton University Press, 2005), 149–58; Judith
Rodin, "The 21st Century Urban University: New Roles for Practice and Research," *Journal of the American Planning Association* 71, no. 3 (Summer 2005): 237–49; Meagan M.
Ehlenz and Eugenie L. Birch, *The Power of Eds and Meds: Urban Universities Investing
in Neighborhood Revitalization and Innovation Districts* (Philadelphia: Penn Institute
for Urban Research, July 2014). As historian Gabriel Winant reminds us in *The Next
Shift: The Fall of Industry and the Rise of Health Care in Rust Belt America* (Cambridge,
MA: Harvard University Press, 2021), "the private sector health care industry is in so many
respects a delegated arm of state power" (23).

8. Clay Gowran, "Medic Center's Success Credited to Theobald," *Chicago Tribune*,
December 23, 1962; John Thompson, "A Costly Dream Takes Shape in Blighted Area,"
*Chicago Daily Tribune*, November 16, 1947; George Tagge, "Gov. Green Set to Spur Chicago Slum Clearing," *Chicago Daily Tribune*, January 23, 1945. Harvey M. Karlen, *The
Governments of Chicago* (Chicago: Courier, 1958), 105, identifies the Chicago Plan Commission as the principal agency urging Illinois legislators to approve and fund the Medical District.

9. Gowran, "Medic Center's Success"; "U. of I. Branch in West Side Area Planned,"
*Chicago Daily Tribune*, May 19, 1947; Thompson, "Costly Dream Takes Shape."

10. "U. of I. Branch in West Side," including quotation; Joel Rast, *The Origins of the
Dual City: Housing, Race, and Redevelopment in Twentieth-Century Chicago* (Chicago:
University of Illinois Press, 2019), 199–200.

11. George Schreiber, "Taxpayers to Foot Bill for Half Billion in Civic Projects," *Chi-
cago Daily Tribune*, January 3, 1960; "New Nurses' Home to Cost 2 Millions," *Chicago
Sunday Tribune*, July 17, 1949; "TV Takes Look at Emergency Hospital Care," *Chicago
Daily Tribune*, January 22, 1956; Chesley Manly, "Vast Medical Center Grows at Rapid
Pace," *Chicago Daily Tribune*, December 8, 1957 (quotation).

12. Thomas Buck, "14 Million Dollar West Side 'Face Lifting' Awaits Federal O.K.,"
*Chicago Daily Tribune*, December 13, 1959; Buck, "U. of I. Plans Expansion of City Cam-
pus," *Chicago Tribune*, October 21, 1965; "Center Is Daily Entity," *Chicago Tribune*,
December 26, 1965.

13. Marcia Opp, "Presbyterian-St. Luke's Tells $75-Million Project," *Chicago Tribune*,
June 12, 1971; Simpson, *Medical Metropolis*, 37. Donald E. L. Johnson, "University Hospitals Will Anchor Vertical Systems," *Modern Healthcare* 9, no. 12 (December 1979): 50,

determines that the combined Rush-Presbyterian-St. Luke's Medical Center was the "only such system in the country."

14. "Calls City Apathetic on Lead Poisoning," *St. Louis Post-Dispatch*, January 8, 1971. Journalist Laurie Kaye Abraham, in *Mama Might Be Better off Dead: The Failure of Healthcare in Urban America* (Chicago: University of Chicago Press, 1993), demonstrates the multiple obstacles that confronted low-income, uninsured patients in obtaining health care.

15. Colin Gordon, *Mapping Decline: St. Louis and the Fate of the American City* (Philadelphia: University of Pennsylvania Press, 2008), 168, 209; Monroe W. Karmin, "St. Louis: Can the Decay Be Stopped?" *Wall Street Journal*, March 2, 1972; Robert Reinhold, "In St. Louis Even the Old Bricks Are Leaving," *New York Times*, July 9, 1978; James Krohe Jr., "Medical Districts to the Rescue: Cities Find Another Way to Bolster Inner City Neighborhoods," *Planning* 72, no. 4 (April 1, 2006): 41.

16. Karmin, "St. Louis"; Sally Bixby Defty, "Hospitals a Bulwark of Stability in Area," *St. Louis Post-Dispatch*, February 10, 1975, including quotation. Kenneth M. Ludmerer, "The Rise of the Teaching Hospital in America," *Journal of the History of Medicine and Allied Sciences* 38, no. 4 (October 1983): 389–414, explains the intellectual, financial, and political origins of the nation's top-ranked hospitals, including Barnes. And see Ludmerer, *Time to Heal: American Medical Education from the Turn of the Century to the Era of Managed Care* (New York: Oxford University Press, 1999), 261–62, for a discussion of rapid demographic changes in areas around Barnes and other major hospitals.

17. Dorothea Wolfgram, "Prescription for Redevelopment," *St. Louis Post-Dispatch*, June 17, 1975, including quotation; Philip Sutin, "Barnes Area Housing Plan Is Approved by Aldermen," *St. Louis Post-Dispatch*, February 14, 1975. In the 1970s, reports physician and historian John A. Kastor in *Governance of Teaching Hospitals: Turmoil at Penn and Hopkins* (Baltimore, MD: Johns Hopkins University Press, 2003), the idea of partnerships began to replace demolition as the preferred method of dealing with a hospital's often impoverished neighbors. See especially Christy Ford Chapin, *Ensuring America's Health: The Public Creation of the Corporate Health Care System* (New York: Cambridge University Press, 2015), for a valuable treatment of physicians, hospitals, politicians, and the politics of health-care reimbursement leading to the creation of Medicare and Medicaid in 1965.

18. "Don't Forget Your Cameras," *Chicago Tribune*, May 17, 1981; "St. Louis: A Gem Sparkling in the Heartland," *Philadelphia Inquirer*, October 4, 1987; Fred W. Lindecke, "Barbara Bush Concedes Lead by Dole in Iowa," *St. Louis Post-Dispatch*, January 20, 1988; Bill Bryan, "Gregory Hits the Streets with Anti-Crime Message," *St. Louis Post-Dispatch*, March 27, 1992, including reclaim quote; Dennis Judd, "Mean Streets, Cultural Assets; St. Louis Is a Tale of Two Cities," *St. Louis Journalism Review* 127, no. 193 (February 1997); Paris Bouchard, "Central West End Is Safe" (letter to the editor), *St. Louis Post-Dispatch*, June 12, 1999, including quotation regarding a 60 percent improvement in safety. Central West End "revitalization has been sporadic and uneven," report historians Joseph Heathcott and Maire Agnes Murphy in "Corridors of Flight, Zones of Renewal: Industry, Planning, and Policy in the Making of Metropolitan St. Louis, 1940–1980," *Journal of Urban History* 31, no. 2 (January 2005): 170, "as gentrification placed high pressures on a segment of the housing stock near the redevelopment area, while neglect and disinvestment continued in the surrounding blocks."

19. Linda Sunshine and John W. Wright, *The Best Hospitals in America* (New York: Henry Holt, 1987), 190; John Pekkanen, "The Best Medical Services and Specialists in

the U.S.: Part I," *Town and Country*, February 1978, 71–82; Edwin Kiester, "America's Best Hospitals for Women," *Ladies' Home Journal* 93, no. 1 (January 1976): 86–88, 90, 124, including quotation; Diane Partie, "Best Medical Care in America," *Harper's Bazaar*, September 1978, 238.

20. "Breasts define women," observes historian and science writer Bettyann Holtzmann Kevles in *Naked to the Bone: Medical Imaging in the Twentieth Century* (Reading, MA: Addison-Wesley, 1997), 250; "Hospital Opens 'One-Stop' Site for Breast Care," *St. Louis Post-Dispatch*, April 6, 1992; Guenter B. Risse, *Mending Bodies, Saving Souls: A History of Hospitals* (New York: Oxford University Press, 1999), 569, including Quotation. Medical historian Keith Wailoo, in *How Cancer Crossed the Color Line* (New York: Oxford University Press, 2011), 167–75, directs our attention to an apparent increase in breast cancer rates among white women residing in affluent Marin County, California, during the 1990s. Such scary news no doubt encouraged similarly situated women in the St. Louis region to perform breast self-examinations and to seek medical attention at Barnes and other hospitals. But in line with the racial themes developed in this chapter, as Wailoo reminds us, African American women died of breast cancer at a much higher rate.

21. Denise Smith Amos, "New Cancer and Outpatient Centers Part of Plan," *St. Louis Post Dispatch*, December 22, 1995, including quotation; Kastor, *Governance of Teaching Hospitals*, 35–36. Winant, *Next Shift*, explains that "profitable institutions could sell costly services—often on national or global markets" (230).

22. Winant, *Next Shift*, 210 (quotation). O'Mara, *Cities of Knowledge*, 402; Robert Sharoff, "Keeping the Fruits of Research Close to Home in St. Louis," *New York Times*, February 7, 2007; Andrew Pollack, "In Biotech Brews, Questions of Consistency," *New York Times*, June 11, 2007. During the 1980s, Mallinckrodt and Monsanto Corporations had awarded $27.3 million in grants to Washington University researchers to work on antibodies and other biotechnology areas. Simpson, *Medical Metropolis*, 4, determines that "biotechnology played an essential role in rebranding . . . [Pittsburgh and Houston] as . . . global center[s] of innovation." Finally, Bartow Elmore, "Ecological Imperialism Revisited: Genetic Engineering and Presidential Foreign Assistance Policy, 1980–2015," in *The President and American Capitalism since 1945*, ed. Mark H. Rose and Roger Biles (Gainesville: University Press of Florida, 2017), 306–28, emphasizes the fierce and persistent efforts of U.S. presidents to enhance the standing, reach, and intellectual property rights of U.S. biotechnology firms.

23. Tom Stein, "Biotechs Gain VC Respectability," *Investment Dealers' Digest*, October 26, 2001, (quotation); Simpson, *Medical Metropolis*, 101; Daniel J. Kevles, "*Diamond v. Chakrabarty* and Beyond: The Political Economy of Patenting Life," in *Private Science: Biotechnology and the Rise of the Molecular Sciences*, ed. Arnold Thackray (Philadelphia: University of Pennsylvania Press, 1998), 65–79.

24. John Dubinsky, "Mark Twain Bancshares Records," *St. Louis Post-Dispatch*, January 11, 1976; Jon Sawyer, "Mark Twain Banc. Outlook Is Rosy," *St. Louis Post-Dispatch*, April 17, 1980; Patricia Miller, "Barnes Leans on Knight to Negotiate Changes," *St. Louis Business Journal*, January 25, 1993, including quotation; Laurie Sybert, "$12 Million Jump-Starts Biotech Corridor," *St. Louis Business Journal*, October 24, 2003; Sharoff, "Keeping the Fruits of Research Close." Cortex was a nonprofit venture among Washington University School of Medicine, St. Louis University, Barnes-Jewish Hospital, the University of Missouri–St. Louis, and the Missouri Botanical Garden.

25. Linda Tucci, "Biotech Corridor Gets Promise of a New Name and Money," *St. Louis Post-Dispatch*, November 5, 2002; Rachel Melcer, "The Coasts Are Calling as Bio-

tech Startups Scramble for Wet Lab Space," *St. Louis Post-Dispatch,* October 28, 2002; O'Mara, *Cities of Knowledge,* 63, 71–75.

26. Matthew Franck, "Blunt Gives Up Life Sciences Funding," *St. Louis Post-Dispatch,* March 9, 2007; Rachel Melcer, "Biotech Leaders Are Back to Square One," *St. Louis Post-Dispatch,* March 10, 2007.

27. Jacob Barker, "Microsoft Will Anchor New Cortex Tech Hub," *St. Louis Post-Dispatch,* March 9, 2017; Mary Mack, "Cortex Looks Ahead: Cortex Special Feature, Chapter 4, 2017 and Beyond," *Entrepreneur Quarterly,* c. 2017, https://eqstl.com/cortex -looks-ahead-cortex-special-feature-chapter-4-2017-beyond/; Simpson, *Medical Metropolis,* 118–19, identifies 5,700 persons employed in Houston's biotechnology firms.

28. Barker, "Microsoft Will Anchor"; Mack, "Cortex Looks Ahead"; historian Joseph Heathcott, email to the authors, February 27, 2020, in authors' possession.

29. "Chicago's Most Influential Technology Players," *Crain's Chicago Business,* November 3, 1997; Gary Ruderman, "A High-Tech Mother Hen," *Chicago Tribune,* July 30, 2001. Economist Enrico Moretti, in *The New Geography of Jobs* (Boston: Mariner, 2012), 178–203, writes about the failure of cities such as Philadelphia, Chicago, Cleveland, and St. Louis to emerge as important biotechnology clusters, despite sizable investments and the presence of substantial, scientifically oriented universities..

30. Andrew Wang, "District on a Debt March," *Crain's Chicago Business,* February 13, 2012; "What's Stifling Chicago Biotech," *Crain's Chicago Business,* July 23, 2018; Jay Kozlarz, "Illinois Medical District Unveils Big Plans for the Future," *Curbed Chicago,* April 3, 2019, https://chicago.curbed.com/2019/4/3/18293798/illinois-medical-district -redevelopment-mixed-use-innovation. During the decades after 2000, the University of Pennsylvania's hospital leaders were equally avid about biotechnology's promise. Starting around 2010, they sought to devise ways to make the transfer of biotechnological ideas from laboratory to patients more efficient and more likely to take place. They labeled the new process translational medicine. Elazar R. Edelman and Garrett A. FitzGerald, in "A Decade of Science Translational Medicine," *Science Translational Medicine* 11, no. 489 (April 24, 2019), explain the deliberate process by which translational medicine researchers worked at the University of Pennsylvania and elsewhere. Penn's Institute for Translational Medicine and Therapeutics included the award of fellowships, advanced degrees, and certification programs to guide younger researchers into translational medicine.

31. "Barnes-Jewish Hospital Begins Renovations on Emergency Department Waiting Area," press release, August 5, 2014, https://www.barnesjewish.org/Newsroom/In-the -News/ArtMID/1493/ArticleID/164/Barnes-Jewish-Hospital-begins-renovations-on -emergency-department-waiting-area; Ellen Futterman, "Inquiries about AIDS Quadruple Here," *St. Louis Post-Dispatch,* August 2, 1985; David Greising, "When Will Chicago's Violence Evoke True Citywide Outrage?" *Chicago Tribune,* August 10, 2018; Stephanie Stahl, "Coronavirus Latest: Temple University Hospital Treating Highest Number of Covid-19 Patients in Region," video, April 9, 2020, https://philadelphia.cbslo cal.com/2020/04/09/coronavirus-latest-temple-university-hospital-treating-highest -number-of-covid-19-patients/; Alan Yu, "A COVID-19 Snapshot: How the Philadelphia Region's Hospitals Are Managing," April 21, 2020, https://whyy.org/articles/a-covid-19 -snapshot-how-the-philadelphia-regions-hospitals-are-managing/; Hiroko Tabuchi, "In the Shadows of America's Smokestacks, Virus Is One More Deadly Risk," *New York Times,* May 17, 2020; Southeastern Pennsylvania Household Health Survey, "2020 Online Report Card Adults 18+," http://chdb.org (accessed 2020); James Bennett, "Fulfilling the Promise of Our Cities," *New York Times,* May 11, 2020; Yaryna Serkez, "Who Is Most

Likely to Die from the Coronavirus?" *New York Times*, June 4, 2020; Elizabeth L. Tung, Kathleen A. Cagney, Monica E. Peek, and Marshal H. Chin, "Spatial Context and Health Inequity: Reconfiguring Race, Place, and Poverty," *Journal of Urban Health* 94, no 94 (November 2017): 757–63; Khiara M. Bridges, "Race, Pregnancy, and the Opioid Epidemic: White Privilege and the Criminalization of Opioid Use during Pregnancy," *Harvard Law Review* 133, no. 3 (January 2020): 770–851. Historian Andrew Hurley, in "Floods, Rats, and Toxic Waste: Allocating Environmental Hazards since World War II," in *Common Fields: An Environmental History of St. Louis*, ed. Andrew Hurley (St. Louis, MO: Missouri Historical Society, 1997), finds that "class and race have been imprinted on the allocation of environmental amenities and disamenities in St. Louis, especially in the years since World War II" (243). David Farber, *Crack: Rock Cocaine, Street Capitalism, and the Decade of Greed* (New York: Cambridge University Press, 2019), 1–9, links the downtown and suburban global capitalism of the 1980s and later to diminished economic opportunities for young African American men and women residing in the nation's cities. Finally, historian Eric C. Schneider, in *The Ecology of Homicide: Race, Place, and Space in Postwar Philadelphia* (Philadelphia: University of Pennsylvania Press, 2020), identifies neighborhoods "of violence, bound in place over time" (xxi).

32. "Ask any Chicagoan, and he or she will have at least a general sense of where those places are," observes political scientist Joel Rast, in *The Origins of the Dual City: Housing, Race, and Redevelopment in Twentieth-Century Chicago* (Chicago: University of Chicago Press, 2019), 31.

33. A. K. Sandoval-Strausz, *Barrio America: How Latino Immigrants Saved the American City* (New York: Basic Books, 2019), 101–2, 115–17, 127–28, 180–82.

34. U.S. Bureau of Labor Statistics, "Labor Force Statistics from the Current Population Survey," 2019, https://www.bls.gov/cps/cpsaat18.htm; "Occupational Employment and Wages in Cleveland-Elyria—May 2019," https://www.bls.gov/regions/midwest/news -release/occupationalemploymentandwages_cleveland.htm; Winant, *Next Shift*, 230, 256. Historian Christy Chapin kindly directed our attention to the way hospital employment reproduces the nation's racialized economy.

35. University of Pennsylvania, "Facts," 2019, https://www.upenn.edu/about/facts (accessed 2020); Ehlenz et al., *Power of Eds and Meds*; Norman Krumholz, "Cleveland's Neighborhoods in Black and White, 2000–2914," in *Continuity and Change: Legacy Cities amid Decline and Revival*, ed. J. Rosie Tighe and Stephanie Ryberg-Webster (Pittsburgh, PA: University of Pittsburgh Press, 2019), 117; LaDale C. Winling, *Building the Ivory Tower: Universities and Metropolitan Development in the Twentieth Century* (Philadelphia: University of Pennsylvania Press, 2017); Winant, *Next Shift*, 6. From 1900 up to the present day, determines Simpson, in *Medical Metropolis*, hospitals "gradually, but decisively, changed" (10) from local assets to major centers of economic activity. The precise relationship between the "eds" and "meds" side of the equation requires specification on a case-by-case basis.

36. Alan Mallach, *The Divided City: Poverty and Prosperity in Urban America* (Washington, DC: Island Press, 2018), 51, 56, 59.

37. Jared N. Day, "Health Care and Urban Revitalization: A Historical Overview," *Journal of Urban History* 42, no. 2 (March 2016): 247–58, reports that "scholars and policymakers now clearly identify health care as an industry comparable with steel, oil, gas, and the railroads in the nineteenth century" (247). The comparison, at first startling, alerts us to an important difference between members of the two groups. Unlike the industrial executives of the late nineteenth century, successful hospital administrators like Danforth and Dubinsky cultivated a deep network of local, state, and federal officials

alongside heads of insurance firms and employees' unions. Along those lines, Catherine A. Conner, "'The University That Ate Birmingham': The Healthcare Industry, Urban Development, and Neoliberalism," *Journal of Urban History* 42, no. 2 (March 1, 2016): 284–305, carefully delineates the racial, class, legal, and ideological factors that guided expansion plans at the University of Alabama at Birmingham's medical campus.

## CHAPTER 10

1. Melvin G. Holli, ed., *Detroit* (New York: Franklin Watts, 1976), 196–209.

2. June Manning Thomas, *Redevelopment and Race: Planning a Finer City in Postwar Detroit* (Baltimore, MD: Johns Hopkins University Press, 1997). Also see Daniel J. Clark, *Disruption in Detroit: Autoworkers and the Elusive Postwar Boom* (Urbana: University of Illinois Press, 2018).

3. George Galster, *Driving Detroit: The Quest for Respect in the Motor City* (Philadelphia: University of Pennsylvania Press, 2012).

4. Steven Yaccino, "Lessons for Detroit in a City's Takeover," *New York Times*, March 14, 2013; *Crain's Detroit Business*, March 17, 2013; Nathan Bomey, *Detroit Resurrected: To Bankruptcy and Back* (New York: W. W. Norton, 2016), 1–6, 18–29; email interview with John Gallagher, April 16, 2018. Also see Kimberly Kinder, *DIY Detroit: Making Do in a City without Services* (Minneapolis: University of Minnesota Press, 2016).

5. *Crain's Detroit Business*, October 9, 2014; John Gallagher, "One Downtown, Two Empires," *Detroit Free Press*, July 27, 2014. Conrad Kickert, in *Dream City: Creation, Destruction, and Reinvention in Downtown Detroit* (Cambridge, MA: MIT Press, 2019), discusses Ilitch in chapter 11 and Gilbert in chapter 13.

6. John Gallagher, "Champion for Detroit," *Detroit Free Press*, February 11, 2017; Jonathan Soble, "Trouble Turning a Corner," *New York Times*, February 10, 2017.

7. Eric J. Hill and John Gallagher, *AIA Detroit: The American Institute of Architects Guide to Detroit Architecture* (Detroit, MI: Wayne State University Press, 2002), 62; *Crain's Detroit Business*, February 19, 2017.

8. Gallagher, "Champion for Detroit." Starting in the 1950s, business leaders in Chicago, including Arthur Rubloff and Philip M. Klutznick, launched urban redevelopment projects. Like Ilitch and Gilbert, Rubloff and Klutznick brought solid political connections to their real-estate developments. Unlike Ilitch and Gilbert, Rubloff and Klutznick also directed construction of apartments and shopping centers beyond the city's famous Loop and out into the suburbs.

9. Michael Betzold and Ethan Casey, *Queen of Diamonds: The Tiger Stadium Story* (West Bloomfield, MI: Altwerger and Mandel, 1992), 137; Valerie Basheda, "Archer Critic Young Backs Mayor on Tiger Stadium," *Detroit Free Press*, March 17, 1996.

10. *Detroit Free Press*, May 4, 1994; Betzold and Casey, *Queen of Diamonds*, 127 (quotation); Thomas, *Redevelopment and Race*, 157–61, 169–71; Heather Ann Thompson, *Whose Detroit? Politics, Labor, and Race in a Modern American City* (Ithaca, NY: Cornell University Press, 2001), 205. Also see Wilbur C. Rich, *Coleman Young and Detroit Politics: From Social Activist to Power Broker* (Detroit, MI: Wayne State University Press, 1989); and Coleman Young, *Hard Stuff: The Autobiography of Coleman Young* (New York: Viking, 1994).

11. Basheda, "Archer Critic Young Backs Mayor on Tiger Stadium," (quotation); John Gallagher, "Welcome to Detroit's New Playground," September 5, 2017; *Crain's Detroit Business*, February 19, 2017; Dan Austin, "Madison-Lenox Hotel," Historic Detroit, http://historicdetroit.org/building/madison-lenox-hotel (accessed April 10, 2018).

12. Austin, "Madison-Lenox Hotel."

13. Gallagher, "Champion for Detroit;" Robyn Meridith, "Court Removes an Obstacle to a New Stadium in Detroit," *New York Times*, July 6, 1996; Nichole Christian, "Detroit Sees Park as Star Player in Redevelopment," *New York Times*, April 11, 2000 (quotation).

14. Basheda, "Archer Critic Young Backs Mayor on Tiger Stadium;" Tina Lam, "Ilitches Give Reins to a Daughter, Son," *Detroit Free Press*, June 20, 2000; Christian, "Detroit Sees Park as Star Player in Redevelopment."

15. Mike Ozanian, "Chris Ilitch Dishes on Detroit's Downtown Development Project," *Forbes*, October 2, 2014, http://www.forbes.com/sites/mikeozanian/2014/10/02/chris-ilitch-dishes-on-detroits-downtown-development-project; Gallagher, "Welcome to Detroit's New Playground;" Thomas, *Redevelopment and Race*, 157 (first quotation); *Crain's Detroit Business*, October 20, 2014 (second quotation).

16. *Crain's Detroit Business*, July 20, 2014 (quotations); Ozanian, "Chris Ilitch Dishes."

17. Patrick Rishe, "District Detroit: The Most Compact Sports District in America Is Revitalizing Downtown Detroit," *Forbes*, November 24, 2016, http://www.forbes.com/sites/prishe/2016/11/24/district-detroit-the-most-compact-sports-district-in-america-is-revitalizing-downtown-detroit; Mitch Albom, "Pistons Go Back Where the Team Belongs in Detroit," *Detroit Free Press*, November 24, 2016.

18. Gallagher, "Welcome to Detroit's New Playground;" *Crain's Detroit Business*, November 1, 2015.

19. Joann Muller, "Private Funding of Detroit Rail Project Is a Gift Horse the Feds Can't Ignore," *Forbes*, May 30, 2012, forbes.com/sites/joannmuller/2012/05/30/private-funding-of-detroit-rail-project-is-a-gift-horse-the-feds-cant-ignore/?sh=44245e27344e; Frank Witsil, "Creating Vibrant Core for Detroit," *Detroit Free Press*, September 3, 2017.

20. John Gallagher, "How Hot Is Downtown Detroit's Housing Market?" October 3, 2016; Mitch Albom, "Saying Goodbye to a Friend of the Fans," *Detroit Free Press*, February 12, 2017.

21. "Mike Ilitch," *Your Dictionary*, accessed January 21, 2022, http://biography.yourdictionary.com/mike-ilitch; Gallagher, "Champion for Detroit" (quotation).

22. "Forbes 400: Daniel Gilbert," *Forbes*, last updated February 1, 2022, http://www.forbes.com/profile/daniel-gilbert; Steven Yaccino, "Detroit's Leaders Carry On, But Know Who's Really in Charge," *New York Times*, April 13, 2013; Tim Alberta, "Is Dan Gilbert Detroit's New Superhero?" *Atlantic*, February 27, 2014, https://www.theatlantic.com/business/archive/2014/02/is-dan-gilbert-detroits-new-superhero/425742/. Gilbert sold mortgages to bankers, who in turn packaged them into mortgage-backed securities. He also relied on bankers' lines of credit to finance his mortgage business, which kept his investment to a minimum. Gilbert entered the business in 1995 and was immediately able to write mortgages nationwide. (Up to 1994, in contrast, federal regulations had limited commercial bankers' ability to write mortgages outside their home state.) For a description of Gilbert's finance methods, see Joann Muller, "Billionaire Dan Gilbert's Advice for Creating Wealth: Avoid Debt and Spreadsheets," *Forbes*, October 3, 2014, https://www.forbes.com/sites/joannmuller/2014/10/03/billionaire-dan-gilberts-advice-for-creating-wealth-avoid-debt-and-spreadsheets/#144f37a53b9d.

23. John Gallagher, "Dan Gilbert: The Next Mr. Detroit?" *Detroit Free Press*, June 30, 2011, John Gallagher, "Gilbert Quickens Downtown Growth," *Detroit Free Press*, September 20, 2011 (first quotation); Yaccino, "Detroit's Leaders Carry On, But Know Who's Really in Charge" (second quotation).

24. *Crain's Detroit Business*, October 19, 2014; John Gallagher, "From the Burbs to the Big City," *Detroit Free Press*, October 11, 2011; Joann Muller, "Gilbertville: A Billionaire's

Drive to Rebuild the Motor City," *Forbes*, September 29, 2014, https://www.forbes.com /sites/joannmuller/2014/09/29/gilbertville-a-billionaires-drive-to-rebuild-the-motor-city.

25. John Gallagher, "More Projects, More Jobs, and More Hope as the City Grows" *Detroit Free Press*, December 14, 2016; David Segal, "Motor City Missionary Against Tall Odds," *New York Times*, April 14, 2013 (quotation); Alberta, "Is Dan Gilbert Detroit's New Superhero?"

26. *Crain's Detroit Business*, March 12, 2012 (quotation); Gallagher, "Gilbert Quickens Downtown Growth;" Bedrock Real Estate Services, "Bedrock Properties," accessed April 16, 2018, http://www.bedrockmgt.com/real-estate; Mark Binelli, *Detroit City Is the Place to Be: The Afterlife of an American Metropolis* (New York: Metropolitan, 2012), 295; *Detroit Free Press*, April 29, 2016. For the growth of Silicon Valley and the subsequent search among state and local leaders to recreate that success, see Margaret Pugh O'Mara, *Cities of Knowledge: Cold War Science and the Search for the Next Silicon Valley* (Princeton, NJ: Princeton University Press, 2005).

27. Yaccino, "Detroit's Leaders Carry On, But Know Who's Really in Charge" (first quotation); John Gallagher, "Name for New Arena Stays in the Family," *Detroit Free Press*, April 29, 2016 (second quotation); *Wall Street Journal*, November 1, 2014; *Detroit Free Press*, January 17, 2013, June 12, 2016.

28. Gallagher, "Dan Gilbert;" John Gallagher, "What Will Rise on Hudson's Old Site Becoming Clearer," *Detroit Free Press*, February 22, 2017; *Crain's Detroit Business*, December 14, 2017 (quotation), February 26, 2018, May 21, 2018.

29. Jon C. Teaford, *Cities of the Heartland: The Rise and Fall of the Industrial Midwest* (Bloomington: Indiana University Press, 1993), 222 (first quotation); *Crain's Detroit Business*, December 14, 2017 (second quotation); Galster, *Driving Detroit*, 225.

30. *Crain's Detroit Business*, December 14, 2017; Gallagher, "What Will Rise on Hudson's Old Site Becoming Clearer."

31. Frank Witsil, "4 Projects to Bring 24K Jobs," *Detroit Free Press*, September 21, 2017.

32. *Crain's Detroit Business*, January 1, 2016, January 7, 2018; Susan Tempor, "Could the Amazon HQ2 Talk a Broader Vision for Detroit?" *Detroit Free Press*, October 15, 2017.

33. *New York Times*, January 18, 2018; *Detroit Free Press*, January 18, 2018; Robin Runyan, "Dan Gilbert Addresses 'Elephant in the Room' in Failed Amazon HQ2 Bid," *Curbed Detroit*, January 24, 2018, http://detroit.curbed.com/2018/1/24/16928978/dan -gilbert-amazon-hq2-bid.

34. Runyan, "Dan Gilbert Addresses 'Elephant in the Room'" (first quotation); John Gallagher, "Dan, It Wasn't Just City's Bad Rep," *Detroit Free Press*, January 28, 2018 (second quotation).

35. Gallagher, "Dan, It Wasn't Just City's Bad Rep." Nor did Ilitch and Gilbert's downtown-centered prosperity extend north to long-impaired cities like Flint. See, for example, Andrew R. Highsmith, *Demolition Means Progress: Flint, Michigan, and the Fate of the American Metropolis* (Chicago: University of Chicago Press, 2015).

36. Gallagher, "Dan Gilbert"; John Gallagher, "What's Best for Detroiters?" *Detroit Free Press*, August 7, 2016; JC Reindl, "181 New Condos, Apartments on Way to Midtown," *Detroit Free Press*, December 3, 2016; Gallagher, "Dan, It Wasn't Just City's Bad Rep." For evidence that members of the city's planning department had acquiesced to Ilitch and Gilbert's downtown rehabilitation and had turned their attention to outlying areas, see Gregor Macdonald, "Planning for the Other Detroit," *Next City*, May 21, 2018, https://nextcity.org/features/view/planning-for-the-other-detroit?utm_source=Next+ City+Newsletter&utm_campaign=34175ca563-Issue_286&utm_medium=email&utm _term=0_fcee5bf7a0-34175ca563-43866161.

37. *Detroit Free Press*, October 4, 2017 (first quotation); Zack Guzman, "Billionaire Dan Gilbert's Mission to Rebuild Detroit as a Hub of 'Muscles and Brains,'" *CNBC*, October 17, 2016, https://www.cnbc.com/2016/10/17/billionaire-dan-gilberts-mission-to-rebuild-detroit-as-a-hub-of-muscles-and-brains.html; Alberta, "Is Dan Gilbert Detroit's New Superhero?"; *New York Times*, April 14, 2014 (second quotation), July 13, 2014. Also see Sam Williams, *The CEO as Urban Statesman* (Macon, GA: Mercer University Press, 2014), for a defense of the Gilbert-Ilitch approach.

38. Segal, "Motor City Missionary Against Tall Odds" (first quotation); Gallagher, "Dan Gilbert" (second quotation).

39. *Crain's Detroit Business*, September 22, 2014; Gallagher, "Dan Gilbert"; Alberta, "Is Dan Gilbert Detroit's New Superhero?" (quotations). See Matthew Cullen, Kevyn Orr, Rip Rapson, and Jennifer Bradley, "Cross-Sector Leadership in Detroit," *Stanford Social Innovation Review*, vol. 15, no. 1 (Winter 2017): 18, in which Cullen, one of Gilbert's senior executives, reports that "one component [of the firm's work] involved us stepping into roles government would typically play: land planning, tenant recruitment, blight abatement, and place-making work."

40. Gallagher, "One Downtown, Two Empires" (both quotations).

41. Gallagher, "Dan Gilbert" (quotes); email interview with John Gallagher.

42. For the social and economic composition of Detroit's business and political leadership, see Daniel Amsterdam, *Roaring Metropolis: Businessmen's Campaign for a Civic Welfare State* (Philadelphia: University of Pennsylvania Press, 2016); and Donald F. Davis, *Conspicuous Production: Automobiles and Elites in Detroit, 1899–1933* (Philadelphia: Temple University Press, 1988). On the outward location of automobile factories and other businesses, see Heather Barrow, "'The American Disease of Growth': Henry Ford and the Metropolitanization of Detroit, 1920–1940," in *Manufacturing Suburbs: Building Work and Home on the Metropolitan Fringe*, ed. Robert Lewis (Philadelphia: Temple University Press, 2004), 200–220.

43. Historians of urban consumption have produced important publications focused on the growing popularity of shopping, travel, and leisure activities among middle-income Americans, including Lizabeth Cohen, *A Consumers' Republic: The Politics of Mass Consumption in Postwar America* (New York: Vintage, 2003); Bethany Moreton, *To Serve God and Wal-Mart: The Making of Christian Free Enterprise* (Cambridge, MA: Harvard University Press, 2009); Lawrence B. Glickman, *Buying Power: A History of Consumer Activism in America* (Chicago: University of Chicago Press, 2009); Aaron Cowan, *A Nice Place to Visit: Tourism and Urban Revitalization in the Postwar Rustbelt* (Philadelphia: Temple University Press, 2016); and Hal Rothman, *Devil's Bargains: Tourism in the Twentieth Century American West* (Lawrence: University Press of Kansas, 1998). On the role of the president of the United States in promoting a consumer-oriented nation, see Brian Balogh, "Consumer in Chief: Presidential Leadership in America's 'Consumer Republic,'" in *The President and American Capitalism since 1945*, ed. Mark H. Rose and Roger Biles (Gainesville: University Press of Florida, 2017), 21–35.

44. Historians R. Daniel Wadhwani and Christina Lubinski, in "Reinventing Entrepreneurial History," *Business History Review* 91, no. 4 (Winter 2017): 768, determine that "entrepreneurship has become a central language—perhaps the central language—of contemporary capitalism and crucial to how economic actors understand business." Historian Thomas K. McCraw, in *Prophet of Innovation: Joseph Schumpeter and Creative Destruction* (Cambridge, MA: Belknap, 2007), finds that economist Joseph Schumpeter's use of terms like *entrepreneur* "have become so ubiquitous and ingrained that we cannot

separate his foundational thoughts from our own" (ix). For examples of the regular invocation of the term among contemporary Detroit leaders to describe Michael Ilitch and Daniel Gilbert, see, for example Gary Peters, "Remembering Michael "Mike" Ilitch," Congressional Record-Senate, February 14, 2017, S1159-S-1160; "Detroit Entrepreneurs Mike and Marian Ilitch Gift $40 Million plus Use of Land to Wayne State University to Build New Business School in Detroit," *PR Newswire US, Regional Business News*, October 30, 2015, "Entrepreneurship's Greatest Challenge: Rebuild Detroit," *Inc* 35, no. 5 (June 2013): 124; and also Tom Walsh, "Entrepreneurs Ready to Get City's Economy Rolling," *Detroit Free Press*, July 31, 2008, for a report on Gilbert's "boot camp" for urban entrepreneurs who were in turn supposed to "start a revolution of grass-roots economic growth in the city."

45. Roger Biles, "Harold Washington and the Planning Tradition in Chicago," *Journal of Planning History*, vol. 17, no. 2 (May 2018): 79–96; Lizabeth Cohen, *Saving America's Cities: Ed Logue and the Struggle to Renew Urban America in the Suburban Age* (New York: Farrar, Straus and Giroux, 2019); Christopher Klemek, *The Transatlantic Collapse of Urban Renewal: Postwar Urbanism from New York to Berlin* (Chicago: University of Chicago Press, 2011); Tracy Neumann, *Remaking the Rust Belt: The Postindustrial Transformation of North America* (Philadelphia: University of Pennsylvania Press, 2016); Gregory L. Heller, *Ed Bacon: Planning, Politics, and the Building of Modern Philadelphia* (Philadelphia: University of Pennsylvania Press, 2013); Francesca Russello Ammon, *Bulldozer: Demolition and Clearance in the Postwar Landscape* (New Haven, CT: Yale University Press, 2016); Mark H. Rose and Raymond A. Mohl, *Interstate: Highway Politics and Policy since 1939*, 3rd ed., rev. (Knoxville: University of Tennessee Press, 2012). And for a similar focus on expressway construction and the concurrent demolition of downtown buildings even among small-city leaders, see David Schuyler, *A City Transformed: Redevelopment, Race, and Suburbanization in Lancaster, Pennsylvania, 1940–1980* (University Park: Pennsylvania State University Press, 2002). "Policy choices," historian Kim Phillips-Fein reminds us, reside at the center of urban physical, financial, and social change (*Fear City: New York's Fiscal Crisis and the Rise of Austerity Politics* [New York: Metropolitan, 2017], 316).

46. Heywood T. Sanders, *Convention Center Follies: Politics, Power, and Public Investment in American Cities* (Philadelphia: University of Pennsylvania Press, 2014), explains the process by which consultants sold new and expanded convention centers by promising additional downtown business. On the financial plight of Detroit's Cobo Center in 2017, including the center's racialized association with Mayor Albert E. Cobo's massive highway and other renewal programs between 1950 and 1957, see *Crain's Detroit Business*, August 28, 2017. For Cobo's determination to push expressways through downtown and into African American neighborhoods, see Roger Biles, "Expressways before the Interstates: The Case of Detroit, 1945–1956," *Journal of Urban History*, vol. 40, no. 5 (September 2014): 843–54, and Eric Avila and Mark H. Rose, "Race, Culture, Politics, and Urban Renewal," *Journal of Urban History*, vol. 35, no. 3 (March 2009): 335–47. On the spatial turn among urban historians, see Michael B. Katz, "From Urban as Site to Urban as Place: Reflections on (Almost) a Half-Century of U.S. Urban History," *Journal of Urban History*, vol. 41, no. 4 (July 2015): 560–66; Raymond A. Mohl, "Making the Second Ghetto in Metropolitan Miami, 1940–1960," *Journal of Urban History* 21, no. 3 (March 1995): 395–427; Timothy J. Gilfoyle, "Michael Katz on Place and Space in Urban History," *Journal of Urban History* 41, no. 4 (July 2015): 572–84; Sharony Green, "Tracing Black Racial and Spatial Politics in South Florida via Memory," *Journal of Urban His-*

*tory*, 44, no. 6 (November 2018): 1176–1196; and N. D. B. Connolly, *A World More Concrete: Real Estate and the Remaking of Jim Crow South Florida* (Chicago: University of Chicago Press, 2014).

47. Andrew R. Highsmith, "Beyond Corporate Abandonment: General Motors and the Politics of Metropolitan Capitalism in Flint, Michigan," *Journal of Urban History*, vol. 40, no. 1 (January 2014): 31–33; Roger Biles, Raymond A. Mohl, and Mark H. Rose, "Revisiting the Urban Interstate: Politics, Policy, and Culture since World War II," *Journal of Urban History* 40, no. 5 (September 2014): 827–28. For the planned decentralization of Detroit's congested near-downtown areas during the interwar years, see Amsterdam, *Roaring Metropolis*, 57. "Since the 1960s," determine planners Brent D. Ryan and Daniel Campo in "Autopia's End: The Decline and Fall of Detroit's Automotive Manufacturing Landscape," *Journal of Planning History* 12, no. 2 (May 2013): 4, "infrastructure development and economic decline have physically fragmented . . . [Detroit], transforming it into a patchwork of freeways, superblocks, and suburban-type housing enclaves." On airport development and changes in New York City's geography, see Nicholas Dagen Bloom, *The Metropolitan Airport: JFK International and Modern New York* (Philadelphia: University of Pennsylvania Press, 2015). Wendell E. Pritchett, "Which Urban Crisis? Regionalism, Race, and Urban Policy, 1960–1974," *Journal of Urban History* 34, no. 2 (January 2008): 266–86, provides a valuable overview of fragmented cities and ideas about regional government in an era of unprecedented sprawl. For urban business executives and successful adaptations to the local political economy in earlier eras, see Eric J. Morser, *Hinterland Dreams: The Political Economy of a Midwestern City* (Philadelphia: University of Pennsylvania Press, 2011); and Joshua A. T. Salzmann, *Liquid Capital: Making the Chicago Waterfront* (Philadelphia: University of Pennsylvania Press, 2017).

# Index

Dilworth, Richardson K. *(continued)*
mayor, 76–77; public housing and, 87;
Rafsky and, 79–82; Society Hill renewal,
80–83, 87, 216; stadium proposal and,
78; urban renewal and, 77, 88; on "white
noose" around Center City, 76–77,
275n11
Dock Street Market (Philadelphia), 79–80
Dodge, Horace, 20
Dodge, John, 20
Dodge Main, 157
Doherty, Robert E., 6–7
Douglas, Paul, 168
Downie, Robert C., 10
*Downtown Cleveland 1975*, 102–103
Downtown Cleveland Corporation, 123
downtown renewal: automobile access and,
28, 57, 90, 92, 95–96, 105–106; business
leaders and, xv–xvi, 47, 267n35, 269n12;
capital accessibility and, 298n6; central
business districts and, 11, 13–16, 58,
92–93, 163; city planning and, 254–255,
313n45, 314n47; convention center
construction and, 46–47, 62–63, 255,
313n46; culture of clearance in, xiv,
265n23, 313n45; department stores and,
30, 45–46, 60, 269n13; entrepreneurship
and, 253–256, 313n44; federal programs
for, 91, 130, 144–145; highway
construction and, 27–28, 91–97, 108,
313n45; hospital growth and, 214–215,
303n1; impact on African Americans,
47, 116, 163, 230–231; impact on basic
services, xii, xv, 231; impact on health
care, 230–231; leisure activities and,
112, 115, 130–133, 138–139, 283n2;
marginalization of poor in, 28, 163, 232,
261n51; as metropolitan project, 266n24;
neighborhood activists and, 163–164;
Pittsburgh model for, 3, 18; postwar
planning and, 11–12, 27–28; professional
sports and, 36, 40–41; public-private
alliances and, 15–16, 32–33, 91, 111–112,
163, 296n38; racial anxiety and, 51,
112; racial politics and, xiv–xv, 7, 13,
28, 47; reduced federal aid for, 111, 142,
178, 202, 300n17; stadium construction
and, 46–47, 114, 132, 138–139, 145–148;
transportation and, 91–97; universities
and hospitals in, 112, 116–117. *See also*
Pittsburgh Renaissance; urban renewal

Dubinsky, John P., 227–229, 308n37
Duggan, Michael E., 247–248
Duncan, Arne, 208
Durant, William C., 253–254
Durham, Israel, 19
Dwight D. Eisenhower Expressway, 106

East Garfield Park (Chicago), 172–173
Eaton Corporation, 129
Edsel B. Ford Expressway, 93–95, 98
Edwards, George, 94–95
Eisenhower, Dwight D., 80, 85
Emanuel, Rahm, 68, 183, 190, 214
Engler, John M., 155, 238
Equitable Life Assurance Society of the
United States, 11–12
Erie Canal, 17, 19–21
Erieview (Cleveland), 104, 120, 122
Evergreen Plaza Shopping Center
(Chicago), xii, 60

Famous-Barr, 30, 32, 45–46, 262n3
Farr, Newton C., 64, 264n8
Farris, Charles L., 40–41, 44, 46–48,
266n24, 266n25
Federal-Aid Highway Act of 1944, 91, 93
Federal-Aid Highway Act of 1950, 96
Federal-Aid Highway Act of 1956, 91
Federal Reserve Bank of Cleveland, 128
Feighan, Edward F., 124
Fein, Michael R., 273n34
Ferguson, Homer S., 96
Ferman, Barbara, 10, 48, 278n35, 295n8
Fernandez, Lilia, 65
Fetzer, John E., 147–148
Field Museum, 198
First Boston Corporation, 4
First National Bank of Chicago, 53
Fisher, Max, 148, 177
Flaherty, Peter F., 112
Flood, Curt, 43–44
Florida, Richard L., 115
Food Distribution Center (South
Philadelphia), 79–80
Forbes, George, 138
Ford, Gerald R., 145
Ford, Henry, 20, 253–254
Ford, Henry, II, 127, 142, 149, 150f, 177,
292n17
Ford, William Clay, 239
Ford Field, 239, 241

Nader, Ralph, 158
National Association for Housing and
Redevelopment Officials, 101
National Association for the Advancement
of Colored People (NAACP), 39, 88, 94,
99, 265n23
National City Bank, 129
National Institutes of Health, 226–227
National Negro Labor Council, 143
National Stockyards (St. Louis), 25
National Urban League, 94
Navy Pier, 198–199, 201
Near West Side Planning Board (NWSPB),
166–167
neighborhood activists: block clubs and,
174; city hall and, 294n1; direct action
tactics, 168–170; divisions among, 295n8;
grassroots opposition and, 163–164,
168, 171, 182, 190; HHCG and, 167–170;
opposition to Harrison-Halsted area
clearances, 166–169; organization of
low-income residents, 294n8; powerful
opposition to, 182–184; protection of
working-class areas, 173–174, 177–181;
residential services and, 177; state and
federal lawsuits, 170–171
Neumann, Tracy, 189, 259n24, 263n7,
269n9
New Detroit, Inc., 127, 144, 149
Nichols, John, 143
Nixon, Richard M., 111, 123
No Child Left Behind Act, 208
North American International Auto
Show, 147
Northerly Island (Chicago), 200
North Loop (Chicago), 52f, 65–67, 197, 202
North Side Revitalization Program, 115
Northwestern Memorial Hospital, 221
NWSPB. See Near West Side Planning
Board (NWSPB)

Oakland-Hastings Freeway, 100
Obama, Barack, 45f, 208, 213, 295n12
Obama, Michelle, 213
Ohio Bell, 129
Ohio River, 11, 24
Old Philadelphia Development Corporation
(OPDC), 70, 82–85, 88
Olds, Ransom, 20
Olympia Development, 237–239, 241, 251
Olympia Stadium, 145

O'Mara, Margaret Pugh, 226
One Mellon Bank Center, 113
OPDC. See Old Philadelphia Development
Corporation (OPDC)
Owings, Nathaniel A., 56–58
Ozark Expressway, 107

Pacyga, Dominic A., 273n36, 301n21
Park Avenue Hotel, 237
Pattillo, Mary, 210
Peduto, William M., 189
Pei, I. M., 120
Pennsylvania College of Podiatric
Medicine, 217, 303n2
Pennsylvania Railroad (PRR): Center City
redevelopment and, 75–76; closure of,
232; Interstate Commerce Commission
and, 5; Mellon and, 4, 10, 15; objection
to smoke legislation, 10; Philadelphia
and, 17, 19; removal of, 75–76; stadium
proposal and, 77–78; territory and, 5,
257n3; union negotiations and, 5
Penrose, Boies, 19
Peoples First National Bank and Trust, 10
Perk, Ralph J., 120, 122–124
Pettibone, Holman D., 54, 58, 60–64,
68–69, 166, 264n8
Philadelphia: African American population
in, 72, 76, 274n4; antidowntown
coalitions, 88, 278n35; biotechnology
research and, 307n29, 307n30; blue-collar
conservatism in, 87; business leaders
and, 263n6, 275n7; central business
district and, 26; Chamber of Commerce,
81; Citizens Charter Committee, 72;
City Planning Commission, 79, 82;
class-based rhetoric and, 277n28;
colonial era in, 18–19, 260n30; economic
decline in, 190; government-funded
development in, 17; Great Depression
and, 26; highway construction in, 85–86,
106–107, 278n32; hospital growth and,
215–219, 303n1; industrial change
in, 16, 19; manufacturing and, 29,
71–72, 232, 274n4; maritime trade in,
18–19; Metropolitan Hospital, 84–85;
Pennsylvania Railroad and, 17, 19, 75;
political economy and, 17, 71; political
leadership in, 19; population shifts in,
17–18, 21; postwar renewal and, 278n36;
poverty in, 89; professional

Philadelphia (continued)
sports and, 107; public transit in, 107;
racial animosities and, 87–88, 218;
racial politics and, 28, 86–87, 278n35;
racial segregation in, 76–77, 275n12;
Redevelopment Authority, 79–83;
Republican Party in, 19–20, 81; smog
issue in, 18; textile factories in, 18–19,
260n30; white flight from, 76; white
racial hate rhetoric and, 76–77, 275n12.
See also Greater Philadelphia Movement
Philadelphia Development Authority, 217
Philadelphia downtown: automobile access
and, 106; business-political alliances and,
69, 77–78, 80, 83; Center City area, 74f,
75, 216–217; Chinatown urban renewal
and, 217, 303n2; deindustrialization of,
72, 274n4; Dock Street Market removal,
79–80; failure to lure middle-class, 190;
highway construction in, 28; hospital
growth and, 216–217; Independence
Hall redevelopment, 72, 79–80, 82, 84,
217; Market East, 84, 88; Penn Center
and, 75–77; Pittsburgh model and,
73; postwar renewal and, xiv, 27–28,
274n5; property values and, 73; racial
animosities and, 76–77, 275n12, 276n17;
Rafsky and, 70–71, 79–83; relocation of
African Americans, 76–77; Society Hill
renewal, 80–84, 87–88, 277n23, 278n32;
stadium proposal and, 77–78. See also
Center City (Philadelphia); Greater
Philadelphia Movement
Philadelphia Eagles, 78
Philadelphia General Hospital (PGH), 218
Philadelphia Industrial Development
Corporation (PIDC), 218–219
Philadelphia Phillies, 78
Phoenix, 49, 267n38
Pier and Exposition Authority, 199
Pirie, John T., 59–61, 63–64, 68
Pittsburgh: City Planning Commission,
11; Convention Bureau, 12;
deindustrialization of, 116, 189, 232,
283n2; distressed city program and, 188–
189; downtown redevelopment and, xiii–
xiv, 3, 113; as leader of urban renewal,
263n7; Lower Hill neighborhood, 13;
neighborhood improvements and, 112,
115; The Point neighborhood, 11–12;
political economy and, 49; poverty in, 33,

116, 188; racial inequalities in, 188–189;
smog issue in, 9–10; unemployment
in, 188; unions and, 21, 116; Urban
Renewal Authority, 12; wealthy as social
arbiters in, 5, 257n4. See also Pittsburgh
downtown; Pittsburgh Renaissance
Pittsburgh and West Virginia Railroad, 11
Pittsburgh Coal Company, 4
Pittsburgh Cultural Trust, 114
Pittsburgh Development Fund, 116
Pittsburgh downtown: casino development
in, 188; central business district
revitalization and, 113, 115–116;
convention center construction and, 114,
188; corporate boosters and, 187–188;
as creative class destination, 115–116;
cultural development and, 113–114; high-
rent units and, 15; physical restoration
of, 12; postwar renewal and, 6–7, 11–12,
27–29, 187–188; professional sports and,
114; removal of African Americans from,
3, 7–8, 13, 15, 56; removal of blighted
areas, 13–14; stadium construction and,
188; underground parking and, 12;
universities and hospitals in, 116; white
prosperity and, 3. See also Pittsburgh
Renaissance
Pittsburgh Partnership for Neighborhood
Development, 115
Pittsburgh Pirates, 114, 117
Pittsburgh Renaissance: ACCD and, 6–9,
11–15, 56, 263n7; air pollution campaign
and, 3, 6, 9–10; bipartisan cooperation
and, 15; business leaders and, 3, 6,
14–16, 56; culture of clearance in, 13–14,
259n22; emulation of, xiii, 3, 12–16, 28,
32, 56, 59, 263n7; Four Gateway Center,
12–14, 32; Golden Triangle and, 32,
59, 76, 188; Lawrence and, xiii–xiv, 8,
12–16; Mellon and, xiii–xiv, 4–8, 12–16,
51; policy tourism and, 14–16, 259n24;
professional sports and, 114; public-
private alliances and, 15–16, 32–33, 112–
113, 187–188; racial politics and, 116
Pittsburgh Renaissance II, 113–115, 117
Pittsburgh Steelers, 114
Plensa, Jaume, 201
Poletown Neighborhood Council, 158
political economy: business leaders and,
5–6, 255, 314n47; Chicago and, 17, 49, 63,
183; Cleveland and, 17; Detroit and, 17,

relations and, 119–120; tax incentives and, 129; tourism and leisure activities, 130–133, 142; UDAGs and, 129–130

Wabash Railroad, 11
Wadhwani, R. Daniel, 274n2, 312n44
Walter P. Chrysler Freeway, 100
Walt Whitman Bridge, 106
Wanamaker's, 75, 80
Washington, Harold: Black-Latino-white liberal alliance, 194–195; business-political alliances and, 183; convention center construction and, 198; downtown renewal ambivalence and, 68, 183, 273n35; neighborhood advocacy and, xii, 68, 183, 194; North Loop redevelopment and, 66–67, 202; TIFs and, 202
Washington University, 45, 222, 226, 306n22
Washington University Medical Center Redevelopment Corporation, 223
Washington University School of Medicine, 222, 306n24
Watts, Anna, 83
Watts, Henry M., 83
Wayne State University, 117, 239, 241–242
Webb and Knapp, 53, 82–83
Weber, Rachel, 273n36, 298n6
Weisberg, Lois, 197
West Garfield Park (Chicago), 172–173
Westinghouse Electric Corporation, 9–10
White, Bill, 43–44
White, Michael R., xv, 137–139
whites: association of African American neighborhoods with blight, 93; associations of African Americans with disease, 263n4; breast cancer deaths and, 306n20; distrust of public housing, 87; downtown renewal and, xii–xiv, 3, 8; migration to northern factory work, 13,

17; nostalgia narratives and, 271n25; suburbanization and, 25, 44, 46, 76, 88, 111, 141–142, 172, 197, 255, 262n1, 263n3, 267n38; upscale downtowns and, 16
white supremacy, 278n33
Wilensky, Harry, 263n7
Williams, G. Mennen, 95, 98–99
Williams, Mason B., 258n7
Wilson, Kathryn E., 303n2
Winant, Gabriel, 15, 226, 304n7, 306n22
Woodlawn Organization (TWO), 169
World War II, 9, 18–19, 27–28, 53
Wright, Bruce N., 152

Young, Coleman A.: automobile industry and, 142, 157–160, 180; blame for economic decline, 142, 289n2; business leaders and, 142, 144, 150f, 157–159; casino development and, 153–156, 161; clearance of neighborhoods for redevelopment, 157–160, 162; conflict with Melvin Ravitz, 154–155, 178–180; criticism of failures, 160–161; Democratic Party and, 143; downtown renewal and, xv, 142, 144–149, 152–153, 178; FBI investigation of, 161; focus on services, 112, 142–143; industrial redevelopment and, 156–162, 180; as mayor of Detroit, 141–143; misuse of CDBG funding, 158, 178; professional sports and, 145–148, 237, 239; public-private alliances and, 127, 145, 149, 153, 161; riverfront development and, 144–149, 153, 161; tourism and leisure activities, 142; union organizing and, 143, 161; white dissatisfaction with, 142–143, 290n6

Zeckendorf, William, 53–54, 57, 83, 277n24
Ziegler, Charles M., 98

**Roger Biles** is Professor Emeritus of History at Illinois State University and the author, coauthor, or editor of several books, most recently *Mayor Harold Washington: Champion of Race and Reform in Chicago.*

**Mark H. Rose** is Professor of History at Florida Atlantic University, and the author, coauthor, or coeditor of seven books, including *Interstate: Highway Politics and Policy since 1939* and *Market Rules: Bankers, Presidents, and the Origins of the Great Recession.*

Also in the series *Urban Life, Landscape, and Policy*:

Michael T. Maly and Heather Dalmage, *Vanishing Eden: White Construction of Memory, Meaning, and Identity in a Racially Changing City*

Harold L. Platt, *Building the Urban Environment: Visions of the Organic City in the United States, Europe, and Latin America*

Kristin M. Szylvian, *The Mutual Housing Experiment: New Deal Communities for the Urban Middle Class*

Kathryn Wilson, *Ethnic Renewal in Philadelphia's Chinatown: Space, Place, and Struggle*

Robert Gioielli, *Environmental Activism and the Urban Crisis: Baltimore, St. Louis, Chicago*

Robert B. Fairbanks, *The War on Slums in the Southwest: Public Housing and Slum Clearance in Texas, Arizona, and New Mexico, 1936–1965*

Carlton Wade Basmajian, *Atlanta Unbound: Enabling Sprawl through Policy and Planning*

Scott Larson, *"Building Like Moses with Jacobs in Mind": Contemporary Planning in New York City*

Gary Rivlin, *Fire on the Prairie: Harold Washington, Chicago Politics, and the Roots of the Obama Presidency*

William Issel, *Church and State in the City: Catholics and Politics in Twentieth-Century San Francisco*

Jerome Hodos, *Second Cities: Globalization and Local Politics in Manchester and Philadelphia*

Julia L. Foulkes, *To the City: Urban Photographs of the New Deal*

William Issel, *For Both Cross and Flag: Catholic Action, Anti-Catholicism, and National Security Politics in World War II San Francisco*

Lisa Hoffman, *Patriotic Professionalism in Urban China: Fostering Talent*

John D. Fairfield, *The Public and Its Possibilities: Triumphs and Tragedies in the American City*

Andrew Hurley, *Beyond Preservation: Using Public History to Revitalize Inner Cities*

Made in United States
Orlando, FL
10 January 2023

28511457R00196